STRANGE EXPERIENCE

STRANGE EXPERIENCE

THE AUTOBIOGRAPHY OF
A HEXENMEISTER

LEE R. GANDEE

133
G-15a

PRENTICE-HALL, INC.
Englewood Cliffs, N. J.

Strange Experience: The Autobiography of a Hexenmeister
by Lee R. Gandee
Copyright © 1971 by Lee R. Gandee
All rights reserved. No part of this book may be
reproduced in any form or by any means, except
for the inclusion of brief quotations in a review,
without permission in writing from the publisher.
ISBN 0-13-850966-2
Library of Congress Catalog Card Number: 76-157053
Printed in the United States of America T
Prentice-Hall International, Inc., London
Prentice-Hall of Australia, Pty. Ltd., Sydney
Prentice-Hall of Canada, Ltd., Toronto
Prentice-Hall of India Private Ltd., New Delhi
Prentice-Hall of Japan, Inc., Tokyo

To
Anne Elizabeth Withers
a great teacher who told me when I was fifteen
that to be a genuine person
anyone must be himself
to
my friends and family
who have loved me as I am
for what I am
and
in spite of what I am
and
to all who revere the integrity
of selfhood in themselves and others
I lovingly dedicate this book

CONTENTS

Homo duplex, homo duplex! The first time that I perceived that I was two was at the death of my brother Henri, when my father cried out so dramatically, 'He is dead, he is dead!' While my first self wept, my second self thought, 'How truly given was that cry, how fine it would be at the theater.' I was then fourteen years old.

This horrible duality has often given me matter for reflection. Oh, this terrible second me, always seated whilst the other is on foot, acting, living, suffering, bestirring itself. This second me that I have never been able to intoxicate, to make shed tears, or put to sleep. And how it sees into things, and how it mocks!

Alphonse Daudet

Prima Materia: The eternal struggle of opposites which maintains the Universe in balance, and from which all things come into existence. Here, the two salamanders may be understood as positive and negative polarity. The face symbolizes the consciousness which guides and sustains creation

1

INTRODUCTION

The Fish Triskelion: Symbol of man's spiritual total identity

When an obscure person such as myself writes an autobiography, his only justification is that he feels his life involves much more than himself. I think that what is true of me is to some degree true of everyone.

I was raised in rural West Virginia, where—cut off from every outside influence—descendants of seventeenth- and eighteenth-century immigrants retained their ancestral folklore. Almost from birth I lived in a haunted house, and when I was less than two years of age, I was taken by foster parents to become part of a family in which astral projections, poltergeists, apparitions, hexes, and communications with the dead were taken for granted.

I descend from men and women who were considered witches because they exercised certain unusual powers. Perhaps I am endowed with a degree of psychic sensitivity. I have experienced healings and used spiritual power to heal; I have always lived where psychic phenomena occur, and have been compelled to seek an understanding of it. From earliest memory I have had intimations of previous lives, and I have recognized places seen for the first time; I have dreamed in foreign languages that I do not speak when awake. In middle life, I have had experiences which convince me of reincarnation, and I have met a man who remembered shared previous life experience. My life has been a strange one, so the autobiography is really an account of a strange experience.

It is this experience which seems to justify the writing. If my reincarnative glimpses are valid, as I believe them to be, I have been on earth for thousands of years. I have been both woman and man. I believe that everyone has been, or must be, for I conceive that only having experienced life as male *and* female can the human spirit comprehend what it is to be completely human, or enter life with an understanding of and a compassion for the needs and emotions of one's mate. I know that the first incarnation that I can remember was not my first, but in it I was a female on Cyprus in about 1700 B.C. If this is true—and the whole drama of my life seems explicable only if it *is*—then this autobiography is a millennials-long chronicle of a human soul.

My birth occurred under circumstances seemingly calculated to make my life one of exceeding great limitation, for I was born in a hovel on a hillside in West Virginia at a spot overlooking the mouth of Polecat Run, where even today the road dead-ends. The community speculated on the identity of my true father, and before I was three I was given without adoption to another family. My childhood was a nightmare because of the psychic atmosphere of the locality and the beliefs of the people around me. I was constantly sick, accident-prone—forever cutting myself, falling, stepping on nails, knocking my toenails off on stones, even once getting in the way of a bullet fired on the opposite hillside at a squirrel—and until my childhood gave way to puberty, I was grotesquely fat. I had no playmates, and was terrified of other children. I was reared with Puritan strictness by a foster-grandmother who believed that the End of Time was already a hundred years over-due, and I was taught to believe in eternal Hell for all but a righteous few—a very few.

At the age of about eleven, I found myself very strongly sexed, with no accurate knowledge of sex, and no outlet that did not incur the strongest of guilt feelings. When at fourteen I began to anticipate sexual experience with some uninhibited mountain girl—*let* hell burn with brimstone—I instead fell in love with a handsome oversexed boy a year older than I. For ten years we shared a strange, exclusive love as deep as any that can be shared by two people; yet he was strongly heterosexual, and we both wanted children. I do not propose to state the outcome of that experience now—only to say that for the past twenty-eight years I have been married; that my eldest child was born nine months and thirteen days after my marriage; and that I have another daughter, and a son.

Either I am not a very good psychologist, or the psychology that I have studied is not very good, for I have found little to explain why an individual with every male characteristic should fall in love with a man. I have found even less to explain an individual's deliberate rejection of one self and the substitution of another—such as I effected when I decided that since I could not bear children fathered by the man I loved, I would father my own with the gear provided me for parent-hood. However, if my male identity already existed, (as I now am certain was the case), then this story is a study in multi-dimensional psychology, such as I am sure must develop when the West accepts the truth of reincarnation, the alternation of sex in successive lives, and the explanation of selfhood as a complex thing dependent upon the accu-mulated (and subconsciously remembered) experience of many lives.

In that context, this is a complex of autobiographies, for I believe the man I now am has reincarnated many times in a male body: once as a Hebrew who followed Moses out of Egypt and watched as *Ehyeh Asher Ehyeh* came down in fire on Mount Sinai and the mountain was "all on a smoke," as the Bible says. He was an Italian duke in the early Renaissance; a Satzburger at the time of the first (Hussite) persecution; an immigrant to South Carolina before the Weberite Delusion; next in an immediate reincarnation, a guerilla fighter in the American Revolution; next, a Confederate soldier in the Civil War—the last two as a member of the same family group and all three within a few miles of each previous life-locality. Today I am again living in the same community, and through the marriage of my second daughter, I am looking forward to grandchildren of that same family connection.

In the present book, I do not attempt to go into the mechanisms of these things, for in 1970, Jane Roberts's book, *The Seth Material,* * provided a theory of personality which for the first time explains both the kind of identity and the kind of consciousness that my experience makes me accept as the real. There, in a hundred pages or less, "Seth" sets forth the concept in half the space it would take me. Rather, I shall tell of the personality that I rejected—or more exactly, sacrificed— hoping to make credible the substitution of the alternate personality.

So, you are given one lifetime and two autobiographes of it. And since the substitution was the great event of my life, and since reincarnation is the central theme, considerable space is given the interlude when I loved "Stud" as a woman would—for I now believe that it was due to Karma—punishment for the scandalous life I lived on Cyprus when "Stud" was my loving and faithful husband. You must try to understand me, then, as a multi-dimensional personality, for though I said I substituted a male identity for a female one, I did not dispossess the woman's ego, but merely gave the other precedence. As I write, whichever one is better informed, or more concerned in telling of a given experience, does so. We are not two personalities fighting for control of the same body, but two who have found it to mutual advantage to cooperate, and aid and abet each other. The woman in me still lusts for a handsome man, and though she is waiting for death and rebirth to be a flesh-and-blood woman again, she remembers, and her memories are those of a whore's pleasures. The man, on the other hand, is what you might expect of one who saw Moses come down from the

* Prentice-Hall, Inc., Englewood Cliffs, N.J., 1970

Mount with the tablets of stone, and who gave up wife, children, house, land, and life for his faith when the Hussites defied Rome and the Holy Roman Emperor. It is a discipline in tolerance for him to share a body with a whore. She has made him see what it is to love, and lent him an easy zest for life that the old, fanatic, Hebrew, heretic, Patriot, and Confederate lacked. We have come to respect each other, these two egos who share this well-occupied body. We have come to like, even to love each other. We are happy, and know that together we are more than the two, separate, would be. So if "I" speak of myself as "we," it is not the royal plural, but recognition of this double personality. We have a woman's tenderness; a man's strength; we laugh and cry like a woman; we also do those things which a man must do regardless of his feelings.

Since ours has been a very strange experience, it has whetted our appetite for all varieties of strangeness that involve survival or relate to the personality, the identity, the nature, or potentials of man. We are intensely human, and each has loved and been loved, and found richness even in poverty. The Weberite Delusion of two centuries and a quarter ago involved hypnosis and magic, and our interest in these matters has been keen. We have practiced hypnosis, but we are not a witch, exactly.

Rather, we know that a great many things that have been called witchcraft are quite natural, and we see no reason not to use any available natural powers to do what we wish. I, the whore, always did anything I pleased, let it hurt others as it might, and I paid dearly for it. The other I is wiser; yet I have convinced him that he need not be a Pharisee. We have come to a sort of mutual agreement, which gives us a code for conduct precisely that of witches. ("An it harm none, do what thou wilt.") We seek to live in harmony with each other, with others, and with Nature. We are at peace. We say to you, as you prepare to read of our strange experience, Peace be unto you. May you find in it something which will bring you to a realization of your own inner peace. Our autobiography is one of flesh and spirit, of body and soul, in which the constant goal has been one of integration—of unification and self-realization. If it has any moral, it is that if male and female, saint and sinner, can attain a satisfactory integration in the same body, anyone can.

In *The Seth Material*, the concept of time seems much nearer our own than does the prevailing one, for we have reason to believe that past, present, and future are what he calls one "spacious moment." So in this "spacious moment," now, (forever now) we are waiting to be born; come to the place with us, and we shall tell you just how it was with us when we came back into space and time.

BY A ROUTE OBSCURE AND LONELY

The Great and Seven Lesser Seals: Refers to the six steps
of Creation, and to the completed Creation; protective
watchfulness for all things great and small

By a route obscure and lonely,
Haunted by ill angels only,
Where an Eidolon, named Night,
On a black throne reigns upright,
I have reached these lands but newly
From an ultimate dim Thule—
From a wild weird clime that lieth, sublime,
Out of Space—out of Time . . .

Edgar Allan Poe

Others have told me of the night before I was born, and I know how it must have been, for I have been young and in love and alone in the same place in springtime, and I am my mother's son.

The valley was full of misty moonlight, and blooming apple trees shimmered, stirred by vagrant winds from the south. My mother could not rest. An inquietude partly of youth, partly of spring, but mostly of the heart kept sleep from falling, filled her mind with fantasies, and summonsed her feet. Her husband lay beside her, drugged with fatigue, resting from a day of toil, in another world. I was restless in her womb, a child marked by the moon and Venus and drawn by the night—drawn by the earth and fated to be born under an earth sign. The planets were in a baleful conjunction, and the date was one that witches call unlucky.

The disturbing moonlight called her. She crept from the bed and to the window. Without what sensible folk would call a reason, she opened the door and gazed toward the mountain. Beyond it a young man stirred in his sleep, dreaming of her, his hair a tangle of silken darkness above his handsome face. One of **his** raven curls twined around her heart and tightened, cutting and torturing her.

The moonlight glistened on her wet cheeks. She felt cold dew on her feet and nightgown, and something white and fragrant swayed beside her. Without knowing how she came to be there, she found herself in the orchard. She glimpsed a face with a crown of darkness above it and put out her hand eagerly to touch it. Her fingers touched only a twig of apple blossoms; the face was only a fantasy of moonlight or of her mind. It was not her lover come again to the orchard to meet her—he had not come since apples lay on the ground. Then she was filled with panic, remembering that after the apples had been gathered, her husband had turned the black sow loose in the orchard. She was afraid of the beast, for the sow was very large, and vicious when she had piglets—a real peril to a girl.

She began to run, and sharp stones hurt her feet; briars caught at her gown. Dark things of the valley and of the soul trooped in around her. She had run to the fence and clambered up the rails when giddiness overcame her and she fell—she lay outside the fence, her forehead bruised by a stone. A dark slumber held her, and when she roused from it, it was dawn and she saw her husband standing in the dooryard calling her name in alarm. She staggered to her feet; he saw her, ran to her, carried her to the house. He put her in the bed and ran to the adjoining farm for her foster mother, Mrs. Hively.

When Mrs. Hively saw her, she said, "Tom, fetch Ret as fast as you can, and pray she gets here in time!" Ret was Retta Elmore, the midwife.

Retta saw the girl, examined her, and shook her head. "Delcie's in an awful bad fix," she pronounced. "Hit ain't fur enough along to live. How long they been married—six or seven months?"

"They were married the first day of last September."

"And today's the eighth of May," Retta computed. "When did you figure hit was due?" she asked the husband.

"If it was mine, it'd be in June at least," he muttered.

"Tom!" Mrs. Hively scolded, "You don't *know* he isn't yours! You know yourself Delcie hasn't come to time!"

"I don't want it to live, or me either," the girl moaned, surprising them, for they thought that she was again unconscious.

"You better go on out," Retta directed the husband. "This hain't a fit place for a man."

He hesitated, then went out and sat on the porch, hunched on the steps with his elbows on his knees as the women made ready for the birth or miscarriage, whichever it chanced to be.

The girl underwent labor without assisting it. In spite of the ax Retta put under the bed to cut her pain in half, she fainted time after time. When she was conscious, she made no effort to do as the midwife bade her. She seemed unwilling that the child should see the light of day.

At ten-fifteen, when the sun was growing high, I was born.

"Hit's a boy, like you said hit would be. But did you ever see one so little and puny!" Retta exclaimed. "Set them scales on the table and I'll lay him in the scoop—hit won't hurt him. Two pounds and four ounces—he hain't goin' to last the mornin' out nohow!"

"He's got to live!" Mrs. Hively exclaimed. "He's to be *my* son—and what's been given won't be taken back."

Retta stared at her, awed by her intensity. "Tell me—it'll not git no further—is he Tom's? I never seen a baby with so much hair, and his eyes as black as a witch-child's."

"As long as Tom doesn't think it's his, what difference does it make? As for his hair and eyes, Delcie's father was like that—his hair was so black it had blue lights in it."

"There's bound to be more talk," Retta said. "Tom so pale-eyed and fair-skinned, and the way she was stuck on that dark Blackwell boy, and him the kind no girl was safe with. Folks is already sayin' around that you'da done better to let her marry Blackwell like she wanted to. They're more two of a kind than her and Tom is."

Mrs. Hively frowned. "There's more to marriage than just what goes on in bed. One or the other has got to have a little common sense, and Tom has sense enough for them both."

"Poor Delcie *is* flighty," Retta conceded. "But a better-hearted girl'd be hard to find. And at drawin' a picture, or makin' up words to a tune, I never knowed the beat of her. If the boy lives, he's bound to have a lot of her in him."

"I'm going to do a better job with him than I did with her. I let her do too much as she pleased. Anything like her I see start in him I'll head off before it can take hold. I never had a son, and I'll take him; there's nothing they can do about it. Even before they were married—I had everything planned. And what I plan, I carry out one way or another. You know that!"

"Yes, you git what you want, sure enough," the other woman sighed "but I ain't sure hit's right, or what the end of this will be."

I know now that my birth was part of a tragedy, a drama spanning many lifetimes, of which the prologue was spoken in another language centuries ago. In our sleep, however, in the dim Thule "out of space—out of time," all of us had forgotten the forebodings of the first act; we did not know the play was confusing only because the preceding portion had been forgotten.

The setting was entirely new—a singularly unimpressive one but as meaningful as my birth itself.

The house was a wretched shack on the Hively land, located on the bank where Polecat Run (or Elmore's Branch) flows into the Littlepage Branch of Gabe Creek. The shack stood just inside Kanawha County, but the bulk of the land lay in Roane. All I remember of it is that when I was about four, Mrs. Hively took me there to fill a pail with straw-berries, and said it was where I was born. One could look through cracks in the floor and see leaves on the ground, and the walls were pasted with tough paper sacks and pages of old newspapers and magazines to keep out some of the wind and cold. It seemed very poor and mean, and unfit for human habitation, for the Hively house had tight floors, fancy wallpaper with roses, and paint on the doors, windows, and mantlepieces. Soon after that, Mr. Hively's nephew, Orrin Hively, bought the land, tore down the shack and built a neat bungalow there, and gave me little blocks and scraps of the dressed lumber—delightful playthings·

But perhaps I do have other memories of the house, for I vaguely remember ugliness. At first I was conscious only of lightness and dark-ness, blurred forms, the sound of much weeping and a little laughter, and voices speaking a language that somehow seemed familiar. Yet I do remember ugliness, and to shut it out, I closed my eyes and sought to return to the place from which my birth had exiled me. By then that world had dissolved into myriads of pinpoints of light which flowed and drifted like golden pollen floating in a stream. But when I closed my eyelids, held my breath and lay very still, the points of light formed pictures, as dots do in a newspaper photograph creating shadowy illu-sions of form and dimension which I could not identify or relate to one another, but which were familiar and intensely meaningful.

Many were of faces and of strangely dressed people. Others were of statues, details of architecture—columns, obelisks, arches, portals, crenellations, whole facades and interiors—geometric designs, land-scapes of waters, deserts, cities, and mountains which have always been waste. With them, audible to a sense beyond hearing, sometimes came sounds—chants, chorales, an organ, drums and instruments of brass, the sounds of all stringed instruments, the surge of the ocean, the roar of wind or fire, shouts, cries, explosions, and speech in what I now know was Greek, Hebrew, Latin, Italian, and German, and others I never have heard spoken in this life. I suppose it is often so when an ancient soul is

resurrected, again embodied, and brought forth from a living tomb of
flesh.

What difference did it make, then, whose son I was, or whose the
gossips supposed? As Jesus said, perhaps for the same reasons, "I am the
son of man." I was born of the race, begotten by a thousand fathers,
and formed in the wombs of a thousand mothers. I am Man, dust of the
earth, made human when God first breathed a spirit into my nostrils. I
am allegorically Adam and Adam's seed; I was, I am, and ever shall be a
son of the Father, as is each man brought forth of woman.

So to be born was nothing unfamiliar, for I have been born once
oftener than I have died. But I had never been born on Littlepage
Branch of Gabe Creek before, or under the same circumstances.

It was necessary this time that my spirit should have been reem-
bodied in a haunted valley. Gabe Creek and Littlepage Branch were
named for Gabriel Littlepage, a hermit who in the last decade of the
eighteenth century took refuge in the forest and built a cabin by a
spring almost in sight of my birthplace. All his cabin's chimney stones
appear to have been burned, so perhaps the home was destroyed by
fire. The oldest man in the community claimed that Gabriel had come
home from a hunt and found the cabin in ashes with the remains of his
wife and child. Indeed, there was memory of something terrible burned
into the stone. The spot where the cabin stood filled me with horror.

Whatever occurred there, Gabriel left the site and denned under a
shelving rock near the main fork of Gabe Creek. For decades he stayed
there—unshorn, unkempt, bearded like a mad prophet, clad in rags and
skins, his only companion a limping grey dog or wolf (most legends said
wolf), exiled from the habitations of men and wet with the dew of
heaven, as was Nebuchadnezzar before his reason returned to him.
About once a year he appeared at Charleston to barter for supplies with
furs and ginseng root, and sometimes he went to the Kanawha Salines
for salt. Those on the trail from Wood County to Charleston dreaded
him, for he had prodigious strength and ranged for miles and was suspected whenever anyone disappeared or was found murdered and
robbed.

A few persons said that half-deranged or not, old Gabriel was a man
of learning and of keen intelligence. The wealthy Littlepages of Charleston (whose stone mansion still stands) denied that he was of their kindred. But for some reason, they kept visiting Littlepage Branch long

after Gabe Creek was settled—ostensibly to hunt, though I feel sure
they could have found better hunting much nearer Charleston.

Sometime shortly before the Civil War, old Gabe stopped turning up
in Charleston or on the Wood County Trail. And when the Campbells,
Gabe Creek's first permanent family, arrived, they found the skeletons
of Gabriel and the wolf under the rock. The skulls showed that both
had been shot. A rusty flintlock lay with the bones, and on a large
beech tree touching the front of the rock, they found carved the name
and birth and death dates of Gabriel Littlepage. The date of death was
the old man's eightieth birthday, and from the circumstances, it seemed
evident that he had shot his only companion and killed himself. The
Hivelys came from Rock Creek in 1872 before the beech was gone, and
like the Campbells they shunned the place as one of eldritch noises and
uncanny presences.

Once Campbell was hunting a cow that had wandered up the creek
toward the Hively place. Just as he neared the fork a sudden storm
arose. Tornadic winds broke timber, terrifying clouds boiled low, lightning flashed almost continuously. He ran to the rock and as he cowered
under it—deafened by thunder, the roar of the storm, and the smashing
timber—lightning shattered the beech. The concussion knocked him
senseless. When he came to, the storm had gone as quickly as it had
come. Blue sky appeared through the scattering clouds, and as he
crawled out through the riven branches he saw the inscription on the
snag and in horror realized that the month and day were the same as
the dates cut on the tree: The day of the storm would have been
Gabriel Littlepage's hundredth birthday had he lived to see it. It convinced Campbell that the storm was not a natural phenomenon, but
proof that the hermit was still present, conscious, and exerting a terrible influence over nature.

That was almost a century ago, but the Reverend James Early Abbott (my distant cousin, whom I shall identify hereafter as Cousin
James Early) moved to the Jackson place at the head of that branch
around 1920 and still lives there. Soon after he came to Gabe, he told
me, he was walking up the creek to Gabe's Rock one night and heard a
tree crash down behind him. He needed the road open for his wagon, so
early next morning he went with an ax to clear it, but found not even a
fallen branch anywhere. Old residents told him that he might expect to
hear a tree fall at any time, anywhere on Gabe, and that eased his fear

that it was a token of approaching death. Finally he grew accustomed
to the noise and said it did not bother him when he heard it.

My friend Stud was foolhardy in his boldness if faced with natural
dangers, but he clung to me utterly unnerved if we were out walking on
a windless day and heard the crash of the tree, seeing perfectly that
nothing fell to account for the sound. I think the noise affected most
persons as it did him, and even I never heard that phantom falling tree
without a chill coursing down my spine and thoughts of old Gabriel
Littlepage racing through my mind. It filled me with melancholy, un-
easiness, and a feeling of devitalization, as if something invisible had
drawn life-force out of me. I always half-expected a shape to appear, or
to hear a demented voice or insane laughter—no, I take that back. I do
not believe that Gabriel Littlepage played pranks, either in life or afterlife. When one sensed Gabe's nearness, he detected shame and remorse,
but chiefly sorrow. One somehow knew that both God and man had
dealt very bitterly with him. I prayed for his soul each time I heard the
falling tree, and possibly because I did this, I heard it very often.

Gabriel's Rock hung out of the hillside so close to the washed-back
creek bank that one could merely edge in front of it on foot, and it was
so low that a team and wagon could not pass under it. So, before I was
born, it was blasted away to make room for the road to the Jackson
place. One night the preacher's son, Cousin Otto Lee Abbott was driv
ing his roadster past where the rock had been, when a dark animal-
looking thing leaped onto the hood and clung there momentarily, sil-
houetted against the fog. Once in the daytime, too, a grizzled beast
limped from the woods there and so frightened Retta Elmore's dogs
that they crept whining under the house. She ran out to see what was
causing such commotion in the farmyard and it daunted her also, for
she said it looked like a great starved dog. She thought of a wolf, but no
one had seen a living wolf on Gabe since the settlement began. Many
nights my hair has stood on end as I heard eerie howling on some dark
ridge or in some stygian hollow. But there were many huge dogs on
Gabe, and however wolflike the sound, I was never certain that it was
not made by one of them, for they howled more than the "Hound of
the Baskervilles."

Mother was ashamed to live in a hovel as wretched as the house
where I was born. As the Jackson House at the head of the Branch, just
over a low hill from the Hively place, was a proper dwelling with

dressed weatherboarding, planed ceilings, turned porch posts and paint, she gave her husband no rest until he agreed to rent it.

The Jackson Place had a fine orchard both of apple and of cherry trees, lush pastureland and ample water, and a black cove of very rich ground. Her husband was ambitious and planned to rent, then buy the land, because it was good, and perhaps also to please my mother, for he loved her. So, motivated on her part by pride and on his by practicality, they leased the place.

But even by Gabe Creek standards, the Jackson house had a wan-chance, ill-betokened reputation. I do not know who built it or when, but I think it was standing when the Jacksons bought the land. Several years before I was born, old Mr. Jackson went insane there, claiming that he was continually pursued by something bent on killing him.

From the bizarre, his behavior became utterly irrational, and when at last he fled screaming even from his own sons and hid in the woods, the neighbors hunted him down, captured him, and took him to the asylum where he soon died. His widow lived on for several years, earning her living with a loom, weaving carpet from rags people brought her. Except for the parlor and the kitchen, every room in the Hively house was carpeted with her handiwork. She was a most adept weaver, and her roots, mosses, and barks made subtle, lovely colors. She too died—I suppose in the winter of 1916, some months before I was born. Before she was in her grave, her daughters had a bitter quarrel over her belongings, in particular over her loom and the barrels of dyed carpet strips. Thomas Gandee began clearing the black cove of locust brush even before the Jackson heirs patched up some kind of arrangement and removed their mother's belongings from the house.

When they sent word that it was empty, Mother and a few girls who consorted with her went with brooms and pails to scrub the rooms and hang the curtains she had made. They worked all morning scouring floors and washing windows, and finished the downstairs—which was all my parents were able to furnish, and as much room as they needed. It took longer than they anticipated, so when they finished past noon they were famished. As they deliberated whether to go home and eat before tackling the upstairs, one of them remarked, "Old Grandma Jackson's canned stuff's still in the cellar. It's a pity it's locked."

"I saw a ventilating-hole open," one girl commented. "Maybe we could reach through and get our hands on something."

"On a copperhead, as like as not," one of the others giggled.

Mother went to investigate, and with a hooked stick drew a jar in reach, a half-gallon of black cherries. The girls passed it around, sharing the rich juice and eating handfuls of the sweet, delicious fruit.

"Hit sure makes you feel queer eatin' canned stuff a dead woman put up, don't hit?" Ollie Elmore prattled.

"She'll not need it where she is," Mother said lightly. "But I'd hate to think what those daughters of hers would say if they knew I took it."

They all tittered, for the Jackson women were known far and wide for their miserliness and sour dispositions—but just at that instant something moved at the ceiling, and the girls stared horrified as a dark stain streaked wetly down one of the fresh-hung kitchen curtains, reddening it from top to bottom.

"Blood!" Ollie shrieked.

"No, it's the color of the cherry juice," Mother choked. "It's old Grandma Jackson's way of showing me she knows I stole her fruit!"

They fled, and Mother begged her husband not to move there. But he had toiled too hard to clear the black cove; he had rented a wagon to haul the furniture next day, and had driven the black sow and her pigs over the mountain to their new pen. When Mrs. Hively got word of what had happened in the kitchen, she asked Mother if she had been raised to steal from the dead and pilfer from the living, and admonished her to mend her ways unless she wanted more than a good scare in this life.

Whatever made the stain, it set in the curtain, and no soaking or bleaching ever had any effect on it. Mother burned it to be rid of the reminder. Her husband, who never believed anything he could not understand and had been to a teachers' institute (albeit never to high school) and considered superstition contemptible in a schoolteacher, said there must be some reasonable explanation. He climbed up to scrutinize the ceiling, and went upstairs to examine the floor, but he found no stains on either, and nothing to account for the one on the curtain.

Mrs. Hively offered him a reasonable explanation—that the stain looked like cherry juice to her, and that mother was quite capable of staining the curtain herself and lying about it if for some reason she had changed her mind about wanting to move. He knew that the girls in Mother's little coterie could lie for her more convincingly than anyone ever told the truth, so he gave no sympathy to Mother's genuine fear of the house, for he had not been married to her a week before he learned that she could simulate any emotion with great realism. When anyone asked him about this incident or subsequent ones that he himself did not witness, his comment was, *"You* know how Delcie is!"

Mother went through torment in the Jackson house. When her husband was not teaching school, he hired out every day he could find work, and when he was doing neither he went to the fields at daylight and worked until dusk—so Mother was alone six days a week. At any time she might hear footfalls in the rooms upstairs, the sound of the carpet loom or the creak of a rocking chair, sometimes indistinct voices or mad, sardonic laughter in some distant room. After each prolonged rain, a red scum like old blood oozed from the ground under the front porch, and soon reappeared if scraped away with a hoe. When it appeared in old Mrs. Jackson's lifetime she explained that the house was said to be built over a walnut stump which oozed the stain. No one dared call it "the peddler's blood" to her face, but it kept alive the rumor that before the Jacksons lived there, a peddler had disappeared somewhere between Henry Hively's house and Dorans's on the ridge, and members of the family then living there were later seen wearing things that Henry and the Schoolcrafts had seen in his pack. Thomas, of course, pointed out that blood cannot stay red and wet upward of thirty years, whereas walnut roots stay in the ground indefinitely. Much later, Cousin James Early told me it came once after he moved there—looking like where someone had bled a butchered hog—but he prayed to be relieved of all that disturbed the house, and it never came back. Prayer and godly occupants such as he may have been all that the house needed, for it has grown quiet since he has lived there.

But in 1917 and 1918, it was intolerable. On the stair which came down between two walls and was closed only by a portière, my parents sometimes heard a whispered bumping. Then the bottom of the curtain would push out, and a ball—like a carpet-rag-strip ball of old Mrs. Jackson's—would roll into the room and disappear behind something, or under the bed, or under another portière into the closet. Her husband could see this ball and sometimes hear noises, and in a different way, they troubled him as much as they did Mother. Search as they might they could never find it after it disappeared. Mother said that once, as I sat on the floor, it rolled so close to me that it brushed me, and I fell over trying to catch it. I vaguely recall once, after I started walking, that I was standing in the doorway when it rolled out past me across the porch: it fell off into the flowers and shook them. Mother said this really happened, and her excitement probably fixed it in my memory.

Perhaps Mother's worst experience had no apparent connection with the house. One night soon after my brother Jesse was born, Mother was lying awake, with me asleep at one side and him at the other. It was a moonlight-haunted night, and the room was faintly illuminated from outside. She had only enough oil to warm over her husband's supper and prepare breakfast, and he would have reproached her for extravagance had she wasted oil for a lamp she did not work or read by.

So she waited in the gloom, alone with only two sleeping infants in a house so still the ticking of the clock in the front room seemed loud and disturbing. She could hear dogs howling at the Phillips place next door, and at the Hively and Schoolcraft houses down the branch. She hoped that they had begun because her husband had passed by.

As she lay waiting, three pale, chatoyant lights appeared at the wall opposite, luminescent and pulsating, and slowly floated across the room and into the tall headboard of the bed, where they disappeared. Since the middle light was large, and the others small, she interpreted them as tokens or fetch-lights, portending death for her and both us children. Had not her husband arrived just then, stamping on the porch, pounding on the door, and calling to her to let him in, I cannot say what she might have done. She was so unnerved that she could hardly grasp the key and turn it, and he had to shake her and slap her sharply to restore her coherence enough to tell what she had seen.

Next morning, however, she saw people coming and going at the Phillips house. And when she went to inquire, she found that Joseph's wife, Amanda, had given birth to triplets the evening before—a boy and two girls, all dead. And when she saw the boy laid out in the wide casket with a sister at either side, it came to her that the lights had been for them—death tokens as she had supposed, but only to inform her that death was a nearby visitant. As Joseph Phillips was a brother-in-law of my uncle Grover Gandee, it was not thought strange that a Phillips token should be seen in a Gandee house.

One of the times Whitney Pickering was on his deathbed—as he gave himself out to be, hopefully, each time he was ill—Grandmother started baking a batch of funeral pies, raisin pies that she carried to wakes. And as our pie safe was full, and she seldom made raisin pies for home use, I asked her, "Are those for Whit's wake?"

"No," she replied absently. "There's nothing ever wrong with Whit except the belly-ache from some mess Rachel cooked, or some bait he fixed if she was too drunk. What I felt was a woman's token. Something started sewing at my dress—it was that plain, the hands and the sewing, just as if you were mending it without taking it off. It has to be for a woman." She always baked pies on the strength of such forewarnings, for always within three-and-twenty hours after she saw, heard, or felt such a token, some nearby person died. I recalled no instance when she had been wrong, but I hoped she was, for I liked raisin pies immoderately. But that same afternoon, the talented seamstress who relined Grandmother's coat when the sleazy silketeen wore out, and restyled it every two or three years with new collars and trim, choked to death on a peach seed. As for Whit, he was up in time for the funeral.

While at the Jackson house Mother derived any comfort she may have had from the nearness of Amanda Phillips and the consolation that however much our house was disturbed, Amanda's was worse. One night as the Phillipses huddled around the stove, a child's voice began crying outside in the snow and it circled the house at incredible speed. Joseph Phillips could see nothing through the window and would not venture out. As they listened, heavy footfalls stamped to the kitchen door, and something began to shake and batter it. The door seemed about to tear off its hinges, so Joseph shoved the heavy cupboard against it and the family retreated upstairs. The bedlam kept up below. They heard the door break in, and the sound of the cupboard being shoved back across the rough floor. They heard dishes being smashed, furniture turned over, glass shattered, and pots and pans thrown about, and all the while the child's wailing never ceased. At last all grew quiet, but they remained upstairs in the cold until daylight.

When they did venture down, the door was locked and undamaged. The cupboard still stood against it; nothing was broken or out of place, and the only footprints around the house were those of the family from the day before.

Another time Amanda was in the yard feeding her chickens when she was surprised by the sounds of a wagon and men's voices in the distance. Wagons hardly ever used the road, though about twenty years before, one had gotten stuck in the stiff clay nearby—and the oxen

were beaten until one pulled off one of its hooves in the mud and had
to be shot. Amanda was so curious she stopped scattering grain and
stood watching for the wagon to come into view. The noise kept coming closer, but no wagon appeared, and she became frightened. It came
on until it sounded as if it were in the air above her. The chickens
dashed themselves into the wire fence in panic; she fell to her knees
praying, but the creaking wheels, jangling harness, and loud unintel-
ligible voices passed overhead. She still saw nothing, and the sound died
away in the distance just as it had come. Grandmother averred that the
suffering of the ox had left something that haunted that stretch of
road. Maybe she was right: cruelty must be paid for, here or hereafter,
and I can think of few punishments more fitting than being returned to
the scene of one's misdoings and made into a thing feared and fled from
by the living. I know now that a disembodied spirit perceives only as
the illumination of its own light permits (and if that light be darkness,
how great is that darkness!). But emotions have their own colors and
vibrations which the dead can see as light, and the gray-green glow of
fear is a most ghastly one which strikes terror to their innermost
depths. So if a spirit is forbidden the place of shades and shackled to
the scene of its own misdeeds, whatever fear it engenders, it feels itself
as fear. There is no escape. This was revealed to me by a spirit who
called himself Michael Moon. He taught me many things, and took me
with him into a dark valley where the dead fled screaming from us—or
else greeted us with reverence and joy. When I marvelled, he explained
that those suffering guilt saw us as devils—deformed, made hideous,
lurid, and terrible by the distortion of their own vision and by the illumination that their auras shed. But those spirits at peace saw us as angels, perfect with the perfection of their own sight and radiant with the
light of their own purity. So though the dead pass through the same
valley, it may variously seem the gateway to Elysium or the open
mouth of Hell. However, some spirits are not permitted to enter directly, but are compelled to remain in this world and reenact their misdeeds until remorse prepares them for transition under conditions within their power to bear. Earthbound, these are the spirits which cause
hauntings.

When I questioned Amanda as to the truth of what happened at the
Jackson place (for mother was my only source of information) she said:
"Land's sake! Don't you doubt ary word Delcie told you about what

went on here. It wore us all down till we was nothin' but bleedin'
nerves. And that was only the beginnin' of it! You couldn't set foot
outside—day or night, it didn't make no difference—that the weeds
didn't begin to shake, off to one side of you. And if you tried to see
what caused it, you couldn't see nothing. Or if you thought that maybe
you *did* see somethin', you couldn't for the life of you make out what!
It was awful, for you never had any notion what caused it, or why it
happened. None of us was what you'd call wicked, and it never seemed
to bother some that was. From what I've heard said, old man Jackson
was a good Christian, but you've heard how he used to go on about
somethin' that kept follerin' him, ain't you? Well, I allow he went off-
in-the-head, like they say—I come mighty near doin' it myself—but I
don't doubt ary bit somethin' *did* keep after him."

"Don't you suppose it's old Gabe's wolf?" I suggested.

"That shook the weeds, maybe; but 'twasn't no wolf that stomped
on the porch and sounded like it busted the door down and tore up the
place that night. All I know is that when Joe and me first come here,
everybody said Gabe's always been thataway. Nothin' ever hurts nobody, but something's always goin' on that keeps you afeared of your
shadow and in continual dread."

One moonlit night I took one of the Abbott girls home from revival
meeting and asked her if the Jackson house was still disturbed. She said
that once as she was sitting before her vanity, taking off lipstick before
going to bed, a light floated across the room and into the mirror. She
said it was the only thing she had ever seen there that frightened her.
But she walked so fast up the ghostly hollow that I was obliged almost
to run to keep abreast of her, and I caught the feeling that she was
eager to be indoors. When I came back—perhaps because I remembered
what Amanda had said—the weeds by the path began shaking. I tried to
believe it was a hound following me and kept looking back. But then it
came to a bare space: no dog crossed the open ground, but the shaking
resumed on the near side. I stopped glancing back and ran.

At the next farm, Lewis Schoolcraft's black yearling was asleep in
the road and when it leaped up startled, my heart almost stopped. Then
as I fronted Gabe's rock where something had jumped down on Otto
Lee's car, Elmore's old horse took fright under the trees across the
creek and lumbered off through the bushes—looking like anything but a
horse until it emerged into the open meadow. I went through college

without ever again seeing one of the girls on the head of Gabe home
from anything.

When Rolandus Rex Rohr—a newspaper publisher as extraordinary as
his name—sighted and measured around the head of Gabe, he seemed
interested in rocks and cliffs. I can imagine that a lead mine might be
found in a cliff, but when he got nowhere with his prospecting, he
moved in and asked permission to investigate the slough below Littlepage's Spring for signs of petroleum. He shoveled in the muck and
quicksand, digging up roots which glowed with foxfire and stirring the
wills-of-the-wisp to unusual activity. He kept claiming to find traces of
oil, but when a well was drilled on the hillside just above the swamp, it
produced only gas. Grandmother never believed he was seeking oil any
more than that he'd been looking for lead. Like some of the others who
speculated, she believed that Gabriel Littlepage brought more than his
flintlock and ax with him and concealed a treasure somewhere. Indeed,
there were strange marks on stones, and among the keepsakes that
Grandfather kept was an inexplicable eighteenth-century piece of Spanish silver. I think he said he found it in the lower garden.

I doubt that Mother ever knew with certainty, but she believed that a
corpse lay under the muck, and that the floating lights which sometimes hovered over the swamp were due to its decay or to the ghost of
the boy whose body she believed it was.

The facts are that after Mr. Hively's father grew old, he took a boy to
raise to help him. The lad disappeared—supposedly having followed or
been lured away by a band of gypsies. Mother believed that the old man
sent the boy into the corn loft to throw down corn, and that the boy
hit him on his bald head with an ear and laughed his silly laugh; that the
old man waited until he was climbing down, hit him with a wooden
handspike, and broke his back. Then to conceal the crime, he killed
him. If it happened, Grandfather only helped sink the body. Mother
said that the boy was a moron—maybe even an idiot—and nobody took
any interest in trying to find him.

I learned early not to rely on Mother's fantasies; to presume murder
just because she believed one had been committed would have been
naive. Not mother, but Caroline Cummings, an illiterate old soul who
liked to barter plants with Grandmother, made me end believing that
the slough hides the boy's bones, though all she said about him was,
" . . . Hit wuz no fault o' his'n 'e wuz a witless innocent. Weak-brained

wuz 'ow God made 'im, an' on 'is dyin' bed, I 'low ol' Jim wished 'e
could call back every wallop 'e ever taken 'im!" She paused and wet her
lips with her tongue. " 'E seed 'im, Ol' Jim did, them four awful days
an' nights 'at 'e wuz dyin'—an' yelled out to God an' Satan 'seechin'
'em to take 'im away—when 'e wuzn't goin' on about the Dog!"

What she said linked the boy with known fact. Of all the deaths I
ever heard described—and people on Gabe took morbid pleasure in telling of bad ones—that of Mr. Hively's father, James, was the most har-
rowing. Grandfather and his brothers—Zuinglius, Henry, Lincoln and
Hant—were all strong men, but it took all of them to hold their father
in bed when he rallied and screamed out in delerium, striving to beat
off a black dog. Grandmother said it was a beautiful dog the old man
had killed years before with a pitchfork out of hate for its owner, but
Caroline spoke of a different thing entirely: The Black Dog is a demon
which comes for the dying only when a terrible guilt is on his soul. (I
do not know if this Dog is a superstition anywhere else, but I heard of
him several times in West Virginia. Later, I found him—or a similar
demon—as a grim deity in the Voodoo pantheon.) Caroline said that her
husband, "Hyrum," was at the house the final night, and that as the old
man's spirit was leaving the body, the Black Dog became visible for an
instant, seized the soul, tore it from the old man's lips, shook it, leaped
off the bed and ran out into the night with it, leaving the room reeking
with the smell of brimstone. She said that other fiends peered in
through the door and windows, and that she would have preferred to
have her spirit taken by any one of them than by the Dog.

When I could not fall asleep—I was then about six—Mrs. Hively composed me by saying that the old woman was grossly ignorant, and that
those fiends came out of our copy of *Pilgrim's Progress*, which she had
loaned Hiram.

"Of course Caroline couldn't read it," she said, "but that's where
they came from. Remember how you used to think *you* saw them when
you were little?"

When I was three, the fiends in the pictures had seemed as real to me
as they must have to the old lady. The one on the cover lurked under
the lambrequin over the fireplace. Another haunted the cinnamon vine
that brushed the window, and the most frightful of all stayed in the
basement, and terrified me each time I peeped through the ventilating
hole and glimpsed it lurking behind the sauerkraut jar and the pickled

beans. So when Grandmother reminded me, and made me recall how she had carried me, kicking and screaming, and made me touch the fiend under the lambrequin (which proved to be only a tassel which stirred in the rising heat from the fire when wind blew down the chimney), I would relax, dutifully repeat after her:

> "Matthew, Mark, Luke and John,
> Bless the bed that I lie on.
> If I should die before I wake,
> Receive my soul, for Jesus' sake;"

sigh, and after a time drift into tolerably quiet slumber.

When I was very young there were no elfin wee folk on Gabe, or pixies, or nymphs, or sprites, or tricky leprechauns—only shadows and ghosts, and fiends, and evil spirits. I know from this life alone what it must have been to be a child in Puritan Salem, or even a child in the Dark Ages. Such religion as Gabe had was Puritan. There is no guilt like Puritan guilt, no phenomena as fearsome as that born of the Puritan conscience, no fiends like those of Calvinism. The end result of such religion is psychological disorientation. Coupled with German mysticism and Scottish supernaturalism, it can produce veritable nightmares of fantasy and self-deception. Devils assume reality; psychological archetypes take on embodied shapes, and ideas become first personifications, then objectifications—or such objectivity as ghosts and eidolons have makes them visible and self-existent.

The Black Dog hounded my childhood footsteps. However by the time I reached puberty, which came early for me at eleven or twelve, my dreams and nightmares changed from those of the Dog to others of a Cat and a Black Man. The Cat, larger than any panther, burned like Blake's Tiger in the forests of the night, fearful in its symmetry, to stalk the soul. It is the symbol of fear, a feline demon which is so swift that few men can escape it if they go abroad in the darkness of the world (as all men must), naked and weaponless against such a creature, their only hope escape or a desperation so great that it turns to face the demon as I did once in a dream. (To my great astonishment, in the dream, thus faced, the Cat shrank to a kitten, and I played with it.) Fear often does this, I learned, when I faced it afterward when I was awake—I have learned much from my dreams, even from nightmares.

The Black Man is a Negro savage who symbolizes to the white subconscious all that is animal and instinctive in civilized man. What a difference it would make if both races understood this! With what surprise
the young idealist would realize that at its deepest level his concern for
racial equality relates not to the Negro race but to himself, being but an
unconscious desire to liberate and make acceptable the actions and
impulses denied him by an artificial and over-civilized society. The
more repressed and conventional the individual, the more likely he is to
mistake the Black Man of his subconscious for the black man on the
street, and insist that the latter be "kept in his place." The more in-
secure and rebellious he is, the more likely he is to seek equality for the
Negro.

One night after I had cried myself sick to go home with Mrs. Hively,
my father—though not many then thought him that—brought me, riding his blind mare across the low gap from the Jackson place, and thrust
me into her waiting arms, saying merely, "Here, take him. That's what
you wanted, and now he wants it. Delcie has her hands full enough with
our baby." He probably meant merely that Jesse was all that Mother
was able to take care of, but when Grandmother repeated this speech
(as she always did when I showed the least restlessness for my parents),
she stressed *our* in such a way that the words meant that Jesse was the
only child that my father considered his own.

At first I was quite sure I was not his son. And not until I was grown,
and he proved to be a father to me, and I came to resemble him a little
was I sure; not until my own son imaged him was I positive he was my
father—he *is* my father. Poor Dad—it shook him to the shoesoles when I
visited him recently, and asked him right in front of his wife if he
thought he was my real father. He turned pale, and then red, and said
feebly, "Why—why yes; I *guess* so," and my stepmother looked at us
and asked me, "Can't you tell by looking in the mirror?"

I can tell by the looking glass, but he's had fifty-four years to mull
over the possibilities, and I'd think he could give me better than "I
guess so." Poor old soul, it must be hard to be 79 and still have to be
looking for enough in a son to convince oneself beyond any doubt. It's
certainly hard to live 53 years and still be looking for enough in oneself
to justify belief that one is the son of such a good man. But there is a
rabbinical saying: "He is not the father who begets the son; he is the
father who gives the son a father's love"—or something to that effect.

By that criterion, even if he was not my father when I was born, he became one to me.

By that same criterion, Mr. Hively was my father as long as he lived. As for Blackwell, even when spiteful boys called me his bastard and I fancied a resemblance, he was never my father at all. Yet in a sense I *was* his son, for I say, myself, that when a woman conceives, it is by the man who is in her heart; it is for his sake she closes her eyes to the man who impregnates her.

If Father did stress *"our,"* maybe that was what he meant. By the time Jesse was conceived, Blackwell was himself married, and Mother may have considered herself her husband's wife for a time—resigned if not satisfied.

After about three years, my parents left Gabe and moved to Will's Creek, where in 1921 Mother gave birth to her last child, Ray. Then they moved to Charleston. They sometimes came back to visit me, but the Hivelys were the only parents I knew, and to this day some of the people on Gabe call me "Hively." As long as he lived, so did James Andrew Daugherty, Grandmother's cousin, who perceived the spirit and knew that mine was that of a son of the couple who reared me, thus that of a kinsman, a cousin of his.

3

THE DAUGHERTY INFLUENCE

The Eye of God: The four diamonds stand for the four seasons, so the prayer is for God's perpetual watchful protection and guidance. This is a sign based on dynamic balance and movement through time

> *Though the subject of this work is the polter-*
> *geist proper, the phenomena of hauntings must be*
> *constantly mentioned as they are inextricably*
> *interwoven with the poltergeist. It is impossible to*
> *refer to one without mentioning the other.*
>
> Raymond Bayliss

If I ever belonged to anyone, it was to Eva Taylor Hively. Mine was a belonging of the spirit, of Karma, a thing of centuries, strong enough to overrule the blood. Mrs. Hively did indeed take me, as she told the midwife she would. Had she not done so, my life might not have been much different from my brothers', who never did or experienced anything very unusual, and were wonderfully normal, rational men free from doubt or uncertainty about themselves or the universe—conventional even in the unconventional things they did.

At least, this was my previous image of them. However, my younger brother was emotional and sensitive, and Jesse, as he grows older, occasionally betrays a dream within him. He always was as intense as I am, as fond of material success as I am of beauty. He loves as I do, only he loves his son, and I love mine and every other son. He belonged to my father unquestionably, and is very like him.

Had Mrs. Hively taken Jesse, he would have been as like me as an identical twin, as torn by the certainty of the psychic as I am by the reality of the materialistic, and at ease with neither. But had she taken Ray, by now he would be a recluse, surrounded by a strange assortment of birds, animals, books, and bizarre companions, some of them visible and more invisible; and the neighbors would speak of him as "touched," and go to him for irrational advice when life becomes too rational for sane folk to endure. Reared by my parents, he suppressed his real nature in his effort to attain material success until the stress and suppression grew greater than his enormous physical strength, and his heart failed him.

I went to Ray's funeral and sat dry-eyed, wondering that so much strength had proved more fragile than my own. I stood dry-eyed at the grave as his lodge brothers and comrades conducted their rites and blew taps for him. But after they all were gone, I went back to the grave, and found his flowers blown over. Seeing their beauty in the dust, cut off in their finest flowering, so like his, released me, and I wept for my brother with irrational grief, for I did not know him in life as I knew Jesse. But when his freed spirit at last communicated, I wept for myself in him, knowing that had my parents reared me it would have been *me* in the grave and him standing by. I wept in belated understanding, for the spirit by the grave never wore uniform, belonged to no lodge, and was of finer ether than is my own, and had Mrs. Hively reared him he would have been the dreamer, the visionary, and the one with knowledge.

Grandmother was a most unusual woman. She came of the fine old Taylor family of Virginia, and was admired as highly intelligent, shrewd, beyond reproach in morals and comportment, indomitable, and endowed beyond common with practicality. By local standards of the time and place, she was well-educated and informed: she took the newspaper and some magazines and had nearly a hundred books on subjects ranging from household medicine to the cultural and political history of Greece. She even had an indirect book on sex hygiene and the arts of love *(Man's Strength and Woman's Beauty*—I suppose she bought it trying to learn why she could not have children) as well as a few novels by good authors, one of romantic poetry, one on Spencerian calligraphy and steel-pen drawing—from which Grandfather drew deft, flourished copies of deer, birds, flowers, and elaborate letters (With the same technique, he drew graphic but imaginative sketches of naked men and women, and the two together, which he kept concealed in his locked trunk. He kept the key under the clock, supposing to his death that no one knew of it.); several religious books, and Bibles in every stage of wear, with the most worn one on display on the parlor table. The history of Greece and the book on sex were not displayed, and were forbidden me, to a Calvinistic mind, these illustrated books were less than decent and certainly not for the eyes of children, so they were kept secured in the locked bottom drawer of the dresser. By the time I was five I discovered that the drawer *above* was not locked and came out, leaving the books in reach, and as I began reading the Bible when I was three, I all but memorized them—mostly because they were forbidden, and because the Greek gods were so beautiful and so different from Jehovah and Jesus. It was not lost on me that Jesus was put to death for doing good, whereas they were not punished for doing evil. I decided that the Greek gods had it better.

But the circuitous language of *Man's Strength* conveyed very little clear information. I learned many words without their meanings.

I knew, too, that men used the "organ of copulation" in "consummating that union which is the natural and providential expression of instinct and the culmination of connubial felicity." But I could not have expressed this in simple speech.

I think the first real shock I ever gave Grandmother was when I asked her how babies came. She told me that mothers found them when they went out early when the dew is on, hidden under cabbage leaves. But Grandfather had already said that storks dropped them down chimneys for the mother to catch as she knelt at the fireplace. And I had doubted, for storks were never seen on Gabe, and mothers had babies who had only tin stovepipes poked through holes in the roof. Every family I knew had cabbages, so Grandmother's explanation sounded just a bit more likely, but I still wanted to know where they came from, not where they were found. So I said doubtfully, "I supposed they were born, like the calf was."

Grandfather laughed and said, "Well, I'll be dad-gummed!" and Grandmother turned red and replied, "Well, of course they are—those are just stories for children—but you are too young to know anything about birth."

It seemed the height of illogic, for I had undergone birth when I was about five years *younger*. But I did not press for more.

When the Black Man began appearing in my dreams seeking to kill me, my sexual instinct was hardly awake. But when I woke from my dreams of the Black Man, invariably I was sexually aroused, and I later discovered that the white man's fascination with the Negro has similar sexual overtones. It hardly need be said that I came to puberty without adequate sexual knowledge.

However, when Grandmother told tales about talking animals, or Grandfather told about giants and dwarfs and water-maidens, they always said, "Those are just stories," making sure that I understood the real meaning of the legend, parable or allegory. But Grandmother's most remarkable and incredible narrations were factual accounts, which she concluded by saying, "I don't know how to account for such things: I only know they happened."

Because I believed her, I have been able to enter realms denied men whose range of belief is more limited. Like her, I have always said, "We know so little: we do not know what is possible to man, and with God all things are possible." No generation ever needed more than ours the ability to accommodate the unbelievable, for the truth that seems incredible today may have to be believed tomorrow. "It is foolish to say that anything is impossible," she taught. Then she would tell of the Hebrew children in the fiery furnace, of the Axe-head which floated for Elisha, of the loaves and fishes which fed the multitude, of the water which became wine and of many other miracles, and say quietly, "Most men now would say those things are impossible," in such a way that it reflected on the foolishness of such men who doubt and deny.

Her kinsmen were all respectable, and most of them highly regarded. Many of them told much the same things. James Andrew Daugherty was my favorite of all those who visited frequently, for he had traveled far along unfamiliar paths. He talked with the dead; spirits were his familiars and his household guests. The simple fact that such a man—a policeman and thirty-second-degree Freemason who saw visions, talked in symbols and allegories; a Spiritualist and a worker of white magic— was acceptable to her, made him so to me.

As long as I sat quietly, he and grandmother paid me no attention and related the strange things of their youth. I would drink it all in, spellbound, until Grandmother noticed that it was past my bedtime and would pause to put me to bed, where I could lie pretending to be asleep and still hear most of what was said, fully expecting to have the cover snatched from the bed by invisible hands.

Psychologists, many of whom are much more learned than wise, are wont to make much of the traumatic effect that terrifying stories may have on a child. Frankly, I would not have missed hearing them for the world—and I believe myself the better from having heard them. Of course I suffered as soon as the lights were out; but as soon as the tales sank down into my subconsciousness, they had a catalytic effect upon ideas and mental processes. Particularly in religion and philosophy they tended to integrate disconnected and dissimilar strands, furnishing the dark background of death and mystery against which—and *only* against which—the dull monotone of the commonplace contrasts as a balanced meaningful pattern, ineffably beautiful and wonderful, a counterpoise of life-that-ends-in-death and death-that-ends-in-life, equal parts of the web of being.

Anything which helps integrate the consciousness or widen its range of perception is good for the individual; knowing that the dead are conscious and active in the lives of the living can only give serenity as one contemplates advancing age and approaching death. Such knowledge prepares the way for realization that physical bodies are no more "alive" than are the spirits of the disembodied. Conversely, knowledge that the living can affect the spirits of the dead makes separation less a cause for grief for *us* than an opportunity to make their disembodiment less of a hardship on *them.*

I soon became aware that the Daughertys perceived things that most people cannot or do not see. They boasted of their "second sight," their intuition, and their awareness of psychic entities and influences. They also had what they called "the power"—an ability to stop bleeding, cure burns, and cause things to happen. James Andrew had it in the highest degree of all, but Grandmother was not far behind him. No one thought of them as witches because they were not malevolent, but I suspect that if families transmit the ability to exert "the power," the Daughertys did so.

Enna Whitehead, Grandmother's sister, was "all Taylor" and a bit resentful (perhaps envious) of her relatives who "took after" the Daugherty side of the family. One day Enna exclaimed, "J. A.'s as fey as anybody ever gets to be! Do you suppose he really does see and talk with spirits?"

"I suppose so," Grandmother said casually without looking up from her mixing bowl of cake batter. "Just because you can't see and hear doesn't mean that those with the second sight can't. You know some of it's true, for Mother said so herself. I'd think you could remember all the talk we heard as children about what happened in Greenbrier County, and those things that used to go on at home."

"Oh, I guess I remember a little of it," Enna conceded, "but it was a long time ago, and I was hardly more than a baby."

Their conversation referred to phenomena which occurred in the Taylor home between 1873 and 1885. Grandmother's parents had married in 1870, and set up housekeeping in an old log house.

Grandmother was born in 1872 and was about a year old when the phenomena began. Ira Taylor and his wife, Sarah Daugherty, had finished their work for the day. Sarah had fed Grandmother and rocked her to sleep in her cradle. The couple had seated themselves for their evening meal, and had their heads bowed as Ira said a grace, when the house was shaken on its foundations by a deafening crash—the sound of splintering timbers, falling boards and shingles blended into one noise. They supposed that the primeval oak growing over the house had fallen on it, and that the shed rooms had collapsed. Horrified, they ran to see if the baby had been killed. But she was sleeping peacefully, and the room was intact. Then they opened the door to the other shed room and found it equally undisturbed. Ira went outside and found not even a fallen twig.

They decided that such an eldritch noise must be a warning, and because other—lesser—noises disturbed them frequently, as soon as he could get lumber dressed and stone cut, Ira built a frame house by Left Hand Creek and moved down off the mountain.

The new dwelling was a local showplace befitting a Taylor, with precisely cut stone chimneys, meticulous carpentry, smooth-planed ceilings, colorful wallpaper, and paint inside and out. The front porch had elaborate scroll-sawn ornaments in the latest fashion; the side portico was even more ornate. It was Victorian, but the lines were symmetrical, for the imbalance and blindness to proportion reflected in late Victorian and subsequent architecture had no place in the decisions which shaped that house. To please his wife Ira hired an itinerant painter to come and paint a decoration over the parlor mantel—a cross with doves for peace and tulips for faith, a strangely Pennsylvania Dutch design for the house of an Anglo-Scotch-Irish family. It was to protect the house from evil, and the family must have felt very strongly about it, for two years ago I found that Grandmother's brother, Ellet, still keeps the panel on which it was painted, though he tore down the house over forty years ago.

For some reason the Daughertys were greatly drawn to the Pennsylvania Dutch. Alexander Daugherty, Sarah's father, knew enough to qualify as a *Hexenmeister*, and drew birth and marriage records full of hex symbols and like Pennsylvania Dutch drawings in everything but language. He lettered his in Old English rather than in *Fraktur*. The crosses, doves, and tulips of Alexander's were exquisite. Those on the overmantel were maladroit, and done with such poor paints that the doves have disappeared entirely and the tulips are flaking off. But their use was for protection, not for ornament, and the family's faith in them was not lost on me, for I realized that Grandmother kept using the symbols in her needlework as long as her arthritic fingers could guide a

needle. Neither Ira's house nor Grandmother's ever was struck by lightning, damaged by wind, or set on fire by accident, and no one ever sat
down in them to a scant meal or went out from them without adequate
clothing. Shame never entered their doorways, and though Death came
and went, He came as a friend and in peace. Of course, the drawings did
not account for these things, but the attitude which accounted for the
drawings and the needlework did.

After moving down to the new house, Ira tore the floor and partition
wall out of the old shed rooms and used the log house as a stable for his
steers and yearlings. He kept the two-story part full of corn and fodder,
taking the cows down to the new barn at the creek, where Sarah could
tend them. Since hunters began lying out in it and building fires in the
chimney despite the nearness of the fodder and hay, he expected the
place to burn down some night, and so took off the door to the stable
and left it open so that the cattle could escape.

Two or three years went by, when one morning just after midnight
he was roused by an old woman called Granny Sides or Seitz, who had
been trudging home through the snow from delivering a baby somewhere lower on Left Hand. She was too out-of-breath to do more than
gasp "Fire!" and motion toward the mountain behind the house.

Ira ran to the back and saw the hilltop aglow, roused Sarah and two
of her brothers who were spending the night, bundled into warm
clothes and crossed Left Hand with them to a spot high enough to give
a view of the building. The four of them watched with Granny Sides as
the roof fell in, and the walls finally collapsed in a fountain of sparks
and flame.

"I run to let you know so's maybe you could let out any stock
penned there," the old woman explained when she caught her breath.
"Hit tuk fire real slow, hit 'peared to me around the chimley or the end
wall upstairs. I seed hit as I rounded the bend at July, and I run as fast
as my old legs would take me."

"Do you suppose the steers would have enough gumption to come
out?" Sarah worried. "Stock goes crazy in a burning building."

"Anybody who caught it on fire surely would run them out," Ira
fumed. "That's the least they could do."

Next morning, what he saw when he came over the crest of the slope
chilled him to the marrow. Instead of a smouldering heap of embers, he

1625289

saw the house as he had left it the day before. The steers ambled out, lowing for fodder, and there was no trace of fire anywhere.

Ira studied the sprinkle of snow and found no human tracks except his own. Unwilling to return to a building that he could watch burn down by night and find intact by morning, he rounded up the cattle to drive them down to the new barn. Hearing something clatter at the house, he glanced back, and glimpsed something which capered along the ridge of the roof and disappeared at—or into—the chimney. Telling of it, Grandmother would always say, "He said he couldn't see it very well, but he knew it couldn't be a naked Negro boy, and an ape of any kind was out of the question. So he did not go back to try to get a closer look at it. He hired somebody to haul down the feed, and never did use the old house for anything after that."

When Granny Sides finished telling about it, the hunters never went back, either, but took to lying out under the Bottomless Hole Cliffs on the north hillside. They are sinister looking, and the old folks said that the hole goes down all the way to hell, but nobody ever saw anything supernatural at the cliffs.

Ira and the Daughertys called the incident the work of Satan. Granny Sides was certain it was witchcraft. I do not know what to believe, though I might have done as Ira did—let the house grow up in brush and rot down without ever going back to it.

If it was an hallucination, who implanted it in the old woman's mind, and how did she convey it to *four* rational people who were asleep until she woke them?

Moreover, as far as anyone knows, nothing tragic, evil, or unfortunate ever occurred there, for Ira's father, William Taylor, who built the house around 1850 when he arrived from Tennessee, and his wife, Mahala Cromwell, reared a stout lot of sons and daughters there. All did well in life, and in their day the house was as peaceful as a Communion table. Enna said her mother caused it somehow; not by willing or doing, but by *being*—being a Daugherty, I suppose.

The capering black thing—what could it have been? Time and again, people have reported such a thing in West Virginia, but not many have been as reliable as Ira Taylor who, people said, told the truth even when it was to his disadvantage.

I cannot imagine Satan's bothering to caper along the peak of a West

Virginia barn in the winter. Ira believed that he roams the earth continually, visibly, in any guise he chooses, seeking souls to ensnare and destroy; but from that day to this he lost any chance of ensnaring any soul on Left Hand in the vicinity of that barn. Righteous as Ira may have been, I doubt that he was holy enough to incur Satan's personal malice—even if I believed in Satan, which I don't. So wiser men than I must speculate and explain what happened, if they can.

Enna Whitehead was wrong in attributing everything to the Daugherty influence, for Ira Taylor had encounters with mysterious phenomena even before he married Sarah—in fact even as a child. As quite a small boy, he was sent with hot lunch for his father, who with his neighbors was working the public road in lieu of cash payment of taxes, somewhere near the mouth of Lower July. Ira was delighted because he had his mother's permission to go on to 'Tater Run to spend the afternoon with his Grandmother Cromwell, who baked memorable Dutch cookies each time he came. As he came in front of the prow of Battleship Knob above July he thought he saw his father's coat on a rock beside the road—and as he did not see him or any of the other men, he called to him. The coat slid off the rock and vanished into the ground.

He ran and found his father quite some distance down the road toward Grandmother Cromwell's, and he would not even go on alone but insisted that his father take him and come for him when he started home.

When he and his closest friend, a youth named David, were about seventeen, their fathers decided to send them with a wagonload of corn to be ground at the new mill in Walton, which had new burrs and ground very fine meal—far better than that ground by the old tub mill in Left Hand, people said. They had to wait their turn, and when their grist was ground, the sky looked rainy and it was almost twilight. So, delighted by the necessity of spending the night in Walton, which had a dozen houses or so and seemed quite a city to them, they besought the miller to take them in. He finally agreed, but charged them a quarter apiece for their lodging, supper and breakfast, muttering that he was not set up to lodge anyone as he had only a poor excuse for one spare room.

The miller's expansive wife set them a hearty supper, however, jovially bade them welcome, and soon after finishing the dishes said, "Me and Hezekiah turns in early, but the young ones set up late. Your bed's fixed, so turn in when you feel like it." And with a huge treenware mug of posset in one hand she went upstairs. The assorted young people— the miller's children and his wife's children by previous marriages and the younger ones who were half-brothers or half-sisters of both other sets—all were congenial and lively. Ira and David quickly felt at ease with them, so they remained up until almost eleven o'clock—later than they ever had before. They guessed riddles, played games, made popcorn and pulled taffy, and one of the girls told their fortunes with cards—scandalously wicked fun, Ira thought, for playing-cards were anathema in any Taylor house. And before retiring, the miller's eldest son made a quantity more posset with so much rum in it, it made Ira's head feel light.

When this young man decreed it bedtime, Ira and his friend followed the others upstairs to the room they had been assigned. It contained only a rickety cord bed with a cornshuck mattress, boxes and barrels, a broken dresser, and a makeshift chair or two. They undressed in the pitch-dark cold and felt their way into bed, delighted to discover that the Miller's wife had piled wool-filled comforters over the thin coverlid under which they had expected to shiver all night. Soon, warmed within by the glowing posset and externally by the bedding, they stripped to the skin, and Ira was in a delicious relaxation of comfort and drowsiness when he was stirred awake by the old bed's quivering and creaking. The shaking kept up an unconscionable time, pausing briefly, then resuming, and at last he nudged his buddy in the back and whispered, "You've been at that long enough to do it a dozen times! I can't get to sleep."

"I'm not doing that!" David exclaimed.

"Next time just go on and finish," he snickered.

The quivering and rustling began again, and Ira was startled to have his friend flounce over, touch his loins and begin searching for his hand and arm. "Are you shaking the bed with your foot some way just to scare me?" the youth whispered intensely.

"You don't need to try to put it off on me!" Ira said almost crossly. "You're shaking it now with your own foot."

"Don't pull the cover off me!" the youth pleaded.

"Didn't you just tug it off me?"

"Not the first time!"

They hauled the comforters to their ears and lay so close they could feel the length of each other's bodies and detect any movement whatsoever. But though they lay petrified, the bed shook worse than before.

"Ira, I'm scared!" David whispered.

"You too?"

"Yell! Make them bring a light or something!"

"They'd think we're crazy. Maybe we're drunk or something."

Just then pandemonium broke loose in the room. A new-born baby began screaming. Hobnails scuffed the floor. A woman gave a shrill desperate cry. Something thudded, and someone fell and smashed a chair. There were sickening sounds of soft flesh striking something solid, and all grew deathly still. Then, as the boys clung to each other in terror, their heads under the cover, it was snatched away. The bed tilted sidewise, dumped them onto the floor with the mattress on top of them, and fell back with a crash that shook the room. Before they were out from under the mattress, off the icy floor, in ran the miller in a nightshirt with a flickering lamp. And as they grabbed for comforters to conceal their nakedness, in came the miller's wife with another lamp, and one of the sons, naked, half-shrouded in a coverlid, with a blown-out candle.

"Don't be scared, boys," the miller said fatuously. "This's nothing that'll hurt you! It's over for the night when the baby stops screamin' and the bed turns over. It's been thisaway ever since I bought the damn house, and we know just what to expect. It'll be as quiet as a church now for the next ten or twelve days, but I declare, tonight was as bad as I ever heard it."

"It's my fault," his wife said. "When you boys offered the money, I told Hez it wouldn't happen yet for two or three days. I couldn't stand to think of you boys freezin' all night out at the mill and maybe takin' sick. That's the truth of it."

"I wouldn't 'a had this happen for a Yankee dollar," the miller apologized. "It's plumb embarrassin', for I know you'll wonder what kind of folks we are to have this sent on us. It wasn't nothin' *we* done that caused it. Anybody in Walton'll tell you the house was thataway before we came here."

"It was some hellish thing somebody done," the woman sighed. "Them that lived here must 'a knowed about it, but nobody in Walton lets on. So, it's just somethin' we got to live with. You boys pile back in bed now and don't pay no mind to me. I've had three husbands and seven boys; nothin' I might see's anything I ain't seen many a time before."

"You can't pull out in the middle of the night, and it rainin'," the miller reminded them. "You can keep the light if you want it and it's all over now."

" '... If you want it!' " his wife chuckled, "Hez, you wouldn't stay in here yourself without a light now. But he's tellin' you the truth," she said seriously to the boys. "It ain't goin' to bother you no more tonight. I've got the bed made up, so crawl back in before you catch cold or somethin'."

She went out so the youths could get back into the bed without further embarrassment, and the miller spread their other comforter over them. Neither closed an eyelid the rest of the night, but as the miller predicted, the room remained perfectly quiet.

When the two reached home they told of their experience, and on their fathers' next trip to Walton, they inquired and found that everyone knew that the miller's house was subject to this phenomenon. One man said that he too had had the covers snatched from over him—and the bed not only dumped him to the floor but fell on top of him—so the men could not doubt that their sons had told them the truth.

As Ira told of the experience—which he did often in later life—he said he kept having nightmares in which he relived it. But finally he dreamed that the phenomenon took place when the room was lighted: he saw a new-born child brought screaming into the room by a brutal-looking man who knocked down the girl who tried to snatch it from him. Then he took the infant by the ankles and dashed its head against the chimney front several times and threw it into a roaring fire in the fireplace, where it was consumed. After that, Ira was certain he had seen as well as heard what had sometime taken place in the room, and was satisfied.

But grandmother was not satisfied, and neither am I. Knowing what tragedy had occurred goes nowhere in explaining how years later the sounds of the crime could become audible at intervals as if it were being reenacted in the dark. Nor does it explain what dark forces began by vibrating the bed, jerked off the covers as if with human hands, and tilted the bed sidewise—sometimes upside down. It does suggest that places subject to uncanny phenomena have been scenes of violence, or tragedy, or intense dark emotions.

Something of this nature must have occurred on the ridge near the
Taylor place, for even before the Civil War, Ira's father saw a specter
which by my time was referred to as "the Black Nun." Mother once
saw it; one troubled afternoon so did I, and others have reported seeing
it.

To me it looked more like a flying skeleton than like a nun, though
the long black garment which fluttered loosely in rags about it as it
sped past resembled a nun's habit. I was sitting tormented by worry on
the Lilly Rock, the highest and most isolated spot on our farm, watching Noah Young's three sons playing at his barn below in the high
meadow. A sheet of tin had blown off, and the children were climbing
through from the loft, clambering to the peak and sliding down onto
the low shed roof, laughing and squealing with make-believe consternation when they slid too far and fell onto the soft, dry dungheap just
below.

The Black Nun appeared at the northwest end of the meadow, seeming to move about three feet above the ground, and at a rate which I
would guess to equal that of a car driving at 70 miles an hour. That's
why I can say it wasn't—and maybe never had been—human. It swept
past the barn on the side behind the peak of the roof, so the boys did
not see it. But they soon scampered out and down the mountain, and
later, when I asked the eldest why they ran away, he said they "suddenly felt scared" as if something awful was close by.

It *was* awful, too; a dull, rusty, scarecrow-form of flying black rags,
with no visible face or features, which jellied reason and chilled the
bone. It simply came into view at one end of the open meadow, and
went out of view at the other side, without apparent purpose, with
nothing to give warning of its coming and with nothing occurring afterward to give it any apparent meaning. Always it goes at that same frantic speed, following no path, going through brush like air, up slopes so
steep a living person would have to scale them with care to each step
lest he fall off balance.

But why *I* should have seen it remained a mystery—until at my request a psychic friend asked "Adam," a part of his own unconscious
mind. "Adam" said that the Nun is an embodiment of an evil thought-
form—a psychic scapegoat—which someone created to bear his hate or
some other evil—a symbol given a form half shadow, half substance, as

one does when he creates a tulpa, or eidolin, or dopplegänger, or materializes an ectoplasmic shape to give a spirit a visible body or a voice, or creates a ghost, or causes one already created to become visible. "When you see a thing fleeing its creator, desperately wishing for annihilation . . . how can you help being appalled?" "Adam" questioned. He suggested that the Nun always is seen running because, being activated by emotion similar to that which created it, it seeks to escape a further burden of evil. It is somewhat conscious of selfhood and something like a spirit, but with no hope of heaven and knowing only the respite of sleep and the longing for annihilation—"a thing similar to the banshees and geists of Europe," he added. "Do recall and find if there were negative thoughts, fights, bitterness in the days it was seen," my friend urged me.

As I pondered what I know of those who have seen the Nun, I realized that the explanation seemed to fit the circumstances. William Taylor is not a clear personality to me, but I know that he hated with intensity. His stepmother treated him and his brother abominably, giving them merciless whippings, and confining them for whole days in a dark outbuilding without food or water when their father was away riding over the two counties where he owned land. The boys endured her abuse until William was sixteen and his brother eighteen. Then their uncle gave each of them fifty dollars, and they took their rifles and two of their father's horses and ran away to Tennessee. The horse was all William ever received of his father's wealth. From ancestral plantation, slaves, and extensive landholdings, he was reduced to a log house, a hill farm, and hard labor. He came to Left Hand bringing only his intelligence, his pride, his aristocratic ideas, and his hatred of his stepmother. Then he became so caught up in the Millerite Delusion that he and his wife dressed in white ascension robes and on the predicted day climbed a hill at midnight to wait the return of Jesus.

With such hate in his heart, one could hardly go up to meet the Lord. Perhaps in the tension of his spiritual conflict at that time, he wrapped a symbolic woman in the black flames of his hate and sent her fleeing across the hills. It is singular that though no one who ever told of seeing the Nun thought her human, all called the specter "her" or "she." Perhaps, after his stepmother's death, her spirit became attached to this weird eidolon. If so, the hills of her stepson's home must seem the

ridges of hell, and the valleys between them, vales of thick darkness in
the Valley of the Shadow.

Mother saw her only a few days before she married my father. The
state of her emotions then may be guessed from what I already have
said. She did not know then that she had been given a drug to interrupt
her menses, as I believe, or that Grandmother had intercepted her lover's letters, which Grandmother admitted to me, but her reluctance to
marry a man she did not love was matched by unwillingness to bear a
child before marriage: her love was counterpoised by the belief that her
lover had made her pregnant and abandoned her. Long after I was a
man, Mother told me that her distress was so great that had not her
mother's spirit appeared to her and bade her live for the sake of the
child that she would bear, she would have eaten poison mushrooms and
killed herself.

I know the circumstances of one of the other sightings. An old man
everyone called "Poor Old Uncle Dick" Williams (a very good but
simple-minded old fellow) had shown a man great kindness in his
orphanhood, and had earned his deep gratitude. On that occasion, the
man had heard that the poor old soul was very ill at his son-in-law's
house, and had gone to visit him. He found "Uncle Dick" near death;
the old man told him that two days previously his son-in-law had found
him soiled, and—as he had lain neglected in his excrement for hours—it
had dried on him. The son-in-law dragged the old man out of bed, clad
only in a shirt, to the creek near the house, jerking him to his feet each
time he fell, cursing him and striking him with a stubby broom. When
they reached the water, though there was ice along the edges, he forced
the old man to bend over, dipped the broom, and viciously scoured the
filth from him. The sick man developed pneumonia, and when the visitor saw the bruises, felt the fever, and saw his torn skin, he hurried up
July to tell the Williams men on the mountain of their father's abuse.
Then he came on to Grandfather's to ask if charges could be made
against the son-in-law. On the path up July, the Nun flapped past him,
"like a big black buzzard against the snow," he said, filling him with
horror.

"Poor Old Uncle Dick" died in a short time, but his sons refused to
bring charges against their brother-in-law, since they realized that were
he imprisoned his large family would become a burden upon them. But

the old man's indignant friend said he placed a death-curse on the son-in-law, and I never doubted that he did. For the son-in-law took cancer of the genitals, and was castrated in two separate operations, each of which seemed to arrest the malignancy for a year or so. But about the fifth year he died, after the cancer spread inward. To my mind, hate sufficient to create and localize a cancer to inflict such punishment is enough to activate the Black Nun or almost any other kind of terrifying psychic phenomenon.

I had my own dark emotions when I saw the Nun, of course, but it is not yet time to tell of them. But she drew enough life-force from me to give her clear form, and my terror filled her with fear so acute the boys in the barn could feel it. How long she is damned to remain, I have no way of knowing—perhaps until, as my friend's "Adam" says, someone releases her from her bondage by making her aware that grace exists.

James Andrew liked to tell of a fright his father had at Lower July sometime before the McCrosskeys built in the glen there. All the mysterious phenomena on Left Hand seemed confined to the stretch between the two Julys.

It had turned cold suddenly, and he was riding hard on his way home from work, eager to reach Taylors' and borrow a coat from Ira, for he was thinly clad. Before the dour McCrosskeys closed it off, a shorter path from July led to Taylors' on the west side of the creek, worn by them as they went to and from the Cromwell place at 'Tater Run. So James Andrew's father left the public road and crossed Left Hand, and when he reached Taylors' pole bars, he dismounted to lay them down.

Just as he was ready to lead the horse through, it neighed in terror, reared, and bolted. When he turned to see what had frightened it, he found himself confronting what appeared to be only the front quarters of a huge black horse, which bared its teeth and reached for him with its long neck. He screamed and ran, and the long-necked monster loped after him on its two legs. He understood that the ill things of darkness cannot cross running water, so he leaped the rail fence, plunged into Left Hand and splashed up the east bank. The horse-fiend did not follow, but James Andrew's father was in a lamentable state when he reached Taylors' and burst in, soaked through, half frozen, and shivering more from terror than from cold.

Ira soon got him into dry clothes, and Sarah prepared a tub of mustard-water and made him sit with his feet in it before the fire to head off pneumonia, so he came to no harm. However, the unfortunate man was hardly composed when his elder son rode up in alarm, saying the horse had come home saddled, and the family was afraid he was drunk and had fallen off. Ira assured the youth that his father had not been drinking that night, but had fallen into Left Hand by mishap. Ira knew that if the lad heard the truth, the boy would not ride back to Coleman Hollow to calm the family, for nothing could have induced either father or son to go out in the dark when a huge two-legged horse was prowling. And Ira had no stomach for going, himself.

Indeed, James Andrew's father and both the sons were at the Taylor house when the worst disturbance occurred there. Just after dark Ira heard something strike the wall and fall to the back porch floor. He went to the door, and as he peered out, a small clod sailed past his head into the kitchen. He called Sarah and went inside for his revolver, and when he opened the door a piece of gravel floated past him, striking the lamp she held but not breaking it. Then a shower of small gravel rattled against the wall, and the dogs ran in past him. There was nothing near to conceal anyone who might have thrown anything, and no gravel nearer than the bars along the creek. Ira walked about the yard with the lamp and convinced himself no one was lurking there, but clods began falling at his heels; he heard a laugh so distant it might have come from the log house on the hill. Suddenly he saw the revolver as a useless thing, and hurried inside. He locked the doors and took the family into the parlor, where the cross over the mantle seemed more security than the pistol. He bade the others be quiet, and read aloud from the Bible to keep down their hysteria, for after they left the kitchen, the clods and gravel had begun falling on the front porch, striking the walls and rattling on the windowglass—which surely would have broken had anyone thrown such gravel against it, for some pieces were as large as hickory nuts. Even the first clod had not seemed to be thrown, and the stone which struck the lamp moved slowly, with the motion of something in a dream.

After Ira read from the Holy Book a few moments, the dirt and gravel ceased falling, but a noise began on the porch as if someone were rolling nailkegs with a few loose nails in them from end to end of it. Daugherty kept some kegs with nails that he had stolen a few at a time from where he worked, and now he got down on his knees inside the doorway and begged the noise to cease, vowing to make good the nails if the persecution were remitted. As he prayed, mocking laughter and jeers rang from outside, but the tumbling ceased. When it did, a number of much larger stones struck the wall.

"In the name of God the Father, God the Son, and God the Holy Ghost, I command you to say what troubles you to be here, or leave this house in peace!" Ira cried in desperation, using the Hex conjuration that compels a ghost to speak or depart.

For a moment all grew still, and the family hoped that the command had silenced whatever was outside. But before they could relax, noises began again. A hurdy-gurdy began playing somewhere overhead, and it sounded as if a dozen persons began dancing on the porch roof, stamping so hard it sounded as if they must tear off the shingles. Mrs. Hively remembered that quite clearly, and said the music was like that which some gypsies who camped on the Taylor place each year played when they made a dancing bear perform, and to which they, themselves, danced. The cries and laughter on the roof also reminded her of the gypsies.

When this began, Ira grouped the family in front of the painted cross and bade them sing hymns as loudly as they could, for he remembered what he had seen capering on the roof of the old house on the mountain. Then he read the account of the Lord's crucifixion, burial, and resurrection. He committed himself and his household to God's protection and care, and they resigned themselves to sit in silent dread of worse phenomena until the disturbance finally ended, about three o'clock in the morning.

James Andrew declared that never in his life save twice when attacked by the Barr's Run spirit (which I myself later came to know only too well) had he been in such a state of terror. When I was in my teens I asked him if in his deep studies he ever had found any explanation for such phenomena.

"Not for all," he considered. "Things always happened around Pa and me. But rocks and clods are poltergeist phenomena, and they say poltergeists are a low order of spirits. Nobody really knows what they are, nor how they do all the things they do. I was a boy then, just changing into a man, and they say that an unhappy person at that age is usually around when a poltergeist starts acting up. I don't reckon I was the happiest boy in the world when I was that age. Maybe it was on account of me."

"Do they ever come inside and make noises and move things around?" I asked, thinking of thumps I had heard, and of books that had fallen off my table.

"Yes, and upset things, and appear in the shapes of animals, make noises of all kinds, talk, and set fires—just about anything."

"Could it have been a poltergeist that shook the bed when Ira and David were staying at the Miller's house in Walton, and what tipped the bed up?"

He raised his eyebrows, tautened his long cheeks, and pursed his lips—exactly as Grandmother sometimes did—an expression which, if translated into words, would have said, "Your guess is as good as mine."

"You know all about spirits;" I pleaded, "tell me why Gabe and Left Hand have had such an awful lot of supernatural things happen. Did something terrible take place somewhere near here?"

"No doubt," he sighed. "Anywhere man ever has lived, something terrible has taken place at one time or another. Indians lived here thousands of years before us, and white men used the trail for fifty years before anyone settled here. Who knows? But I think the living have more to do with what happens than the dead. Did you ever know anybody on Gabe or that part of Left Hand who was altogether happy or fully satisfied?"

I found it a searching question: certainly those who experienced the things about which I knew were not.

SOMETHING NOT QUITE INNOCENCE

Strength and Courage: Here the sign uses a rooster (symbol of watchfulness) rather than the usual eagle

From childhood's hour I have not been
As others were—I have not seen
As others saw—I could not bring
My passions from a common spring.
From the same source I have not taken
My sorrow; I could not awaken
My heart to joy at the same tone;
And all I lov'd, I lov'd alone . . .

Edgar Allan Poe

Until I was thirteen, Grandmother did not alarm herself as to my spiritual state. She took me to Sunday School whenever one was in operation within walking distance, and to meeting whenever any Millerite preached nearer than Rolling Hill Church on Hurricane. When she could not hear Millerite sermons, she often made do with Baptist or Methodist preaching, calling it "a little better than none," and smiled enthusiastically when some fire-breathing Baptist got carried away with the Second Coming, as was not infrequently the case.

I could see little difference among preachers for, one and all, they ranted against drinking, card-playing, bobbed hair, short dresses, cosmetics, and fornication. All but the Methodists included dancing. But, I could detect, drunkenness kept on; bobbed hair grew ever more common and skirts shorter. More and more cosmetics came into use, and as fornication did not cease to be a favorite sermon topic, I judged that sin had remained as prevalent as ever. The only one of the devil's works that the preachers seemed to succeed in keeping cried down was horse racing, but our local horses were seldom more than broken-down plow hacks, so that would not have been much fun anyhow—certainly not anything to compare with fornication, which I decided must be almost universally enjoyed from the frequency and vehemence of its denunciations. More and more I wondered what it was.

When Preacher Metz said that Man's concupiscence gives rise to fornication, and Grandmother explained after church that *concupiscence* means eagerness for physical pleasure, I knew that it was something that one does with the body. And I began to suspect that it was the *pleasure* Metz was so vehemently against rather than the sin, for he was a dour, gloomy, funereal old bone-rack who Grandfather said would

48

sour milk just by looking at it. I felt that just by the nature of things, whatever this old raven was against, I was for, since he chilled me like the north wind. However, the day I reached thirteen, Grandmother began a campaign to get me converted and baptized.

Her belief was that up to that age, if a child dies, it is taken to heaven automatically. Usually when a child did die, she sighed piously and called the death an evidence of God's prescience and mercy—proof that He could see ahead and thwart the devil, who otherwise would have probably succeeded in winning the child's soul.

"Up to his thirteenth birthday, no child is accountable for sin," she pontificated as a prime article of faith. So I felt perfectly secure, even if the End of the World should come, and even though I had stolen Grandfather's fine German-steel knife to use in place of my cheap dull one; had told Grandmother lies whenever I thought I could get by with it; and for over two years I had given myself such pleasure as a sexually precocious boy can provide himself. I took full advantage of unaccountability right up to ten minutes past ten of the morning of my birthday (allowing the other five minutes for possible error in the clock), for I still thought that since concupiscence gives rise to this indulgence, I was fornicating when I did it, and that I could land in hell if I did it after ten-fifteen.

It is one terrible, solemn feeling to believe in eternal hell and see it gaping open ahead, with one's immunity from it at an end: by ten o'clock I had put Grandfather's knife back where he could find it, resolved not to lie to Grandmother any more; and having prolonged my final indulgence and tried to satisfy concupiscence to the fullest degree, I resolved reluctantly to fornicate no more and pondered whether I did anything else that was sinful. I came to accountability with the best of intentions, my spirit submissive, however rebellious the flesh.

Good intentions carried me through the rest of the day without sin. The second day I caught myself just in time to keep from lying to Grandmother, and by a heroic struggle of will I resisted the urge to masturbate. On the afternoon of the third day, however, salvation through righteousness proved a vain hope (I was afraid from the first it might); so having yielded once, I realized I must go as a sinner for conversion at the next revival. Until then, I might as well sin as often as I pleased and hope that the Day of Judgment could hold off until revival-time.

So when a gross-looking, pot-bellied, tobacco-chewing little Millerite preacher, Wall, by name, whose breath smelled like a stale spitoon, came to Gabe and pitched a tent on the school grounds, I went the first night, and testified that I was a sinner, and was repentant (though in truth I was much sorrier to give up fornication than to have indulged in it). I said that I realized my only hope of salvation lay in the grace and forgiveness of God, asked for the prayers of the Church, affirmed that I accepted Christ as my personal Saviour, and asked for baptism.

As the elders gathered to give me the hand of fellowship and the holy kiss, the singing and clapping which broke out galvanized Old Lady Agnes Kieffer into a shouting spell; through some power she threw aside her cane and bounded about the tent like a kangaroo. Her son, an Elder, closed his eyes and stood quivering and jerking, saying, "I see Jesus! I see Jesus!" The clapping accelerated. A woman sprang up and started leaping up and down. Two girls began shouting, and as the hysteria mounted—venting the repressions the community had kept pent up since the last revival—the meeting became a mass emotional catharsis quite hypnotic in its effect. The God might as well have been Damballah, the faces black, and the hills outside those of Haiti or Senegal, for this was primitive religion. The preacher was ecstatic. Two back-slidden persons declared themselves reconverted. A girl cried out that she had committed fornication—I wondered how a girl could, having no penis—and fell on her knees at the mourner's bench. When the tent was somewhat quieted (but before the excitement died down), the preacher took up the collection, and even dollar bills went into the hat.

The following nights produced similar excitement. As word spread that a Holy-Ghost revival was in progress, people came across the mountain from Buffalo Lick, off Hurricane, from Cotton Tree and Doctor's Creek to attend. By the end of the week there were five or six converts to be baptized and nearly a dozen back-slidden already-baptized persons added to the church. The Elders (Granny Kieffer's son, Cousin Dexter Staats, Lewis Schoolcraft, and Bill Lowe) were in transports. The Gabe Adventist Church had been hovering between life and death for thirty or forty years, paralyzed by Jesus's inexplicable delay in returning and wasted by the falling away of Adventists to the Baptist and Methodist churches. But now it appeared that the Millerites might even become strong enough to build a church and find a regular preacher jointly with Rolling Hill. Grandmother was as delighted as

any, but when she listed the constant, the converted, and the reconverted, Grandfather, little given to enthusiasms, said merely, "This is
July: count them in January."

The ensuing Sunday afternoon, we converts, all dressed in white,
resorted to the Mouth of Gabe to the deep hole where I was just beginning to learn to swim. The swimming hole wasn't as large as many
private pools are today, but it was seven feet deep in one place, sand-
bottomed, and had a wonderful slope. To drown oneself in it would
have required downright ingenuity, and as Grandfather had himself
learned to swim there, he declared it perfectly safe. Each time the paper
carried news of drowning, he showed it to Grandmother, saying, "That
just goes to show you what can happen if you don't know how to
swim." Finally he got her to agree to let me learn, though he never
found a rebuttal to her argument that no one *ever* drowned if he stayed
out of the water.

The tobacco-chewing preacher soused us under. I strangled and came
up sputtering, but no one paid any attention and the crowd sang and
shouted so loudly that the ceremony attracted people on the road. A
few got out and came to watch, and one overdressed lady from New
Jersey called it "a quaint, old-time, country baptism," and looked at us
as if we were aborigines holding a tribal ritual. Her companion averred
that it was the first outdoor baptism she had ever witnessed, laughed,
and remarked that it seemed unsanitary. I had never witnessed an
indoor baptism, and found myself thinking of tanks such as a few
persons had for dipping cattle, and imagining that it would take one of
that size for her. I wondered where churches kept them when they were
not in use. The two women deeply antagonized me, partly because they
were outlanders, partly because of their fine clothes, and because they
clearly regarded us as gazing-stocks, interesting in our primitive way,
but inferior. Had they spoken to me as I emerged from the water, they
might well have gotten such a look as Americans receive in rural Mexico
when they take snapshots of peons in regional costume.

Monday afternoon the Seabolt twins, Ray and Gay, came and asked
me if I wanted to go to the swimming hole. It was hot and sultry and
the idea of the cool water was irresistible, so I went. We stripped to the
skin and went in. I was neck deep in the pool when my feet touched on
something unspeakable and I yelled in surprise.

"You get on a turtle?" Ray asked.

"No. It's cloth, and it's squashy. I think it's somebody drowned!"

We got a long pole and at last fished up the object. It proved to be a large burlap bag, weighted with rocks and the remains of five large, long-drowned cats.

"Godamighty!" one of the boys gagged, when we dumped the water-logged carcasses onto the sandbar. "I just swallowed a mouthfull of that water!"

I had a yellow-green feeling in my stomach. "Aaagh!" I retched, "I strangled when I was baptized. I like to have swallowed the whole pool!"

We poked the disintegrating cats back into the bag and threw it into the current below the pool, then went upstream and tried to wash away even the thought of them. But the sensation they gave us stuck, slimy and foul as the carcasses.

Grandmother insisted that the loathsomeness in the water had no bearing at all on the purity or efficacy of my baptism—but it did. To this day, the word evokes a memory of dead, eyeless, liquifying cats and the tactile sensation of the oozing burlap. For the first time I wished I'd been converted a Methodist, so I could have been sprinkled.

Still, my spiritual strength had been fortified by the revival, and during the week I did nothing at all that I considered sinful, and though the urge of sex was not diminished, I stoically withstood it, though the repression brought three days of migraine.

The preacher had promised to return the following Sunday, and our newly-organized congregation was waiting. But he did not appear. After an hour of disappointed waiting, Cousin Dexter, whose persistent nasal condition beaded the tip of his nose with a drop of water and gave him a sniff by which one could measure time, wiped his nose, gave a very loud sniff and attempted half-heartedly to raise a tune. Alcie Carpenter, who with training could have been an opera soprano of distinction, siezed it as soon as she recognized it and turned it into a hymn. Others joined as they were able, though she soared high above them. Then Cousin Dexter suggested a psalm and read the first verse, followed by the congregation in unison.

The psalm was in progress when an old roadster, with only its driver, rattled into view. The fat preacher had come in this conveyance once or twice with its owner, who claimed to be a preacher, too, though he looked more like a half-starved, shifty-eyed bootlegger. We expected to be told that the car had broken down, for it looked as if its most recent mile was the last to be expected of it.

The skinny man got out, and the Elders met him at the door, where they stood talking in very low voices. The fellow-preacher looked embarrassed and would not step inside, but shifted from one foot to the other on the porch.

"Well, why ain't Preacher Wall with him?" a woman in the front of the room demanded in a shrill loud voice, ignoring St. Paul's admonition that women hold their peace in church and if they wish to know anything, ask their husbands later.

"The rotten son-of-a-bitch is in jail!" one of the Elders answered, forgetting that for the time being, the schoolhouse was a house of God.

"What was it he done?" the woman shrilled eagerly.

"This feller says Wall got drunk last night and beat up on his boy and his old lady," Elder Schoolcraft informed her. "Says he purt' near done 'em in. Had to take 'em to the hospital!"

There was no closing hymn, no benediction that day, and Gabe Creek saw no more of Millerite preachers in my time. And I never went to a Millerite service again.

Well did Chaucer write:

> . . .That if gold ruste, what shal iren do?
> For if a preest be foul, on whom we truste,
> No wonder is a lewed man to ruste;
> And shame it is, if a prest take keep,
> A shiten shepherde and a clene sheep.
> Well oghte a preest ensample for to yive,
> By his clennesse, how that his sheep sholde lyve.

Being naught but a mere "lewed" boy, the rust sank deep into my metal. Pinwheels of flickering light spun in front of my eyes, and I felt my brain pulling apart with the onset of migraine. So as the crowd scattered, I dodged into the woods out of sight, not caring that God slew Onan for spilling his seed upon the ground—not caring for anything! By the time I was home, the migraine had vanished.

The fiasco of the Millerite reorganization was a punishing blow to Grandmother. "I don't know what to say," she lamented.

"I'll be right surprised if he feels like going to any church for a spell," Grandfather rumbled. "I wish I'd set my foot down and when he was thirteen let him find his own way in religion! If you hadn't 'a' kept harping on him so to get converted, he'd 'a been a sight better off; he wouldn't 'a' suffered this setback!"

"You're right, Hilary," she sighed. "I know how he must feel. He thought that low-down Wall was a real man of God."

She was mistaken in that, for I had undergone conversion in spite of him, not because of him, and actually had found him repulsive. But I took heartless advantage of her lost sense of infallible rightness in deciding what was best for me, and grabbed for independence. I was envious of the Seabolt brothers, who went where they pleased, associated with whom they pleased, climbed trees without being ordered out of them, spoke without thought of sentence structure, syntax or grammar, and knew just where to hit to make the blow count if anyone started trouble with them.

Grandfather had never approved the strictness of Grandmother's supervision, but not until the Wall incident did he intervene. She was by far shrewder and more forceful than he, and could make him seem wrong even when he clearly was in the right. He could not parry her sharp-witted specious reasoning which often was intended merely to confuse him. Nevertheless, he was German enough to be obstinate, and sometimes won through sheer stubbornness. After the Wall incident he insisted that I be allowed to act like a real boy—at least some of the time.

After a while, though, I realized that religion cannot be condemned because those who profess it sometimes do not possess it; even the nauseating cats came into perspective as only a deplorable coincidence. I decided that anything which did not harm anyone else and apparently did not harm me could not be any great sin, and took literally the Biblical command "Resist not temptation" and grew quite comfortable. The next time the Seabolt boys asked me if I would like to go to Epworth League at Wellford I went with them, enjoying the opportunity to be out with young people, free of supervision, even if I did not relish the inane League programs and the banal literature.

The building at Wellford was a real church with a pulpit and pews, and seemed impressive compared to Gabe Schoolhouse, where one sat in ink-stained, knife-scarred seats made for children, and the preachers stood behind the schoolmaster's desk on the same level with the congregation. Had the church offered nothing but a place to sit, I would have gone regularly anyhow just to be with the four youngest Seabolts and their friends.

A most wholesome, likeable, intelligent boy nicknamed "Ace" soon became my favorite companion, for he had been away to reform school and was wise beyond his years. He was guilty of nothing that our community considered a crime, and was admired by those who knew that moonshining was all that stood between his family and starvation and that he had let himself be incriminated rather than betray his father. Robust and strong, full of devilment and good humor, he undertook to salvage what was left of boy in me. He urged me to exercise, taught me to enjoy rough-and-tumble games, got me out of my clothes and into the swimming hole, and made fun of my precious grammar until finally I gave in and said, "Hell, Ace, if you want me to say 'ain't I?' instead of 'am I not?' then 'ain't I?' is what I'll say!"

"Aint it easier?" he laughed. "I just want you to talk like people do."

He got me out of my Victorian prudishness and told me all he knew about sex (which was a great deal more than I had gotten out of the book) and set my mind at ease, saying that if masturbation really made boys go crazy, there wouldn't be a sane man in seven counties. But when two lewd girls began sneaking up to spy on us as we swam, I was all but overcome at the thought of their seeing me.

"Let 'em look!" he muttered. "What you got ain't one to be ashamed of, and with them kind, lettin' 'em see it don't make no difference. They hang around here hopin' some guy'll know what they want and take a notion for a piece. I wouldn't touch 'em with a ten-foot pole, for they're plain-out white trash, and no tellin' what they got; and they stink worse'n a bucket of dead craw-dabs. But if they got such an itch for cock that they'll walk three miles just to look at ours, the shame's on them, not us."

That struck me as logical, so I forced myself to wade out of the pool when he did and dress in sight of them. But afterwards, it amused me to think that they yearned for what we did not offer: I ended by wading out, facing them, and dressing with very deliberate display of the treat they were missing. I even began to wonder how bad a bucket of dead

crayfish smells. After I realized that what I had been doing was merely
what the book referred to as "self-abuse," I found the idea of *real* fornication all but irresistible: if the enjoyment I knew could be called *abuse*,
what was it the concupiscent understood as "pleasure."

As Grandmother worded it, I "got set in with Ace and his bunch" at
League. They lived on Doctor's Creek, Hurricane and Cotton Tree, and
seldom were all together except at Wellford. However, singly, or in twos
or threes, they used the Gabe swimming hole almost as much as did we
and we stayed on good terms with them, though we regarded them as
"a pretty rough crowd." Their roughness consisted mostly of profanity,
dirty talk, blustering, sexual promiscuity, and a little drinking. They
were uneducated, hard-working, poorly-dressed farm boys whose lives
were as limited as the narrow hollows in which most of them lived. Sex
was one of a very limited number of pleasures possible for them, and
their approach to it was direct, even animal. Their leader was a handsome, precocious fifteen-year-old called "Stud," as mature as Ace, who
was two years older. Ace told me that Stud and his gang often obliged
the two girls—Stud regularly, and the others whenever impulse got the
better of discretion.

I have parallel sex vocabularies. One is socially acceptable, culled
from a legal dictionary, scientific and medical tomes and the writings of
Petronius, the Marquis de Sade and Proust. It covers every possible
activity—even some that not everyone knows *are* possible. But I give
Stud and his gang credit—they had a vocabulary just as extensive and
considerably more vivid. Some of it came from Anglo-Saxon; some was
forged in the heat of action from any crude material in reach; some was
improvised on the frontier by inventive men who perhaps hovered
shivering under the same bearskin and found each other warm, then
hot. This vocabulary—unspeakable to the refined and for years unprint-
able—I used only at the swimming hole until I found it again in use in
the Air Force.

Once when Stud had a falling out with the seventeen-year-old we
called "Sheepy," Stud called him a malodorous epithet coined from the
local verb for anal intercourse, and—after they had knocked each other
down several times—landed an uppercut from which Sheepy was glad to
stagger up and run. As Stud wiped blood from his lip with his skinned
knuckles, he bleated after the fleeing youth with such contempt that I
had no remaining doubt that Stud believed him guilty of intercourse

with sheep as well. *Man's Strength and Woman's Beauty* said nothing about these things; I was both scandalized and horrified. Grandmother kept predicting the End of the World because of Man's heinous wickedness, and she hardly could have known that such abominations took place right in Clendenin, where Sheepy had a homosexual buddy. I expected to look up and see fire descending from the sky—well, not really *expected*, but it would not have surprised me greatly.

While I was thus being educated at the swimming hole, Grandmother was engaged in making me learn to embroider! No other act, she believed, so effectively disciplines the impulse to stir constantly, so well inculcates deftness and precision, cultivates patience, and so quiets the mind and emotion. So though Grandfather was outraged, and I all but overcome, she compelled me—by making my trips to the pool dependent upon it. The more patiently I embroidered the more often and the longer she allowed me to go.

I ran through chain, blanket, eyelet, lazy-daisy, outline, French knot and cross-stitch lessons in single sittings, and turned out a pile of ten-cent-store runners, scarfs and cushion tops of no artistic merit, but well and neatly done. Then came the time for fancier work: crewel, pargello, flame and satin stitch—the elegant and artistic medium to which Grandmother gave her own talent in design. For the satin-stitch exercise she laid out a design of roses, made a fine pair of pillow cases, crocheted wide pineapple-lace edging, and secured a quantity of white floss.

When I saw the beautiful wide bands of roses, I flatly refused to do them in white-on-white: if I never saw the pool again, I would not work them unless in natural colors. She knew I meant it and relented, securing lovely shades of scarlet and green. By the time I had one flower and leaf worked I began to be eager to see the whole design completed. I worked almost eagerly, and in the fifth week I finished them. She scrutinized them, declared them fine enough for a bridal bed—and told me to put them up for use if we ever had any special company. I loathed sitting with embroidery hoops in my hand, of course, but I enjoyed the feeling of creating something beautiful. I was actually proud of them.

I was outwardly demure, a very Saint Cecilia, as I sat embroidering, even when I fumed inwardly to start to the pool. But when I got there I tried cultivating Stud's group to prove to myself that I had not been castrated by embroidery scissors. I played at being as rough as any of them, swearing for effect, expressiveness and sheer satisfaction. I even bought a pack of contraceptives and one of cigarettes and made sure they saw the former and observed me smoking the latter. It may have fooled most of them, but not Ace, who knew boys very well indeed.

From the first, I had liked and admired Stud above all the rest of the crowd. The reason for his nickname was not hard to guess even if one knew nothing of his exploits. I did not envy him much on that account, but he was handsomer than I and had a perfect body, rippling with smooth, strong muscle; beautiful in its symmetry, balance and proportions. He was perfectly coordinated, moving with feline grace, and his quick, warm grin, impulsive good nature, and rich deep voice appealed greatly. He did everything I yearned to do but didn't, held back by prudence, convention, Victorian up-bringing, or—in the case of the two girls—mere fastidiousness.

One day Stud laughingly told of the intercourse he had enjoyed with the two girls the night before. Afterward, I said to Ace, "It's a damn shame Stud's low-down, ain't it?"

"Stud's a great guy!" he said quickly. "I thought you liked him!"

"I *do!*" I said, "But you heard what he said he did with those two stinking white-trash girls. How could he! Of course, I don't suppose he did—not twice with each one—a guy couldn't do that in one evening!"

"Stud could, and he probably did," Ace chuckled. "He's dumb to take the risks he does. He's goin' to wake up mighty sore and mighty sorry one morning. But that don't mean he ain't one damn fine guy!"

"Why doesn't he ever have anything much to say to me?" I sighed.

"He things you're stuck-up," Ace said reluctantly. "he'd never try to make friends with you."

"Why not?" I said, surprised and rather hurt.

"You don't know how hard up his folks are. That's one thing. He's as proud and independent as Satan. He's pure German from the Dutch Ridge, and he thinks of you as a Taylor—that's another. He thinks you feel you're a lot higher-up than the likes of him, and he's afraid you might snub him."

"Hell, I'm mostly Dutch, too. You know I'm not like that, Ace!"

"No, you ain't stuck-up," he admitted. "But you are almost like a Taylor. You're high class: you talk that way, think that way, act that way, look that way, and you *are* that way."

"Shit," I scoffed. "What's so high class about me?"

He laughed. "It's either your nature, or the way your Grandma raised you. You even had to make yourself say what you just said. It didn't sound like 'shit' the way Stud or one of us would say it."

"You mean there are different ways to say it?"

"If it comes natural, it sounds natural. From you, it don't. Anybody can tell its just a front."

"*You* told me to talk like people do," I reminded him. "If I didn't try to talk and act like them, they wouldn't even speak to me."

"I didn't mean talk and act like something you ain't. I meant what's natural for you, not for your Grandma, but not for Stud and them either—for *you!* If that bunch don't take to you the way you are, plenty of other people will when you leave here."

"But I'm not outside, I'm here. I have to have friends! I'd do anything to make Stud like me."

"Then it's up to you to let him know it—he wouldn't believe me if I told him. And if in the back of your mind you think he's low-down, forget it! He's smart as a whip: you wouldn't fool him a minute."

"He's tough, but I think he's wonderful."

"He ain't as tough as you think he is. Under what you see he's as tender-hearted and easy-hurt as a girl. He just puts on a better front than you do—and he's had it rough. Outside that, you two are an awful lot alike."

"Alike?" I gasped, astonished and vastly flattered.

"Yes;" he repeated, "down deep you feel the same way about everything that matters."

One afternoon about a week later, Stud and two of his gang were with me at the pool. The girls stole up to the very willows and tied knots in our pants legs before any of us noticed them.

"Hey!" one of the boys yelled when he saw them. "Leave them clothes alone and clear the hell out of here! We come here to cool off. It's too hot for fuckin'!"

The girls hooted in derision, and Stud splashed to knee-deep water, cupped his testicles in his hand, and yelled: "This what you come after? I thought I give you enough Sunday night to last all week!"

They giggled, and the taller girl threw his pants into the top of a low willow.

"That's okay!" he laughed. "You sure are fixin' to get what you come for!"

"Chase 'em away, Stud," I urged. "The next thing, they'll take our clothes and run off with 'em."

He splashed out stark naked, flew up the creek bank, and after them into the tall corn. Soon we heard them shrilling when he caught up with them and tussled with them. He kept demanding, "You give up?" and laughing, and they squealed and giggled.

"Old Stud's about to get him some more," one of his pals chuckled.

"Ain't you goin' to take one of 'em?" his companion asked him.

"Shit," he said (it *did* sound natural from him), *"you* can if you want to! I wouldn't touch one of them bitches without I had a tub of germ-killer handy!"

Stud and the two girls moved up to the sandbar where the July freshet had washed out the corn. I was scandalized that both girls went with him at the same time.

"What does the one he's not with do?" I asked the boy nearer me, "Just look on and wait?"

"Hell, she wouldn't miss watchin' it for nothin'," he grinned. "It gets her hotter for her turn."

"I'd think they'd be too embarrassed."

"Them? *Embarrassed?* God!"

"Which one is Stud's regular girl?" I asked.

"Both of 'em is," he chuckled. "He don't give a shit for either one except for that, and they don't for him, but he's so damn big he's got to have a girl that's stretched like a cow, and them two besoms poke full-growed cucumbers up 'em when they can't find a guy. You or me'd get lost in 'em."

Stud was with them at least an hour. When he returned he glistened all over with sweat, and looked exhausted. His knees were red and sand-scoured; his pubic hair was sticky and plastered down, and his heavy genitals hung forspent.

I felt that to show camaraderie at such a time should prove conclusively that I was not stuck-up. Unlike the two others, who had sneaked to watch—and had masturbated while doing so, to judge by their comments when they came back—I was almost at the point of orgasm from imagination. The erection added informality and testified to my genuine interest.

So when he waded near, I grinned, and said, "Stud, you look like a guy who's done a hard day's work."

"I sure wore myself out," he chuckled, "But you don't know them two! Every guy this side of Charleston could line up, and all of 'em couldn't get 'em satisfied. Why didn't you all come with me? There was plenty for everybody, and a heap left to go to waste."

"They—I mean, I don't think I could do it in front of anybody. I'm too bashful."

He eyed my throbbing erection, which seemed to offer conflicting testimony. A devilish grin dimpled his cheeks, but his eyes were not twinkling; they were dark and inscrutable.

"Yeah? I allow you could," he said. He reached, felt me appraisingly, then gave me a few gentle, expert manipulations and a tantalizing squeeze which produced ejaculation. Too late I said, "Stud, stop that," and pushed at his hand, realizing that there was nothing convincing then either in the prissy protest or the half-hearted gesture.

He gave a snort, sank backward slowly into the cool water, and vastly amused, chortled, "If just thinkin' about it got you like that, and that made you shoot off, I sure allow you *could*!"

Stud's buddies left before I did, and he told them he wanted to stay a while longer. Presently he submerged in the deep hole and surfaced beside me, brushed his unruly, curling forelock out of his eyes, and gave me a sheepish grin.

"I hope you ain't mad at me for doin' you like that," he apologized. "I don't know you good enough to do a thing like that for fun. I done it to embarrass you 'cause I felt ashamed. I'm sorry."

"I'm sure not mad at you," I murmured, realizing that unless I mattered to him he would not have felt ashamed. "Ace says you're a great guy."

He smiled. "You mean you been talkin' to him about me?"

"I asked him what I could do so you wouldn't think I'm stuck up or anything," I explained. "I'm not. It's just that Grandmother raised me, and never would let me go anywhere, or do anything, or be with any-body until just lately. I hardly know how to fit in."

"You mean you ain't always sure what to do or say around us? I thought you was stand-offish 'cause you thought we ain't as high-up as you are."

"No, Stud, I'd give anything to be just like you."

"That ain't no high-up ambition," he chuckled. "I'd give anything to be like *you*. You got education; I ain't got none."

"Ace says we're a lot alike," I said. "There's so much you could tell me and show me to help me learn to fit in."

"I hope you know what you're lettin' yourself in for," he said doubtfully.

"Come home and have supper with me," I invited. "That way we can get acquainted."

"Your Grandma might not like havin' me brought in on her without no warnin' or nothin'!"

"She wouldn't care. Grandfather's so Dutch he always has her cook enough for two or three extra, and she's always complaining about food going to waste. You'd like her if you got to know her."

"Hively, Dutch? I thought you was Taylor kin. They aint Dutch."

"Grandmother was a Taylor," I explained, "but Hively used to be Heifle—it's Swiss, but you know how it is; folks call it Dutch." Then because I wanted to stress our ethnic similarity, I said, "Anyhow, they only raised me. I'm a Gandee—Gänther was the name in German. Like the rest of my German folks they tried to make it sound English. I'm related to a lot of German families: Schüldisch, Westphal, Müde, Karber, Zarber, Hoffmann, Reubel—nearly all have made the names sound English. Your family's German, too, isn't it?"

"Yeah, it sure is, but I never knowed you was Dutch."

"I'm real proud of it," I said.

"Folks don't come no better than we are," he smiled. "We don't ask nobody for nothin', and we don't take nothin' off nobody, and we stick together, but there aint nobody farms as good as them folks out on Dutch Ridge, or works harder." As he boasted I could see that the ethnic barrier had fallen. He seemed much more at ease.

Grandmother had a very good meal that evening: canned beef, drop noodles, new potatoes in butter sauce, green beans, sliced tomatoes, coleslaw, and a warm peach cobbler with whipped cream. Besides, there was a chocolate cake from the day before, and the usual assortment of pickles, relishes, and preserves that she kept on hand. When Grandfather took a good look at Stud after he heard his name, he said, "I used to work some with your grandpa and his brothers Mark and Luke. You sure favor them. When the grub goes around, dish in and eat yourself full. It brings back old times."

After a morning in the hayfield, an hour of intercourse, and an afternoon of playing, Stud had a gargantuan appetite. Grandfather kept filling up his plate for him, and after he ate the dessert, forced a huge wedge of cake upon him. After Stud went home, Grandfather belched, rubbed his great stomach contentedly, and murmured, "It did me a world of good to watch that kid stow away the grub. You don't run across many that knows how to enjoy eating the way he did. That young fellow's a regular go-getter, I bet—worth three or four of the kind you can hire to do anything nowadays."

"Yes," Grandmother smiled complacently, "I could tell he enjoyed everything he ate. He seems a nice, decent, well-meant boy, and he does look strong and intelligent and energetic."

"Then I don't suppose you mind if I get to be good friends with him," I said innocently.

"No," she replied. "His family haven't an ounce of refinement, of course, but they are honest, hardworking, Dutch Ridge people, and they'd starve before they'd go on relief. Just don't start talking the way he talks, that's all. I never heard worse grammar."

"He may not say things right, but he makes a lot of sense," Grandfather declared. "He'd be a wonderful good one for our boy to pattern after. He's all man, that one; he'll amount to something."

The next time he saw me, Stud told me how much he enjoyed his visit and insisted that I have supper with him soon. I went one afternoon the following week, and was served groundhog meat for the first time in my life. Grandmother assigned anyone who ate groundhog to the lowest class in her social heirarchy. "Groundhog-eater" shared a place with "low-down white trash," differing from it only in that the latter also implied degeneracy. But I knew Stud's family ate groundhog of necessity, and I would have eaten a baked buzzard for Stud's camaraderie, so I forced it down. And when Grandmother asked me pointedly what kind of meat they had, I told her they had some kind of pork. (I suppose one can rationalize that any kind of "hog" meat is pork.) Logic could not account for Grandmother's feeling that groundhog meat defiled the very plates on which it was served, when she heaped her own rose-bordered platter with fried chicken—a luckless hen who that very morning might well have followed to the outhouse to devour fresh excrement. Actually, groundhog was tasty, and groundhogs are very clean beasties that eat only herbs. I never called anyone a "groundhog-eater" again, and began to take closer looks at all my prejudices.

"SEEK ME A WOMAN
THAT HATH A FAMILIAR SPIRIT"

The Earth-Star Flower: Life seen as beauty, with faith
reaching out and with love in the four directions, becoming
themselves part of the greater flower

Then said the woman, "Whom shall I bring up
unto thee?" And he said, "Bring me up Samuel."
And when the woman saw Samuel, she cried out
with a loud voice: and the woman spake to Saul,
saying, "Why hast thou decieved me? for thou art
Saul." And the king said unto her, "Be not afraid:
for what sawest thou?" And the woman said unto
Saul, "I saw gods ascending out of the earth." And
he said unto her, "What form is he of?" and she
said, "An old man cometh up; and he is covered
with a mantle." And Saul perceived that it was
Samuel, and he stooped with his face to the
ground, and bowed himself. And Samuel said to
Saul, "Why hast thou disquieted me, to bring me
up? . . ."

1 Samuel, 28:10-15

One often finds himself wondering why occult events so often occur in remote places, and why perfectly familiar locales never turn up in print. In my case I understand, for not many people in either West Virginia or South Carolina write on such topics. To most writers, West Virginia is only an unfortunate place where coal miners suffer exploitation at the hands of capitalistic interests, corrupt unions, and sordid politicians. To writers South Carolina is a place where Negro children suffer malnutrition and where the Civil War began. Only folklorists and a few other specialists realize that in both states an archaic culture persisted until well into the twentieth century. I was not aware of it until my professors at William and Mary took interest in the fact that I sometimes used Scottish words, dialect, or forms which have changed in meaning or grown obsolete in standard English, but were in common use in Shakespeare's or even in Chaucer's day. Both states have areas settled in the eighteenth century by folk who were already two or three centuries behind the vanguard of cultural changes. They were isolated, and their descendants passed down from generation to generation the ideas and beliefs of their parents. This kept them from the fallacies of over-reliance upon human reason and disbelief in that which is beyond reason. Through the Enlightenment and the Age of Science—the materialistic science of the nineteenth century—they remained children of the Age of Faith. By now the automobile, radio and television have changed them profoundly, but the change has come only in the lifetimes of the middle aged. Long before the current vogue brought witchcraft to university campuses, the old people of both places knew that the hills and hollows hid witches and *Hexenmeisters* who exerted strange powers. Before spiritualism became a religious movement, or mediumship a profession, if one knew to whom to apply, he could go to such a person as did King Saul to the Witch of Endor and hold conversation with the dead.

In my youth and for many years before there was a woman known in West Virginia as the greatest of those who had familiar spirits. One might apply to her, retire with her to her parlor, and, after she had brought them up, talk freely with his dead relatives and friends. She died before I was old enough to visit her, but she had great influence nevertheless upon my thought and belief. So not long ago I was surprised and delighted to buy a paperback and find mention of her for the first time, and learn her Christian name, Elizabeth.

As far as I know, she was little-known even in the Spiritualistic movement, except to the small churches in southern Ohio, Kentucky, and West Virginia. Until I read the paperback I never knew her full name. Everyone who ever mentioned her to me called her "Old Mrs. Blake," in such a way that "Old" conveyed respect, reverence, and admiration. It was she who introduced James Andrew to spirit communication, converted him to Spiritualism, and guided him into mediumship.

I am well aware that the Biblical reference to Saul's visit to Endor indicates only that spirits *can* communicate—not that anyone should *let* them! And those who put headings to Bible topics headed this one, "Saul seeketh a witch." But they also put the date of Creation at "Year before the common Year of Christ, 4004," and just as I believe they erred by several billion years, so do I think they were wrong in calling the woman a witch. To be sure, King Saul was quite wise in seeking to prevent communication between his people and the dead: for the soil of Israel was full of the bones of their enemies (though not as full as it will again become, as I shall predict at greater length at the end of this book). The psychic atmosphere still contained the presences of the old heathen gods of Canaan. Their influence, plus the malice of the dead, would have produced some tragic results had. the people asked discarnates for advice. Lying spirits, still burning with desire for vengeance upon the Jews, would have answered them, trying to lead them to their utter undoing. Later, St. Paul would not have enumerated discerning of spirits as one of the great spiritual gifts, had the danger of contacting malevolence not been great. It still is.

But the woman of Endor was not a witch, and the dead Samuel reproved *Saul* for disquieting him, saying not a word of reproof to the woman. She seems to me a good, kindly, considerate soul—one who felt such compassion that she butchered her calf, baked bread, and compelled her visitors to refresh themselves before going forth to meet their doom. And such a good woman was Mrs. Blake.

Mrs. Blake, whom I judge was born before 1860, lived about two miles up the river from Chesapeake, Ohio, just across from Huntington, West Virginia, in a small white frame cottage. She tended a garden, and aside from her great gift of mediumship, she seemed an ordinary, working-class housewife and mother—not very well educated or well-to-do, her parlor filled with the same kind of inexpensive bric-a-brac, nondescript furniture, and inartistic, poorly-framed pictures one might have found in any village parlor along the Ohio River. All I remember of it is the piano, which was remarkable because it played with the lid closed—and it was not a player piano!

A tin ear trumpet lay upon it—the most unusual thing to be seen. Sometimes it levitated and moved around the room of itself, people said; for most, voices came from it. But it was mute when I saw it, for Mrs. Blake had gone on. Her daughter kept the piano and trumpet only as keepsakes, and seemed ill at ease when the locked piano broke the commonplaceness of the room by sounding a faint few bars of a hymn.

"That's Mother now," she murmured. Incongruously, I felt that the playing was like that of a self-taught village housewife, and was disappointed. I suppose one expects spirit music to be celestial, in harmony with the golden harps of heaven.

When anyone applied to Mrs. Blake she took him into the parlor and sat with him until a voice came from the trumpet. Then, if the visitor was not afraid, she left him alone to talk privately. She would go out to her garden or into the kitchen, or back to whatever she had been doing when the visitor arrived. James Andrew would spend whole afternoons, talking mostly with his considerably older brother. They had been close indeed, and when the man died, James Andrew—who had depended upon his older brother for some of the things that men with better fathers receive from them—grieved for him immoderately.

I do not know when he first went to Mrs. Blake, but I think it was around 1900. In any case, by 1936 she had been dead several years. It is not easy to fix exact dates for a person known only from hearsay, but the record of great psychics will not be complete until someone tells her story. No doubt there still must be people around Huntington who knew her personally, and could attest to marvelous things about her powers (which sufficed to locate a will hidden behind the trim above a door in a house she never had visited, and to find a diamond ring which had been asphalted over, a foot below the surface of a parking lot).

Most people would not believe in spirit communication though one returned from the dead. Sad to say, this is truest of men of Science and of the Church. But to the open-minded, Mrs. Blake's mediumship brought a transformation in the concept of death. Accepted, it would bring a transfiguration, for to most people the face of death is dark, the tongue of death is still, and their fear of death is great. But her testimony and the evidence give the face of death a smile; its tongue, comfort and hope. And the fear would become something akin to anticipation—in fact, death would become an experience not regarded as much different from birth. For providing evidence of survival, thus opening the way for me to view death without fear, I thank Mrs. Blake and bless her memory. One by one I have lost all who were closest and dearest to me in my childhood and youth. But thanks to her, I know that they are as alive as ever, and I have glimpsed them. They have come to me and spoken, foretelling things which later came to pass, drying the very tears I wept for them. And when I do not see and hear them, I know that they have gone on, some to rebirth, others to serve, and one I love most dearly, to the education for which he yearned so strongly while in the body.

James Andrew came to regard Chesapeake much as one does the hometown of a beloved kinsman. His brother did not materialize, but his voice came through the trumpet in the same tones, inflections, and speech patterns that he had used when in the flesh. The two discussed things that they shared in memory; the brother gave James Andrew encouragement when he needed it, and urged him to develop his latent mediumship. He also urged him to change his mode of living so that life would be better for him beyond the flesh, and introduced him to other spirits who instructed and helped him and became his familiars.

In the Spiritualist vocabulary, these familair spirits are called "guides." James Andrew knew his guides by name, and came to know as much about their background and personalities as he knew of his neighbors'. One was Elenipsico, who was murdered (along with his uncle, the great chief Cornstalk, and another great Shawnee chief) by treacherous whites at Point Pleasant, West Virginia, while on a peace mission.

When James Andrew began working in Point Pleasant, Elenipsico earnestly entreated him not to live there, so he bought a home in Henderson, across the Kanawha River. The Indian told him that after the murders, the Shawnee medicine men held a great solemn pow-wow, and placed a curse on Point Pleasant, not to be lifted for three hundred years—one century of misfortune and calamity for each life taken.

Indeed, the place has seen tragedies. Though its location should have made it a great city at least as large as Pittsburgh or Cincinnati, it is to this day a small, unfortunate place where industries come to grief through fire, explosion, flood, or human error. Only a few years ago, its main bridge collapsed and drowned scores of persons in the Ohio River. Elenipsico's word seems to keep holding true: the curse still has over a century to last, but when it lifts at the time stated, beginning in the year 2091, Point Pleasant, West Virginia, will mushroom into the principal city on the Ohio River. Before that, however, possibly in the bicentennial year of the murders, the river will destroy as it did in the Ohio flood legend of the Shawnees, covering the valley from hillside to hillside; and the floodwalls will be like barriers of sand that children build to hold back the sea. There have been many floods along the Ohio, but no white man has experienced any like the great flood that the Shawnee legend speaks of, nor can he imagine the one of the Shawnee prophecy. People along the river tell of sighting the great Spirit-Birds. It is almost time for another catastrophe. Woe to poor Point Pleasant! (Woe to any place which kills seekers-of-peace! Thus said Elenipsico.)

When James Andrew moved to Henderson, the spirit of the young chief left its haunts—a rock shelter overlooking the river—and went to stay at his house. The night before "The Great Powder-Plant Explosion" which occurred during World War I, he woke James Andrew and told him what would take place the following day. James Andrew dressed, went to the house of a friend who worked in the POWDER Plant, and woke him. He was so impressed by James Andrew's having crossed the river in the dead of night to warn him that he stayed home and tried to persuade *his* friends to do so, but they paid no heed. That evening, he was the only one of them alive, for every other man in the department where he worked was blown to bits or crushed to death in the explosion.

In many instances, American Indian spirit guides may be only figments of the imagination, but a good man's life was saved because Elenipsico did not wish James Andrew saddened by the death of that particular man, and I imagine that man would have been the last to say, from that day onward, that *all* Indian guides are fantasies. He would also have been the last to say that spirits do not have foreknowledge of events—unless (dark possibility!) Elenipsico himself caused the explosion.

Once James Andrew took me up to the rock shelter where Elenipsico had kept himself before encamping in the upstairs rooms at the house. He said that the Indian was with us, and besought the young chief to make himself visible to me. He refused, but made the sound of a tom-tom and spoke a few words. He did not use the "How! Me Elenipsico," kind of dialect I associate with imaginary Indian guides. He spoke good English—with a British accent, in fact—as his uncle Cornstalk did in life, for that matter, if old records are to be credited.

Any visit to James Andrew was memorable, but one Sunday when Enna Whitehead was visiting us, she and Grandmother decided they wanted to go. So the three of us drove up about ten o'clock, taking James Andrew by surprise.

No man would have dared think of preparing a meal around Grandmother and Enna. So almost as soon as they were out of the car they were in his kitchen—surprised, I think, to find he had plenty of food on hand, and kept his kitchen as clean as theirs. He killed a hen for them, and then left them as they bustled to dress it, make dumplings, bake bread and prepare the usual things. He talked with me as we sat in the porch swings. He went in from time to time to see what progress they were making, and about ten minutes before the meal was ready, he announced he was going somewhere to get some ice cream for dessert. Before he left, he whispered to me, "You're not scared to stay here. alone, are you?"

"Of course not," I assured him, "Why?"

"If Ennie starts nosing around—and I never knew her to fail—you just might see some excitement." Then he got in his car and drove off.

I went in just as Grandmother was poking a pan of biscuits into the oven, frowning as she tinkered with the thermostat.

"I want you to see how well Andy keeps house since his wife died." Grandmother said to me. "I've been in many a woman's kitchen that didn't come up to this one!"

Just at that time a faint sound in the room upstairs caught Enna's ear, and she looked straight at Grandmother.

"Maybe this *is* a woman's kitchen," she whispered loudly, motioning toward the ceiling. "I'll just bet some hussy stays with him, and she saw us get out, and took upstairs before we came in."

"At *his* age?" Grandmother snorted.

"Ha!" Enna exclaimed, "That old goat might fool you! I'll bet a nickel there's some woman up there."

"I wouldn't get too curious about who's up there," I commented.

"He's always whispering to you, telling you something," Grandmother said. "*Is* there a woman upstairs?"

"A spirit, maybe."

"Oh, law!" Enna exclaimed. "Since when does a spirit rock in a chair and tiptoe around?"

"I bet you're afraid to go see," I teased her. "You could say you were looking for the bathroom."

"So I could," she said. She rolled down her sleeves, primped her hair, and with a great burst of dignity puffed up the steep staircase. We heard her open doors and then come flying back down the stairs at breakneck speed.

"Evvie!" she squealed. "There's nobody up there!"

"Nobody *you* could see," Grandmother corrected her, without looking up from the peas she was dishing out.

"What scared you so?" I asked her.

"It was the chair!" she puffed. "It was just there in the middle of the floor, rocking when I opened the door. With nobody in it, I tell you!

And something jumped up out of it and made for me! I know it did!"

"There's an Indian ghost . . ." I began.

"Now hush!" Grandmother commanded. "Can't you see she's about to fly to pieces? She never could see anything that wasn't solid flesh and blood!"

Just then James Andrew came in with the ice cream, and when he saw Enna he chuckled. "You look like something mighty near got you," he teased. "I knew I'd not be out of the yard before you'd go snooping upstairs."

"It just rocked! What makes it rock?" she said, almost hysterical.

"It has curved pieces under the legs," Grandmother snorted. "That's the way it's made. And the biscuits are getting cold. Now stop it, and get to the table or the dinner won't be fit to eat."

Enna and James Andrew grinned. For sixty years they had bick-ered—two exact opposites who were the best of friends—and for that long Grandmother had treated them both as children. After all, Enna had spent all her life among the Daughertys! She managed to eat a very hearty meal.

I think James Andrew felt he could talk with his brother any time he chose to visit Mrs. Blake, but on one visit she told him he couldn't.

"He can't get through," she told him. "There's some new girl—calls herself Margaret. She says she wants to talk with you."

"I don't know her," he told her.

"She says you do. Here, take the trumpet. Maybe you'll recognize the voice," she insisted.

"This is Margaret," the voice began. It startled him, for the voice was familiar, though he could not call to mind whose it was. "I'm to speak in place of your brother," it continued. "They say tell you he's in a dark place, and can't talk to you any more for a long time—it will seem long to you—they say seven years."

"I can't think of no Margaret who is dead," he murmured, disappointed.

"Why, you do so know me!" she exclaimed. "I'm your cousin. I'm Ira Taylor's daughter Margaret that everybody called Maggie. I hate Maggie, so here they let me have my way and call me Margaret."

"I reckon Margaret is Maggie's right name," he considered, "But Cousin Maggie's not dead!"

"I was well when you were at home last week. That's what you're
thinking."

"You are a lying spirit," he rebuked her. "I was there all right, and
Maggie was well—she still is. If anything had happened, they'd have
written."

"They were not meant to write. This is meant to be proof to them.
Pa won't believe, no matter what, but tell them I said I got dreadful
sick one day and died the next. And they buried me with my little
white Bible with the gold cross on the cover, and a wreath of white
carnations. They buried me in a white casket that Pa got in Clendenin—
a homemade one would have done just as well, and they should have
used the money for something they needed, but it was beautiful, and it
helped a little, for people all said it was a lovely funeral and that made
them feel better."

She detailed fact after fact about her death and burial, told by whose
grave hers was dug in the coffin-shaped Taylor cemetery, and named
persons who attended the funeral.

So James Andrew wrote them, dreading the reply. Mrs. Blake had
told him long before that lying spirits can dissimulate with incredible
realism, assuming the personal characteristics of the individuals they
pretend to be, and producing information which only those individuals
might be expected to give. He could think of no end that such a decep-
tion might serve, but he could hardly believe that Maggie, so robust and
full of life and rollicking fun the previous Thursday, could on Wednes-
day afternoon be with the dead.

The reply came quickly. Everything had been as the voice related it,
except that Margaret said her death resulted from acute inflammation
of the brain, whereas the doctor called her tremors and convulsions "an
exceedingly rare form of St. Vitus's dance." I suppose a country doctor
cannot be blamed if he loses a patient with a rare disease that other
doctors have not been known to cure.

The effect of this message makes it perfectly clear why orthodox
denominations decry spirit communication so vehemently. Ira held that
the devil is as omniscient as God and that the message was given by
Satan to deceive—probably what most churchmen would say, especially
since the girl's brothers stopped attending church. They no longer
believed what it taught as to the afterlife, feeling that if it erred in so
important a matter, it might be unreliable in everything.

The message made a complete Spiritualist of James Andrew, of course, who thenceforth pursued psychic investigation with mind, body, and soul. Grandmother was torn with religious doubts from that time on. Grandfather, who never belonged to any church and whose only religion was to do good according to his lights, said that if the woman of Endor called up Samuel, he could see no reason why Mrs. Blake might not call up the dead. He also said that one world at a time was all he could cope with, and that he preferred to wait and see what the next world will bring rather than take the word of either the living or the dead. "Live as if you expect a reward," he sometimes said, "but don't count on it. Doing good is enough reward in itself." I think he accepted the spirit world as he did the one in which he was embodied, for though we were constantly aware of his presence as a spirit, he never sought to communicate after his death.

I had heard of this visit ever since I could remember, and when I was about fourteen I had James Andrew tell me of it himself. I had no way to get to Chesapeake and no money to offer Mrs. Blake, but I resolved to visit her as soon as I could, and ask her to bring up Gabriel Little-page. I very much wished to ask him why Gabe was as it was, why the rich Littlepages had cultivated a friendship with the Hivelys, what Rolandus Rex Rohr had been seeking. True answers to such questions might be worth a far greater sum than the old lady ever accepted from any of her clients.

At the time though, I still wondered whether Ira Taylor might not be right that spirit communication was the work of Satan. One would have had enough to dread if only Gabriel Littlepage guarded a treasure, and with Satan besides—it all seemed very risky. I decided to ask Cousin James Early, for he was the only preacher in whom I had any remaining confidence after the fiasco of my conversion and week-long career as a saint. I knew that he would not beat around the bush, and I knew his life to be better than his preaching.

"I never heard about that before," he mused, when I told him of Margaret Taylor's message, "but it's a fact that Mrs. Blake calls up the dead. Charlie went to her once."

"Charlie Short, your wife's brother?"

"Yes. It sure made a believer out of me."

"You?" I exclaimed.

"Oh, that was a spell before I took to tryin' to preach," he smiled.

"Before religion meant anything to me, I was a pure old hell-raiser like all us Abbotts. I reckon that Charlie had the most to do with turnin' my thoughts to God, for you can't have proof that the soul lives on, and not start thinkin' how and where yours will be. That depends on how you live, and you have to love God and keep his commandments to live right. And if you try livin' right and see what a heap of good it does for you, it leads you to want to tell your friends. And when you start tellin' about the good life, you find you're preachin'. That' how it was with me."

"What happened when he went to see Mrs. Blake?"

"Charlie? Well, a voice come through a hearin'-horn of some kind, and it was his brother—his natural voice, and as plain as ever he spoke in this world. He give his names and most folks never heard his first name, for he never used it. And he proved who he was by tellin' Charlie something that nobody knowed except just them two. 'Do you recollect them dynamite caps we stole when we was boys?' his brother asked him. And when Charlie said he did, he said, 'Well, *I* sure do, but here I've got back my toe that got blowed off.' Charlie went on and told me how they sneaked into the dynamite shed and took the caps, somewhere where their Pa was workin', and when his brother blowed off his toe they made up to tell he mashed it off with a rock because they knowed their Pa'd take the hide off 'em if he found out they'd been foolin' around the dynamite and stealin' caps. I don't know how they got him to believe it, but you can get your feet tore up mighty bad goin' barefooted. Maybe he just figured he wouldn't get the truth, no matter what, and let it go, figurin' a tore-off toe ought to learn 'em whatever they needed to be taught."

"Maybe Charlie was thinking about that, and Mrs. Blake only read his mind," I suggested.

"She didn't stay in the room. When she was sure he was gettin' the voice all right, she went back in the house somewhere and started ironin' clothes. She just stopped by the door now and again when she was takin' a bunch of sheets or something to put away, to ask if he was gettin' along all right and gettin' through to his party."

"How did he use the trumpet?" I asked.

"Just like any old-time hearin'-trumpet, I reckon. You stick the little end to your ear and listen, and when you answer back, you just talk the same as you would to anybody else."

"They tell me the trumpet floats around the room sometimes, and voices and singing come from it," I commented. "You don't think it's the work of the devil?"

"If it is, he's cuttin' his own throat," he replied with a wry grin. "Charlie's brother up and told him Charlie'd better change his ways or he'd end up in the same fix as him, sayin' he didn't reckon it was Hell he was in, but it'd do for that in a pinch. He said he could get out, though, as soon as he got straightened up."

"That sounds like Purgatory," I mused.

"It couldn't have been that. He was raised Baptist."

"Then what is it?" I asked.

"All he knowed to call it was a *state*—it's all I know. And its one state I don't want to find myself in when I leave this world."

Margaret also had referred to the place of her spirit as a "state," and had described her surroundings as beautiful, with her Aunt Lavinia and her grandparents, and some of her friends helping her to make herself accustomed to it. To her, the state was one of happiness.

"It certainly doesn't sound like where Margaret went," I pondered.

He gave me a knowing look. "That figures," he said drily. "I allow Charlie's brother had more to straighten up on account of one payday Saturday night on Frye's Alley than Margaret Taylor had to account for in her whole life."

I was a bit shocked to have him name the red-light center of Charleston so familiarly, but then, maybe he *had* been a pure old hell-raiser in his young manhood.

"... SEX IS ..."

The True Lovers' Knot: For romance or love in marriage.
(A visual representation of endless love)

> *Sex is, as any student of advertising and publish-*
> *ing knows, a highly intriguing phenomenon,*
> *charged with explosive possibilities, and accom-*
> *panied by an infinite number of strange, beautiful,*
> *and terrible ramifications. With it are involved the*
> *most intense of human emotions; love, hate, jeal-*
> *ousy, treachery, betrayal, cruelty, sacrifice, devo-*
> *tion . . .*

Gina Cerminera

When James Andrew visited overnight, he slept with me, and it was from his pillow that he mumbled the most wonderful and exciting tales—of spirits and haunted places; of familiars, eidolons, mediums, astral projection, magic, and such things—all of which Grandmother would have forbidden had she heard him.

I was certain that if an old man of seventy could bewitch me until after midnight with things of the spirit, Stud could enchant me until morning with things of the flesh. I decided to be perfectly honest and confess that I had never even kissed a girl; that I regarded him as wiser in such things than Ace; and that on mature deliberation, I believed I could engage in intercourse in front of other persons after all—if they were he and the other girl. (In fact, I would have undertaken it just to watch them.)

Besides, I thought it possible that Stud knew some secret that accounted for his splendid development, and might confide it to me. I was not yet fifteen and hoped that there might still be time to benefit. I supposed that any youth would like to be larger than he is, and I knew that if I were a girl, the more like Stud a man were, the more he would appeal to me. (It did not occur to me to wonder why thinking of Stud should make me know how a girl would feel, or why the thought even occurred to me at all. Certainly around Grandmother I had no chance to fathom how a woman feels, or understand the erotic workings of a female mind any more than my own.)

Stud soon promised to come, and I spent the morning making ready for him. I changed my bed, borrowing Grandmother's dazzling, lavender-scented "special company" percale sheets, and sneaking out my gorgeous rose-bordered pillowcases. Grandmother had read a book on

the language of flowers, and had told me the pineapples symbolize hos-
pitality, and that the secondary significance of a rose is secrecy. The
lace expressed my attitude, and the flowers suggested the kind of conversation I anticipated. I swept—even under the bed—dusted and waxed
the furniture, set every object in exact order, cut a large bouquet of
zinnias in the same scarlets as the roses, as well as some of gold, and
arranged them in an antique salt-glaze jar for the study table. I charred
spicewood shavings to give the room fragrance; and before he came I
bathed, shaved, doused my face with spice-scented shaving lotion,
scoured my teeth with soda, and trimmed and cleaned my nails. I wanted Stud to see that I had gone to some effort to have things nice for
him, partly—but mostly I wanted to observe what his response would
be. If we were really alike, as Ace had said, I knew he would betray his
appreciation of the cleanness, the order, and the beauty I had set out.

Stud brought nothing with him, so he did not go to my room until
bedtime. When I switched on the light, he paused at the door in surprise
and said: "So this is where you roost. Boy, ain't you got a pretty
room!"

"I like it because away back here I can play my radio and not bother
them in the front of the house."

"How many books you got?" he asked, moving to the table to examine those ranged on it and in the end shelves.

"Too many, I think sometimes—two or three hundred."

"God, have you read all that many?"

"Until I was thirteen reading was all I had that gave me any pleasure.
During school I still read two or three every week."

"This word book—this dictionary—it's got words I never heard tell
of. Is this where you get them you're always usin'?"

"I guess all I use are in it," I smiled. "As I read, I'm always running
across words I don't know and I look them up."

"That's one kind of book I ought to use," he considered.

He examined my closet, manifested great interest in the antique converted flintlock rifle, powder horn, shot pouch, bullet mold, charger
and percussion caps Mother's father brought from Virginia, which I
kept hanging above the table. He felt of my opaque, autumn-hued
cretonne curtains. He sniffed the fragrance and I explained that I had
smoked that morning and had burned spicewood to cover the smell of
the cigarette.

"Land, I was just fixin' to smoke one before we turned in," he said.

"Well, do." I grinned, offering him mine in their brass, enamel-medallioned Chinese box. "I want one, myself." As he hesitated, I added, "the smell will be gone by morning."

In the bureau I had laid out pajamas I had never worn, but since he brought none, I decided to sleep in my shorts. When he undressed, and had on no underwear, I took off mine also, and went to bed.

"It sure feels great to turn in after a hard day," he sighed blissfully. "Your mattress beats Aunt Mat's feather beds, and them pillow cases is so nice it's a shame to sleep on 'em. Them roses is right-near like real flowers, and maybe prettier, and that's some real fine lace. Your Grandma sure makes first-rate fancywork."

"She knows every stitch that ever was," I chuckled.

"I wish poor old Ma had a chance to make pretty things," he murmured. "She purely loves 'em, and so do I."

I smiled: Stud might not think fancywork so pretty if he had to sit hours on end and make it himself! Still, Ace had been right—the hard-fisted, daytime, visible Stud was a phoney.

Changing the subject from fine needlework to the secret of developing a youth's penis does not come about naturally unless a deliberate transition is made. When I stretched out to turn off the lamp, I pretended to lose equilibrium and threw back my arm for counter-balance, allowing my wrist to brush Stud's genitals so that in apologizing, I could shift the focus of attention.

"Hell, after the way I done you that day at the swimmin' hole, you don't want to let touchin' nothin' of mine bother you none," he assured me.

"I've been meaning to ask you—did you do anything to make you get so well-developed there?"

"Nah," he scoffed. "I'm just made that way, natural. It kind of runs in Pa's family, I reckon. If you think I got a big one, you ought to take a look at Cousin Bud's sometime."

"Nobody ever told you some charm to use?" I persisted.

He snickered. "Oh, when I was eleven or twelve and just beginnin' to know I had it, Bud was fourteen, and as big as I am now. He told me if I wanted it to get like his, I'd have to give it lots of exercise. He was always playin' with his, so I believed him. I plumb worked at it—three times a day, regular and faithful. I didn't count it no hardship," he chuckled, "but I did believe him, 'cause it growed right onto six inches—but it'd 'a' growed just the same even if I hadn't."

"Usually I don't do that but twice a day," I confided. "Maybe so much did help."

"Nah," he laughed. "Take Cousin Sam, Ma's nephew out on the Ridge. He's three inches taller, forty pounds heavier, and a heap stronger than me. He done it as much as me or Bud ever did, 'cause I told him what Bud told me. But he still ain't got good five inches. Just be thankful you're like you are. I'd hate to be too little, like Sam, but I'd about as lief be like him as like Bud! A girl would head for a tree if a guy pulled out one like his."

I laughed. "Do Sam and Bud fool with theirs right in front of you?" I asked, wondering how else he could know so much.

"Heck, we been swappin' that together ever since we was kids," he chuckled. "We aint near as bashful as you made like you was."

"Those buddies of yours were gawking, and I couldn't let on I enjoyed it," I breathed.

"What if it was just you and me, and nobody around, and you knowed I was fixin' to do it?"

"Are you telling me you *are?*" I murmured archly.

"I sure wouldn't want it to surprise you, if that's all that'd be to stand in the way of you enjoyin' it," he said roguishly, and I felt his big warm hand find me. A giddy feeling shivered through my abdomen as he toyed deliberately, rousing me to unbearable anticipation.

"Stud," I whispered hoarsely, "Please don't ask me to do anything that isn't right."

He quickly removed his hand. "You talked like you enjoy havin' fun, and you sure felt ready. You near-about told me to go on and fool with you."

"I meant like that queer in Clendenin did for Sheepy and Bill and those."

"Huh? What made you think I was buildin' up to ask you to do *that!* I thought we'd maybe just have a little fun, like if you was Bud or Sam."

"Well, I don't see anything wrong in that, but I won't do those other things."

"Me neither," he breathed, put his hand back on me, and took mine and laid it on himself, where it explored, comparing, estimating, and enjoying its discoveries.

"Do you do this with Bill and those?" I whispered.

"Huh-*uh*, they'd be too sure to run their mouths. You ain't goin to blab to Ace or nobody are you?"

"Of course not," I assured him. "I'd better get up and get a towel."

"Yeah," he agreed.

I took deliberate pains to repay him fully, and both receiving and giving were so enjoyable that after we whispered a while, I agreed eagerly when he suggested we swap again. He must have enjoyed it as much as I, or he would not have suggested a repetition. Besides, his involuntary gasps and spasmodic tightening of the abdomen were impossible to counterfeit, and there was something like appreciation in the way he clasped my shoulder and squeezed it as he said good-night.

He turned onto his side and fell asleep almost instantly, beginning a soft, quiet snoring which did not in any way disturb me. The clock struck eleven; twelve; one; two—Stud slept without stirring. However, I was far too keyed-up to think of sleep. This first sharing of sex, albeit with another youth—or more likely *because* it was with another youth—loosed titanic upheavals in my hidden mind. For the first time in months, the pinpoints of light drifted again. Faces, shapes, and landscapes formed of them, as did incomprehensible symbols. I heard strange, modal music, smelled aromatic perfumes, some hauntingly bitter, like rue or wormwood—and when I finally did fall asleep, I dreamed fantastic, unsettling dreams.

Perhaps because I so often had mused that Stud looked like a god in Grandmother's Greek history—Hermes, I decided, since both were fleet runners—these dreams borrowed from Greek mythology. I dreamed of the Fates, of a golden centaur with Stud's face and torso, and of Cerberus, the three-headed dog who guards the gates of Hades and keeps the shades from escaping. These classic dreams were interwoven with others of the Black Man, who, when he neared me, was Stud— black, savage, and fearsomely beautiful. He pursued me through nightmare terrain with a spear, and at last impaled me, though the wound seemed painless. I dreamed of Stud in his own form, and in that dream I was a girl and he ravished me. All in all, the sleep was more wearing on

me than wakefulness had been, and I woke from it fitfully, finding him
still at rest and snoring peacefully.

My first real sleep finally came from sheer emotional exhaustion, and
I awoke with a start to find Stud straddling out of bed over me, and
light stealing in around the blinds.

"You looked so wore-out I tried my best not to wake you," he
whispered, "but my back teeth's floatin' and I got to go outside."

"Use the bathroom," I yawned. "It's just through the door there."

When he returned and crawled back in bed, I asked, because it was
custom, "Did you sleep well?"

"Like a log," he assured me. "Did you?"

"Oh, so-so, I guess, but I sure feel rotten this morning. I think it's the
migraine about to set in."

"What's that?"

"Oh God, Stud, it's an awful sick headache that lasts two or three
days. It starts with whirling colored lights and balls of fire or flashes of
lightning in front of your eyes. Then your brain feels as if it's pulling in
two, and half your head kills you, and you feel as if an egg-beater is
turning everything inside you into meringue."

"Land's sake! What brings 'em on?"

"I don't know—nervousness maybe. I get them if I get terribly excited, or want something terribly and can't get it, or if I get furiously
angry, or if I worry."

"You didn't worry about what we done, did you?" he murmured
with concern in his voice.

"About that? No, really I didn't. I've made up my mind that if it
doesn't harm anyone, a person can do anything he pleases. It was just
the excitement and pleasure of having you with me."

"You got a heck of a way of puttin' things," he said half ruefully.
"That was just a nice, kind, can't-get-mad-at-it way of sayin' I made
you sick."

I chuckled, realizing that he was right. "Maybe it'll go away—sometimes they do. Anyhow, I'd have had one before dark if anything had
kept you from coming."

"If you get 'em when I come and get 'em if I don't, you're in a bad
fix," he said seriously.

I suddenly realized that despite all my plans, I had not mentioned intercourse or girls to him all evening. At the moment they seemed uninteresting.

"What got it going was what I dreamed," I murmured. "I dreamed enough last night to set any guy nuts."

"I dreamed some too," he mused, "I don't often—but they was nice dreams."

"You remember any of them?"

"Yeah. One was real nice. I dreamed we was in real deep water—I never seen any waters bigger'n Kanawha at Charleston, but I reckon it must 'a' been the sea. And you and me was swimmin' or more like floatin' in it, and rompin' and playin' tag, and havin' a wonderful time."

"I dreamed about the sea, too," I reminisced. "Or maybe I was awake—I thought I was awake. There was an island, and a town with a temple on the hill behind it, and . . ."

"God! I dreamed that too! It was off to the side of where we was. A big white buildin' with posts up the front sort of like the big church on Koontz Avenue in Clendenin?"

"In a grove of trees, with pine trees on beyond!"

"Yeah!"

"The one I saw was a little like the Parthenon," I said, "only smaller and plainer."

"What's that?"

"It's a temple in Athens. It's the most beautiful building in the world."

"Well it sure was pretty, up there on the side of the hill among the trees, with the town and the blue water. But how in hell could we *both* dream it? We sure never saw nothin' like that—leastways I never did. Did you?"

"Only in pictures."

"That was too real for any picture. There's bound to be some place that looks that way."

"Did you dream about rocks?"

"Well, there was some great big white ones stickin' up in the water, but it wasn't at the same place."

"It must be telepathy!"

"Telepathy?" he said uncomprehendingly.

"Grandmother's cousin, James Andrew Daugherty, says that sometimes people are able to know what is in someone else's mind. He says if you think very strongly, and see a picture of what you think, and feel very strongly—particularly if you're trying to work magic—you can send a picture of the thought to another person. And if he's sensitive, he sees it, or enough to get the idea of what you're thinking. That's what must have happened—maybe while I was awake."

"That's funny," he said, "I been noticin' that sometimes before you say somethin' I know ahead what you're fixin' to say. I know with Ma, and sometimes Bill, and a few more, but I never knowed there was a right name for that—*Tel-eth-a-py?*"

"*Te-lep-a-thy.* You must be sensitive. J. A. says I am."

"You must be *real* sensitive when it comes to me," he observed.

I did not understand what he referred to, so I grinned ambiguously, said "Maybe," and added, "There's something unusual between us. The first time I saw you I felt I'd known you for millions of years, and I liked you and felt something pulling me to you. J. A. says it's polarity, but I don't understand all he says, yet."

"I don't know nothin' about polarity," he sighed, "but you drawed me, somehow, too. How does it work?"

"Have you ever used a magnet?"

"Uh-huh; Bud got some out of some junk he was tinker'n' with and tore up. Tacks and cut-nails sticks to 'em, and it beats all to watch 'em—they look like any other pieces of metal."

"A magnet has two kinds of polarity—kind of electro-magnetic charge. One end is negative, and the other is positive. If a negative end touches a positive end, they stick, but two negatives or two positives won't. J. A. says people are like that. When a positive meets a negative, they draw each other. He says most guys are positive and most girls, negative.

"Well, a girl sure draws me," he giggled, "but that wouldn't account for *us* feelin' drawed. You're a guy—I didn't know till last night just how much guy you are. You could 'a' kept on as long as me.

"I just used male and female as examples. It's more an attraction of opposites. You've heard of people with magnetic personality, haven't you?"

"No, but I see what it means. I'd say you got a real magnetic personality."

"And I feel that you have one, so if there's anything to it, we have different polarities, even if we are both boys."

"I don't know if there's anything to it or not," he chuckled, "but I'd

as lief call what draws me *polarity* and say I'm drawed by your magnetic personality as anything else I could find to say. And five minutes
ago I couldn't 'a' said neither one, 'cause I'd never heard the words,
even. If I start runnin' around with you as much as I think I'm goin' to,
it's goin' to be sort of like goin' to school. I'd give my right arm to have
the education you got."

He reached over and squeezed my shoulder as he had before he'd said
good night. As he left his hand resting on my shoulder, I took his other
hand and squeezed it, and lay happily when he laced his fingers with
mine instead of taking his hand away. We lay with our eyes closed,
almost dozing.

"Stud," I breathed, suddenly aware of something, "My migraine! It's
all cleared away!"

"Great!"

Hand tightened on shoulder, and fingers pressed fingers. I gave a
lung-filling, chest-emptying sigh of happiness. Grotesquely, a picture
from *Pilgrim's Progress* etched itself on my inner vision. It was
Christian, freed from his Burden. Emotionally I searched for my own
Burden and did not find it. The feeling of loneliness, or of aloneness, lay
lost beside the path we had taken in the night.

When I returned Stud's overnight visit, I saw at a glance why my
room had impressed him. His room never had been papered or painted.
His father's house on the Ridge had burned, and when his father had
sold the land in order to make a new start, there had been nothing left
for furniture. What the family now had was what relatives had given
them after the fire and what his father had improvised or had picked up
for a trifle at country sales.

In one corner of Stud's room stood a sagging iron bed similar to one
Grandmother had put away in the feed-house loft, except that Stud's
lacked the brass ornaments atop the posts. On it was a thin, lumpy,
cotton mattress over old folding-springs so limp that the mattress sank
to the slats at night. The pillows were stuffed with flock. A barn-red
dresser with a cracked mirror and two unmatched old oak dining chairs
by an improvised stand—a barrel to which Stud had nailed a square
top—occupied the other main wall spaces. Over the mantle in a peeling
gesso frame hung a tipped-out enlarged picture of Stud's maternal
grandfather. Over the bed Stud had tacked two calendar pictures of
half-naked girls, and between the uncurtained, green-shaded windows

hung a huge calendar showing a hunter with two bird dogs. The only comfortable seat in the room was a bent-willow rocker which faced Stud's crude tool chest, implying that when anyone sat in it, he talked to someone sitting on the box. The bare floor was scoured white, and the oil lamp immaculate. Aside from the voluptuous girls, it was a Spartan, orderly, clean room—nothing more could be said of it. Totally unexpected was a well-arranged bouquet of wild rudbeckia and ageretum in an old blue fruit jar on the stand, with a New Testament displayed by it.

"Stud, your flowers are beautiful," I told him, seeing nothing else to admire sincerely.

He turned red. "Yeah—them damn hateful sisters of mine laughed at me when I brought 'em in, and called me a sissy—asked me if I thought you was comin' courtin'! I told 'em I'd bust 'em if they didn't shut up. I never knowed till the other night a guy could let on he liked flowers, but I seen what them of yours done for your room. Them's only weeds from along the path at the branch, but I thought they was pretty, and God knows I ain't got nothin' else that is."

"You'll have all the beautiful things you want, some day." I assured him.

"If workin' hard'll get 'em, I sure mean to," he said grimly. "Uncle Paul did. He went up to Akron, and now he's rich."

"What do you keep in the big, long box under the bed," I asked, intrigued, for it looked like a small coffin box.

"Oh, them's only my rocks," he said reluctantly. "I found an arrowhead—a real pink one. I never saw no pink rock before so I kept it, and since then I've had a conceit of savin' all kinds I run across. One's got a little fern on it, as plain as anything."

"A fossil?"

"I bet you think I *am* nuts, now, savin' rocks—and you'll laugh at me the same as the other guys do when they see 'em."

"Heck no!" I said. "Rocks are fascinating."

He dragged the box out. "What was it you called the little fern?"

"A fossil. It was buried when the rock was being formed, when it was still mud, and minerals took the place of the vegetable matter when the leaf decayed."

"You mean ferns was here before rocks was?"

"Why, yes. Ferns were on earth among the earliest higher forms of plant life, millions of years before man was. Lots of rocks, and coal, and gas, and oil all have formed since ferns appeared on earth. Coal is full of fossil ferns."

"So I found me a million-year-old fossil!" he exclaimed with delight. I got to remember that word so I'll know the right name for it—fossil, *fos-sil.*"

We spent the entire evening examining and discussing the rocks, and I told him all I knew from books I had read. He had flint, chert, and a few quartzite arrowheads; different kinds of sandstone, shale, steatite, slate, and conglomorates with many kinds of pebbles. He listened in sheer fascination as I told him how the different kinds were formed. He had a fragment that I felt sure was a meteorite, and when I told him it probably fell from the sky, he was incredulous.

"You mean to say they got rocks in Heaven, and maybe a piece fell out and I found it!" he exclaimed.

"No, Stud," I chuckled. "The Revelation says the walls of the New Jerusalem have chalcedony and jasper in them, and they are kinds of quartz, and that's rock. But I meant the sky—out in space. The moon is mostly rock, scientists say, and every time you see what folks call a shooting star, its a rock that fell into our atmosphere and caught fire from friction."

"Well, I seen a shootin' star that looked like it fell on the hill, and right there was where I found that! How do you find out all them things? Books, I reckon. Where could I get hold of me a book that would tell about 'em?"

"When school opens next month I'll bring you some from the library," I promised.

"I'll sure remind you," he said eagerly. "My! I learned me some fancy, high-soundin' words out of this: *fossil, meteorite, chert, conglomorate, steatite, sedimentary, igneous*—I knowed flint and sandstone already. What was the other one I misunderstood and you laughed so— the name of that streaky-lookin' piece?"

"The one I said looked like a piece of *schist?*"

"Yeah," he guffawed. "Ain't that a hell of a name for a pretty kind of rock like that! Before, they was just all rocks, and I didn't know nothin' about 'em. I can't wait to read them books you bring me! Will you help me if I can't make nothin' out of 'em?"

"Sure," I beamed. "You bet I will."

I realized that we could not whisper after we lay down, for the wall was but the thickness of a single board. But before Stud blew out the lamp he opened a drawer, took out a towel and held it up inquiringly. I nodded. After we said goodnight we lay an hour or more, communicating by touch until fully satiated. We breathed our real good night inaudibly, and I fell asleep almost as soon as he, not resisting slumber as I did the first night for the same reason one sometimes tries not to wake from a wonderful dream. I now knew to be real all that had seemed fantasy the first night—for many times before then I had imagined him beside me, sometimes so vividly that his image seemed lying in the bed, as I suppose that of Urbain Grandier did in the beds of the Nuns of Loudun as they hungered for *him.*

There was already a hint of autumn in the late August evening, and it grew chilly after nightfall. Only a thin blanket was on the bed. We lay close together, and I awoke once and found his arm over me—whether for warmth or to give warmth, I could not say. "If two lie together, then they have heat," the Bible says. "But how can one be warm alone?" it asks, knowing there is no answer. I slept with no dark dreams, waking only to enjoy his warmth and nearness, quiver inwardly if his hair or maleness touched my skin, and after touching him, or feeling his strong arm over me, I contentedly fell back asleep. Once, feeling his face touching mine, I kissed him softly, taking care not to wake him.

I taught him many new words. He taught me new, subtle, complicated meanings for words I thought I knew. I was not willing to realize I loved him, but soon enough he taught me the aspects of *love* that I had never suspected—its beauty, that those who do not love call ugliness; its hunger, that in a cruel way is satisfaction; its happiness, that hovers on the verge of sorrow; and its joy, which is paid for in the coin of grief.

A year flew past. One of us spent each Friday night with the other, or Saturday night if one of the Clendenin boys came with me on Friday to hunt the following morning. We spent every Sunday together, and sometimes he came during the week. Stud began reading for sheer pleasure when I brought him *The Earth for Sam* on the second day of school. He revelled in its account of ages past, and made me teach him how to pronounce the "high-sounding words." With his grammar, hearing him speak accurately of conditions in the Silurian period all but threw my mental processes out of gear. Had he cared to learn grammar, by the time he was seventeen he could have spoken perfect English. But if I suggested it, he would grin his disarming grin and say "Hell, Lee, you always seem to get what I'm drivin' at, and that's all talk's for, ain't it? Just tell me if I'm pronouncin' it right—this word here, *paleozo-ology?*"

"Yes," I would sigh, "it comes from Greek. It means literally old or ancient animal-life science. It's a branch of paleontology."

"Yeah, I figured that," he would say. "We done went through what *that* meant."

In my last year of high school, when I made a despairing appeal to improve his grammar, he looked at me and grinned. "Lee," he said, "I only got to go through the fourth grade and you know it. If I ever do get to go to school and get an education, then I'll try to talk educated. But it just don't seem right, somehow, to be ignorant and talk edu-cated. To seem something I ain't, is worse than bein' ignorant and talkin' that way."

At the time it exasperated me, but now I rather agree with him. Stud was genuine. I have since seen shams—articulate men with impressive degrees and impeccable grammar, yet either profoundly ignorant or fools—teaching the young and effecting untold damage because their glibness and prestige made ignorance seem learning, and that which is foolish or false in their teaching seem profound and true.

Exasperated or not, I was never as happy as when he was with me, and he was with me whenever possible, for I was a different kind of friend from any he ever had known—one who brought books and helped him understand them—one who realized his instinct and hunger for beauty, and urged him to understand what makes things beautiful.

I brought him a book almost every week. After satisfying himself with a basic knowledge of geology, trees, wildflowers, animals, and birds, he discovered that books had also been written about agriculture, and began clamoring for those. We spent our Sundays in the woods and fields, studying and identifying. He climbed trees and brought down mistletoe to compare its roots with those of dodder, astonished that even plants can live as parasites. He dug up Indian pipes and beech drops to study the only saprophytes we could find other than mush-rooms. He was mystified, as was I, as to the nature of a jellylike organ-ism—a gelatinous slime mold—we found creeping beside a log, for it seemed to share both animal and vegetable characteristics. Then, often to seek "right answers" to his questions, or find "right names" to give him, I learned anew all that I had learned superficially, for I knew that I had a pupil worthy of a master teacher, and I caught his enthusiasm.

I also taught him the classic principles of beauty—a six-fold rule based on the forms of Nature, showing him how things that he thought beautiful were so because of balance, rhythm, harmony, unity, proportion, and fitness or function. I explained symmetry, and made him stand naked before my long mirror to study the exquisite balance and proportion, the harmony of line, the pleasing rhythm and perfect unity and functionalism of the human body.

"You see now what I meant when I said that you are beautiful, don't you?" I asked, for previously he had laughed when I told him he was.

"Yeah, I got a real good bilateral symmetry and balance, and the lines do have rhythm and harmony; and I'm real pleased that my body's all in one piece—if any of it was gone I'd miss it right away; and it's meant to do certain things and it does 'em fine. It goes by all the rules. I'm beautiful—about the way a blue-tail lizard is."

"Yes," I smiled, determined not to rise to his teasing, and pretending perfect seriousness. "God designed them according to the same principles. The shape, and size, and functions are different, that's all."

A puzzled frown wrinkled his forehead and was replaced by an astonished look of sudden realization. "It finally got through to me what you're talkin' about! I was thinkin' that *beautiful* means the same as *pretty*. It means a damn sight more than that to you, and now I see what it means. I'm the shape I *ought* to be as man, and a lizard is the shape *it* ought to be. That way of seein', I *am* beautiful! Everything that lives and grows is, if it's whole, and ain't stunted, and is all it was meant to be. You're sure right, I'm what God meant a man to be! You see everything by that way of seein', don't you?"

" 'The earth is the Lord's and the fullness thereof; the world, and they that dwell therein,' " I quoted.

"You make me feel like it's right near sacred!"

"God put a lot of time in on making it as it is," I reminded.

"All the way back to the Paleozoic."

"Longer. Back to the beginning."

"Tell me all you know about beauty! I want to know all there is to know!"

"You do. Now you've seen it, and you've seen God in it. That is all there is to know. Beauty is a gate, as love is an everlasting door. It is through the gate of beauty, or the everlasting door of love that a man goes out to God, or God comes in to him."

"I never figured on bein' preached to, me naked in front of a lookin' glass," he breathed.

"Who's preaching?"

"You and the glass both," he replied.

He studied, and his wonder grew as he discovered the order and vastness of the Universe. He became fascinated with stars, and tried as vainly as I to conceive distances which must be measured in light-years. His Heaven, which, like that of my own childhood, had seemed almost in shouting distance overhead, moved back behind the stars into the void. But simultaneously it drew near and established itself within him. "It purely makes my head swim," he murmured one night as we stood looking at the sky, as I tried to point out the constellation of Andromeda. "If each one of them stars is like the sun, bigger than the earth, and they're as far apart as they got to be to look the way they do, then I can't hope to get no idea of how big it all is. God, compared to the size of that, I ain't as much as one little speck of dust in a corn field! If God's busy keepin' all that goin', what time or attention has He got for somethin' like me!"

It is good that a man should know his size, but he sounded so wistful that I sought to comfort and reassure him.

"Do you see the Pole Star?" I asked him.

"Yeah, Arcturus; you showed me how to find it by the Dipper."

"It's at least forty light years from us."

"Yeah?"

"Well, you may not be any more than a speck of dust in a corn field, but you are conscious of something forty light-years away. Think about yourself as a being whose consciousness can reach out to something that distant, and recognize it, and give it a name, and when you wish go back and locate it in something vastly bigger."

"My consciousness! It's conscious of all the stars in the heavens. It's conscious of the whole universe!"

"And you think God has no time for a thing that can take in the universe?"

"You're gettin' me till I don't know *what* I think. If you know about

the things you make me think about, and dream and wonder, I wish
you'd come out and tell me, plain."

"I *don't* know. I only know that it's good to think, and wonder, and
dream."

He was silent a long time, then he asked, "Lee, is there some other
words like *gate* or *door?*"

I wondered what he wanted to say with the other words. "Well, an
entrance can have pole bars the same as a gate; and the door to a palace
is called a portal," I replied.

"I'm beginnin' to need them words. Now I can say you opened the
gate of beauty, and unlocked the everlastin' door of love; you laid
down the bars of wonder, and took me through the portal of dreams.
You give me ways to go out, and God ways to come in."

"You're quite a poet, Stud."

"Nah, I ain't no poet. I love you."

"Which one? The little speck of dust, or the one that can find the
Pole Star?"

"What's dust in me loves what's dust in you, and what in me looks to
the stars loves what in you looks to 'em." he said softly.

"Why Stud, that's just the way I love *you!*" I whispered. By now,
you see, we were no longer boys. He was past twenty and I was past
nineteen. We had studied and learned together and loved for half a
decade. We were no longer boys; we were two people who loved, body
and soul.

Had this love been homosexual, or *merely* homosexual, there would
be no place for it in a book purporting to tell of the unusual, for perver-
sion is older than Sodom and Gomorrah, and it would be naive to call
it strange. But our love—especially when I came to realize its true
roots—was the strangest experience I have had. The circumstances made
it deviatory, but before God, it was not perverse.

At the first, I realized that Stud was by nature demonstrative, and in
need of demonstrative affection. The two sluts had given him sexual
experience, but sex without love satisfies only momentary need. Bud
and Sam would have blushed at the thought of kissing him, however
unselfconsciously they "swapped" masturbation. Stud's six sisters,
envious of his sex, and more of his good looks—for what was strength in
his face was coarseness in theirs—constantly bickered with him. His
taciturn father loved him, but showed it only in trying to discipline him

into being a good and upright man, and his "Poor Old Ma" was too
burdened and careworn to do more than absently call him "honey,"
occasionally, and sometimes lay her hand upon his head. So, because I
realized his hunger for affection, my yearning to demonstrate mine
impelled me to break the taboos. I found that he loved to have his back
scratched, and I scratched it; I massaged him; and diffidently at first,
but soon with eager enjoyment, he accepted these attentions and returned them. Once when I thought him asleep, I carefully kissed him,
and my heart skipped several beats when he opened his eyes. But instead of reproof he gave me a smile, and to my utter confusion, raised
his head from the pillow, pulled me to him and gave me a kiss.

"Stud, you mustn't kiss *me*!" I stammered.

"Hell," he grinned, "you done it to me first."

"I thought you were asleep!"

"Yeah, and that was the third time you done it when I was playin'
possum. If you feel like kissin' me, do it when I'm awake."

After that night I was consumed with jealousy of the two girls. It
seemed an outrage that two creatures so unworthy could enjoy more of
him than I. Masking the jealousy even from myself, cloaking it in concern for his well-being, I begged him to leave them alone—at least use
every precaution—but he laughed, assured me that they did something
to prevent pregnancy, and said he knew all the boys who shared them,
and knew that these boys had no disease. But hitchhikers from the out-
lands used the road, which was as open to the public as the girls were;
and from some transient, they contracted gonorrhea.

Stud and Bill took it at once. After Bill lamented to me, Stud
avoided me for days, then came, and on pretext of going on a hike to
study nature, instead led me to what he called our "palaverin' log" secluded in deep woods, where we had our most serious conversations.

"I'm so ashamed I could drop dead," he began. "Them damn,
stinkin' dirty, low-down bitches! Many a time I've kept on with 'em
after I felt all I had to shoot was dust, tryin' to satisfy 'em, and they let
me catch the clap without sayin' a word!"

I pleaded with him to tell his parents and go to a reputable doctor
instead of trying hearsay remedies, but he seemed not to hear a word
and kept on fuming.

"I hear you," he said, as I persisted. "I plain-out don't dare let 'em
know! Pa'd horsewhip me, or maybe even run me off—and I couldn't

blame him a damn bit, either. They ain't got no money to lay out on medicine and doctor bills, and I only got a dollar and sixty cents left of my own that Aunt Tillie give me for workin' in her garden."

"Stud, hear me!" I begged him. "No father could know his only son is in the shape you are, and not do everything to help him. If that goes on, it can even make a cripple of you!"

"Is it that bad?" he gasped. "Bill said—"

"Bill said! That book of Grandmother's says it can work back into the prostate gland. That's what kept Grandfather from ever having any kids. Your dad must know what it can do. He'll find some way to raise the money."

"Damn a bull-headed fool that never listens to nothin'! Ace and you warned me a million times, and begged, and pleaded. Pa's threshed hell out of me three times already for bein' with them hussies. If he finds out this, it won't be no rope plow lines this time; it'll be the black-snake!"

"Even if he does, you'll get over *that*. Tell him, and go while the doctor can still cure you."

"I'd as lief he took the blacksnake to me as for Ma to find out."

"Look," I said, "she loves you, and she's a very sensible woman."

"I reckon. She even knows somethin's wrong. I got pus on the sheet last night."

"I told you what it did to Grandfather. It certainly messed up his life, and Grandmother's, and Mother's, and Dad's, and mine. If they'd had any children, Grandmother wouldn't have raised Mother and kept her from marrying the guy she wanted; and if he'd been my dad, Mother'd have kept me."

"I sure don't want to mess up nobody else's life," he pondered. "I'd about as lief be dead as think I couldn't have any kids. I reckon all I can do is tell poor old Ma, and maybe she can keep Pa from clean killin' me."

That was the day I saw the Black Nun. The Lilly Rock atop the north mountain somehow seemed a place for seeing clearly and far, and I went there only when I needed vision while dealing with my emotions. Stud went home down along the side of the hill, and I climbed on up to the rock when we finished talking. I was sick with fear—fear that Stud would not go to the doctor, fear that he was beyond cure, fear that Grandmother would hear enough to forbid me from associating with him. I hated the girls for having contaminated him; I hated him for having incurred contamination; I hated myself for loving him so much his contamination mattered; I hated myself for being such that I *could* love him; I hated my body for being male. It is surprising that just one thought-form whipped across Youngs' meadow. My state of mind was enough to have sent them one after another like fence-jumping sheep.

That evening I swore Grandfather to secrecy and told him, asking him to offer Stud's father a loan.

"That goes to show what can happen when a pup starts thinking he's a big dog," he said. " *You* know how to keep from getting it, don't you?"

"Ace told me. I know the danger."

"I figured he would, if I could fix it so you could start running with him. He was bound to learn something at that school he was at."

I realized suddenly how great his understanding was. "Will you loan Stud's father the money?" I entreated.

"I'd *give* the money to see that boy cured," he sighed. "But I don't figure his old man'd take a loan—he's too independent. I figure he'll offer to sell something."

The following day he ambled off down the road, carrying a letter to the Post Office, and late that afternoon returned leading Stud's father's fine milk cow. Grandmother declared that we did not need another cow, and seemed so surprised I knew Grandfather had told her nothing. In a reasonably short time, the doctor succeeded in curing Stud.

After we resumed our former intimacy, I asked if Stud's father gave him the dreaded lashing.

"Naw," he grunted. "He just looked through me, so I felt less than an inch tall, and he said: 'Son, your ma just told me what you got that has you swoll so. I hope you know now why I had to try to whale some sense into that hard head of your'n. I only hope and pray this learns you!' And I hope to tell you, it sure did!"

"I didn't think he'd whip you," I murmured. "Not after you already were in trouble—he's rough, but you mean the world to him. You must know that now. Maybe it was worth it."

"I reckon I always did know that," Stud breathed. "It wouldn't 'a' hurt near as bad if he'd laid my back open and rubbed salt in it, as it did seein' him set there with tears in his eyes, and hearin' him say in a low voice: 'I reckon you understand how much this shames your ma and me, what a sacrifice it puts us to,' like he done—and poor old ma, just standin' there with her eyes on the floor, cryin', and not sayin' a word. I swear to God, I ain't goin' to touch another low-down rip as long as breath is in my body!"

7

TESTIMONY OF HEALING

A *Petschaft* or *Wunder-Sigel* Design: For curing sickness or
stimulating sexual activity

There is no pain in Truth, and no Truth in pain.

Mary Baker Eddy

My middle and late teens were as rich in varied companionship as my previous years had been solitary. Perhaps aside from Stud and Ace, my dearest friend was from Clendenin. He was Norman Rhodes, called "Darkie" because of his deep-olive complexion—though he was otherwise not very brunette. He was as unlike Stud as any other youth could be. Stud, extroverted, impetuous and sensual, had a glorious body and a warm, turbulent, emotional nature. Darkie, quiet and deliberate, small and wiry, had a beautiful spirit, a halo of goodness, and unshakeable serenity.

In its own way, my love and my need for the one was as great as for the other, and I find no inconsistency in my having loved and needed them both in totally different ways. I am an animal with a physical body, but I am instinct with spirit. With honesty or safety I cannot deny either, for though I have two natures, one of the flesh, the other of the spirit, they compose and share one being, and are interdependent upon each other.

In those days I was groping, first for identity, then for knowledge, and after knowledge a philosophy, and I had only instinct and vague memories to guide me. They told me that Stud's sensuality needed the balance of someone else's spirituality. If anything, Stud was too real to seem entirely good. Darkie was too good to seem entirely real. When I alternated them, I knew they balanced. When Stud grew a bit overwhelming, and discussion of sensory and sensual things palled, a night spent in Darkie's chaste, unspotted bed listening to his uplifting conversation set everything back in perspective and in equilibrium. Conversely, being too long with Darkie called for Stud, and revitalization borrowed from his earthiness and great physical vitality.

Darkie's wry smile, his droll, dry, unstinging wit, and his patience, made him a friend one might choose as his only one if forced to choose. He was the only Christian Scientist youth in Clendenin, and I quickly associated his religion with his remarkable personality. In fact, the two were inseparable.

No one I asked knew anything about his church. In fact, few even had heard that such a denomination as the Church of Christ, Scientist,

existed. I hesitated to ask him about it, fearing that he might be reluctant or embarrassed as was a Catholic boy when I asked about his local-
ly abominated religion. When Grandmother learned that the Mother
Church was in Boston, she developed a cool reserve, as if by being a
"Yankee Church" it lost any interest it might otherwise have had to
her. Her world lay entirely south of the Mason-Dixon line, and east of
the Ohio River. (She was born only seven years after the Civil War, and
all her people were Confederates.) She also felt that since nothing scientific could be Christian, Darkie's church had to be one or the other.

"But you like him!" I remonstrated.

"Yes," she admitted, "I only wish Stud and your other friends could
have as much good said of them as Darkie deserves to have said. But
that has nothing to do with his church. There are good people in all
churches, except maybe the Catholic—and on the other hand, I've even
known a few Adventists who were the devil's own."

It is extraordinary that my memory of the Rhodes house is as vague
as it is. I can see other rooms of that time so clearly that worn places on
the linoleum appear. I can see individual pieces of furniture clearly
enough to detect the pattern of the material with which they were
upholstered. I can see the knothole in the ceiling over Stud's bed, and
the pattern of the grain of the wood around it; but of Darkie's house, I
have only nebulous impressions, like those of a leafless branch seen by
the light of the new moon on a night of fog. I do not recall how the
house looked, other than that it was low and white and clean, cramped
between the mountain and the river near the upper end of Koontz
Avenue, where Clendenin narrows to a single row of houses before
being pinched off entirely by the hill.

Had they lived in Versailles, surrounded by gilt furniture, mirrors,
and brocade, the family would still have impressed me more than their
surroundings. Each had a strong, distinct, and pleasing personality, and
together they complemented one another in such a way that the family
seemed greater than the sum total of its members. Darkie did not dread
his father as did Stud, but adored the old man—he seemed to me older
than Grandfather—and showed him open affection. His father's age
notwithstanding, Darkie had an elfin little sister, as vivacious and
sprightly as Darkie was reserved and deliberate. They all idolized Darkie's tiny, fragile-looking mother and turned to her as to a pillar of

wisdom, strength, and inspiration. Not beds and sofas and chairs, but peace and harmony is what I remember there—they gave the house the feeling of a shrine. Love emanated from the walls, and to sojourn there was to visit in Elysium.

Such homes are so rare that one knows not what to make of them. I was perceptive enough to recognize the atmosphere as one only religion and worship can give a place—and religion of a most unusual sort. It requires holy magic to charge a place with goodness so strongly that a sensitive person can detect love, happiness, and contentment when he steps inside even an unoccupied room. Other houses have atmospheres filled with the residue of hate, fear, suffering, horror or madness, and are called haunted. I suppose the Rhodes house was haunted, too, but in a blessed way.

When I was ten, someone had notified the authorities, and Grandmother was forced to send me to school. They tested me for placement and were nonplussed to find that I could read at any level, could perform at a seventh grade level in mathematics, and could relate Greek history and parrot sex information in an adult manner that shocked them.

My social adjustment, though, was that of a defective child of kindergarten age. With adults I comported myself with adult decorum, but other children terrified and baffled me, for I was never allowed to be a child in this life.

The school officials had to put me somewhere, so they put me in the sixth grade. There I stayed until I learned to mimic the behavior of a seventh grader, utterly bored with the assignments given; giving answers in language consciously borrowed from the essays of Ralph Waldo Emerson, and unconsciously from the King James Version of the Bible; releasing myself from captivity by periodic illnesses which appeared to be all known varieties of measles, whooping cough, scarlet fever, chicken pox, pneumonia, influenza, and if nothing else could be acquired, colds of unbelievable severity.

Finally the sixth-grade teacher promoted me. In the seventh I came to realize that children are almost human—or maybe a seventh grader *is becoming* almost human; and in the eighth I even made a few hesitant friends. Nevertheless, at fourteen, the wild, free boys at the swimming hole (some of whom had never known childhood, either, because of the exigencies of poverty, and all of whom had escaped the regimentation of schools) were my chosen companions.

So, the first autumn I was in high school, I was fifteen. Darkie was the same age, though he was a grade ahead. In compassion he did what he could to help me adjust to high school life, which by comparison with the nightmare of grade school, soon became tolerable, then agreeable. Either because I had acquired immunities or because I no longer needed all the diseases as escapes, I ceased being ill.

Before I knew Norman well enough to think of him as Darkie, he once saw me limping and ran to me.

"Oh, I was running like a fool in the school yard and tripped on something," I explained, favoring my twisted ankle.

"Don't think about pain," he urged. "Let me treat it for you."

He sounded much like Grandmother when she told me to stand still and let her treat a cut to stop the bleeding. His voice had the same quiet assurance of power and authority—the same faith in the efficacy of what he was about to do.

"Do you know words to say for a sprain?" I asked. (Not even Grandmother knew a charm for a sprain.)

"I am affirming for you. You are Spirit, and Spirit cannot be injured or in pain. Pain is unreal, a belief in error. True Man cannot be hurt, and I see you as True Man. There can be no accident in God's Perfect Universe. Know this, and the belief in error will disappear."

I supposed the words were an enchantment; since Grandmother's spells worked immediately, I expected the pain to stop at once. I put my foot down gingerly and could bear my weight on it. It did seem remarkably better.

"Thanks, until you're better paid," I breathed. "It's going to be all right now. Thanks again!"

He smiled his warped, droll grin. "Sure it is," he beamed. "If you wish, I'll have Mother treat it, too, when I get home. She's as good as a regular practitioner."

"She knows a lot of such charms?"

"She makes very powerful affirmations," he replied.

I supposed affirmations to be a special kind of incantation. "She uses magic to heal, I mean," I said, making the statement half question.

"No, it's divine Truth that heals," he said quietly. "She knows the

Truth about the condition that Mortal Mind sees as injury, or sickness, or disharmony, and Truth destroys the belief in error, and it disappears."

"Is that part of your religion?" I asked in surprise.

"That *is* our religion," he nodded.

The fascination of finding a religion with the power to heal took my thought away from the ankle altogether. Very soon after that Darkie brought me a worn-out copy of *Science and Health, With Key to the Scriptures,* by Mary Baker Eddy, and I began trying to understand Christian Science. It is by no means easy.

However, without understanding it, I did apply it, and the ankle did not bother me, though it remained weak. In those days, having walked during the years when most children run, and being somewhat behind those who had run, I ran everywhere. One afternoon I ignored school rules and ran down the stairs to the gymnasium. As I cleared the bottom two steps to the landing in one bound, I turned my ankle again, much more severely than the previous time, and could barely limp on down and across to the office.

Again Darkie and his mother gave it treatment, and to the best of my understanding, do did I. Again it gave very little trouble, and seemed to heal with preternatural speed. It hurt in cold, wet weather, but Mrs. Eddy's book scoffs at the effect of climate, so I denied that it hurt under those conditions,—and it seemed strong until I lapsed back into mortal error and could feel how weak it really was, and had to reaffirm all over again. However, by the end of school it gave practically no trouble, and I rejoiced that Truth had overcome error in my flesh.

I suppose that in absolute Science, belief in flesh is itself error, for flesh is matter, and matter is defined as error and unreal. So the whole effort was one of replacing one unreality with another. It almost surprises me now that I did not dematerialize myself. Stud advised me to tape up my ankle and keep off it all I could, but this smacked so of mortal error that I deliberately missed the bus the following afternoon in order to spend an hour with Darkie, and walked home. The six-mile hike—eight, counting the mile from school to Darkie's house and the mile back—seemed to have no adverse effect at all on the stretched ligaments.

About a month after the end of school, Stud called from old Aunt Tillie's to ask me if I could spend the night. Grandmother agreed, so, eager to get the milking done early, I called the two cows until my throat was sore. Not even a tinkle of their bells could be heard on the mountain. Vexed, I started the steep climb. When I reached the third bench I heard them in the extreme distant corner of the pasture—maybe in the peach orchard, or even through the fence on Carpenter's side.

One cow was a mischievous, clever, temperamental Jersey with deceitful, loving-looking eyes like a doe's. She was called Pet, and that was her exact status with Grandmother, who raised her from a calf, and declared her the finest milk cow in the county. The other, Bessie, was a dull thing of no certain breed, which Grandfather fattened for beef after he bought Stud's father's cow. Bessie followed Pet in everything, being too stupid to think up mischief of her own. When they heard me, Pet raised her head, peered up over the briars and wild pea vines, and gave an insolent moo. Then she began to climb to the very crest of the hill to the line fence.

I knew I would have to go all the way to bring them down, so I clambered up, holding to bushes and climbing straight up the slope when I could, rather than taking the zig-zag paths the cows had made. When I came near enough to throw rocks almost to the cows, Pet mooed again, and the two, sportive as yearlings, raced down the hill, leaving me high on the mountainside. The Jersey often played this game, bovinely amused by my frustration and exasperation, knowing that by holding her milk she could inform Grandmother if I dared lay a hand on her. They did not stop until they reached the first bench, from which they meandered on down to the milkplace with perfect decorum.

As soon as I was off the steep slope, I also started running, and on the sled trail on the second slope I turned my foot on a round stone and fell headlong. From the blinding agony and the unnatural position of my foot, I realized that this time I had dislocated my weak ankle. When I tried to stand, nausea overcame me, and I felt myself about to faint. I sank down, lowered my head to keep consciousness, and waited for the nausea to pass.

I hardly knew what to do. Dusk was ready to start gathering. I knew Grandmother would be frantic if night came and I did not appear. She could not climb the mountain, and Grandfather was ill. It was too far from the house to hope to make my voice heard, and much too far to try to crawl. I had nothing with which to cut a forked stick for a crutch, and I could not find a dead branch on which I might hobble. I tried hopping on one leg, but the jarring brought back the nausea.

Then one of Mrs. Eddy's gems of Truth came to my mind and I clung to it. "Let not the flesh but the spirit be represented in me. . . . There is no Truth in pain, and no pain in Truth." I affirmed with all my powers that I was Spirit, and that Spirit cannot be injured. I denied the dislocation as an erroneous claim of mortal mind, and visualized myself intensely as an uninjured, perfect Spirit. I succeeded, but I also unintentionally projected my consciousness—something I had, until I was thirteen, done at will.

"I" stood up readily and started to go down, when "I" observed my physical body lying on the ground. I willed the uninjured spirit back into it, and it reentered. I stood up and sensed bone grate on bone as the dislocated joint slid back in place. Then, as the foot was straight again, and I was not conscious of any sensation from it, I hurried on home.

Grandmother had already milked. And when I told her what had happened she began bustling to boil water and hunt in the pantry for the box of Epsom salts. I told her I would rely on Truth alone to heal me. When she began to argue that nothing is as helpful as salts-water, I replied, "God is! Now please let me alone!"

The answer took her aback. She knew that when a matter of conviction is involved, no one was ever more stubborn than I can be. Moreover, she could see the rapid swelling of the discoloring ankle, and realized that something was happening—or had happened—to make me able to walk freely on it without apparent discomfort. It awed her.

"Sometimes I don't know what to think about you!" she muttered She poured the hot water over the supper dishes, put the salts back on the pantry shelf, and went to washing dishes, baffled.

My ankle turned black, but merely felt thick and awkward, and I felt no pain. In a few days the blackness changed to a gruesome rainbow of other colors, and gradually faded back to normal. The swelling went down and disappeared. From then until now, that ankle has been as strong as the other.

"It's some kind of magic power you got, ain't it?" Stud demanded after he had seen the ankle.

"It's the power of Divine Truth," I murmured. "I'm treating it with Christian Science."

When I showed him the tattered book, he looked at it, read a page or two, declared that he could not make one word of sense out of it, frowned a puzzled frown, and said it *must* be some kind of magic.

"I know you can do a heap of things if you know the right words to say," he admitted. "Aunt Mat knows how to stop bleedin' like your Grandma does, and Uncle Luke used to know somethin' to charm rats away. But them kind of charms is mighty hard to come by."

"That *is* magic." I said. "I can stop blood, too. Grandmother taught me what to say."

"Will you teach me?" he besought eagerly.

"I'm sorry, Stud, I'm not allowed to," I said reluctantly. "As long as I live, I'm to tell only three others, and they all have to be women, and all younger."

"That must be what Aunt Mat meant," he considered. "She said she'd told as many as she could."

"If you tell more than three or anybody older, or of the same sex you are, it breaks the spell. You can't do it any more, and the other person can't."

"Heck! A person has a time tryin' to learn any kind of witch work like that. Great-grandpa could charm bees so they wouldn't sting. I can't find nobody that knows that, or will let on, and I'd give a pretty to know it."

"That about bleeding really isn't witchcraft. I *can* tell you that much; the words come straight out of the Bible."

"God," he gasped, "that's the last place I'd look for any kind of a magic spell!"

"I think it's full of magic, if you only know where to look. Magic is only a word for power that people don't understand. This that set my ankle is the power of God."

"If it ain't the power of faith," he puzzled. "I swear I didn't see nothin' in what I read that'd make God heal you."

"It's not the God that they preach in all *our* churches. The book explains God as Principle."

"Like a Sunday School Principal?"

"That's a different word. *Principle*, like a fact in science or a law in mathematics."

"And that heals you? Don't try to explain. It's away beyond my understandin'."

If I could stop here, there would be nothing particularly unusual about my testimonial—except that in my concentration on spirit, I accidentally sent out a *doppelgänger*, or underwent astral projection. Almost all Christian Scientists have experienced permanent healings, some more dramatic than that of a dislocated ankle. Christian Science has to its credit the healing of almost every disease and condition imaginable —other than gonorrhea and syphilis. It is almost impossible to contract those diseases mentally, and once you have them, it is almost impossible to feel spiritual enough to effect healing.

What makes my testimonial of Christian Science healing strange is that I am not a Christian Scientist.

To begin with, my sensibilities rejected the adulation and veneration accorded Mrs. Eddy by her followers. I found it egregious that her word should be read alternately with the Word of God in lieu of sermons, and given equal weight with Scripture in the teaching. She was a precise, Victorian lady, opinionated and dogmatic, who always made me think of Harriet Beecher Stowe. Convinced that her word was Divine Truth, she inevitably (like the Stowe woman) had a son who was a great disappointment to her, a source of embarrassment; a cross of shame. She was enough like Grandmother, and I enough like the son, for my sympathies to lie with him. And because I know what manner of woman she was, I felt that she required scrutiny with both eyes fully open. When such women as Mrs. Eddy make mistakes, they are mistakes in fundamentals, which have far-reaching effects. I began to search for her fundamental error as soon as I read her official biography, for she seemed altogether too perfect. I have known good women; I have known great women; but I have yet to find a perfect woman (or man either). Should I find one, I would bow down and worship, as I bow before the figure on the Cross; but I am certain that I must go through life unbowing, other than to the good I find even in the worst of men.

Stud's remark—"If it ain't the power of faith"—kept troubling me. I knew that Christian Science healing is not ordinary faith healing, which is usually a result of hypnotic suggestion engendered in mass hysteria and is no permanent healing at all (since when the suggestion fades, so does the apparent benefit). So for a long time I searched for the explanation, and at last found the answer. The power *is* that of faith; it is not the *Truth* of Mrs. Eddy's belief which heals, but the *belief* of her Truth. As long as anyone *believes* that Christian Science is Truth, he can heal with it. It works *precisely* like magic, which is a far less casual statement than "It works like magic." And I could see from the effect this magic had on the Rhodes family, it *is* holy.

But it was not meant for me. The Christian Science teaching is illogical, for it defines God as infinite Good. The Christian Science God is real, but not total. I am a total person, and I must have a God of totality. If a thing is infinite, it cannot be limited, and *good* limits. It does not speak of the God who said to Moses, "Say . . . I AM hath sent me," He who slew the firstborn of the Egyptians, and drowned Pharaoh's army in the Red Sea. What of this God who said, "I form the light and create darkness: I make peace, and create evil; I the Lord do all these things."

From the beginning, *He* is the God I worship. He is *Ehyeh Asher Ehyeh*, He who spake out of the burning bush. It was He who came down in fire on Sinai; who spake and there came flies; who spake and the locusts came.

This God is unto each man what that man believes God to be. The reason that Christian Scientists prosper, enjoying health and happiness, is that to them, He is the God who forms light and creates peace. They deny that He creates darkness and evil, and would deem it blasphemous to call Him the Lord of Flies. Yet God is Slayer of the Firstborn, by the testimony of the Sacred Word, Slayer even of His Own Son. Older and wiser faith sees Him more clearly than Christian Science. As Brahma the Creator, as Vishnu the Preserver, as Shiva the Destroyer, it calls him Trimutri, the World-Soul. Yet he is *Ehyeh Asher Ehyeh*—Infinite Being. Only so can He be God of Light, God of Love, Slayer of the Firstborn, and Lord of Flies.

My soul would know the darkness of God so as to appreciate the light. I would taste sorrow, the keener to taste joy. I would know total God with total being, so that in years ahead when I behold Him approach as Lord of Famine, as Lord of Earthquake, or as Lord of Death, I may love and worship Him though He may slay me, in the faith that to whatever He slays, He gives life again.

His miracles are not restricted to Christian Scientists; they are freely available to all who believe—even Methodists. At Wellford I met a Methodist preacher who had lived near Gandeeville, and when he learned my name, he said he knew Grandmother Gandee-Raines, Uncle Grover, and father's sister Virgie Wilson and her husband, Thomas.

"Now there is one fine woman," he said, "I've never known anybody who walks nearer to God than Virgie does."

"I don't know her very well," I said, for I had a deep feeling that if one were to walk near to God, he would have to be quite restrained, and have a stiff-starched piety. Virgie was a stout, bustling, loud-voiced woman who laughed a great deal, hummed as she cooked, and bantered at the table.

"She has had true miracles granted her," he continued, "and so has her brother-in-law. You know he is afflicted?"

"Yes, a cripple, and maybe a little off in the head."

"Maybe—but he's a real Christian. Once he was at a revival in the winter time, and the stove in the church was red hot. He got filled with the Holy Ghost and began shouting, and started walking the backs of the seats, stepping from one row to the next, never losing balance, lame as he is. *Nobody* could do that unless he was filled with The Power. Then he sprang down, and went up toward the stove, shouting 'Glory! Glory! Praise be to God!' with his eyes shut, and tears running down his face, shouting and clapping his hands, and embracing everybody he bumped into, saying 'Praise the Lord!' Well, he bumped into the stove, and threw his arms around it, and laid his cheek up against it, saying 'Glory!' until they grabbed him and pulled him away. And you know, that hot iron did not burn his face, or scorch his clothes! When they all saw that, that meeting turned into something to remember! Not one sinner who came there that night left without giving his heart to God."

"Did you see that?" I asked him.

"My father and mother did. That was the night father was converted, and started to try to raise me to want to preach. He said he wanted that kind of religion when the world is on fire."

"Did something like that happen to Aunt Virgie?"

"Maybe her's was greater. She's the kindest, most generous, tender-hearted person in the world. It was back in 1922, the year after the late freeze killed everything that was planted, and all the fruit and berries. In 1921, all anybody had was what he planted after that frost, and fall came so early they lost a lot of that. The whole country was on short rations that winter."

"I remember," I agreed. "Grandmother had up over three hundred cans of stuff from the year before, but even so we ran low."

"Sometime in the winter they got a new preacher at Gandeeville, and Virgie knew how little money the church could pay him, so she gathered up all she could spare and took a ham, a crock of sauerkraut, and some eggs and butter to him on a sled. They say the preacher's wife cried for joy to get that food, for they had been on beans for a week or more. Well, when spring came and the preacher wanted some to plant, he went to see if Virgie could spare him seed potatoes."

"Did she?"

"Yes; they had planted, and had three bushels left. Three bushels wouldn't begin to last her till the new ones came in. But she said if the preacher was doing without, so could they; so the preacher took two bushels. And you know—I reckon you've seen how they put away the grub—one bushel would not last that family a week."

"What about the miracle?" I reminded him, for I thought he had gotten off on how generous Aunt Virgie was.

"That's what I'm coming to," he said. "They went on using potatoes the same as ever, and that *one* bushel lasted until the crop came in, and they had some to throw away out of it. Whenever she came back for more, the basket was as full as ever."

Aunt Virgie stayed with me in later years. I asked her about these things, and she smiled a smile that few can justify.

"Yes," she said, "it's the truth. I thought of the Widow of Zaraphath and her oil and meal, and of the ravens that fed Elijah, and I prayed that God would feed my house in that time of hunger, and God replenished them."

"It's hard to believe," I said in awe.

"Is it?" she asked quietly. "Doesn't all our food come from God? Read how many times God provided food when there was need and when the earth could not provide it the usual way."

"I know," I nodded. The preacher had been right: I have not met many like her.

She told of other instances in which she had been given help. Once one of her sons was sick, I think with typhoid, and lingering at the point of death. She had been up seventy-two hours with him, without sleep, praying continually.

"I was worried out of my mind," she breathed, "for he was so low it looked like die he would, and no doctor could come, and I had done all I knowed to do, but he got worse instead of better. Then a voice came to me and said, 'Lie down and get some sleep.' But I thought it was just part of me crying out for rest, so I fought to stay awake. Three times I heard it. So the third time, I did lie down, and was asleep in no time, and began to dream. I dreamt I was barefooted, and an angel was by my side. He motioned me to go with him, and we went through the barn lot into the pasture field. There were thistles all around, and he said, 'Pull them.' And I did, and he said, 'Boil the roots and make a tea,' and I woke up. So I went to the place without even putting my shoes on, and found thistles there and made the tea, and poured some of it down the boy. Soon as I had the dose down him he went to sleep. I thought he had died, and called Tom, but he come and looked, and the glass of the mirror fogged when we put it to his mouth and when I knew he was just asleep I fell down on my knees and thanked God. When he woke up, his fever had broke, and by next afternoon he was well on the mend."

"Maybe you did hear a voice," I mused.

"Why, what else could it have been?" she asked in surprise. "I had to sleep so the angel could reach me in a dream. If one had come to me, awake, I'd have thought I imagined it because I was so tired. With all the boys who die every day, I couldn't have believed God would send an angel to save mine. I ain't worthy."

God must have thought otherwise, for her son lived and is still alive to this day.

8

"THE WORD OF GOD,
THE MILK OF JESUS' MOTHER,
AND CHRIST'S BLOOD..."

The Sign of Creation, Manifestation and Materialization: An affirmation of the Hex rule "As below, so above," and of man's power to create through mental and spiritual action. The flanking symbols are Earth-Star signs, calling for all the good things of earth and earthly joys

> *I say: any and every man who knowingly neg-*
> *lects using this book in saving the eye, or the leg,*
> *or any other limb of his fellowman, is guilty of the*
> *loss of such limb, and thus commits a sin . . .*

John George Hohman

The realization that Christian Science is a form of magic came as somewhat of a shock. I was not surprised that holy persons can use magic,
for Stud's Aunt Mat was as good as bread, and in her own way, Grandmother was a holy woman. That Grandmother spoke a verse of the
Bible and stopped bleeding—even in animals, when someone phoned
and asked her to try—seemed natural to me because it was familiar.

My great-great-grandfather Zachariah Lee could command rain so
well he could stop a shower at will, or bring up one in a few hours. Now
there was a Hex! But one day he grew angry because lightning had
struck his favorite shade tree and almost frightened his great-grandson
to death, so he stepped to the edge of the porch, shook his fist at the
clouds, and cried, "Bust my tree and scare a little boy, damn you! This
is old Zach: let's see you flash one at *me* once!" A Hex should not say
such things. The lightning obeyed him; he was killed instantly.

Only after I was in college did I realize that something was involved
here that is not accounted for in ordinary psychology. In college I also
took philosophy. When I saw that even atheists may have Puritan standards as to right and wrong, I began to wonder what unique value religion has. Its practical values seemed to come from psychology, and its
helpful effects in controlling behavior, as well or better from ethics or
philosophy. All that seemed left was worship, and I found that very
difficult in churches. They are not big enough to inspire awe, or beautiful enough to inspire reverence, or quiet enough for meditation. More
and more, I became interested in magic, more and more in the God in
Nature, less and less in churchly religion.

Though I still used Christian Science effectively when I believed
some particular affirmation, I became interested in Hex, or Pennsylvania Dutch White Magic. This was the kind Stud's Great Aunt Mat
practiced, as well as did the others in our community who used "The
Power" in any of its forms.

The title of this chapter comes from the "sympathetic words" of
John George Hohman's *The Long Lost Friend.* Part of an incantation
called "A Good Remedy for Bad Wounds and Burns", it is printed as
below, followed by three Hex crosses: "The word of God, the milk
of Jesus' mother, and Christ's blood is for all wounds and burnings
good. + + +"

By way of instruction Hohman said, "It is the safest way in all these
cases to make the crosses with the hand or thumb three times over the
affected parts; that is to say, over all those things to which the crosses
are attached." It is a typical pow-wow, or Pennsylvania Dutch conjuration for curing. I find it effective, though for wounds and for burns
I use two separate ones which work more quickly for me.

Unless one is already himself a Pow-wow, the instructions may not
be clear. Hohman lived at Rosenthal, near Reading, Pennsylvania, and
wrote the booklet in 1819. The language has not changed much since
then, but John George was a Pennsylvania Dutchman, not unlike the
Carolina Swiss after they began speaking English. A barrister com-
plained of them, "Their natural way of expression is such that not all
the artifice and cunning of the legal mind could, by design, contrive its
equal for obscurity and ambiguity of meaning."

Here and there, with other incantations, Hohman let fall other hints,
but not enough to clarify fully what one does when he pow-wows.
When three crosses are printed after the "sympathetic words" (incantations), the following procedures should be performed: First, the words
"In the name of God the Father, God the Son, and God the HolyGhost,
Amen" are spoken. Then, the pow-wow makes the sign of the cross
three times—over the affected part of the body if the person being
treated is present, or if the person is not present, in the air in his direction. In any benevolent work, the crosses are made by closing the right
hand into a fist. Using the thumb, first make a downward stroke, then
raise the hand to the right and cross the first stroke horizontally toward
the left.

The use of the left hand and of a crossing from left to right is for
malevolent purposes—useful when one is cursing a malevolent condition, in which cases the two malevolencies counter each other, as do
two negatives or two positives in polarity. Any effort to heal, as for a
wound or a burn, that does not require the destruction of anything

could be called benevolent. If healing first requires destruction, as of a cancer, a tumor, or the core of a boil, the Hex is a curse to destroy the *cause* of the trouble and could be called malevolent.

For ritualistic reasons, I stand with my back toward the East when giving present treatment, in order that help may come to the treated person from that direction in deference to the Sun, and all that the Sun symbolizes. When I give absent treatment, however, I face the direction of the person treated. In absent treatment I speak the Pow-wow aloud. But if the person is present, unless the conjuration is in German or in words whose meaning is not known, I whisper them inaudibly. This is done for the same reason that one keeps prayer secret—and Jesus Himself commanded that prayer be made in secret. In speaking a Pow-wow, as in the ancient religion, the head is covered, as I believe it still is in synagogues during prayer or worship. For this purpose the old users of Pow-wow kept a special hat or bonnet in a dark place, and brought it out only for this ritual. In emergency cases I have covered my head with a towel, a handkerchief or a newspaper, but I keep a hat in my wardrobe for use whenever possible.

In some old "Papers"—the handwritten incantations kept by users who knew too many conjurations to remember them all—occasionally one finds an incantation followed by J. J. J. or I. I. I., or Y. Y. Y. However written, this indicates that instead of "In the Name of God . . . etc.," the saying is to be followed by "In Jesus' name, Amen."

The incantations marked with crosses or the three letters should be said at specific time intervals. Unless there are special instructions, the first is said and the signs are made when the Hex undertakes treatment. The incantation is repeated and the signs are again made a half-hour later; the third repetition and third signs are made an hour after the second, making a total of nine signs in the course of the treatment. The four-square cross originally invoked the Lord of the Four Directions—the Universal One God. It is the Hex symbol of power, of universality, and of the pairing of opposites—of negative and positive, of male and female, of active and passive or of any pair of opposites which must be in balance for wholeness, for perfection, or for generation. In the context of Physics, it could stand for opposite polarities.

After the old religion gave way to, or made room for, Christianity, it transferred its conjurations to the new gods. (White Hex called the new teaching the God-spell and recognized it as the highest magic—one in which priests transformed bread and wine into the very body and blood of Christ by the ritual of the Mass.) Nevertheless, when doing research for his dissertation, "The Practice of Using to Heal among North and South Carolina Lutherans," a student at the Lutheran Theological Southern Seminary in Columbia, South Carolina, found a woman in North Carolina successfully using an incantation which invokes Thor as well as the Trinity! It must bridge the transition between pagan and Christian belief in Northern Europe.

When he remonstrated with her, incredulous that a Lutheran should still invoke Thor (albeit many pow-wows refer to the Virgin Mary and other saints), the good old soul, country bred and uneducated, told him that the word *Thor* was part of the incantation that had always been handed down. But what it meant, she did not know, for she only repeated what the old ones taught her. I can believe her, for when my cat was snakebitten, I used an incantation, *"Slongabis, Slongagift, geh im sond,"* repeated thrice as one strokes down from the wound to touch the ground with the thumb, and I have no idea what *Slongabis* and *Slongagift* mean. I only know that David Shull wrote them in his "Paper" in Pennsylvania in 1859, and that the cat recovered overnight from both swelling and sickness. That incantation invokes neither the Trinity nor Jesus, and requires only that one repeat it and touch the ground at the end of each downward stroke, then draw the cross on the ground with the thumb. It may go back to the old religion, and to a forgotten language. It was titled "To Cure Snakebite in Cattle"—but it works fine for a cat, maybe because *cattle* once meant any kind of domestic animals.

In one of his comments, Hohman said that what is prescribed for man also applies to animals. I presume the reverse is also true. Still, I would not rely on this charm, not having seen it tried on a person, unless I were snakebitten where I could not induce bleeding and hasten to a doctor.

Until he decided that God must take her ignorance into account, the researcher was rather disturbed to find that the old lady's incantation worked successfully notwithstanding its suggestion of divided loyalty. He dutifully included it with the many others he collected. I gave him my favorite pow-wow for burns and referred him to retired Lutheran pastor Wessinger at Newberry, South Carolina, who has lived and preached among users all his life, has great respect for their powers, and enjoys their complete confidence.

Pastor Wessinger, though he still serves rural congregations that cannot attract a full-time minister, must be past eighty. He told me that in his youth there were still a few Hexes in South Carolina who could walk in front of the fire in a burning field or forest, and the flames would stop and go out at their path, and not rekindle on the opposite side even in a high wind. He said the woman who handed down my pow-wow for burns could thus extinguish fire, but the only recent attempt I have heard about did not succeed. The enchanter walked in front of the flames, was cut off from escape from the field, and was forced to run for his life and jump in Lake Murray. But with what sublime confidence old Granny Slice, the good witch of Dutch Fork, would start across a blazing woodland, and how people marvelled when the fire died at her tracks! People in the Dutch Fork tell of a house which stood in the path of a raging fire in Little Daniel Koon's lifetime. He arrived on horseback, only in time to jump off, circle the building, and gallop on to a point where he could safely begin the walk. The house was all that remained unburned in the wake of the fire.

But I know of none left like Granny Slice and Little Daniel Koon, and though I have sought the incantation they used, I have not found it. The old pastor said he had never heard it, nor had he seen a firewalk. "But my parents saw them, and I saw a tract of pine where Granny Slice had walked and stopped the fire," he reflected. His people had known the Slice (or Schlaiss) family since the middle of the eighteenth century.

A seminary seems an unlikely place at which to present a dissertation on magic, but the South Carolina Synod is full of people who know that "using" is practiced widely among Lutherans in the state, and I suppose they wished to learn all they could about it. Before I owned a copy of *The Long Lost Friend*, I was quite put out to make a trip to Dutch Fork to ask one of the old Slice men to let me copy from his book an incantation I needed, only to find that his minister (a young man—also named Wessinger) had borrowed it ahead of me and taken it home.

At the seminary and in the Synod, hardly anyone is more respected than the Reverend J. Benjamin Bedenbaugh, D.D. Older South Carolina Lutherans have known him since he was a scrawny, devout, earnest young seminarian, regarded as a genius by his instructors, and affectionately called "Bennie" by the whole Synod. A farm youth from near Stony Battery, in Newberry County, he had known of users all his life.

As a student, and later as a theologian at the seminary, he was subject to agonizing, prostrating headaches. (He is a bachelor, and his headaches reminded me of the migraines I used to suffer.) So when the researcher told him he had found a conjuration for headaches, Dr. Bedenbaugh allowed him to use it in his behalf. I would give much to have witnessed that pow-wow, for it involves pressing the fingers of both hands against the sufferer's temples, recitation of irrelevant-sounding words, and the solemn assurance, "This I tell thee, Bennie, for thy repentance' sake. + + +" It must have been a bizarre sight.

I was told some months afterward that Dr. Bedenbaugh's headache: had stopped, and though I am too much in awe of his reputation and erudition to ask him personal questions, I noticed that he took on a different look. He remained pale, but no longer corpselike; solemn, but no longer funereal; and the pinched, tormented look left his face and eyes.

The dissertation was accepted: the researcher was ordained, and the last time I heard of him he had a church of his own, and was also "using" actively for the members of a Negro Baptist congregation. (This group was on the verge of turning Lutheran because of his wonder-working power, but I think he taught the Negro minister how to pow-wow, instead of leading the church away.)

At that time I was teaching at Lenoir Rhyne College, in Hickory, North Carolina, and knowing of this development in Columbia, I felt it defensible to give help to my students when I saw they should have it. Hohman wrote, "Any and every man who knowingly neglects using . . . in saving the eye, or the leg, or any other limb of his fellow man is guilty of the loss of such limb, and thus commits a sin. . . ." I feel much the same; so though I realized fully that the administration would make fun of it, or condemn it as superstition or witchcraft, I began using "sympathy" when I was on the faculty there.

The first instance was for a boy from Virginia. He suffered a deep, inward nasal hemmorrhage which had persisted for more than twenty-four hours, and had gone to a doctor in Hickory who had not succeeded in stopping it. When I learned of it, he was about to start to a specialist in Charlotte, with friends who were going along, afraid he would collapse or grow too faint from loss of blood to drive his car.

I asked him if I might try to help him, and he agreed, though he said, "What do you think *you* can do?" in complete scepticism.

"I can try, that is all," I told him. "I know an old way."

"Well, try!" he urged. "If somebody doesn't do something soon, I'm going to bleed to death!"

So I took him aside, and said the "words of sympathy" to stop bleeding, made the crosses, and he went on to Charlotte.

However, the bleeding stopped before he was out of Hickory, and the specialist merely examined his nose and throat and did nothing except tell him not to do anything to risk starting it again, and sent him back. Word spread in his dormitory that I was some kind of wonder-worker, and the boys teased me unmercifully, though a few wanted to know the method.

Next a youth from Charlotte fell on a trampoline and cut his eyebrow, injuring his eyelid and eye very severely. That night, he and his friends sat up and soaked the blood and fluid into towels, for it hardly slackened, and the doctor feared that he might lose his eye. It was just before Christmas holidays, but he could not travel to visit his sister in Richmond in that condition. When he did not appear for the last class before the holidays, I went to the dormitory to visit him, for I was very fond of him.

When I offered to try to help him, he sighed, "Well, if you helped Stu like they say, maybe you *can* do something."

I recited the conjuration, and before the vacation began that afternoon, his injury stopped bleeding and discharging fluid. He went on to Richmond. His eye still looked hopeless when he returned, but he was beginning to see vaguely with it, and though double vision persisted for months, by the time he graduated the following spring, his eye was normal. Another case was of a youth who was one of the most strikingly handsome athletes I ever saw, a star on the basketball team. During practice he was struck squarely in the mouth by someone's elbow; the impact knocked out one of his teeth and loosened the two adjoining it. The coach found the tooth and rushed him to the dentist, who set it back in place. But his mouth was so grotesquely swollen and discolored when he entered class next day, I hardly recognized him. After class I stopped him as he left, and asked him what had happened. When he told me, I exclaimed "What a shame! Does the dentist think it will grow back?"

"He said I had maybe a ten percent chance it might."

"Let me look at it."

He opened his mouth painfully and I saw that the gum was black, torn, and oozing blood. I touched his lip, and it was burning with inflammation.

"Looks awful, doesn't it?" he sighed.

"Maybe I could do something to give it better than ten percent."

"Like for Mike's eye?"

I nodded.

"Well . . ."

"Come where we won't be seen," I said, motioning him to my office.

"What is it you do?"

"I use an old, old method."

"Witchcraft? They say you are a witch."

"I bind a charm, but it is the power of God that does the work."

"I don't care if it's the power of the devil, if it works!"

"Close your eyes, and hold your breath till I touch your lip," I directed, and whispered the incantation, which is one of Hohman's:

> Bruise, thou shalt not heat:
> Bruise, thou shalt not sweat;
> Bruise, thou shalt not run—
> No more than the Virgin Mary
> Shall bring forth another son. + + +

He peeked, and being of Catholic background, he looked askance at the crosses crossed toward the left with the thumb.

"That's a queer way to make the sign," he commented. "Why the thumb and the fist?"

"When you have your fist closed, all that is left free is the thumb."

"Why close the fist?"

"It's a roborant gesture to strike against the trouble," I replied, positive he would not know what *roborant* means (who does, and him a star athlete!)—the less understood in such cases, the better the chance of success.

"And that is going to cure me?"

"I did what I can do."

For some weeks the secret was between us, for I told him to tell no one until his teeth were again sound. His face resumed its former perfection. Then one morning he waited and spoke to me after class, with a look not unlike those I had seen on Stuart and Michael.

Yesterday the dentist told me my teeth are fine," he breathed. "They grew back as sound as ever."

"Thank God!"

"I did. Now I want to thank you—I doubted you could do anything."

"I couldn't bear to think of your beautiful teeth ruined."

"You think my teeth are beautiful?" he beamed.

"Gorgeous," I said roguishly. "You know all too well how beautiful everything external about you is. *I* certainly don't need to tell you! But the day after the accident you were not beautiful. You ought to ponder that: physical appearance is not enough. You need a kind of beauty that disfigurement cannot take away."

Perhaps he did ponder. Before he left the college, he seemed to lose some of his egotism and superficiality. He fell in love with a quiet girl I thought quite plain, and his personality took on depth and warmth. When the inner matched the outer, he was superb.

After his mouth healed, other athletes came to me frequently. *Bruise, thou shalt not heat* . . . became something that flashed to mind every time I saw a football or basketball player limping in my direction. I am told the high school coach at Newberry, South Carolina, "uses" regularly for his boys. For a time, I did almost the same for the college team.

I have no proof that this had anything to do with my replacement on the faculty. It was not the reason given me. I was told that my department needed academic strengthening and prestige for purposes of accreditation. That could not be denied: the only Doctor of Philosophy in it was stricken with Parkinson's Disease and the two senior professors were due for retirement. Still, Lenoir Rhyne is a cnurcn college, and as such, not likely to hold any kind of mental, spiritual, or magic healing desirable.

No matter. "Any and every man who knowingly neglects using. . . ." Hohman said, *"neglects."* I would consider it more sinful and contemptible to refrain from "using" for fear of the consequences in such circumstances as mine. If I saved the tooth, or the eye—to say nothing of the life of one of my students, I am satisfied. I did what I thought right, and if I have sustained any loss from use of sympathy, God has recompensed me double.

An unidentified part of my awareness informs me when I should attempt to heal. There are individuals who can be healed, and others who cannot. Perhaps there are some who *should* be healed, and others who should not. I try to detach my conscious mind and my emotions from them as individuals, allowing my intuition to suggest an attempt or not to suggest it. God knows that I attempted to heal relatives I loved, but who made no response; whereas I have felt compelled to attempt healing for some for whom I felt no personal liking, and they were healed. Detachment, and the feeling that I am a channel for healing rather than a healer, seems the most effective state of mind to be in to produce an effect. So, again limited by language, I say, "*I* heal nothing: God heals." But I might add that there is in Nature a potential for healing which my mental action seems to channel when I follow the impulse to direct it, or in rare instances I am under compulsion by some unrecognizable or unnameable Influence. I do not even speculate upon what this Influence may be, but I know when it is at work. I become restless, see strange symbols, and sometimes experience unusual phenomena.

When I need to reinforce vital energy, I do so by contact. I do not know by what process I absorb it from living things (or, if they are deficient, transmit it to them). It may be a subjective experience, for a cedar tree is a symbol of immortality, and an oak a symbol of strength. Since I think in symbols, it may be that all I do is reinforce my thought. However, I find the earth healing, be it merely a plaster of clay on a wound, or the handling of it, which stabilizes the emotions, or walking on it, which in solitary places tranquilizes the spirit anc opens the inner mind.

Following an article on "using" that I wrote for *Fate* magazine, a woman in a distant state wrote me saying she had tried the incantation for bruises given here, to cure a sore in her son's mouth. She said it was an ulcer, which a doctor had treated for several days. The ulcer grew larger and more painful daily, and when she read the article, it occurred to her to substitute the word *sore* for *bruise*. She said he looked in the child's mouth and repeated the "words of sympathy," feeling that if God could heal a bruise, he could as readily cure an ulcer.

It worked. The boy's ulcer healed quickly and gave no further trouble. Not long afterward, I was sent David Shull's "Paper," and among the other pow-wows was this very one, under the heading "To Cure a Sore," substituting *sore* for *bruise*.

After that, I experimented. It is quite possible to adapt a conjuration—even to create new ones. After all, they are not mystical mantras revealed by the holy angels. Someone created each of them to meet a need—and what has been done once can be done again. All that is required is a startling affirmation or command, confidence, and the power of God to bind the spell. "Pain, go; go; go; go. Pain go! . . ." (which some cash-in-advance "users" in Iowa employ for broken bones) sounds modern to me, but its simplicity startles almost as much as reference to the milk of Jesus' Mother. I should like to see the one above used with a drum or an *asson* by a sorcerer who did not know what the words mean. I fancy it would heal just as effectively.

One unfortunate widow whose children had all moved to the West Coast wrote me that she fell on her icy steps and broke the small bone of her leg, but had no money to see a doctor, and no one to look after her cows and pigs and her poultry. She bound splints to it and used the "Pain, go . . ." incantation and kept on about her work. When she did see a doctor after her youngest son came back from Korea, the bone had mended, and she wrote that ". . . it was kinder sore a while, but not what you'd think a broke bone would be."

Occasionally a pow-wow produces that effect. Last year I was cutting a small tree in a clump of old crepe myrtle, and in trying to pull it free, the butt suddenly flew loose from the others which bound it and struck my leg. The bone probably wasn't broken, but a very hard lump formed on my shin, and I could not walk without limping. By using this charm and the one for bruises, I achieved a condition in which I was not conscious of pain unless I touched the lump. It did not discolor, and I doused it with turpentine daily for a few days, and forgot about it. I don't remember when I stopped limping, or when the lump went away; when bathing several days later I thought about it, felt for the lump, and it was gone.

I was brought up to believe that the *Power* to pow-wow had to be protected by the strictest taboos. Grandmother made a great secret of her incantations, never telling them even to her husband, who was older. When she taught me her conjuration to stop bleeding—or showed me where to find it, for it comes word for word from Ezekiel (one recites the sixth verse of chapter sixteen)—she told me that in her whole lifetime she could tell only three persons, each younger than she and of the opposite sex, and that I in turn could tell only three women, all younger. It was inexorable; the penalty for breaking it was the loss of the power to use it.

As long as I did not break the taboo, I could staunch the flow of blood as effectively as she could herself. But in college, I told the psychology class of the incantation and the taboo, and when the need for it came, I found that I had no power whatsoever to stop bleeding. It increased my awe of the *Power,* and my belief in the taboo.

For years I could not "speak blood." Ruefully I sought out wise women who could be wheedled into confiding other conjurations for other purposes—many of whom were happy to pass the charms down to someone who still believed in them. Any I secured, I kept as secret as guilt.

In the Dutch Fork, in the past century, lived "users" who had power second to none anywhere. One old lady renowned for her success was dead before I settled here, but her daughter is also a "user," so I visited her to beg any secrets she might teach me. I found her friendly, and proud to tell of her mother's "gift." Her mother's "Paper"—it was a good-sized notebook—had been stolen, but she sent me to her brother who showed me the little German trunk in which it had been kept dark, along with his mother's "using bonnet," her spectacles, her wand, and a strange dirk which I supposed was her athalme, or witch's ritual knife.

We were sitting on her porch as we talked about "using," and it seemed to me that she spoke far too freely, for my wife, the woman's daughter-in-law, and several children were present. When I mentioned her mother's fame as a "user" who could cure burns, she beamed. "Yes, she was a wonder at that. People came or sent to her for miles—even on your side of the river. I do it, too, but I think she was better."

When I asked for that charm, she nodded. "Sure," she said. "I believe I remember it—let me think. It's been a good while since anybody wanted a burn used for."

"Where can we go so I can hear it?"

"I'll tell it to you right here. Them others may need to help me recollect the words."

"Will it still work if you do that?" I marvelled.

"You mean letting the women hear it? I know what they say, but it just ain't true. It was just for protection. You know how they used to be about witchcraft in the olden time, and anybody who knowed anything not everybody knows was a witch, even if it was for doing good. I reckon the fewer knowed about your power, the fewer there would be to blab, and they kept it in families because your kin wouldn't be so apt to get you in trouble. That's my thought on that. It don't make no difference at all who you tell, nor how many. It's a power from God to give you a way over nature when you are in need. The more that knows how to do good, the better, it appears to me; and I reckon the more good is done, the more God likes it, too."

The utter naivety of her reasoning was convincing. I took down the incantation, and she showed me the gestures that accompany it.

"Ma always thought the motions done as much as the words," she commented, "but I ain't so sure. The girls is always getting them mixed up. I've told them and told them. When it's the white you are doing, it's the *right* hand you use, and it's down with the thumb and up to the right, slantwise, then across to the left, but it appears to me they do as well with the wrong motions as with the right ones. I reckon the white work is all you'll be wanting to do?"

"Your mother knew how to do the black, too?" I said in surprise.

"A witch can do either kind," she said quietly. "It's the same power. Jesus could heal, and he could kill—he killed a fig tree. It all works the same. Sometimes it takes the black to do good, and sometimes you may do bad with the white. It's what you do that makes either one good or bad. Jesus knew all about the power of God, and we know."

"You think Jesus was a witch?"

She laughed. "No," she replied, "but if you was to do here in Dutch Fork what he done in Israel, a heap of folks would call *you* a witch."

"But you think it was the same power?'

"It's got to be. There is only one God, only one Power, and only one Nature. If a witch don't know nothing else, he knows that."

A new incantation is like any other new thing one gets—one is impatient to put it in use, to see how it works—and here I must say, they do not all work with equal effectiveness for all people. I know one which never failed the person who gave it to me, yet it never has done the slightest good when I tried it. (I don't like it—never did like it—and I suppose that is the reason why. I like conjurations that say surprising things, and it is as dull as lukewarm water.)

So, I was almost glad when my sister-in-law called on the phone to tell that her son, Frank, had burned his foot that morning. "Ask her if she wants me to try for it," I urged.

"Lee wants to try to talk the fire out of his foot," my wife told her. When she hung up, she turned to me and said, "Don't just stand there and fidgit. Frankie burned his foot pretty bad. Go on and witch for it."

I hastened to my room, put on my hat, faced the direction of the boy's home and recited my new incantation . . .

His foot healed rapidly. He wore a rag around the burn for several days, but it seemed to give him little trouble. I was rather disappointed, for I had been accustomed to immediate staunching of the flow of blood, and felt that a burn should heal instantaneously. But it left no permanent scar, and in that respect probably healed better than it would have with ordinary treatment.

Frank was quite young then, about ten or eleven. Six or seven years passed, and I almost forgot I had ever treated him. However, he remembered—as I discovered when he appeared one evening with a chum of his who had been burned.

I had not met his friend, but I knew of his family, and the boy himself evoked compassion. I had seldom seen minor burns which looked so painful. Frank explained that the boy had been welding under a car at school, stripped to the waist, working in a cramped position, when something caught the torch. A shower of sparks and molten particles rained on his chest and stomach. The blisters were from pinhead to dime size, and the pain from them was so acute that he had not been able to sleep the night before. As I looked at his torso—not a pleasant sight where the silky hair was burned off and the smooth skin was sprinkled with red marks, blisters and raw spots—I could well accept his apology for coming in stripped to the waist, saying he could not bear a shirt to touch him.

"Frank thinks you can cure me," he said hopefully. "Will you?"

For a thousand years, the ritual answer to that question has been, "I will try." A "user" should never promise a cure; he may find himself unable to concentrate sufficiently. He may become involved emotionally—even find himself questioning whether the individual *deserves* help. Fatigue, distraction—and emotional, psychic, and physical factors often too obscure to recognize—may intervene. If the cure does come from God, it comes only through the agency of the human mind, and man does not know his mind well enough to make guarantees. If one can avoid emotion, hold off the temptation to judge the individual, and concentrate fully on the pow-wow, usually one succeeds if he has any power at all.

The etiquette of pow-wow requires that the sufferer ask the "user" to "try," but those who come seldom know that, so they always begin by requesting a cure. If I feel led to use sympathy for the case, I reply, "I do what I can do; I will try." It is not the most confidence-building reply one might make, but it is the only safe answer. If a Pow-wow has success in ninety percent of his attempts, he is excellent. If in seventy percent of his attempts he succeeds, he should not be discouraged. But I left Frank's poor burned friend standing while I digressed; so now back to him.

"Sure, I'll try for you," I told him. "Cross my threshold and advance toward the East, and I will get my hat."

"Which way is East?" he asked, bewildered by the unusual directions.

"That is the east wall where the drawing of the star in a circle hangs. Stand to face that."

He looked at the Hex drawing of a double earth star so made that it enclosed a circle in which a serpent climbed a staff upon a heart. There were smaller hearts between each of the points of the star, and a large heart beneath was flanked with bluebirds standing on branches of olive. 'What does the German on it say?" he asked.

" 'Haymet iss wau da Hotz iss'? It's dialect. It should read *'Heimat ist wo der Herz ist.'* It means 'Home is where the heart is.' "

"Where did you get anything like that?"

"I drew it."

"What does it all stand for?"

"It's for love and happiness."

"Does it work?"

"I don't look unhappy, do I?"

"Frank says you know about all kinds of queer stuff."

"Maybe," I breathed. I moved between him and the wall after I raised my hands to the east, and turned to face him. "Now close your eyes," I said, "and don't look till I say so. When I touch you, hold your breath and slowly count three times three three times, and I will do what I can do." (I wanted to puzzle him as to the counting, to distract him.)

He flinched when I touched his forehead and tensed as if in dread. It was his first experience with the occult, and I imagine he was a little uneasy in the room, strange to him with its dried herbs, symbolic objects, bones, its clutter of books and curious drawings, its prehistoric relics, and its oddities.

"That is all," I breathed, "Open your eyes and check the time. In half an hour I shall use for you again, then again after a full hour."

"The burns don't seem to hurt quite as bad," he commented.

We played rummy while we waited for the second treatment, and I observed that he began toying with the burns unconsciously as he studied his hand. He had not touched them before. When the time was up I said, "It's time again. How do they feel by now?"

"Why—they don't hardly hurt none at all! I'd quit thinking about them."

I am not sure what degree of sensation his statement describes, but it cannot be very acute. I repeated the treatment, reminded him to watch for the hour to be up, and we returned to our series.

When Frank won it, he turned to Frank and said "We'd best leave now. I'm dying for sleep, and I can't afford to stay out of school no more than I have to."

"It's fifteen minutes yet till the time," I reminded him.

"You don't need to do it again; the burns are okay," he said.

"I'd better finish it," I insisted. "It's better to go the full set."

So he stayed for the final try and went home. Next afternoon he passed me on Main Street, with his shirt on, honked his horn, waved, and, smiling from ear to ear, yelled "Hi!" Frank later told me the burns healed and never caused him any further discomfort.

This incident was proof to me that a taboo can be broken without impairing the effect of a pow-wow. However, my most astonishing experience with the charm for burns came when I used it on myself. On

July 3, 1968 I was working at renovating my house and had a pile of scrap to burn. Weeds and brush had grown to the edges of the lawn, so no clear spot was available for the burning. In a lightly weeded area behind the former slave cabin lay a brushpile of cedar branches four or five years seasoned, so I decided to clear a firebreak around this old heap, burn it, and use the spot to burn the trash from the house. I felt that the light branches would make a very quick fire with not enough sustained heat to dry the weeds past the firebreak, even though the weather was dry and here and there the field had much old broomsedge from previous years. So I kindled the heap of branches and stood by with a rake to put out any sparks.

It was burning briskly when I recalled that the heap lay atop a pile of old fat pine posts. When the branches made them hot, tar flowed from them, and the heap blazed into an inferno which blasted the growth back yards past the firebreak and kindled it in all directions. I fought it frenziedly, for the slave cabin is also built of heart pine, and if it caught, I felt sure the big house would burn with it—a loss no insurance could make bearable. Neighbors rushed to help, and among us we kept the fire from reaching the slave quarters, the garage, or the woods. But when it was out I realized I had been severely burned.

Where my body was covered, my sweat-drenched clothing had protected me, but I was wearing only an undershirt, which left my arms exposed. Blisters formed on them from shoulder to wrist, some as large as fifty-cent pieces. The pain was maddening.

"I wish somebody lived near here who could use for me!" I exclaimed as my daughter smeared ointment on the burns and flustered with bandages.

"I thought you knew how," she replied.

"Why, I do!" I realized. "It might work on the person who does it. Let my arms alone! I am going to try!"

I went to my room, hung a mirror on the east wall, raised my tortured arms in appeal, and gazing into the mirror, tried for the first time in my own behalf.

> Lonza's bread! Christ is our consolation:
> Christ will not forget
> To remove the inflammation.
> In the name of God the Father, God the Son,
>   and God the Holy Ghost, Amen.

The image in the mirror made the Hex crosses toward the stranger in the hat. The bizarre thought came to me, "That man feels no pain." For his smudged, reddened face was rapt, detached, apart from consciousness of any kind save of the spell.

As I made the third cross, something took effect that I cannot name. I was no longer observing from the mirror but for an instant aware of my suffering body. The anguish of burning changed to a sensation of numbing cold. Goose flesh stood up around the burns and on my whole body. When it passed, all pain had ceased.

An old Daugherty incantation for burns which Grandmother never knew in full included lines about the Angels of the Four Directions, one line of which ran:

The one from the North brought ice and frost . . .

I felt certain that that incantation sought to procure the uncanny, blessed chill that took away my suffering—something known to the conjurers of centuries ago, but not mentioned in any psychological text I ever have read. How much, one wonders, did they know that contemporary parapsychology must rediscover? Must the scientist at last turn to the witch for knowledge? I am sure he could obtain some.

When the half-hour passed I repeated the incantation, but knew that the first had sufficed. The sticky unguent ran, and the inept bandages kept trying to unwind. To my daughter's horror I took them off, washed my arms thoroughly with soap and water, and left them unbandaged. I dusted the raw spots with sulphur, hid my arms with a long-sleeved shirt, and went back to my work. At least I now had plenty of room to burn scrap safely—an acre burned bare!

Each day as I toiled, my sweat absorbed soot from a defective flue and dust from the attic. It spotted the raw flesh black, while the sulphur crusted it yellow. My arms looked gruesome. As the skin came off I dusted finely powdered burnt alum on the flesh to keep granulation tissue from forming, and kept on working. When my wife came from Hickory, she joined my daughter in admonishing me to go to the doctor—but only half-heartedly. The burns were healing rapidly, and I felt no pain—not even discomfort—so why go? She admitted that no one could expect or ask more than that.

Sometime in September a black wasp stung me, and I reacted with intolerable itching. Then I phoned the doctor, who told me to come at once, for several local people had almost died of wasp stings in the past

few years. When I arrived, he told me to take off my shirt, and when he
saw my arms, he gasped.

"You have had frightful burns! Who's been treating them?"

"Oh, I take care of them myself," I replied. "When I got burned back
the first of July I used for them, and I dust them with sulphur and alum
as they heal."

"You should have gone straight to the hospital."

"I didn't have time to fool with the hospital. I was too busy renovating the house."

"How could you stand to work with the pain?"

"After I "used" there wasn't any pain."

He grinned an exasperated grin, then chuckled. "That's rich. You
witch third-degree burns and treat them as nothing, and come running
to me with a wasp sting!"

"I don't know anything to do for that. I always go to a doctor when
I *need* one."

⁻He seemed to give me a shot as a kind of personal satisfaction, insert-
ing the needle deliberately. "A doctor should treat bad burns," he
muttered.

"Don't my arms look as far along as they should?"

"July, August . . . yes. They are healing all right—and you say you
felt little pain?"

"They were killing me before I treated them."

"But afterward? With your clothes rubbing the raw flesh where the
skin came off, you didn't feel much?"

"I didn't feel any pain at all."

"Then I don't blame you. If you had had regular treatment you
would have felt pain—plenty of it! Before you go, I want my associate
to look at your arms," he told me, and when the other doctor came in,
he said, "Look at these. He uses sulphur and burnt alum on them like
doctors did in the seventeenth century. He was burned back in July."

"It must have been as good a way as those we have now," the other
doctor commented. "They look fine to me."

"Could a person have such burns without pain while they heal?"

"Impossible!"

"He says he 'used' for them, and has felt no pain at all."

"Incredible!"

"I don't know," the older man meditated. "When I came here I would have said so, but I have run onto some funny things around here —some damn funny things!"

I grant that the treatment may merely have disconnected my consciousness from signals which my brain would otherwise have interpreted as pain, but that is theoretical. Now over a year later, all the scars have disappeared except the three largest.

> . . . Christ will not forget to remove the
> inflammation. + + +

Hexes do many other things besides pow-wow. Usually they have ordinary occupations, trades, or professions. Christopher de Witt, a great Hexenmeister who died in Germantown, Pennsylvania in January 1765, was among that colony's earliest clockmakers, and was also a noted botanist, astronomer, astrologer, and philosopher. He specialized in "casting nativities"—drawing astrological horoscopes for children soon after their births—but he also raised a notable variety of medicinal and magical herbs and prepared medicines.

Other Hexes prepared amulets, drew *Annängsel* (cryptic parchments lettered with abbreviations, figures, geometric, and mystical signs, used as talismans). Some prepared candles, burned them ritually, and applied soot from them by means of a *Petschaft*—a metal stamp which printed Hex signs on the bodies of the sick or injured, and allegedly cured according to the ingredients in the candles and the rituals and incantations used at their preparation and at the time of stamping.

Father Conrad Matthai, the last Hexenmeister of the Wissahickon Rosicrucian monastic group, had no visible means of support, and was so near—or far—out of this world that he needed little. His distinctive specialty was securing information from distant places, lying on his bunk in trance, sending out a *Doppelgänger*, and appearing and conversing with persons elsewhere, sometimes even in Europe, giving or securing messages for his clients. Before the telegraph, his was the swiftest communication service between Pennsylvania and London, and it has not been improved upon since in its field, (this isn't really true). It *is* rare, though.

Since pow-wow is only one area of a much larger field in which parapsychological activities affect nature and call into effect laws which are inactive without such factors, it behooves a pow-wow to familiarize

himself with the other areas: witchcraft, Christian Science, faith healing, astrology, Spiritualism, hypnotism, parapsychology, and plain psychology. It will broaden his understanding of his own area, and the
benefits are manifold.

When a man realizes that he is able to affect nature and alter circumstances by the power of his mind, he suddenly ceases to feel absurd or
meaningless. He realizes that man is only a little lower than the angels—
which the Bible says he is. "I have said ye are gods," quoth Jesus, who
is regarded as authoritative by many. When man discovers his power, he
does assume godlike ability to create, alter, or destroy. I dare not say,
"Ye are gods," as Jesus did, but I do say that man is profoundly meaningful, exceeding powerful, and sovereign over the Earth and all that
pertains to it.

When an individual realizes this, he cannot call existence absurd. He
can integrate his personality and shape his destiny as he wishes. He can
even assume his right relationship with God, which is to embody in
matter the spirit in him, which is of God, and to manifest in the plane
of matter what God cannot manifest without a material agent. God has
mind or *is* Mind, and has consciousness, or *is* Consciousness, but God
does not have hands. Man does. God does not have lips or a tongue;
Man has them. God does not operate a typewriter or print books, or
build schools and universities. These things man must do.

And when man does what God cannot do, but needs have done, he
fills the role intended for him and assumes his right identity. Then is he
godlike.

"And God said, [Let us make man] . . . in our image, after our likeness, and let them have dominion . . . over all the earth. . . ." Let everyone be reminded that God is a spirit, and the image and likeness of God
must be man's *spirit.*

Merely to stop the flow of blood from a wound by uttering words
from the Bible gives the Scripture a very different kind of meaning
from that usually assigned it. A searcher who knows that only one verse
in the Bible can be used to stop bleeding will begin searching for other
secrets in it. Truth is concealed, not revealed, in the Book. It had to be
so, otherwise the Bible would have been destroyed or altered by those
in custody of it.

When he finds that a verse in Ruth will cause the whole Book to turn
when suspended in a certain manner (when a key is tied across the

verse) to answer questions, whereas no other verse in any other book will serve to move, he begins to comprehend the very strange power of this Book. If he is interested in the mystical power of numbers, he will find some very singular things when he begins studying the arrangement of the King James Version. More and more, I am convinced that this arrangement of the Bible by verse and chapter was reached by conscious—or more likely unconscious—division of the text to enable occultists to identify hidden mysteries by their numerical implications.

The secret of pow-wow is concealed in the first Gospel. The words are Jesus' own. One is a key number, the number of unity. Thus what the Bible says about the unity of anything should appear in a first book, a first chapter, or first verse. Three is the number of spirit, and six of creativity. So in the first book, in a location numerically suggested by three or six, should be a statement of prime importance regarding spiritual creativity, and it does. Matthew 18:18 reads, "What ye shall bind on earth shall be bound in heaven, and what ye shall loose on earth shall be loosed in heaven." This is the secret. Jesus referred to it as "The keys to the kingdom of heaven." The same words are reiterated in another place. Repetition in the Bible is always a clue. What is said twice is worth reading twice—many times, until it is comprehended.

The Catholic Church holds that this was spoken only to St. Peter, despite the plural pronoun, and the crossed keys on the Papal seal refer to it. However, Jesus said "What *ye* shall loose . . . what *ye* shall bind," and ye *is* plural. It is meant for every man. Moreover, it is not a promise to Peter to confirm his authority, but a statement of principle, of universal law.

This law makes magic, prayer, Hex, pow-wow, and every other activity which consciously binds anything by mental action effective. Perhaps even more important, it makes effective anything that is bound by habitual mental action, even though no conscious act of binding takes place. If one continually thinks about disease, fearing it, lo: he binds it, often upon himself.

Binding, however, implies more than idle thinking. To truly *bind*, there must be concentration and emotional intensity. In pow-wow, the concentration comes from remembering the odd incantations and the gestures, and the emotion is faith. In a black Hex, the concentration comes from the incantation and the ritual, and the emotion either from fear (of the devil and his demons) or from horror induced by some act of the ritual. In idle-minded hypochondria, disease is induced by the fear that one will develop the symptoms, by fear of contagion, and by some strong emotion—hate, envy, greed, or whatever—held simultaneously, though not necessarily in connection with the contemplation of disease.

All anyone needs is to know this simple truth which Jesus stated, have the power to concentrate, and the resourcefulness to surround himself with strong emotion as he binds his charm, be it faith, love, fear, fury, lust, or horror, and he can get what he wishes.

Anything more that can be said on the subject is mere elaboration. Follow these instructions, and you can be a Hex, a faith-healer, a saint who works miracles, a Satanist, a Christian Science Practitioner, a Pow-Wow, a Witch-Doctor, or whatever you please. "What ye shall bind on earth . . ." is a metaphysical *law*. It does not matter in the least who does the binding, or whether what is bound is good or evil, whether in Christianity or in witchcraft. The laws of nature operate for all alike; as the lady said, "It's the same power."

If you have stopped blood, you are a Hex yourself, and there is no Hex you cannot perform if you have the faith. See? What the old woman in Dutch Fork told me was true. There is no taboo except what one taboos himself, for the taboo says a man cannot tell a man, or anyone more than three, and I have told the thousands who read *Fate* that charm. It *can* be taught publicly. Now, as one Hex to another, I say, "Let thy walk be Jesus' limp; thy speech be Jesus' stammer." It means, "You can't ever come up to His performance: but as long as you try to do good, you're doing the same things He did, so do your best." It's taken as a kind of blessing, and a hope that the Hex to whom it is said will always do good with his *Hexen*.

OF DREAMS AND DOPPELGÄNGERS

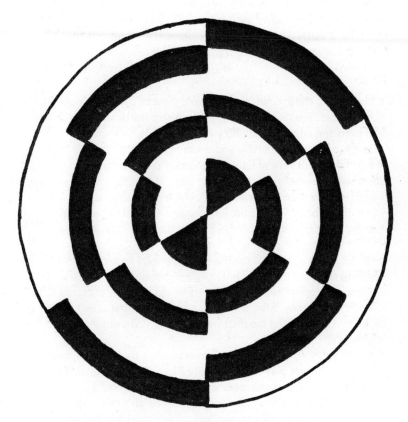

Growth: At each step a plane higher in the process of evolvement, be it of materialization, of development, of prosperity, or of Spirit

Professor Joseph Jastrow epitomized the general criticism with the succinct statement: "What Freud does not sufficiently recognize is that dreams do not all follow similar courses because dreamers have different psychologies."

This was backed by extensive studies of thousands of dreams which only by extreme distortion or greatly strained assumptions could be interpreted according to Freudian findings. . . .

Walter B. and Litzka R. Gibson

When I was a child, Grandmother made most of my clothes except my Sunday best. She took Grandfather's tentlike shirts when the collars and cuffs frayed, or his size fifty-four pants when the crotch wore through, and by deft cutting and stitching made the sound cloth into sober, faded, but very practical garments. For my summer underwear, she saved flour sacks which, in those days, still came printed with dyes intended to fade and bleach out quickly, leaving good, useful white cloth like tight-woven muslin. Even when I was fifteen, she was still making them into shorts for me, though the print stayed in much longer after she stopped making her own strong lye soap.

When I undressed with the boys at the pool, I hated to display any that had not yet bleached white. Once she made a pair that had "100 Lb. net wt." printed beside the fly—it would not have occurred to her pure mind as funny. Stud was alone with me the first time I wore them, and when he glimpsed the inscription, he laughed until tears ran down his cheeks.

I laughed, too, as he turned me to read what the seat said, finding a calla blossom, and part of "White Lily Flour." He sighed wistfully, and said, "Your Grandma sure does all kind of sewin' good. I always have wanted me a pair of shorts for summer. I wouldn't mind what they said on 'em. As far back as I can recollect, I ain't never had but one wool union suit at a time, and when the weather warms up, and it starts itchin' and sweatin' me, I got to peel out of it and go with nothin' on under my pants. With them six good-for-nothin' sisters of mine, Pa just can't afford nothin' for me. To be decent they got to have dresses, and slips, and bloomers, and lately brassieres for two of 'em, and no difference what they got, they keep hollerin' for more."

So that was why he never wore underwear—not from choice, as I supposed, but because he could not afford any.

"Stud, we're the same size around the waist. You take these if you like them," I offered. "Grandmother made me a whole stack."

"Hell," he said softly, "I can't take yours. She'd be bound to miss 'em and want to know what you done with 'em. I can't stand to have nobody but you know we're so damn hard up we can't buy clothes."

"I've got a nice pair of store-bought ones from that stuff Mother mailed me Christmas," I considered. "Tuesday's your birthday. I'll give you those as your present."

"You mean you been keepin' 'em saved back, 'cause you like 'em too much to wear 'em, and you'd give 'em to *me?*" he breathed.

"Oh—it's not that. They're red striped, like peppermint candy. I—I don't like red—not on me."

"Yeah? I bet you just *hate* 'em, don't you! You don't want to be givin' me no present! Come on, let's get in the water!" he said, and ran and plunged into the deep hole.

I knew he remembered my crimson tie that I wore on special occasions, and the red roses on the pillow slips. His face, and his glistening dark eyes before the water camouflaged them, showed that he knew I loved him enough to wish him the very best I had.

As I took the shorts and undershirt out of the holly paper in which they came, rewrapped them in white tissue, and tied the package with red Christmas ribbon, I was really grateful for the first time that Mother had sent the shorts. I had prayed she would visit me that Christmas day—presents did not matter.

When I fell asleep, I dreamed it was Stud's birthday. I took the gift to him, and in the dream he went to his room, buttoned the door, put them on, tilted the mirror and admired them with ineffable pleasure. He fingered the soft, smooth fabric, arranged himself where they bound him, grinned, and said, "Now that I got these, I reckon I wouldn't be embarrassed with a town girl in Clendenin!"

Then the dream changed to the post office at Wellford. There was a parcel, and when I took it home, Grandmother handed it back to me to open. I took out three pairs of jockey shorts with matching T-shirts. "See how you like these," she said. "You're getting grown, and these give support. I'm going to start buying this kind for you if you like them."

When on Tuesday I told Grandmother I wanted to take Stud his present, she said, "I suppose you'll be for staying with him as usual," not even hinting that it was a question.

"I'd sure like to," I said eagerly, "if he can still come to spend Friday night."

"Well, eat supper here before you go. I know they raise everything, but you eat a lot of bread, and they have to buy their flour."

I milked the cows early and ate supper, so it was almost dark when I reached his house. His parents had somehow bought him a pair of khaki pants and a sport shirt, so when it was near bedtime he buttoned the door, tugged off his tight dungarees, tilted the mirror, put on the shorts and shirt and admired himself like a strutting peacock. He felt the bright, silky fabric, and to hide his deeper feelings, said lightly, "Boy, ain't I somethin' in 'em! Bet I could get me that girl in Clendenin, now."

Since the first part of the dream had occurred like a replay of a film, next morning I hurried to the post office, and sure enough, Grandmother had a parcel.

When I reached home and gave Grandmother the mail, she said: "You open the package. There's a surprise for you in it, anyhow."

"My jockey shorts and shirts?" I asked eagerly.

"How did you know! I meant to surprise you with them! That is sealed just the way they sent it."

"They're those that came three sets for $2.98," I said excitedly.

"Yes, they're the ones," she marvelled.

"I never had on anything that felt as nice as those," I rattled.

"You haven't even *seen* them yet!"

"I dreamed they came and I tried them on."

"So that's how you knew! I didn't have the least intention of ordering those, but when I started to close the order I suddenly could *feel* you wanting them. Did you?"

"Yes," I admitted, "I wanted them so I could feel myself in them as I looked at the picture on the page, and I kept thinking, 'Someday I'll have those.'"

"That may be one way of getting things," she said, perhaps casually, perhaps with a secret knowledge. "But wouldn't it be simpler to *ask* me for what you want?"

Glimpsing ahead was nothing new to me. About five years before, when I was ten, I dreamed a precognitive dream so detailed and improbable—it involved all of the furniture in my parents' house in Charleston, a beaded lampshade, and a Japanese phonograph record of which I had no previous knowledge—that its fullfillment could not be attributed to coincidence.

Such dreams disturbed me with perplexities as to the relationships of consciousness and time. The Bible tells of many prophetic dreams and I have had a few that seem so. Others have given me knowledge of events, schemes, and relationships pertaining to my well-being at the moment.

As I suggested to Stud, telepathy is possibly an explanation. Once, in light trance, when ESP experiments were popular at college, I received telepathic impression of a run of twenty-four cards without an error. The sender was across town in Huntington, West Virginia—over a mile away. That convinced me beyond doubt of two things: that telepathy operates, sometimes with great efficiency; but that its power is unpredictable and extremely variable, even between the same two individuals —for with the same sender I never achieved startling results save that once, and occasionally I fell below the score one might expect from chance. If I was tired, or a little drunk, my scores were low. If I was utterly exhausted, they rose. Actually, on the night I made the perfect score, I tried to project my consciousness to my co-experimenter, and did not see just the cards—I saw him looking at them as he concentrated. In dreams, perhaps, sometimes one projects the consciousness, and I am convinced that consciousness exists not in time, but in eternity.

The most extraordinary precognitive dream I have had since full adulthood came while I was in the Air Corps, stationed at Leesburg, Florida. As a personnel clerk I worked with service records, and troop shipments involved long hours of fatiguing processing. The South Pacific phase of the war was at its bloodiest, and the replacement units were full of hourly apprehension.

One of the most congenial friends I had while I was in service was a young lieutenant named Henry Olson. He half-believed I had supernormal powers, and liked to discuss the world of the occult with me. He seemed afraid that he might not survive the war, so I sought to glimpse his future—which was unclouded—and assured him that he would come out alive and uninjured.

Then I had a dream, evolving from scenes first appearing as pinpoints of light, then taking on natural color, with sound, odor, and tactile sensation like that of reality. (When they occur to me, such dreams and visions, I feel sure, *are* reality—past, present, or future as the case may be. They may be of thousands of years ago, or of today, or of time to come.) In this dream, Lieutenant Olsen and most of our unit were on a troop train, and I was somehow both with them, yet at a base elsewhere.

I was conscious of every movement, sound, and odor on the train, yet conscious that I was in a barrack that was very chilly. I was also aware that both train and barrack were dreams, and that my body was in the chilly tent at Leesburg, Florida. (In the dream, I even supposed that the cold barrack was involved because my body was itself cold as it slept.) Very often, I realize that part of my consciousness is dreaming and another part is awake, conscious of conditions around me. Sometimes the wakeful part evaluates, criticizes, or sits in moral judgment of the dream, giving me the uncomfortable feeling that these two consciousnesses operate independently, though entirely aware of each other's activities. Then there is, of course, a third—realizing that as the first engages in some outrageous or outlandish action, the second is morally censuring the behavior. It is very disturbing.

The dream train finally came to a halt at a railway station, and the troops descended. I scrutinized them as they got off, looking for my own face among them, and went aboard to see if I was still inside after they all seemed out on the platform. I was not, and I regretted it, for the sign outside read "Karachi," and I should have enjoyed a tour of duty in India—even in Pakistan. Then the dream sleeper in the cold barrack awoke, got up and stoked a stove with lumps of coal, put a long overcoat on the bunk over the blankets, and lay back down, shivering— and I awoke in the tent, more or less simultaneously.

I always went directly from breakfast to build a fire in the stove in the Command tent, and the morning after the dream, Hank—Lieutenant Henry Olsen—came in to chat with me before the others arrived, and "Sir" was what I called him.

"Anything new, Lee?" he smiled, saving "Corporal" for later.

"Yes, something wonderful!" I exclaimed. "Now I know where you are going. To India—Karachi. You and most of the guys will be stationed there most of the rest of the war, but I won't be with you."

"When did the orders come in?"

"No orders will be issued for two or three weeks. I saw it in a special kind of dream I have sometimes."

Doubt and disappointment came over his face, but within the month, top-secret orders arrived, and from them I was given a long list of specialties to draw from the replacements. Hank was shipped out. Though I missed him, for he was a genuine friend, I shrugged *"C'est la guerre!"* I said a prayer for his safety and happiness, and merely whispered "Hank, I hope you enjoy Karachi," when we shook hands goodbye.

Then sometime after the war, as I read *Fate* magazine, I was pleased and startled to run upon an article which Hank had written after his return to the United States and civilian life—he was at heart always a civilian—in which he told of his top-secret journey, across the continent, across the ocean, and across an undisclosed land in a sealed troop train. And he said that full realization of what I am came to him as he stepped out of the train onto the station platform and saw the sign reading in three languages, "Karachi."

I have had experiences with other so-called "altered" states of consciousness. I was extremely fat as a child, as I have already mentioned, and discovered an easy way to go to my room upstairs. I stopped at the stair door, and willed myself to astrally project to the hall above. Of course my body followed, but when my consciousness was already up, it was spared the sensation of exertion. I was so fat that climbing made me short of breath, and even outside when I wanted to ascend a steep hill, I did so in that fashion. I would close my eyes, breathe very deeply and hold my breath until pinpoints of light began to flash, and I would slip out and move with the most exhilarating sensation of weightless and effortless flight imaginable.

However, I came to realize it had to be done with great caution, or the results would be, at the very least, embarrassing. The first time I was detected at it, I had gone upstairs, and as I was not taking anything up, or planning to bring anything down, I did not bother to bring up my body but left it at the stair door. After I was in the room, something took my attention until I heard Grandmother speak to me downstairs.

I flew down and into my body instantly and replied, but not in time.

"Ha!" she exclaimed, "You with your eyes open but not seeing me, and so slow in speaking—is something the matter?"

"My mind was just somewhere else, I guess," I told her truthfully.

"My land," she chided, "you were so wrapped up a snake could have bitten you and you wouldn't have noticed."

Even worse, I once left my body propped against an apple tree and went far up the hill, to where I knew spring orchises were blooming under the beech trees. I became so intent upon them I quite forgot about my body until Phillip Smith came by, saw it, and went to see what ailed me. He found me insensate, somehow got me on his back, and was staggering toward the house with me. I was so nonplussed I could hardly concentrate sufficiently to reenter my body. When I did succeed, I said faintly, "Put me down, Phil, I'm all right now."

He did, gladly, but looked at me with deep concern.

"I just started to feel giddy, and sat down," I lied. "Then I woke up on your back."

"You are too fat," he observed. "It can't do you no good—and Lord, you are heavy!" He held my arm until we reached the porch and he called to Grandmother.

"I come up on him in the calf lot," he told her. "He was leaned back, on the ground with his shoulders against the sweet-apple tree. I called to him, and when he didn't seem to hear, I went to take a close look at him. He was limp as a dishrag, and his eyes were open, and I touched his eyeball, and he didn't blink. I couldn't find no pulse, and I couldn't see no breathing, so I got him on my back to bring him in, but he come to and spoke to me. Is he often took so?"

"Good heavens! Did it look like he had been in a fit?"

"No," he considered, "he had his hands folded on his stomach, and looked like he hadn't stirred after he sat down. He hadn't threshed around or nothing."

"I declare!"

"Seems I heard Delcie was part Abbott, and they's some epilepsy amongst them. I've heard tell of a kind where they just stand, and don't take no kind of fits. Just look empty-eyed, same as he did, and don't know nothin' or feel nothin'. That's how he took me—like he was in one of them spells. If he was mine, I'd let a doctor take a look at him— even if I had to go to Charleston!"

As soon as he left, Grandmother faced me with a look I dreaded.

"Listen to me," she said sternly, "I'm going to have the truth out of you once and for all. What happened?"

"I don't know."

"You know *very well* why you propped yourself back against that tree. Why did you sit down like that?"

"I was resting."

"You haven't done a form thing all morning, and you hadn't been up long enough to be tired. You don't pull the wool over my eyes one bit! You might as well tell the truth now as later, for I've got all day; and you'll tell it before I'm through with you!"

"I was afraid somebody might see me just standing," I blundered.

"Standing with your eyes open, and not blinking when somebody touches your eyeball, and your face as empty as a mask? Where *were* you when he found you?"

"Under the apple tree," I writhed.

She slapped me with all her strength. "Lie! Evade! You know very well what I mean! Where were *you*?"

"Up the hill under the beech trees, looking at some orchises. I didn't think about anybody coming along the path."

"Then it's true, what the old people used to say," she pondered. "You say you were looking at some flowers?"

"Yes, the orchises. They're the only ones in this whole neighborhood. A beetle was trying to get inside one, and I was watching to see if he was what pollenizes them."

"Can you hear as well as see when you are like that?"

"Better, and I can see at night, just the same as in daylight."

"George Lucas said old Nancy Greenaway—I think she was Delila Abbott's mother, and a daughter of the Ledgerwood Witch—did that. Only he said people could see her in two places at the same time, and if she had a mind to spy on people, she sent out a bird or an animal instead of going in her own shape, and when she called it back, she knew what people were doing miles away. And I think they told that Great-grandpa Daugherty could do that."

"Did your grandfather have that power?"

"I'll ask Andy the next time he comes. Now hear me. When Phil tells Hilary about this, don't you let on but that some kind of spell did come over you! I'd as lief people thought you have epilepsy as to know the truth, and if you have any sense at *all*, you'll never let anybody find you in that shape again."

"People can't see me," I considered.

"You can thank your stars for that," she said with a wry grin. "If he'd seen you running up behind him while he had you on his back, it would have been the end of Phillip Smith. He'd have been to bury."

She was no longer angry, and not as upset as I expected, so I took the matter lightly.

"Then you won't tell Grandfather, or Father, or anyone?"

"What could I tell them—that I've got a witch on my hands?"

"It's not witchcraft! It's just a trick of breathing, and of sending out my mind."

"Then what *is* witchcraft?" she asked.

Later she advised me again not to do this any more, because she was afraid an evil spirit might find my body and take control of it while I was outside. "Had you thought what might happen if you couldn't get back in?" she asked.

"I almost wish I didn't have to," I sighed. "I'm so fat and ugly, but when I'm outside I'm so free, and I feel so close to everything. I know I'm not fat and ugly when I am outside. I am graceful and beautiful."

"Pshaw," she murmured. "In a year or two you'll thin out and get tall, and there won't be a handsomer boy in Roane County."

I began to wonder what *would* happen if I came back and did find something already inside my body. The Bible did nothing to ease my dread, for Jesus himself said that an unclean spirit "findeth it empty . . . then goeth he, and taketh with himself seven other spirits more wicked than himself, and they enter in and dwell there . . ." I had no desire to come back and find eight evil spirits in my body, and Gabe seemed just where eight evil spirits might very well be in need of a body.

Still, my third-great-grandmother, Nancy Greenaway lived to be very, very old, and George said she was all right up to the day she died, and it was such fun that I did not entirely stop taking the risk. Only, like her, I did it when my body could be left safely in bed. What I went to see is easily guessed, and hence better left untold. But even such nightly excursions came to a sudden halt when a girl turned her face, gasped, and shoved her companion away from her. "Something is standing there!" she cried, pointing to me.

The boy leaped up, fumbling with his pants. "Where?" he demanded, "I don't see nothing."

"There," she said. "It was a man, but he disappeared. He ain't there no more!"

Afraid she might have recognized me, I realized that if even one person had the power to see me, spying on people at night was far too great a risk. But it was fun while it lasted.

Nocturnal habits of human beings are far different from their observed daytime habits, and I came to have a very cynical attitude toward their posturing, for in darkness, when they think they are unobserved, they reveal their real nature. Civilized, moral man dies each evening at twilight. Night man is primitive, without conscience, without restraint, cruel, lustful, cowardly. Man is a consummate actor, who puts on a daytime personality as artificial as his clothing, and acts out the conventions of the role he plays as if he were what he pretends to be. Knowing the truth placed my own sins in perspective. If I burn for them, I shall be in company with many others.

Later, I asked James Andrew if he thought there were real danger of having one's body taken over during such experiences.

"Well," he considered, "it must not happen often, for people are half out during sleep, and quite so when unconscious or under ether, yet you never hear of possession taking place during operations."

"I wonder if there really are evil spirits?" I mused.

"They exist, all right," he affirmed. "They usually are where an act of violence occurred, and people died in a state of strong emotion, leaving something unfinished. They are mostly human spirits that stay earthbound."

"Did you ever come in contact with any?"

"Yes," he nodded, "There is a place near Ravenswood where there is one, on a creek called Barr's Run."

"What does it do? Does it scare people?"

"It watches some money that was hidden there. And scare people? Yes, it scares people!"

"Tell me."

"I'd as lief not talk about that thing. Thinking about them draws them to a person."

But my curiosity was eventually satisfied in full, as I'll relate in the next chapter.

10

A DEAD MAN'S TREASURE

The Double Creator's Star: A diagram of the internal lines of force which hold matter in form. It is a sign seeking permanent enjoyment of abundance

> *. . . Spiritualism can only prove that certain individuals have a continued existence after death and maintain their affiliation with mortal flesh.*
>
> Mary Baker Eddy

I feel bound by no chronology. Time has never moved chronologically for me, but only psychologically, and the farther I have advanced in it, the farther back I have returned. I was thirteen, then nineteen, in six timeless moments of happiness that the calendar measured as years. They were full of discovery and activity; sweet with friendship and love; vibrant with youth and health, and bright with the joy of life—six moments of wakefulness that seemed dreams, six moments of dreams that seemed wakefulness. I sustained one deep sorrow, for Grandfather took cancer of the stomach.

A great amount of unusual phenomena occurred during the last few weeks of Grandfather's life, and continued long after. Grandmother called me to the back porch one morning about a month before he died, and in a hushed voice bade me look at an object she had taken from his pillow.

"That's a feather crown," she breathed in awed emotion. "You always said you wondered what they look like. I always was told that if one forms in a deathbed pillow, it's a sure sign that the dying person has a crown waiting in heaven. Poor Hilary was never converted and never baptized, but the Lord is merciful, and he was a good man in his own way. Aunt Lavinia had one—it was the only other one I ever saw—and she was a saint. It gives me a little hope for his soul."

I examined the intricately imbricated circlet of feathers with amazement. I feel certain that human ingenuity—much less pure chance—could not weave so perfect or so firm an object of feathers. It was about four inches across; twice the thickness of a finger; as perfect and smooth as a growth of nature.

Three days before he died, Grandfather's heavy enlarged picture fell from the wall in the middle bedroom, and Grandmother called me in to see it before she touched it. We both saw that the wire was unbroken, and coiled where it had been wound around the nail. We glanced on the floor for the nail, but it was as firm as ever, a large nail driven slanting into a stud.

"Didn't you look at the coil? It never untwisted. It's things that you can't understand which make a token so strange." She was very right—a human hand would have had to pull the nail and slip it through the coil to remove it.

The next day as Grandmother was washing dishes, one of the glasses she had scalded and set in the cupboard clicked. When she picked it up the bottom fell off. "That's the second token," she sighed. "I wonder what the one tomorrow will be?"

It was warm next day, though it was the nineteenth of October. She had the half-window over the sink open, and sometime in the afternoon, a wren flew in. "Oh Lord!" she said, "Don't touch it! A little bird flew in at the Robinsons' and lit on one of the twins. She caught it, and gave it to her sister. The first one died in three days, and the second, the day after: That's not a wren! It only looks like one. No telling *what* it is!"

In its confusion, or terror—or by intention—it flew though the hall and middle room into the front bedroom and lit on Grandfather's bed. As I opened the front door, Grandmother drove it into the living room, whence it flew outside and disappeared.

"He'll die tomorrow." Grandmother said.

That same evening the clock struck, and when I glanced at it, I said, "That's odd; I wonder what got it out of order?" for the hands showed the time at a quarter of eight.

"He'll die within the next twenty-three hours," she breathed. I knew there'd be a time token."

At dusk the following day, Grandmother's three brothers—Irvin, Ellet, and Guy Taylor—their sister Cora Cromwell, and her husband Bill, and two neighbors were there, keeping the death-wait with us. We were sitting in the living room, silent, with Grandfather's bed just inside the adjoining room. Suddenly we jumped at the sound of something striking the wall, outside at the back of the house. Three times it struck, as it someone had hit the weatherboarding with a heavy piece of wood.

Irvin jumped up to investigate, but Grandmother said, "No, don't. You couldn't see anything. It's almost time."

"Another half hour till a quarter of seven," Cora mused. "I remember when Papa died . . ." (Then, the Taylor clock, which had been

turned to face the wall, had struck twenty-four strokes and stopped,
never to run again.)

Irvin turned and peered through the doorway at the still form on the
bed. Then he went in and bent over Grandfather.

"He's gone," he said.

Just then something struck the gas chandelier, rattling the globes and
making two of the filament mantles fall. The light flared and flickered
grotesquely, and may have caused the fluttering shadow we thought we
saw at the ceiling. Cora held Grandmother to her breast and the men
went in, folded Grandfather's arms, placed coins on his eyelids, and
drew the sheet up over him.

By then Darkie had told me that death is an unreality, and when
Stud heard of the death he came to comfort me. "Damn it, you ought
to know by now you can cry in front of me!" he said. "I would if Ma
or Pa died—I'd plumb bawl my eyes out."

He had led me to the woods to the mossy log where we always sat,
and he stripped off his old, red-and-black-checked woolen shirt, chilly
as the late October evening was, and pressed it into my hands. "I ain't
got no handkerchief, but here—here's my shirt tail. Use it, and get it all
out of you. You got to cry! You're goin' to feel like hell till you do."
How did he know his concern and shivering sympathy would loose my
tears when I had told him the open casket and filling grave could not?
How did he know that only tears can dissolve sorrow and melt grief,
and that sobs loosen the tightness of a throat racked with dry agony?

I sobbed until I choked, and tears moistened the soft old shirt. I felt
him take it and dry my face repeatedly. His arm stayed around my
shoulders, and when I finished choking, I found both his arms around
me and my face pressed against the bone buttons of his union suit.

"There, you're goin' to be all right now," I heard him murmur, and
he held me and patted my shoulder, just as a mother might, comforting
a weeping child. I began crying again, but without the anguish.

"You'll be all right," he breathed, and his embrace relaxed. "Just
take plenty of time, and cry till you stop. Just let yourself go."

"Stud, you're so kind and good," I breathed in gratitude.

"I couldn't take seein' you like that," he said. "It hurt me like I was
goin' through it myself, almost."

After the funeral we did not notice anything other than slight, mysterious noises in the house. But when warm weather again allowed us to
sit on the front porch, then every second or third night we would hear

the wide wooden gate at the front entrance clatter shut—and in exactly
the same time it had taken Grandfather to walk from it to the yard, the
yard gate-latch would click, we could hear the rattle of the gate-chain,
and the sound of the gate swinging shut, pulled to by the weight of the
chain.

One night Grandmother said she felt poorly and she retired early,
leaving Stud and me in the porch swing. He had his guitar, and was idly
playing chords and snatches of his favorite old ballads, when the front
gate clattered.

"Now who do you reckon is comin' in this late?" he asked. "It's
awful dark to be out without a lantern or something."

"It isn't anyone," I breathed. "In a minute you'll hear the yard gate,
but nobody will come into the light. If the moon were out, you could
see it doesn't open."

Just then the yard gate sounded, and he jumped up, frightened.

"It's just the time *he* used to take goin' between them gates," he
exclaimed.

"You're not scared of *him,* are you?"

"Come on! Let's go in!"

"Stud, he thought the world of you," I assured him. "One time after
you left, he said, 'I ain't a rich man, but I'd give all I own on this earth
if I'd had two or three boys like that one.' You can't be afraid of anyone who felt like that about you, can you?"

"Do you ever hear him in the house?"

"Just the scuff of his slippers, sometimes—Grandmother does—and
sometimes the dog knows he's around. She'll wake up and start wagging
her tail, and sometimes she barks and jumps for candy the way she did
when he used to come from the store."

"I couldn't stand it!" he declared. "That kind of stuff never happens
on Doctor's Creek or Hurricane, or out on the Ridge. Them fallin' trees
plumb spooks the hell out of me, but this'd be worse. I don't see how
you can set there, same as in broad daylight, and talk about such as
that! With the feelin' of havin' you-don't-know-what slippin' up behind
you!"

"If you've had that feeling every day of your life, and nothing ever
has hurt you, you get a sort of feeling that nothing ever will."

"*You* set out here if you want to," he said. "But if you do, I'm goin'
to bed and goin' to sleep."

"I'll go with you and turn on the light," I chuckled, pleased to be braver in something than he. Stud never did get accustomed to the noises, and was an utter coward when faced with the supernatural. If I talked about spirits and communication with the dead, he fidgeted, and I was never able to talk him into helping me with a Ouija board or with a table. He thought it witchcraft.

The clattering gates persisted for years, and began occurring in the daytime as well as after dark. When I whitewashed the two buildings in the front lot, I came down several times to see who was coming in, only to find the front gate fastened, and no one in sight except maybe Grandmother on the porch.

After she sold the place to Otto Lee and Toye, and they moved into the two-room house behind hers—for she reserved the right to live in the house during her life—the noise kept on until she died. Soon after that, Mother told me that Toye had Otto Lee take down the gates, but it had no effect on the phenomenon. The last time I went back, the fences were gone too. I did not think to ask if the gates still clatter. If they do, I suppose the family is by now accustomed to the sound. After all, it is Gabe.

The June after Grandfather died, I graduated with honors from Big Sandy District High School at Clendenin, and my father arranged to send me on to college. I was the first in his line ever to go to college, since Hans Jakob Gänther came to Philadelphia in 1736. The one I selected was Marshall, at Huntington, West Virginia—probably because Huntington is across the Ohio River from where Mrs. Blake lived.

When I was settled at Marshall, my first intention was to visit Mrs. Blake, but when I inquired, I was told that she had recently passed on. (Most of those who had known her used just those words, felt that she had entered a richer life.) I went to Chesapeake, anyhow, as one goes to see the homes of the truly great, and found her daughter living in the unchanged house where I heard the locked piano play, as I've already related. She talked at length with me about her mother, and urged me to attend the Spiritualist Church in Huntington that her mother had been instrumental in bringing into being. It met Sunday night in a hotel conference room.

When I did so, the first and most unsettling thing I found was that the minister was a woman. I had seen the female readers in Christian Science churches, but hardly considered them ministers, and with each there was always also a male reader. In the Spiritualist church no man assisted the minister. Women far outnumbered men in the congregation. They all had the single-minded concentration and intensity about their religion that I had first observed in Christian Science.

At once I realized that whatever else it might do, Spiritualism had the effect of forming a true church—a group of like-minded believers drawn together for mutual solace, companionship, help, and inspiration. I found the first meeting interesting, and accepted the literature that earnest women insisted I take. Some of it proved very thought-provoking, though not a small part was banal or patently the work of credulous and utterly uncritical enthusiasts.

I was most interested in the spirit guides James Andrew had said so much about. Mine, he said, was a very learned man, a sober German who at one time had taught philosophy at Bonn. He also spoke of a dark-haired woman (called Zaïda or something) who had some connection with me, the nature of which he was not certain. He frowned as he spoke of her, both in puzzlement and in seeming disapprobation.

I hoped that those at the Church would tell me more, but I found that if they spoke of familiar spirits, it was always of their own. Appalled by the kind of guides, and by the quality of their communications, I soon became very glad that my own guides kept silent, for the group at Huntington was surrounded by a tribe of cigar-store Indians. I found them all suspect—too conventionalized. Tall Pine, White Deer, Yellow Bird, Red Fox or Hailstorm could be counted upon to come through at any meeting with a message such as the following:

"How! Me Tall Pine, friend of paleface. Me heap glad see-um so many here. See new face. Her squaw with power—could be Medicine-woman. Got-um message for lady in pink hat. Her got bladder stones. Her see doctor, him take out stones, her feel better quick. Tall Pine take journey Happy Hunting Ground. Meet paleface spirit say him Elmer. Elmer say tell-um squaw him fine. Say tell-um squaw buy Coca-Cola stock; no buy stock in silver mine. Silver mine no good . . ."

I might myself have given a similar message had I known, as must the congregation, that a man named Elmer had a widow present, for I had overheard the woman in the pink hat tell another that the previous night she had passed a bladder stone; that she felt awful, and just knew that she needed an operation. I suppose the woman who claimed Tall Pine as her own knew that the widow had been approached with mining stock. In any case, a lady stood up, thanked Tall Pine, and said that she had a feeling (no doubt due to Elmer's concern) that the mining stock sounded too good to be true.

All that is well and good—somebody has to look out for the welfare of persons too procrastinating to attend to a health problem or too zany to know a good investment from a dubious one. I even think that as a fantasy-figure, Tall Pine was an entity, and real to the woman who claimed him. I never thought that Elenipsico was a fantasy of James Andrew's, nor do I think that any genuine familiar spirit is. (I only felt an influence from Zaïda. But one night the German professor—fantasy or real—appeared to me briefly, and said simply, "Read Spinoza," and disappeared.) The conviction that there *are* such guides as Tall Pine encourages persons who believe in them to personify and activate repressed parts of their own personality or their psychological needs. If they materialize at all, the activated personifications become eidolons. If anyone "sees" an eidolon, as I think the women saw their Indian guides, it is almost inevitable that he will believe the personified fragment to be a spirit. One needs the gift of discernment of spirits to distinguish between such guides and genuine spirits.

I quickly became cynical about Spiritualism. The minister always wore the same unstylish, wispy evening gown and gave the same thin-textured, sentimental sermons about the "beyond." Her messages afterward were such as any intelligent, observant, alert person with intimate knowledge of his group could give without any psychic perception whatsoever. I never received messages, and attributed this to the group's knowing nothing about me. Had I received such a "message" from "a spirit a long time discarnate, a relative who lived to the East— J.—Jo—is it James, or Joseph, or John?" I had my mind made up to say, "He must be Uncle John Brickey, my mother's great-great grandfather's brother. Thank you for the message," and never attend any more meetings.

However, Mrs. Blake's daughter sometimes gave meaningful messages, and a round of visiting speakers and mediums kept the group entertained, and somewhat entertaining to me. One of the mediums materialized or apported some flowers, and once a pigeon materialized unexpectedly and flew about, finally out the window. I saw no possibility of trickery in either case, for the table belonged to the hotel and had no cloth over it, and the clear vase in which the flowers appeared was out of reach of the medium, who sat motionless in profound trance. (In fact, the flowers did not remain long, but disappeared as inexplicably as they came.) As for the pigeon, it simply appeared flying about near the ceiling, and one would have to imagine extraordinary complicity on the part of the hotel to suppose that it was released through a sliding, concealed panel. Though they had no practical value, either for instruction or edification, I could only believe those phenomena genuine, and they kept my interest alive.

One evening I arrived late and took a seat in the second row of chairs from the back. Someone came in even later and sat behind me in the back row, and all during the service kept up a hushed conversation with a most irritating, prattling little girl. Several times I was strongly tempted to turn squarely around and give them a stare which should silence anyone.

Then when the service ended, I did turn and look. And I must have shown my astonishment, for the stooped, wispy little man rising from the seat behind me was all alone. In the hall outside, he touched my sleeve, and murmured apologetically, "I could see you was right restless, and I'm sorry if little Josie bothered you. Sometimes she just *will* keep on talking."

"I thought she was—I mean, I didn't realize that she is a spirit," I replied, shaken.

"You're the new feller from up at the college they was telling me about, name of Gandee, ain't you? They said you ought to be a medium. You ought to be, too. It ain't many hears little Josie like I could tell you did."

"She was your little girl?" I asked him.

"Sweet little thing," he nodded. "Her brother and her was the only ones Ludie and me ever had, and poor little Bert died when he was two. Then I lost Ludie and her in the great flu epidemic, and I been alone all my life since. Ludie went on and is with Bert now, but little Josie stayed with me. She's all I got in this world, and she's a sight of comfort. Without her, I don't know what I'd have done, the long years since."

"I'm sorry," I said in sympathy. "I'm sure she must be a great comfort to you."

"Yes," he said with a kind of inner happiness, "The nineteen-eighteen epidemic took all I wanted to live for. I went home after I buried Ludie—it was the third day after Josie was buried—and was sitting in the empty room, praying that I'd go, too; and I was grievin' so I called their names. Then little Josie answered. She ain't left me a single day. Seems like time stopped for her. It's going on nineteen years now, and Josie would be a grown woman, nearly twenty-five, but she stays just like she was, my sweet, little, curly-headed angel."

"Can you see her?" I asked him.

"Oh, I see her in my mind, but I don't see her any other way. I just hear her. She doesn't often talk that much, like she did during service, except when we're at home alone. Most folks only hear me talk to her, and say I'm touched in the head."

"Well, I heard her talking about a doll and about Bertie," I assured him.

"It makes me feel real good, when somebody else hears her," he said happily. "Then they know I aint just crazy. But I know; and you know; and Mrs. Blake knew."

"I never heard a spirit talk before," I mused. "I just hear noises and sometimes glimpse things."

"They said you needed development," he replied. "I fgure you could develop very easy."

This experience revived my interest even more than if a spirit identifying himself as Cousin Leo Lycurgus Lee had assured me that his brother, Elijah Newton Shakespeare Lee, was with him in the "beyond" all the names ungarbled.

Finally, we were visited by a medium whose name was sometimes mentioned in the literature. Her sermon was better than the regular—nothing extraordinary, but then she was billed as a great medium, not as a lecturer. Afterwards it was announced that she would go into trance and receive messages, and the church grew as hushed as it can only when everyone present is thinking of the dead, hoping to hear a message from one of them.

She gave two or three messages, for which the recipients thanked her and testified that they recognized the spirit and knew to what the message referred. Then she electrified me by saying, "There is a message fo the young man in the third row—you, with the turquoise suit. Will you please stand?"

I arose, embarrassed but very eager, and the congregation listened intently, for they had not yet heard from any of my connections "on the other side."

"This is no ordinary spirit!" she groaned. "I am in great pain. Do you recognize someone who died in intense suffering?" *(Medium in full control.)*

"No," I faltered. "—Maybe my grandfather. He had cancer, but he was drugged and unconscious for days before he died."

"This is a wound," she continued. "I hear gunfire. I feel pain in my chest. You do not know me." *(Medium loses control, last sentences spoken in her voice, but by the spirit.)*

"No—well, there was a neighbor boy, but he meant nothing to me."

"I am a relative of yours from long ago. Mother had a sister in your family. Mercy? Marcia? Massie? Your grandmother?" *(Spirit in full control of speech using medium's voice.)*

"My third-great-great-grandmother was named Mercy, and they called her Massie. She died at a hundred three, before my father was born."

"Uh-huh, her," the medium grunted, her voice changing, and her face taking on a frightening look. "She was Ma's sister. Ma's name was Bess." *(Spirit in full control of speech and beginning to seize voice.)*

"Is it somebody killed in the Civil War?" I inquired.

The medium was in no state to hear the question. She began to sway, and would have fallen had not the minister and another woman grabbed her. *(Medium's spirit dispossessed, spirit seizes body.)* Her face contorted in terror and anguish, and she gave an agonized, animal sound. She went completely limp, but as the women struggled to hold her up, she jerked up her head, strangely and abruptly squared her shoulders like a man. Then she stood erect, arrogantly shoved the minister aside, and in a totally unexpected man's voice—coarse, deep, and loud—said: "Thuh gold is still hid. Go git it!"

The fear-stricken church gasped audibly. "I don't know what you mean!" I exclaimed.

"You know thuh ol' codger," the voice boomed. "Ast him; he knows."

"Who?"

"They calls 'im Andy," it replied. That was what they called James Andrew!

The medium wilted again, and the women placed a chair and eased her into it. *(Spirit relinquishes body.)* But the congregation wasn't nearly as interested in her as it was in me. I could not have felt more self-conscious if all my clothes had dematerialized.

The medium had the look of a corpse, and several women gathered around her, sponging her face with water from the fountain in the hall. Presently her own spirit reentered, and after a while she arose unsteadily. She was very small and frail; it seemed impossible that the rough male voice had issued from her. She kept feeling her throat as if it hurt.

"There was a message for someone—the young man in the blue suit— you with the copper-colored tie. Did it get through to you?"
"Yes, ma'm," I replied.
"Did you recognize the spirit and understand the message?"
"No, but he told me whom to ask about it. I know him. Thank you."

"Young man!"
"Yes, ma'm?"
"Utter darkness was around that spirit!" she shuddered. "It is an evil and terrible one that had no right to possess me, or to intrude in a church service. I do not understand how it was allowed to speak through me. Beware of it!"
"I believe you!" I shuddered, knowing that James Andrew was reluctant even to speak of it.
"In God's name I forbid that spirit use of my body and voice again. I will not speak for him. But I can tell that you are new in the movement. Visit me before I leave town," she urged. "I must talk with you."

"Thank you, I shall," I promised, wondering if any hoax could be acted out with such incredible realism. But how! Nobody in Huntington seemed likely to know that Mercy Hughes had at birth been named Martha, in memory of an elder sister who was captured by Indians and carried off to Detroit. When a peace treaty was signed, her father Jesse walked from Virginia to Detroit to search for Martha, found her and brought her home. When she saw the daughter she had supposed dead, his wife Grace exclaimed, "This is God's mercy!" and renamed the second child Mercy to commemorate God's preservation of the first. Being Tuckahoe and wholly illiterate, she pronounced it "Massie." How could an outlander such as the medium know the name of my obscure and distant ancestress, and how it was pronounced!

If the spirit knew I was in the congregation, I realized, it must know all about me, and follow me, and might have returned with me to my room. When I undressed and reluctantly turned off the light, I pulled the cover to my chin—"spooked," as Stud would have described the state—expecting something in a shroud of thick darkness to appear in the semi-obscurity of the room. I felt as I had fourteen years before, after listening to Grandmother and James Andrew tell their weirdest stories. Then it occurred to me to follow instructions I had once read in a book on "development" that a woman at church had loaned me, for I felt that even the awesome knowledge that the spirit *was* present would be better than the intolerable, expectant uncertainity in which I lay.

So, half-remembering the procedure, I rattled a prayer, instructed any spirit present to rap once for "yes," twice for "no," and asked, "Do you hear me?"

Behind the headboard of the bed came a distinct tap, as if someone had struck the wood with his fingernail. My hair stood up, and goose-flesh covered me to my toes. Still I felt pleased, for it meant that I could communicate with the entity without a medium.

My elation was short-lived, however, for something unspeakable began to envelop me like a clammy fog, insufflating itself into me with my breath and forcing itself into my body even through the pores. I could feel it, tingling like electricity, in my lips, my nostrils, and my armpits; my genitals stung with the sensation. It pushed aside my senses and evidently replaced them with its own, while my own spirit rose and hovered above the bed like the *Ka* in an Egyptian tomb-painting, seeing the body, which had grown helpless and insensate, reanimate with the senses and will of the possessor. I found myself hoping it was *only* an evil spirit, not a devil.

I was horrified by the face of the body on the bed, for albeit the same flesh on the same bones, it was no longer the one I knew in the mirror, but a brutal, sensual mask—the face of another, much more evil and much stronger man.

As I watched the face change, the body galvanized into action. Its hand clawed open my pajamas, and I saw its penis extent to a turgidity and size I did not dream possible. The hand jerked at it frenziedly, and for the first time, I saw the tight foreskin strip back, and the glans protrude fully. My own consciousness experienced no sensation whatsoever, but winced, knowing that forcing my foreskin even gently caused pain, and that its being savagely forced back over the engorged glans must have been agonizing. If so, the entity paid no heed, but roughly and immediately produced ejaculation. Blood smeared both hand and organ, but without pausing, the invader drove on to a second orgasm, and a third, and continued as long as stimulation could restore even partial erectness.

Then the thing left my body, and my horrified consciousness crept back in. I was aware only of stinging pain. I arose, washed off the blood, and tried to comfort myself with carbolated vaseline. When the bleeding had ceased and the smarting somewhat subsided, I dressed in dry pajamas, and changed the sheet. Then, for the first time since the Preacher Wall episode, I knelt by the bedside to beseech protection, mortally in fear of the entity which spoke of treasure, but had siezed my body to satisfy the sexual deprivation of a century. I felt like a vessel drained dry and set down, and finally fell asleep, too forspent even to dream, though I expected nightmares.

As soon as classes were over the next day, I went to the bank and drew out ten dollars, phoned the medium and asked if ten dollars would pay for an interview. She replied that she had no thought of charging, that mercenary mediums were the main cause of the ill repute of the Spiritualist movement. She considered mediumship a spiritual gift, and assured me that she had independent means which made even a contribution unnecessary.

"I knew that Mrs. Blake used to take money," I explained, "and I think she was a good medium."

"She was a truly great medium," she agreed. "But she had no other income, and had to depend on her gift for her living. If anyone needed help and could not pay her, though, she gave it freely. She even saved lives for which she was given nothing."

"I never heard about that," I said with interest. "What happened?"

"Once when some young boys were playing, their mother left them and drove to her sister's, about three miles away. The older children locked the youngest boy in a coal shed, and could not get him out, as the mother had the key with her car keys. Then somehow the weeds got on fire and caught the building. The children were too excited to think to call their mother, or maybe they didn't know where she had gone. In any case, the child's grandmother's spirit came to Mrs. Blake and told her, and she phoned the sister's house in time for the mother to rush home and get him out alive. He was quite painfully burned and overcome by smoke, but he soon recovered."

"Who told you about it?" I asked, for I wished to check the report.

"The boy did, at Mrs. Blake's funeral—he was then a man," she said. "And his mother testified. At the funeral, all the people talked about was the good that Mrs. Blake did. She was a very dear friend, almost a mother in the faith to me. She was sincere and genuine—one of the chosen—one of the very few."

When I went to the hotel, I told her that I had felt the spirit near me, had tried to communicate by rapping, and found that it replied (but did not tell her any of the rest).

"I would not attempt to communicate," she said gravely. "At the church I could not tell you how dreadful that spirit was. No other spirit ever robbed me of so much vitality, or caused me such pain, or left me feeling so unclean. It is ruthless. If you must, find out what the situation is from the man he told you to ask, but proceed with great caution. Such a spirit could do you irreparable harm."

"Can spirits hurt you physically?" I asked.

"I have seen heavy tables and a piano levitated to the ceiling, and I see no reason to suppose that a force capable of such displays could not injure anyone if it chose. But I never heard of a case in which one did. I should be more afraid that he would seize my body. He is evidently an earthbound spirit, and must have been so a century or more. Only a very evil spirit would remain in thick darkness so long. He cannot have had any moral or spiritual qualities or he would have been released long ago and allowed to progress, or perhaps to reincarnate."

"Why should he want *me* to have the money?" I pondered. "Do you suppose it's because I'm his distant cousin?"

"If he were planning to take over your body, he'd want you to have the gold so he could enjoy it. Or perhaps it's a strategy to get you so engrossed that your spiritual defenses will be down when he makes a psychic assault."

"I surely would be excited if I thought I were about to dig up a treasure," I considered.

"He may have had to wait a hundred years to find someone like you to try to dispossess," she said pointedly.

"How do you mean, like me?" I demanded.

"You are handsome," she appraised, "You have a strong, fine, well-built body; you look masculine, but you have the spirit of a woman—fine, and sensitive, but sensuous, even sensual, and not very stable. You do have an extraordinary amount of libido, don't you?"

I pondered. "Well, I—that is, my—yes, I suppose I do, more than most," I fumbled.

"That goes with the kind of spirit you have," she remarked.

"What *is* wrong with my spirit?" I asked, not defending it.

"There's nothing *wrong* with it. You have great vital power and psychic sensitivity. It is so evenly balanced that it responds to any psychic influence, and that makes it precarious. You react to any strong influence in either direction. Balanced between spiritual and carnal, between good and evil, you are extremely vulnerable. If such a spirit as that one should gain control of you, you would be capable of any evil. But you are capable of saintliness as well. It depends on what influence you allow to dominate you. Again, I urge you not to communicate or seek contact with that spirit until you know you can control any spirit—*particularly* your own.

"How do you know so much about me?" I asked, realizing that all she said was true.

"My guide consulted yours after you phoned me," she replied. He informed me in those matters necessary for me to know in order to advise you."

"Then people do have guides!" I exclaimed. "After some of the messages at the church, I began to doubt in them."

"I can imagine," she sighed. "So many silly and attention-seeking people only pretend that they have guides who speak through them. It makes people think that all of us in Spiritualism are either phoney or unbalanced. It is a great pity, for the truth underlying genuine psychic experience is the greatest truth of all. Yes, guides are sent us—some of them are spirits of the first order, even angels. One guide does not serve all purposes. One with you is an instructing spirit. Another is the spirit of a woman who gives you warmth and insight. They do not protect you. In time of danger, all they can do is summon other, protective spirits; and once in control, the spirit who spoke might be able to hold you despite them if he did not dissipate his energy on physical excesses."

Mention of "physical excesses" made me acutely conscious of my

soreness, and quite convinced me that she knew what really had tran-
spired. I was acutely embarrassed, so I merely thanked her for her kindness and interest. After urging me to study the underlying principles
and philosophy of Spiritualism, and to pray for the gift of Discernment
of Spirits, she wished me a safe and successful life full of psychic activity and benefits, and sent me on my way.

After some indecision I wrote James Andrew, and soon received a
long letter in reply. He recognized the spirit all too well. It came to him
first at Mrs. Blake's, where it merely told him to ask his wife about a
treasure hidden on Barr's Run, near Ravenswood. His wife could recall
only that when she was small she had heard her parents say something ·
about one—and she suggested that they visit her great-aunt, who was
still living there.

The old lady related that in her parents' youth, two brothers named
Stanley had held up the Louisville bank. After killing a man, they escaped and eluded their pursuers until they reached home on Barr's Run.
Taking their mother's kettle from the fireplace, they went out of sight
with a shovel to bury the money. Soon they returned, leaped on their
horses, and continued their flight up the river.

A few minutes afterward, the pursuers arrived and interrogated the
mother. She told them where she supposed her sons had taken the
money, hoping that searching for it would delay them. But instead of
searching, the posse followed the men in the downpour of rain. They
pursued them into Wood County, and caught up with them about four
miles below Parkersburg. In the exchange of gunfire, the younger man
was mortally wounded, but lived long enough to say that the money
was buried in his mother's corn field. He begged forgiveness for his part
in the crime, and besought them to pray for his soul.

The older brother was wounded at the same time, but escaped; and
the Kentuckians found his horse, riderless, near the river bank. They
followed bloodstains into a dense thicket, where they found his sodden,
bloodstained coat and indications that he had made his way down to
the water's edge. There, more blood and disturbed drift seemed to indi-
cate that he had worked loose a log, clung to it, and been carried out
into the current. So little time had elapsed they thought he might still
b sighted if they rode along down the river bank. They soon saw a log
 ating, but no one was clinging to it, so they decided he had lost
strength to hold on—or had lost consciousness—and drowned.

They took the younger brother's body back to his mother, and told her what they supposed had happened to her other son. They then went to search the corn field, but the heavy rain had obliterated all tracks or signs of digging, so they found nothing. The amount hidden was said to be twenty or twenty-five thousand dollars, all in gold coins.

The old lady claimed that for years people searched and dug in the corn field, but no rumor even went around of anyone's having found anything. In time the incident passed into legend, except as an occasional searcher with some detecting device or forked witch-hazel wand or peach limb—dowsed for it without success. Then, linked with the legend of the gold, other stories sprang up which gave rise to local conviction that the old Stanley Field was haunted.

James Andrew went on to say that after hearing the story, he communicated with the spirit again. It instructed him to dig twenty feet southwest of the spring near where the railroad crossed Barr's Run. Because a house stood in sight, he went after dark—though both his Ouija board and his guides had told him to leave the treasure alone—and as soon as the lights were all out at the house he stole in and prepared to dig. He had barely started when a phosphorescent white bull with fiery eyes and glowing horns frightened him away. Of course, at that moment, to James Andrew, *any* white bull in moonlight would have been phosphorescent, fiery-eyed and glowing-horned, but I fancy that what he saw was something other than a bull.

He told his brother-in-law, and quite soon they worked up courage to go back. This time they began digging and had worked perhaps five minutes, when the Ouija they had with them began moving. Astonished to see the planchette move without a visible hand upon it, they were quite unnerved when it spelled DANGER. However, they had a lantern, and one held it as the other dug. Then a roaring, as of strong wind, began. An unearthly glow spread over a rather wide expanse around them, and again a bull appeared, this time black, larger than life, and much more dreadful than the phosphorescent one had been. It advance ; they grabbed their gear and backed away. As they did so the roaring grew louder, and they saw clods and dirt fly back into the hole. The bull came to the hole and stood pawing the spot, and when it again began moving slowly and ominously toward them, they turned and ran and did not stop until they reached their car.

Soon after that, James Andrew developed arthritis, and went to Mount Clemens, Michigan, to take the baths at the health resort there.

At the spa he met a Spiritualist couple from Illinois, and at one of their seances, the Barr's Run spirit urged them to go together to dig up the treasure, bidding them not to be afraid of anything that they might see or hear there.

Their arthritis improved remarkably soon, and they drove to Ravenswood together, bought a lantern and tools, and went to dig. They struck metal, and were in a state of feverish excitement when an unearthly noise began, and the earth and stones began flying back into the hole. They had a Bible, and James Andrew read from it as the other man threw out the dirt, and the woman held the lantern for both. Then she gave a piercing yell, dropped the lantern, and fell to the ground. The horrified men saw something black hunched over her clutching her throat. They dragged her free, somehow got to the couple's car with her, and sped back to Ravenswood. They thought it necessary to rouse a doctor and have him examine her. He was incredulous when they told him she had been attacked by a man as she was walking in the dark, for he said that only claws or extremely long nails could account for the lacerations on her bruised throat, and he phoned the sheriff of Jackson County to be on the watch for a man with very large abnormal hands— probably a lunatic!

The woman was more in shock than seriously injured, and when she was somewhat restored, the Illinois couple headed home that very night. James Andrew stayed on at the hotel. Next morning he trudged to the Barr's Run site, found his car undisturbed, found the trampled Bible and burned-out lantern, and the tools where they had fallen. But the hole was filled, and so carefully camouflaged that it gave no evidence of their digging.

James Andrew urged me to leave the treasure alone, but both need and greed impelled me. By day, I reasoned, such terrors would not come—and even if they did, I could see them in time. Now and again the spirit tried to communicate, rapping behind the headboard of the bed, or inside my locked desk. I gave it no encouragement, and each time it began, I read aloud from *Science and Health with Key to the Scriptures,* and this either silenced it or drove it away.

After my soreness went away, however, I came to feel that no matter how unnerving and excruciating the experience, the spirit had done me a real favor when it stretched my foreskin. Each time I bathed, able to draw it back and wash myself freely, I recalled how unpleasant it had

been to cleanse with a swab previously. I wished I had had the fortitude
to loosen it long before, as Stud frequently had suggested. I developed a
feeling almost of gratitude to the entity.

Christmas vacation came, and the first night Stud stayed with me I
led him to believe that I *had* followed his suggestion. When I told him
of the Spiritualist church, the woman's message, and James Andrew's
account of the Barr's Run treasure, I urged him to go with me during
the holidays to dig up the money, offering him half of any we might
find.

"Do you think I'd go within forty miles of a place where anything
like that happened!" he exclaimed. "One look at a glowin' bull and I'd
never be in no shape to spend money."

"Just think, Stud, those old coins would be worth a fortune—fifty
thousand dollars or more," I tempted.

"Well, I ain't goin' to do it, and that's final!" he exclaimed. "And if
you got good sense, you ain't goin' to neither!" I knew that pleading
would be mere waste of breath. He lay in silence a while, then as an
afterthought, no longer vehement, he asked, "Did your great-grandma
sure-'nuff have a sister named Bess Stanley?"

"I don't know for sure," I mused. "Massie Gandee named her youngest son James Stanley—I do know that."

"If some spook come and tried to claim kin with me, I'd be real
curious," he commented.

Later it occurred to me that Cousin R. M. Droddy at Walton had a
copy of *Border Settlers of Northwestern Virginia*, which includes a
biography of Jesse Hughes and tells of his children, so I wrote him,
asking if Mercy Gandee had a sister who married a Stanley. He replied,
quoting the sketch, that "Elizabeth married James Stanley; lived and
died on Mud Run, a tributary of Big Sand Creek, Jackson County, West
Virginia . . ." How could I doubt that the spirit was authentic! Of
course, Barr's Run is not Mud Run, but the book is not very accurate,
and it does not say how long Elizabeth lived on Mud Run, how early
she moved there, or that she is buried there. I felt certain that no one in
Huntington had researched the Hughes relationship, and each day I was
more certain that I had heard the very voice of a kinsman of mine who
had been dead a hundred years. More and more I rationalized that he
wanted the treasure to stay in the family and that a cousin could not be

all bad. So when I went back to Huntington, I invited him to communicate. Immediately my room became a focus of psychic activity.

He did not possess me—overtly—again, but raps sounded almost every night—sometimes, much to their alarm, even when students were visiting me. At night I could hear papers stirring inside the desk. One night when I had left the curved lid up it fell with a loud bang which made me jump half out of bed. A large copper cent that I kept in the locked drawer disappeared, and two days later I found it under my ashtray. Something kept striking the typewriter keys in the dark. I left paper in the machine, hoping for a message, but always the result was a meaningless jumble of letters and symbols such as a child might make while using the typewriter as a toy.

But if he did not forcibly make use of my body again, I felt that he was insidiously influencing me. I began drinking to excess, and for the first time since I was fourteen I lusted to experience intercourse with a girl. (My feeling for Stud had grown to seem so natural that the urge seemed *unnatural*—but reason could have overcome that. I was held back only by loyalty and love.)

The drinking interfered with my studies, so I resolved to turn again to Christian Science, since it seemed the strongest influence against the entity. I joined the Mother Church in Boston, and attended the local church. However, I still attended the Spiritualist meetings each Sunday night. Ironically, almost from the day I joined the church I began smoking regularly. Previously I had smoked only a cigarette or two a day, or a cigar if I wished to show off. But I bought a pipe on impulse, and it became part of me, seldom out of my mouth except in class, in church, or asleep. Mrs. Eddy was dead-set against use of tobacco—had she not forbidden it, it might not have seemed so irresistible. But I wondered if Stanley had enjoyed a pipe, and blamed the craving on him.

Even though I never went to Barr's Run, this story has an appropriately appalling conclusion. Some years later I wrote an article, "Dead Men Cry Gold," for *Fate* magazine, and as soon as it appeared, began to receive a flood of letters seeking more details. I soon went to Florida, but I struck up a correspondence with a man in West Virginia who went to Barr's Run, and from him received an account which gives me an idea of what I escaped—and *barely* escaped—thanks to Stud.

This man had made the acquaintance of a young couple who lived nearer Ravenswood than he. They were Ouija operators, and by help from their wooden (wooden Ouija boards seem the most effective) board had found $18,000 hidden in a deserted warehouse at Point Pleasant. They were keenly interested in messages about Barr's Run they had begun receiving, saying that the gold was still there, and that they would be shown the location if they would go there and wait till the opportune time. All the messages allegedly came from the same spirit, who said that he was weary of guarding the treasure.

To reach the site they had to leave their automobiles at some distance, stealthily cross posted land where an abandoned house stood, then climb a wooden gate secured by a padlock and chain.

Once, when the three of them had sneaked in and had just climbed the gate, a gray stallion galloped up after them. It came to the gate and passed through it as if no barrier were there, continued to the supposed spring site, lowered its head as if drinking, neighed, and shook its head up and down as if nodding "Yes." Then it reared, and after galloping off a short distance, vanished as they watched.

When the woman was sufficiently composed, her husband sent her back to the car for tools, convinced that the apparition had come to point out the exact location of the spring. But when she did not return immediately, he marked the spot and went to see what was detaining her. He found her lying on the back seat. As she hurried to the car, she told him, she had begun feeling faint and giddy. He decided that the ghostly horse had been too great a shock to her—for she was of a high-strung, excitable disposition—so he took her home, to return another day.

That night the wife fainted and when revived, babbled about the gray horse, and a strangely dressed, dark, long-haired man. However, by morning she seemed quite normal, so her husband was not greatly alarmed by her behavior.

They again met my correspondent, returned to the site, and began to dig, though a rain had begun, and dark clouds, and lightning, and gusts of wind threatened a severe storm. Soon lightning nearby made the use of metal tools seem too risky, so they went back to the car to keep dry and wait to see if only a heavy shower was approaching.

The light drizzle changed into a hard, steady rain. As they sat, the gray stallion galloped past, wheeled, returned, bent its neck, peered through the streaming windshield at them, jerked its neck up and down, and wheeled off in the direction of the spring.

The wife grew quite hysterical. When the thing disappeared, her husband got her under control, took a flask out of the car pocket and forced her to take a swig of whiskey. But then she grabbed it from him and began gulping it as if she meant to drain the bottle! He tried to take it back, and she bit him and clawed like a wildcat. Most of the whiskey was spilled before he subdued her, but the condition she was in made it obvious that nothing could be accomplished that day even if the rain ceased. Again the men postponed their digging—each promising again not to return alone—and arranged a later meeting.

The writer was not sure what happened after that. The young man's work took him unexpectedly to Wheeling, West Virginia, and he later wrote my informant from there, asking him to inquire around Clarksburg—where both my correspondent and the man's wife had relatives—to learn if any of them knew of her whereabouts! Instead of asking them, my correspondent drove straight to Barr's Run, and found a hole at the site where they had agreed to dig. Furious, he went on to Wheeling, hunted up the husband and demanded his share.

However, the man convinced him that he was alone; the Ohio County Sheriff confirmed that the woman had been reported missing, and that no one in Wheeling, at Parkersburg, or in Harrison County seemed able to offer any suggestion where she might be. A search had been going on for her for almost two weeks.

The distracted husband told him that after the second experience at Barr's Run, his wife had acted irrational for three or four days, at times seeming withdrawn, and at others feverishly animated. A doctor said that she was undergoing some difficulty due to irregular menstruation and had the symptoms of a nervous breakdown. He gave her tranquilizers but the sedation made her extremely listless and unresponsive. Then she seemed to improve, asked for the car for a few days, and began preparing for a visit with her family near Clarksburg. When she overstayed the time, the husband went in a borrowed car to her parents' home. She was not there. The husband then began to wonder about Barr's Run. He went on there, found his tools and a deep hole at the treasure site, but no trace of his car or his missing wife.

I was in a state of suspense for weeks until another letter came from my correspondent. The woman had been found, but even her husband had hardly been able to recognize her. From a fastidious, emotionally repressed, church-going young woman (whose only problem—significantly—was a nymphomania which made great demands on her husband), she had changed into a slovenly, foul-mouthed, whorish drunkard. She had taken up with a gang of construction workers, who told the police they were glad to be rid of her. Though she had plenty of money, bought whiskey by the case for them, gave them parties, and coupled with them and their friends to the point of satiation, they said that her public behavior embarrassed *them*. She had a few thousand dollars with her, so my informant supposed she had sold the antique coins to some dealer for a small fortune.

The husband divided the money with my correspondent, who in largess sent me a five-dollar bill in the letter—more than enough to pay for the postage I had spent writing him. I sent it on to a boys' orphanage, determined that at least that much of the Barr's Run hoard would be put to a good use.

I heard from my correspondent once more; he told me that the woman had been committed to a mental hospital for observation and treatment. I have wondered many times since what the outcome was, but I am afraid it was none too good. In cases of possession, medical science is rather at a disadvantage. Doctors refuse to recognize the real condition and tend to treat it as something else. The woman needed exorcism, I imagine, which I do not think that any mental hospital provides.

I have wondered even more how the Stanley spirit adjusted to its unfamiliar circumstances. On reflection, I decided that sex is sex, and it is no doubt just as satisfying in a female body as it is in a male. But it does seem ironic that a spirit so masculine that it manifested itself as a stallion or as a bull should be reduced for satisfaction to whatever body it could seize—and, unless he enjoyed their sensations vicariously—to the grossness of a crew of half-drunk construction hands. I suppose the woman's own spirit was merely forced out, as mine was temporarily, to watch as stranger after stranger profaned the body, and the body itself grew foul, and its lips spoke lewd and obscene profanity and lay besotted. What becomes of such a dispossessed spirit? Does it haunt the places familiar to it when it had its body, or finding no reentry, does it find itself admitted to the same state to which go the spirits of the dead? I cannot say, but death would seem much better.

As a sort of epilogue, years later, in New Orleans, I was idling with my Ouija board one Sunday afternoon when it began to spell.

TOM STANLEY, it wrote uncertainly. A chill ran over me.

"Barr's Run?" I asked.

The planchette moved to "Yes," and I exclaimed with concentration and earnestness: "Leave me alone! In the name of God the Father, God the Son, and God the Holy Ghost, I command you, go; go in peace, but leave me!"

I shoved the board away and sat in a dark reverie, when from the table sounded two feeble raps, the old signal for "no."

It astonished me that the spirit should ignore the command given so earnestly in the three Holy Names, but I became so curious I picked up the planchette and allowed it to write again.

PRAY FER A PORE SINNER, it spelled out. IM JOHNS BRUTHER. HE ANT WITH ME NO MORE.

"John was the older one? Was he the one who caused all the trouble?"

HE SHOT THE BANK MAN, it replied.

"Where is he now?"

DONT NO. HE LEFT AND ANT COME BACK. IM ALONE. I WANT TO GO WHAR MA IS. THA GOT LIGHT THAR.

"Where is she, in Heaven?"

NO IT ANT FUR BUT I CANT GIT THAR. PA AND A PASSEL OF FOKES IS WHUR SHE IS.

"Did you try to warn me when John tried to get me to Barr's Run?"

HE DUN TO MUCH RONG. I DIDNT WANT HIM TO HURT NO MORE FOKES.

"Do you believe in God?"

SHOR.

"Do you believe in His forgiveness and mercy?"

YES BUT ITS TO LATE TO PRAY.

"Then what can I do to help you?" I demanded.

PRAY FER ME.

"Will that help?" I asked in surprise, thinking of Catholic prayers for the dead, which Grandmother had said was practiced for the money.

IT HOLP SUM THAT WUS HERE.

"Are you in a place called Purgatory?"
DONT NO.
"I'm not a priest. Did priests pray for those who were helped?"
ONLY NO THA WUS PRAYED FER.
"And that set them free?"
SUM NOT ALL. THEM THAT WAS SORRY IT DID.

I then prayed that the spirit of Tom Stanley be released from the state in which it was held. I said solemnly: "Hear me all angels, all devils, and all spirits; hear me Lord God. The Lord Jesus Christ said, 'what ye shall loose on earth shall be loosed in heaven,' and the words of Jesus Christ cannot be made to lie. I loose this spirit here and set it free. I forgive him his sins on earth and remit his punishment, dependent upon his sincere repentance. If that is not enough, I take his guilt upon myself. Hear me, Lord God! Hear me, O Son of God! Hear me, O Holy Spirit! Bear witness that I have set him free. Hear me all spirits, all devils and all angels: Unless you have power to make the words of Jesus Christ a lie, you have no choice but release him and let him go."

Then I placed my hand on the planchette to see whether the spirit was satisfied. "Cousin Tom, are you still there?" I asked.

But the planchette did not respond. I never heard from Cousin Tom again.

11

"TO LEAVE THE FRIENDS YOU LOVED . . ."

Hearts and Tulips: Love and faith—a sign for lovers and for happy marriage

To lose the earth you know, for greater knowing; to lose the life you have, for greater life; to leave the friends you loved, for greater loving; to find a land more kind than home, more large than earth—

—Whereon the pillars of this earth are founded, toward which the conscience of the world is tending. . . .

Thomas Wolfe

Stud had come to spend the last night with me before my departure for college and after I whispered good-night to him, he suddenly drew me to him and clutched me in a tight embrace.

I was astounded—almost frightened—for he was quivering, and his burning maleness pressed my loins and his lips crushed mine and held them long and hungrily.

"Stud! What's got into you?" I gasped. "Don't kiss me that way, and don't do that—it hurts!"

"I love you!" he said hoarsely. "I didn't mean nothin' wrong. It's only that I reckon this is the last time you'll ever sleep with me, and it's like the loss of the best part of me, seein' you go. I don't care what you think of me for sayin' it!"

"Why—I'll be coming home all the time," I assured him.

"Yeah, but how can it be the same? You'll make friends there that has learnin', and you'll maybe take up with some girl. You won't never even think of me."

"Nothing could make any difference, you big sweet blockhead! I'll love you as long as I live. I'd think you ought to know by now I love you!"

"I *do* know it," he breathed, "that's what makes losin' you hurt me so. I know too this ain't no place for a guy to make a livin'. I wouldn't hold you here if I could. Only nobody ever showed me such understandin', or ever give me a love so tender and fine. I only wish we could go on to college together. It's pure hell to have to quit school because you ain't got money for clothes or books or nothin', and then grow up and see what all you're missin'. I'd 'a' made the best athlete they ever saw at Marshall and I know I got the mother-wit to learn."

178

"You're like thousands of other boys trapped here in these hills," I sighed. "That's why I have to go somewhere where there's a better chance for my children."

"So must I!" he said fiercely. "The day I'm twenty-one, and Pa can't hold me here, I'm goin' to Akron, where Ma's brother Paul is. All his kids got to go through high school, and Cousin Emma went to business college. Ma says when he went there, back durin' the war, he didn't have no more education than I got, and didn't talk no better. But he went to school at night till he got a high school diploma, and his boss took interest in him, and set him off into engineerin', and now he's head of a whole department in the plant he works at. I ain't goin' to stay no ignorant hill-billy in the head of some damn hollow all my life, no more'n you, Lee. I'd kill myself workin' to *be* somebody."

That night was one of realizations and crises, for he took me in his arms again and we kissed each other, and as I felt him against me, a woman flamed to life within me and cried for him. But "I didn't mean nothin' wrong" was what he said the first time, and we did nothing that we considered wrong—unless loving itself is.

I told him I wished that I were a girl that he might enjoy me. He sighed, took my hand, squeezed it, and kissed me with profound tenderness.

"I sure wish you was," he breathed. "You are; 'cept you got a man's voice and a man's body. I always thought you was one damn fine guy— but I reckon the woman in you is what always drawed me. You was always a hell of a lot more to me than any other guy ever was, and all I never could find in a girl. It'd just be so wonderful nice to have you with me all the rest of my life, runnin' on with me, and goin' over me with alcohol when I'm wore out, and lovin' me, and makin' over me the way you do."

"You wouldn't want to marry me."

"Wouldn't I!" he exclaimed softly. "You'd always be waitin' ready for me at night, and more'n willin' no matter how much of that I wanted; you'd stay clean and always smell good; you'd keep house the way a house ought to be kept; and always have plenty of good grub on hand; you'd look like a million dollars, and give me fine, smart, classy-lookin' kids; and I'd wake up and go to sleep lovin' you and bein' sure you love me. I'd be a damn fool not to marry you."

"But this kind of talk is crazy," I sighed. "We have to have wives to get what we need out of life. It only hurts to talk this way."

"I'd be plenty satisfied just bachin' it with you. Why can't we just stay bachelors and live together? It'd border on bein' married, the way we feel."

"When you were sixteen you told me you'd as lief be dead as not have any children."

"Like as not my boys would be aggravatin' headstrong devils like me that'd worry a person right into the grave, and the girls homely as sin, and mean and sassy like my sisters," he deprecated.

"But you know we never could have a real life," I breathed. "Playing at sex is all right for boys, but we're not boys any more. That's not something for a whole life, or for a whole lifetime. That's just not enough to satisfy."

A strained, diffident look came to his face. Almost inaudibly he whispered, "If what we do don't satisfy you, I—I'd do them other things for you if you'd live with me."

"Damn you, Stud!" I gasped, when what he said sank in. "Is that what you thought I meant? If you think I'm a dirty queer, to hell with you!"

"I don't think that!" he exclaimed. "But it's all I knowed to offer. Them's the only other things we *could* do. Now I went and made you so mad you cussed me! I—I'm goin' to get right up and go home."

"Well, go then!" I snapped. "I don't want to sleep with you anyhow if you'd do those things—God!"

He scrambled out over me and started to pull on his clothes. Tears began to run down his cheeks, and the sight of them was more than I could bear. I began crying, too—stricken by thought of losing him, and remorseful for hurting his feelings.

"I was only tryin' to say I'd do whatever it'd take to make you happy," he choked. "I didn't think you wanted to do them things, but I'd do anything for you, I want you with me so bad!"

"Come on back to bed," I pleaded.

"I don't know who's worse mixed up—you or me!" he muttered. "I keep feelin' like you really *are* a woman, and—oh hell! I'll stay if you ain't mad at me no more."

When settled beside me again, I pushed his unruly forelock out of his eyebrows and kissed him on the forehead, realizing how confused he must feel. "Now, lie on your belly and I'll scratch your back—all night if you want me to." He sighed deeply, turned over, relaxed again, and gradually lapsed into a state of bliss as I went over his back.

Finally he breathed, "That'll do," reached over me, turned off the light, and held me to him so close his musky armpit all but stopped my breath. But it strangely pleased me, and as he held me he fondled my chest as if he searched for breasts.

"You ain't queer," he whispered. "You're out-and-out a woman. Makin' over me one minute and cussin' me out the next; orderin' me to go home one breath, and the next, cryin' and tellin' me to stay. It's a goddamn shame you ain't made like one!"

Six bittersweet years we lived with this realization. He continued to treat the visible man as his comrade, and when we were seen together by day we were innocently swimming, hunting, picking berries, gathering nuts, helping each other at work, or digging ginseng and other roots to sell. But in the darkness, he put his arms around an unseen woman, and we loved in cruel need and hunger. I, with maleness like a genital malignancy which denied me the pleasure of him; he, with the self-denying gentle tenderness of a devoted husband whose wife is cancerous and forbidden. When I stood studying my own body, wondering whether it contained concealed deformities, I found it baffling. I hated myself with helpless, frustrated fury because I also, externally, seemed perfectly male. To have been his wife and borne his children, I would have with my own hands cut off the mocking evidence with a knife, but mutilation could not open my body to receive him, nor emasculation provide a womb for him to fecundate. Once in senseless, involuntary reaction to the mirror, I struck it with my fist and cut my hand, but the bruise and cut that the broken tormentor gave me hurt not at all compared to its reflection.

It was cruel for Stud, too, though at least his was not an inadequacy which caused him to despise his own body, for his body was perfectly fitted to play the only role conceivable to or for him—that of a man. It is one thing, with a fine male body, to think of oneself as a husband. It is another matter, with a body equally male, to hunger to be a wife. I know; I have done both.

While I was at Marshall, I came home each summer and on vacations. We became utterly devoted, and uninhibited in expressing our affection. Our families were not talkative, however, so very few others realized how much time we spent with each other. Stud's wild reputation persisted long after his period of misconduct with girls, and when he reached young manhood his appearance and mannerisms were so masculine that even a sophisticate could hardly have suspected him in love with me. At most, the discerning merely remarked that it was unusual for an educated person and an uneducated one to be such boon companions, saying that college certainly had not made me snurl up my nose at former friends.

Before she had seen Stud a dozen times Grandmother had realized that only his lack of education stood in the way of his belonging to the highest class of all—that of the naturally superior—and she unbent with him, soon bade him call her "Mom Eva" as I did, and grew fond of him. And if he showed up at dark, sweaty and covered with dirt from a day in the field, she read his appearance as a testimonial to his industry, did not complain if he begrimed the towel, and bade him make himself at home. She kept a jar of her incomparable, corn-syrup Dutch Honey set aside especially for him.

Then Stud went to Akron, and for the next three years we saw each other only occasionally. He worked and went to school and made rapid progress in everything except grammar—which was as incomprehensible to him as algebra always was to me. However, in the third year he won his high school diploma and made a special trip from Akron to show it to me.

Both sleeping and awake I prayed that in Akron he would find a good girl who would be to him all that I could not. I repeated that I would not share bachelorhood with him, but he always said, "You say you won't, but you're too much woman not to change your mind."

His forthright, "Them's the only other things we *could* do," haunted me, for I feared I heard it as "Those *are* the only other things we could do," and I wanted neither responsibility for making him a pervert, nor guilt of depriving him of his natural fulfillment as husband and father. I began to feel very sympathetic toward homosexuals, wondering if they experienced feelings such as mine. I found some of them devoted to their partners, but most often found them essentially men making a farce of the sacred role of woman. They seemed willing enough to play

at being woman for pleasure, but I found none who yearned for child-
bed as did I. I refused to burlesque before the world, preferring the
concentration which enables an actor to become the character in a
serious play. Reason told me I must live out a role as the man in the
mirror. I knew that this entailed both loneliness and suffering, but these
one can bear in dignity.

Sometimes I felt premonitions that Fate might resolve my situation—I had seriously considered going to fight in the Spanish Civil War,
feeling that I might be killed and spared the frustration of my love for
him. At other times I had disturbing visions of him—symbolic glimpses
in which he walked into a dark shadow, sank into the sea, or entered a
door which closed after him. I supposed that they symbolized his disappearance out of my life, but they filled me with foreboding.

My subconsciousness must have come very close, indeed, to the
threshold of awareness, as I agonized in my efforts to understand my
feelings for Stud.

I had accepted the belief that God is just, and if justice must be
cruel, then it is. This feeling went far to enable me to reach a quite certain supposition that my unhappiness was punishment for some forgotten sin. When I was told that Zaïda was one of my familiar spirits,
nobody suggested that she might be more or other than that, but I
came to feel that she must be to blame for my wish to be a woman, and
for my yearnings. My reading of Spiritualist and Theosophical literature
had familiarized me with the concept of reincarnation, and I supposed
my unhappiness to be due to karma. All I failed to realize was that the
spirit within me might *be* Zaïda's, and the karma *hers*. Those realizations did not come until much later—not completely until after I began
writing this book.

When I graduated from Marshall in 1940 I knew that war must come
soon. I was certain that it would involve me, and I hoped that it would
bring me death. I went back to Gabe and secluded myself at Grandmother's, finding no pleasure in the swimming hole, where younger
boys now replaced my former associates. When I chanced to meet those
left of my friends at Wellford, they were mostly with young wives, already care-worn and burdened with infants they were ill-prepared to
rear. They were earth's sparrows (whose fall at least, Jesus compassion-
ately assured them, is marked by God); the wiser and stronger, the able,
the ambitious, and the unfettered birds had flown. I wrote a book—a

long, red-tinged novel about the Spanish Civil War. When he came on a visit I let Stud read it before submitting it to any publisher.

He annihilated it, making me acutely aware that it was hollow, unreal, propaganda from front to back, and utter rubbish. (I tore it to shreds and burned it.)

"Next time," he meditated, "don't try to write like somebody else, or about something you don't know, or some place you've never been."

"There won't be any next time," I sighed.

"Oh, I think maybe there will be," he said. "No telling the good you could do if you didn't try to hide the love you have so much of, and if you'd write to the world from your open heart. You'd make people feel big inside, and free, and happy, and not afraid to die, or even to live. That's what you did for me, and I love you for it. It meant a hell of a lot more than all the fun we had together—and that's sayin' something!"

"You make me feel wonderful," I breathed.

"To me, you *are* wonderful," he murmured. "You're no angel, but I've seen you do things a preacher-man couldn't do. You stopped the blood when I cut my foot, and I watched you talk to a plant that looked like it was dyin' and when I next thought to look it had leafed out and was fixin' to bloom. You said it was God that did it; it was, but you did the talking. You're not a witch, and you're not too awful holy. But you still can do those things, so I know you don't have to have wings on your back as long as you love and believe."

We decided to have a final swim for old time's sake before he left, and to say good-bye where we had become acquainted. When we came out, I dried his back, and when he was dressed and said the bus was due, I reached to clasp his hand. But he ignored it, and—wet as I was— threw his arms around me, clutched me to his breast and tearfully kissed me. "I'm not going to ask you any more to come," he whispered huskily. "If you ever want to, I'll be waitin'. And if you ever need me, call. I never can forget you, but if this is how you want it, well, good-bye. I know you're givin' up your happiness for mine."

"Good bye, Stud," I whispered, my voice breaking, and without looking at him, I ran and plunged into the deep hole to hide my tears. I did not look after him, and faced away until I heard the bus stop and drive on.

The pool seemed Styx—I wished that it were Lethe—so I waded out and silently went home. Strangely I felt that I had not lost him, but made him mine forever, and my sickness within seemed past its crisis. The drama of our lives was over, I felt, with one protagonist gone, the other sacrificed, the gods departed, and the Fates satisfied. I wondered if by treating parting as if it were as irrevocable as death, I had killed him somehow, for I felt for him as I do for the beloved dead.

That afternoon, instead of climbing to the Lilly Rock and grieving, I filled out and sent my application to enroll in the graduate school at William and Mary.

12

THE HALF-WAY IMPERTINENT
KNOWLEDGE OF HYPNOTISM

The Rain that Refreshes the Soul: A symbol referring to
spiritual water, the field to be watered as the human soul,
and to the rainbow of promise. A sign asking for inspiration, insight, and creativity

. . . Mr. Phineas P. Quimby visits your city for the purpose of exhibiting the astonishing mesmeric powers of his subject, Master Lucius Burkmar . . .

James W. Webster

. . . Mr. Quimby was led more and more steadily to the conclusion that all effects produced on Lucius were due to the direct action of mind on mind, and that no other hypothesis was necessary. He found that he could influence Lucius either with or without Lucius's knowledge, and that Lucius was also affected in respects which were not intentional on his part.

Horatio W. Dresser

At first I found that my thoughts affected the subject, and not only my thought but my belief. I found that my own thoughts were one thing, and my belief another. If I really believed in anything, the effect would follow whether I was thinking it or not.

Phineas P. Quimby

Mind-science is wholly separate from any half-way impertinent knowledge . . .

Mary Baker Eddy

When I enrolled for graduate study, I decided to prepare to teach English Literature at college level. I took courses including Anglo-Saxon, Chaucer, and Shakespeare, feeling that without knowledge of these three influences and that of the King James Version of the Bible, one is ignorant both of the language and its literature. For my thesis I soon decided upon a study of the supernatural and witchcraft in Shakespeare's plays. When those in the dormitory realized that my interest in

188

these things was more than academic, the curious and the sensation-seeking began taking interest in me.

Among them was a dolt described by his friends as an "amateur hypnotist." I felt that the adjective should have been the noun, but his amazing ineptitude intrigued me: once in a while he succeeded in hypnotizing someone, using rote commands from a book and stumbling through demonstrations described in it. I decided that if such a dunderpate could hypnotize, it must require neither skill nor intelligence, and felt sure I could do better. Accordingly, I found an old book on Animal Magnetism—which is Mrs. Eddy's term for hypnotism. Without noticing that it came out before 1850, I bought that particular volume because it was badly worn—always a good recommendation for an old book. This outdated work equated Animal Magnetism with Mesmerism, so I learned how a magnetizer induces the mesmeric sleep. I practiced a compelling, penetrating gaze to hold the eyes of my prospective subject, fancied that I could feel the "fluid" in my fingers and, determined not to rely on rote (as did the blockhead), studied the commands until I felt I had caught their import and feeling.

I am now glad that I had an early book to go by, for in the mid-1800s, hypnotism still had elements of the unknown and mysterious in it, and accordingly sometimes produced unexpected and extraordinary phenomena. In hardly any other field save parapsychology does result depend so completely upon expectation, for in both it is true that (as a witch is told at his initiation), "If that which thou seekest thou findest not within thee, thou wilt never find it without thee." So, if a hypnotist believes he cannot produce a given result, he cannot. But if one does not know what to expect—or not to expect—the result is due to the subconscious belief either of the magnetizer or the subject, and is likely to be as interesting and significant as are all actions of the subconscious. Contemporary hypnotists seldom, if ever, produce phenomena as fascinating as that produced by Mesmer and Dr. Phineas P. Quimby; not knowing that certain things were "impossible," the early magnetizers sometimes produced them. Needless to say, even they did not match the performances of the Egyptian sorcerers and magicians mentioned in Exodus, or those of later *Hexenmeisters* and witches.

Just to see what the result would be, I gave one subject suggestion that on Halloween I would take him with me to a sabbat. I told him

nothing of what to expect, but instructed him to remember everything
that he experienced and tell of it later. He half-believed already that I
was a witch, and waited for Halloween night with keen anticipation.
At the given hour he went into trance without further suggestion,
and remained in it until he awoke voluntarily about an hour later,
believing with all his heart and mind that he had witnessed a sabbat.

He related that I had taken him on a besom behind me and flown to
a solitary glade near Lake Matoaka, where eleven other witches arrived,
some on besoms, and others riding horseback (the horses really men
bewitched to serve as mounts for this occasion). Then we were joined
by a horned being with cloven hoofs—Satan, no less! My subject described him in awful detail and told vividly of our ceremonies (I should
greatly enjoy a sabbat if witches really *do* hold such rites), and he said
that we flew back to the dormitory, with him holding on for dear life as
the besom descended. Aside from the amused few who had been in the
room the entire time, the students listened to him fascinated, almost
convinced that Satan had presided at a very lively celebration not a half
mile from the William and Mary campus. His absolute conviction gave
poignant understanding of testimony that truthful men and women
gave centuries ago, for what he believed was what folklore says of
witches and what the race mind believes of them. All that suggestion
did was activate everything he ever had read or heard about witches and
about Satan, and turn a fantasy into something that, to him, *was*
reality.

Mrs. Eddy deprecated hypnotism to such a degree that she even
called it "the specific term for error or mortal mind." She devoted over
a page to Mesmer, citing an adverse report of his phenomena given by a
French government commission in 1784, and one by a committee of
French notables which investigated Animal Magnetism in 1837.
(Both commission and committee were such that any favorable report would have been far more extraordinary than any phenomena
they might have encountered.) She quoted Mesmer as believing that
"There exists a mutual influence between the celestial bodies, the
earth, and animated things," and declared: "The planets have no
more power over man than over his Maker."

I felt certain that Mesmer had been right—every atom in the universe
is conscious, and is influenced by every other atom. The First Book of
Moses, called Genesis, says in the first chapter that even before God

said of the sun, moon, and stars "let them be for lights," He said "let them be for signs."

Since childhood I had regulated my planting and gardening by the signs of the Zodiac and by the phases of the moon, so I knew that the "celestial bodies" have effect upon the germination, growth, resistance to disease and drought, and upon the fruitfulness of plants. In my mind I still can hear Stud say, "If you got to nut a pig or anything, you sure better wait till the sign's not in the Lion or in the Scorpion." I had observed the effect of castration in those signs—the profuse bleeding occurring in Leo, and the gross coimplications attendant in Scorpio.

I value pragmatic observation more than the theories of a Victorian lady who probably never grew a cucumber, much less castrated a pig, so I gave no more weight to her opinions about hypnotism than to her comment as to the influence of the planets. In fact, I wondered whether she feared that in hypnotism her students might find devastating insights into her own system. I did not at that time know anything about Dr. Phineas P. Quimby, who (Mrs. Eddy's enemies say) through the study of Animal Magnetism discovered the principles which make Christian Science "work."

Quimby is so important that I must digress to say a little about him. Before he became a spiritual healer, "Dr." Quimby—a clock-fixer with very little education, he was in no way entitled to the "Dr." he affeɛ..a—went through a period of investigation as a magnetizer, traveling ab. ɟt in Maine and Canada demonstrating the marvels of which his subject, a youth named Lucius Burkmar, was capable when in mesmeric sleep.

Lucius became clairvoyant and could describe places he had never ᴊeen. He became mediumistic, and could give exactly the same type of information about the dead as can a good spiritualistic medium. Though neither Dr. Quimby nor he had any medical training whatsoever, he could diagnose disease and prescribe treatment or medication which succeeded in effecting cures. In short, acting together, the two performed almost identically as Edgar Cayce did by himself a century later. In spite of his lack of education, Dr. Quimby had a remarkable mind and realized that his phenomena had profound medical, scientific, and philosophical implications. Without a vocabulary adequate for medicine, science, or philosophy he nevertheless worked out a nebulous system which is revolutionary with respect to all three, advancing ideas in accord with Cayce's later revelations, and the even more recent ones of "Seth" (of *The Seth Material*).

One has to empathize with Quimby and translate his tortured gropings for expression into the contemporary, comprehensible language of atomic physics, biochemistry, endocrinology, psychology, psychiatry, and parapsychology. Only then can one realize his real significance, so even though a portion—in my opinion, not the more interesting or meaningful one—of his writings has been published *(The Quimby Manuscripts)*, Quimby remains yet to be "discovered."

Before Sigmund Freud was out of diapers, Quimby knew all about the problems arising from unrecognized guilt feelings and complexes, the dire results of repressed emotion. He dared hold the church responsible for much of the illness that he encountered, accusing it of creating guilty feelings and fear in the minds of church goers, and of encouraging them to suppress instincts and repress emotions.

One illustrative case always mentioned in connection with Quimby involves a woman who was afflicted with dropsy. Physicians had treated her without effect. The clergy piously urged her to submit to the will of God and meet death with resignation. Quimby sat with her and, he says, "took her feelings"—probed her consciousness telepathically—and saw the real cause.

Several years previously, the woman had been in love with a sailor. They had a lover's quarrel, and still angry, the man shipped on a vessel which was soon overtaken by a storm at sea; he was washed overboard and drowned. The woman began to blame herself for his death, and—in the kind of poetic justice for which one should always be prepared in connection with karmic or psychologically-caused conditions—she undertook to punish herself symbolically, by slowly drowning her body in its own fluids.

Quimby recalled the incident to her, convinced her of the cause of her dropsy, and gave her his assurance that she was not responsible for the man's action, nor for the storm. She accepted his explanation, recovered quickly and fully—and stopped going to church.

Mrs. Eddy "unmasked" Animal Magnetism in such a way that anyone reading her chapter gets the impression that hypnotists are all as sinister and power-crazy as Rasputin. But though most hypnotists do not seek to gain absolute mastery over their subjects or to carry out evil intentions, the danger should never be overlooked or left unmentioned.

In Italy (where even old Roman law provided that a person could be charged with enslaving the personality of another and where witchcraft is particularly malevolent, widespread, and greatly feared), the penal code defines the crime of *plagio* as "exposing a person to your influence in such a way that the subject is reduced to a total state of subjugation." Persons have been convicted and imprisoned for doing this.

I had no interest in gaining despotic control over anyone's personality, and had always found enough persons who sin of their own volition. I was simply intrigued by Mrs. Eddy's inference that hypnosis is a means of securing "half-way impertinent" knowledge, for my mind balks at the idea that *any* knowledge is impertinent.

Impertinent is defined as "intrusive, presumptuous, incongruous, inappropriate, trivial, silly, or absurd." My feeling still is that *presumptuous* knowledge (the theologians of the time notwithstanding) changed man's concept of the universe from the Ptolemaic to the Copernican system. *Irrelevant* knowledge is semantically impossible. *Incongruous* knowledge is the best clue to inconsistency, incompleteness or error in the system where it ought to fit, but doesn't. *Inappropriaate* knowledge always has appropriate uses and may open wonderful new fields to the individual. *Trivial* knowledge is the foundation of many high-sounding degrees, titles, and reputations of many "authorities." *Silly* knowledge is often great fun; and *absurd* knowledge is a great help in dealing with absurd people and situations. I felt that Mrs. Eddy must have had in mind the *intrusive*, unbidden kind which comes as insight, empathic comprehension, or revelation, worth almost any price.

Saint John wrote that he was in the spirit on the Lord's Day, when on Patmos were revealed to him those things which make up his strange book in the Bible. To be in the spirit is to be dead, unconscious, in projection, or in trance, I hoped through hypnosis to learn as much as possible about trance states.

My life had long been enriched by intrusive knowledge. I have many times had inflowings of the awareness of God. Often they came as I gazed at stars, enthralled by the magnitude and splendor of the universe. Once God, and the poem, and the marshes and I became one continuum of experience as I saw the tide fill the Marshes of Glynn. I always see Him in the ocean, and·once glimpsed a vision of the intercourse in which life was first engendered on the earth: The fire of lightning fecundating the chemically estrous water in electromagnetic

copulation of such primal passion that it could take place on no earthly bed save that of the ocean, as the Male Principle of God united
with the Female Principle—positive and negative polarities joining in
the fervency of the Divine Libido as the planet rocked, and the ocean
bed was asweat with lava. Seeing this, I grasped the mystery of the
appearance of life. That is no churchly vision, but it squares with my
own theology and with atomic science.

I had no fear of any kind of knowledge, so I decided that if hypnosis
is possible, it is natural; and if natural, then it is so because of the way
God constituted the mind of man. I wanted to discover all that a subject in hypnotic trance can see. I pored over the old book until I felt I
had grasped its meaning, and then set about seeking a good and willing
subject. I held hands with upward of twenty boys in search of one who
could sense the magnetic "fluid" with which I thought I was filled. And
when I found one who assured me I made him tingle all over, I selected
him.

This suggestible youth had interested me from our first meeting, for
he seemed quite familiar. On acquaintance we found that we both had
Dabney and Shrewsbury ancestors in the early days of the Virginia
Colony. (I am quite touchy about that, because I do not know whether
my own line descends from Cornelius Dabney and his wife Edith, or
from Cornelius and the Pamunkey Indian Queen.) But the exact kin-
ship was so remote that our friendship meant more. Somehow we
began calling each other "Coz" which the boys in the dormitory
took to mean "cousin." But we used it as did the commonality in
England in Elizabethan times (to the delight of the Shakespeare professor), and greatly enjoyed cozing with each other, and cozening
the rest.

Coz was a slender, graceful youth with an imaginative, quick mind,
and a talent for poetry who composed poignant little verses not unlike
those of Sara Teasdale. He was not a consistent student, for he put
forth effort only in courses he enjoyed. His father was determined that
Coz be a business administrator, and Coz was just as determined not to
be. His mother insisted that he be a concert pianist, but he was indiffer-
ent to the piano, though technically he played well. He was mediocre in
all sports, but enjoyed playing tennis with partners no better than he.
His favorite pastime seemed to be lounging, listening wherever boys
congregated. He was homosexual, but so secretive and unobtrusive that

few except his partners and his most intimate friends were aware of the fact.

Only after our hypnotic experiments had gone on some two or three weeks did he manifest any erotic interest in me, but I kept it from getting out of bounds by post-hypnotic suggestion. However, I realized that if any of the dangers Mrs. Eddy mentioned exist, that of sexual involvement between hypnotist and subject is probably the greatest. To judge from my experience, this is not due to any effect hypnosis has on sexual attraction or libido, but to the raising of the threshold of awareness between the two. In the rapport between Coz and me we knew each other's feelings directly and realized that it was impossible to dissimulate, even had we wished to.

This matter came up one afternoon when Coz lay sprawled on my bed as I studied. I chanced to look over at him and idly began to size him up, comparing his boyish gracefulness with Stud's muscular strength. He grinned, moved his hips suggestively, and said, "Why don't you find out how I'd be?"

As I blushed, stammered, and guiltily assured him that I was just admiring his graceful build, he chuckled and said, "You don't need to try to hide anything from me. *I've* been gay since I was fifteen "

"Coz," I reproved him, "I like you a lot, and I feel that if you're gay that's your own business; but I don't want to get involved with you that way, and I won't! So, cut out that kind of talk."

Our first session occurred a month before this conversation; I took Coz's hands in mine and fixed my mirror-perfected hypnotic gaze into his eyes. He passed into trance then and there, and I induced fairly deep hypnosis. I know that modern hypnotists, even Quimby, would deny that there is any kind of "fluid" involved, but I experienced some sort of electrical sensation in my hands, and he claimed he did. I suppose it was mere suggestion, but in any case, during the second session he went into plenary trance, and I gave him post-hypnotic suggestion to enter it directly from then on.

Within a week, I found I could dispense with spoken commands, and induce trance merely by staring into his eyes intently. Soon I dispensed with the stare, and he went into deep trance if I said "relax," or when I told him to look at a picture I kept over my bed. Once, in a shoe store, I said, "I want a pair of felt slippers I can relax in," and Coz went into trance on the spot, somewhat to the alarm of the clerk.

The picture was a small print of a Crucifixion by some little-known German romantic artist. I believe it is known as the *Köln Altarpiece*. I never have seen any other reproduction of it, and my copy came from a book supplied by the German Library of Information when that outlet supplied the most subtle propaganda that could be found for analysis and study. A most unusual portrayal, it showed Calvary as a somber, evergreen-covered South-German hill against a fading sunset, with the cross so distant that the figure on it was indistinct—it might have been that of any crucified man. More of a commentary on the brooding sorrow of Nature for Man's impious cruelty, it moved me more than any other portrayal of Calvary ever did. It also had a strong, strange effect on Coz. He often entered trance unbidden when he studied it, and on such occasions saw things in it that were not painted there. He told of seeing murdered men, sorrowing women, mutilated children, burning cities, incidents of warfare, and horrible crimes.

Two or three times I came in and found him kneeling on my bed in front of it, weeping—not, he said, for the Crucified Lord, but because of the sin and suffering of the world. Since then, I have realized that what he saw *really was* in the picture—figments of emotion-charged imagination drawn from my mind as I meditated upon it, considering those things which perpetually crucify the sons of Man. In effect, *I* had haunted the picture, filling it with thought-forms which became visible to him clairvoyantly when he was in trance. And he left a few thought-forms of his own in it, which I glimpsed long afterwards.

We began our experiments with production of physical phenomena such as one finds described in almost any work on hypnotism. They entertained and demonstrated the control the mind exerts over the body, but I was more interested in the possibility of extending perception, and in the clear indications of telepathic communication I soon found Coz manifesting when in trance. I was greatly interested in determining the kind and extent of information a subject can draw from persons present. I already believed that telepathy accounted for most "spirit" messages, and for the names and descriptions of dead persons I had heard produced by mediums in Spiritualist church services, and presently, I intended to test Coz's ability to perform as a medium.

My book said that persons in mesmeric sleep can "see" objects not possible under normal conditions, so I told Coz to "see" coins boys examined and put back in their pockets. He could give the dates on them with great accuracy. I assumed that he received a mental image of the date or perhaps a picture of the entire coin, for he could give the value of the coin as well, and once detected that a nickel a boy had was of the old liberty-head type, with the Roman numeral V. In the same manner, Coz gave the content of short sentences that students wrote on slips of paper and put in envelopes which I had him hold against his forehead. I say "content" rather than wording, for sometimes he substituted words of similar meaning, calling house "building," and on one occasion reading I am the eldest of three *children* as "I am the eldest of three *brothers."* From that, I felt that he was indeed drawing information from the mind of the writer rather than from the slip of paper, for the boy who wrote the slip said that the other two in his family were boys. But I was still in doubt, not knowing whether the writer might have written "children" and remembered it as "brothers" as Coz pressed the envelope to his forehead, or whether the boy remembered the wording, and visualized his two brothers so that Coz corrected the word to "brothers" because that was what they obviously were. In the light of his later performances, I incline to the opinion that he saw them.

Quite early in the experiments, I found that I frequently drew information from Coz when he was in trance, for sometimes I knew the date of a coin before he gave it, or the content of the slip of paper at his forehead before he "read" it. Occasionally I caught glimpses of persons and places I did not recognize, which he told me were familiar to him. Once I "saw" him engaged in fellatio with a youth we knew, whose outward character seemed so moral that the very glimpse shocked me. As delicately as possible, when Coz was out of trance, I asked him if he ever had had an affair with that particular youth, and he stared at me incredulously.

"With *him?* You've got to be out of your mind!"

"Well, would you *like* to have?" I asked, knowing that what one has had and what one would like to have often are the universe apart and supposing that I had glimpsed a fantasy.

"Wow!" he answered voluminously. "Are you going to get him for me?"

"What?"

"You've hypnotized him before! Please! You *owe* me something."

I added fantasies to the things that can be transmitted telepathically, and realized that I had stuck my foot into some very sticky mud. Coz kept insisting that I hypnotize the good-looking boy and give him suggestion that would make him willing, until—I *did* owe Coz something—I hypnotized Coz instead, and gave *him* suggestion that he was experiencing what he wished with the other youth. And I added with posthypnotic suggestion that he would remember it as the most satisfying experience of that type he had ever enjoyed!

Later, still chuckling inside over the solo pantomime Coz had enacted in trance, it occurred to me what this trick might lead to. So I hurried to Coz's room, hypnotized him again, and gave him suggestion that though the experience had been incomparable, he would never suggest a repetition to the boy, or again feel any desire for him.

Thus came about what must be one of the most bizarre hypnotic situations in history, for as Coz "remembered," whenever he took a fancy to any handsome youth, he importuned me to "get" him. To satisfy Coz, I told him I could get him a youth who exactly resembled a nude photograph Coz kept concealed in his room. I hypnotized Coz and turned the imaginary demigod over to him for his very own, handing him an unseen key to an imaginary door in a pleasure-house of fantasy where he could find his idol always the same, always waiting, and always eager to cooperate. I told Coz the only unfortunate thing was that this youth was in only on Saturday nights, but that the rest of the time Coz would go about his normal activities without thinking of him other than to recall the pleasures of his past rendezvous and anticipate the next. I suppose even yet, if Coz is living, he renews his trance (by locking his door), lies down in the embrace of his magnificent imaginary companion and commits immaculate, illusional sins with consummate satisfaction. So if anyone knows a Virginian, a William and Mary graduate now fifty, who behaves explicably except on Saturday nights, but then at dusk begins to exhibit extreme restlessness, locks himself in his room, and emerges Sunday morning looking somewhat haggard, but in rare good humor, maybe it is Coz.

Coz's astonishing ability to see clairvoyantly made it possible to blindfold him and have him give descriptions of students who came in, giving their physical peculiarities and remarks as to their characteristics. Privately I instructed him to ferret out the individualizing characteristics from the minds of the boys themselves, and sometimes he said things which embarrassed.

After one student came in with his roommate and Coz described him, mentioning his thick-lensed glasses, his prominent teeth and his clothing, he added, "And he has a cold now, and habitually picks his nose and puts the snot in his mouth." The boy turned red and stammered denial, but his roommate chortled, "You do so!"

One boy he greatly alarmed was a visitor from another dormitory. Coz got off to a poor start with him, calling his aqua shirt "blue" (I learned later that the boy himself was colorblind!), and saying the youth needed a haircut, which seemed to me hardly the case.

I concentrated on the boy's appearance, trying to convey the command to mention his large conspicuous ears. "You are entering a deeper state of sleep," I suggested. "You see him very clearly, and will mention the feature about him which is most distinctively identifying."

Coz frowned, and presently said, "He has a large mole. He has several moles."

I scrutinized the youth and did not see a blemish on him. "You are going into the deepest trance possible and you will see with perfect vision. Now be accurate and say what is the most important difference about him."

"He has five brown moles on his abdomen," Coz murmured presently from the utter depths of trance. "They are ordinary moles, and do not matter. But he has a very large one at his scrotum. It is the most important feature of his body, for if he does not have it removed, when he is about thirty-five, it will turn into a melanoma and kill him."

"Good God!" the youth cried, turning pale. "What's a melanoma?"

No one seemed to know, so I ventured a guess. "The only thing I ever heard of a mole's turning into is a cancer—a black rodent cancer, usually fatal."

"Do you have a big mole there?" the boy who came with him asked.

Yes!" he exclaimed. "It even bothers me a little sometimes!"

"If he could see the mole, maybe he can see what it will do," I said. "I think you ought to have it seen to."

"I sure am," he agreed. "My girl's been saying so for months!"

Everyone was greatly amused by his unthinking candor, but when he showed the group the five moles on his stomach and allowed them to examine the large one, their awe of Coz's ability was boundless.

I myself was no less amazed, so later when we were alone and Coz was out of trance and lying idly on my bed as was his custom, I asked him exactly how he received the information, and from what source, but he only grunted that he did not know.

"Did you know the boy already?" I asked him.

"I've seen him around a lot on campus," he yawned, "but I didn't know about the mole."

"Did you already know the word *melanoma*?"

"I don't think I ever heard it until you woke me, and they were talking about what I told him. Maybe if you'd put me under again I could say how I saw it."

"Well, look at the picture and then tell me all you can."

He stared up and went into trance. "Now I see him coming in," he said presently. I supposed Coz meant "into the room," but he continued: "He's sitting on the edge of a bed holding his penis up and looking at the mole. He has a worried look on his face."

"You saw that the first time?"

"Yes. Now it comes off and starts growing enormously large—bigger than he is, and turning black and horrible. He's worried frantic. He looks as if he's about thirty-five years old. Then I see him with a doctor, and when the doctor examines him he says it's a melanoma. I see him in a hospital bed with a woman and a little girl visiting him. Then he is in a casket, and the woman and girl are crying, and there is an old couple crying—his parents."

"You said it would kill him if he doesn't have it removed. How did you know that?"

"I saw him at about the age he is now, and the doctor he is with is looking at the mole. Then on an operating table, and again I see him aged about thirty-five, and the woman and girl are with him in a park near a lake, somewhere, eating a picnic dinner."

"You saw all that while I was trying to get you to answer?"

"It bothers me—you keep trying to get me to mention his big ears— you *said* tell his most important difference. The mole is the most important."

I woke him and we perused the old book, trying to find mention of the possibility of prophetic messages. It spoke of mesmeric sleep as a possible means of determining morbid internal conditions, but not of foretelling future development of diseases or conditions.

"You know, there's a nut of some kind at Virginia Beach named

Edward Casey or something who goes into trances and tells people things like that," Coz mused.

"Does he do it under hypnosis?"

"I don't know. Aunt Helen knows a woman who went to him. He told her the doctors had been treating her for the wrong thing; told her what was the matter, and what to do; and she got well."

It was my first information about a remarkable man—not Edward Casey, of course, but Edgar Cayce.

"I'd think that if a subject can tell such things, doctors would have hypnotists diagnose for them," I said.

"Who'd go to a doctor who did that? Nobody would believe what somebody in trance said."

But the youth with the mole made a special trip home that Friday and was examined. The doctor declared that the mole had the appearance of threatening to turn malignant, and removed it during the Thanksgiving holidays. The boy was touchingly grateful to us.

I tried having Coz describe relatives and friends of the boys and in one case, he gave the correct name of an aunt of one of them, saying that it was Alvina. The boy argued that it was not her name, but Coz demanded that he write her. When the youth did, and the woman declared that she had been named Alvina at birth, but so detested the name that she never allowed anyone to use it after her childhood, I began to wonder how far Coz's mind ranged in its contacts. This identification of persons at a distance was very popular with the audiences we drew, and once seemed convincingly evidential that Coz had just the same power as a Spiritualist medium—whether that be to contact discarnate consciousnesses or to draw information from the mind of a living person, I still am not absolutely sure.

On that occasion I asked Coz to describe the person nearest to one of the boys who had come in. He began: "I see her name very clearly; it is Martha Jane—it's cut on a slab of granite. She's about forty-five, and she has a broken ring on her hand. I see her lying as if asleep with white silk or satin all around her."

"Mother!" the boy gasped. "He's seeing her tombstone and he sees her in her casket!"

"Coz," I directed, "you are to describe the person who is nearest to this boy *now*. His mother is dead."

"She *is* nearest to him," he said from the depths of trance. "She always was, and now she is standing by his chair."

"She's still with me?" the youth cried.

"She's smiling. She bent over and kissed you on the forehead."

"Does this spirit have a message?" I asked, almost involuntarily.

"Kathy," Coz breathed. "She says go back to Kathy."

"Do you understand what he means?" I asked the young man.

"Yes," he faltered. "Kathy was my girl when Mother was alive. Now I'm going with someone else, but I still love Kathy—so did Mother."

"She says Kathy is the only right one for you. She says Kathy still loves you in spite of the quarrel, and has stayed true to you all this time. She also says Christine only believes you will come into all the money."

"She knows about Christine!"

"Your mother says she loves you and is with you all the time—she says she's glad you put the broken ring on her finger—the one with which she was married."

The youth was crying silently, and everyone in the room was hushed. For all of them it was their first message from the dead. But who can say "from the dead" with certainty! The youth admitted that he still loved the girl. He certainly knew he had placed his mother's original wedding ring on her finger. He was engaged to the girl Christine.

Still, who can say with certainty that the message did *not* come from his mother's spirit? I never knew. I do know that he broke his engagement and went back to the girl he loved because of it, and even if the detail of Christine's interest in his money came from the depth of his own subconsciousness, I think it may have been a wise change. He believed with all his heart that his mother's spirit spoke through Coz, that she had kissed him and reassured him of her love and of her presence. In such cases it is unkind to raise questions or implant doubt, for he was profoundly comforted, and his loneliness without father or mother was not as it had been before.

One afternoon when I came in, trying not to think of Stud, who had broken his resolution and written me, I found Coz lying with my pillows at the foot of the bed, gazing up at the *Köln Altarpiece*. He was in trance sufficiently not to notice me, his eyes following movements he fancied he saw in the picture. "Stay in trance, Coz," I directed. "It will grow deeper and deeper. You will hear me, but not notice me. You will keep seeing what is moving and will tell me what you see."

He replied in the remote voice he used when in deep trance, "I see you coming back down the mountain."

Since before he had reported only scenes of sin, suffering, guilt, or horror, I was fascinated, as I was by the word "back." "Go into the deepest sleep you can, and begin when you first saw me," I instructed. "What was I doing up there, and how did you know it was me?"

"It's you—in your own body," he replied. "I'd know those tan pants and that old tweed coat anywhere. Anyhow, you are near enough so I can make out your face."

"What is happening as you first see me?"

"You are in bed naked with another fellow," he sighed. "He's your guy back home. Wow, next to Jim, he's the best-looking thing I ever saw."

I wondered who Jim was, not asking him aloud.

"You know—Jim Hungerford, my Saturday-night guy."

I had not given Coz any name for his fantasy-companion. "Stud's handsome, all right," I agreed. "What are we doing?"

"Nothing. You are just lying with your arms around each other. He loves you. It's in his eyes, and in his face, and in his tenderness. Before Jim came along I always wished somebody like that would hold *me* in his arms and sincerely love me. I needed so terribly to be loved, and nobody ever really did."

As he said nothing else, after a time I asked, "What are you watching that makes you have such an odd expression on your face?"

"I can't describe it. It's like something in a movie. You are changing into somebody else. You were there in his arms nearly as male as he is. Then you began blurring, and when the blur cleared you were not yourself, or even a man any longer, but a beautiful woman with a heart-shaped face and a mass of long, black, flowing hair. She is as beautiful a woman as he is man."

"You are seeing me as I yearned to be with him," I murmured. "That is the part of me who loved him. Her name's Zaïda."

"He is lying asleep now with his hand still on her, and she is lying with her lips touching his cheek. I see tears on her face."

"Yes, always," I murmured.

Puzzlement filled his expression, and he breathed, "Now you're in two places. You are still in the bed, but I see you on the seashore. I don't know how I know it's an island, but I do. There's a town and a temple above it on the hill."

"We dreamed about it once," I breathed, "It's all a fantasy."

"It's fading away. It is growing dark. You and he are gone. It's cold, and empty, and terrifying! I'm so alone! So fearfully alone!" He had a tortured look on his face, one of terror and anguish.

"Coz," I said with concern. "Everything's all right! I'm here with you; it will grow light again. Here, take my hand. You will know then that I'm with you, and you'll not be afraid."

He clutched my hand and the look of fear disappeared as his eyes began following movements in the picture again.

"The frame is melting away," he murmured. "It's not the picture now; it's the mountain. I see a balance taking form."

"What kind of balance?"

"Brass, like one Mother keeps wax fruit in on the sideboard. But it's so huge the top is as high as the hill beyond it. You are standing in one of the pans, and your guy is in the other. It just weighs even because he's holding out a heart to you, and you're offering him a heart of stone. Then three old hags come and take the stone away from you and force a heart like the one he has into your hand. Then the balance weighs for him."

"What are they like, the three women?"

"Weird looking. They look as old as the earth, but they have wreaths of flowers on their heads."

"Those are the Fates," I mused.

"Now a woman with a veil comes up carrying a newborn boy. You reach for it to hold so you will balance with him, but the old women will not allow her to give you the baby. They make her lay it in the other tray with him. You seem to see that you can never weigh equally, and climb down out of the tray as the old women laugh and mock at you. You turn and lay the heart of flesh at his feet, and, weeping, start up the hill."

"Coz," I sobbed.

"As you climb, a demon flies down in front of you and forces a knife into your hand. She is horrible. Her skin is scaly like a snake's, and her long, hanging breasts and her wings are leathery like the wings of a bat.

Serpents writhe in her hair, and blood runs from her eyes. She keeps motioning to you to kill yourself with the knife."

"I couldn't, Coz; it was not my body."

"She keeps clawing at you, and you take the knife and cut off your beautiful hair and give it to her. Then she claws at your breasts and keeps demanding them, and you cut them off and she takes them and flies away."

"That was one of the Erenyes," I breathed, "one of the Daughters of Night."

"With blood flowing from those horrible wounds you stagger on up to the top, and sink down at the cross, and your blood covers the ground with that from His feet and hands and the wound in His side. You lie there dying."

"But you said you saw me coming *down*," I breathed, after he watched solemnly for what seemed a long time, and tears began running down his cheeks.

"As you lie there, your wounds close, and after a long time you arise, and are back in your own body, a man's. Your clothes appear on you, and you bow before the cross and start coming down."

Not wishing him to remember even a vague impression of the half-pagan, half-Christian passion he had witnessed, I told him that he would forget utterly that he had seen any of it, and would suppose when he awoke that I had just come in. ". . . When I say five, you will wake fully, rested and relaxed, and in a pleasant state of mind. You will suppose that you merely fell asleep. You will remember nothing. Even in trance you cannot repeat any of this you just told me."

When I awoke him, he opened his eyes in surprise, saw me, yawned, and said, "Goodness, I must have fallen asleep as I was looking at that crazy picture. Have you been here long?"

"Only a little while," I replied casually. "You look as if you had a nice nap."

"I came as soon as I got out of that damned laboratory," he said, glancing at his watch, "to find out what was wrong. When I met you as I was coming from lunch, you looked as if you had been crying."

"Me?" I exclaimed, feigning surprise. "You must have been imagining things."

"I don't think so. I could feel something wrong as I waited. I tried to find your mind and see what it was, and saw you sitting under a mimosa tree reading a letter, and you were crying then. It's your guy back home, isn't it?"

"The letter was from him," I admitted.

"I think maybe I saw him. I had a dream or something, but I can't remember any of it. All I know is that you deeply, sincerely love him, as you told me."

"He has to have someone who can give him children. He has a big warm, wonderful heart that nothing but a family could ever fill."

"And you love him so much you are giving him up so he can have them," he meditated. "And the letter put you through all that again! God, I'm sorry—and I thought you were only gay! Is there anything I can do to make it easier?"

"No; I'm all right now," I murmured gratefully. "I've climbed the hill already and come back down."

He glanced up at the *Altarpiece* with comprehension—almost with recall. "That's why you keep that picture with you, isn't it? You see it as your own hill."

"Sooner or later, it's everybody's hill, I imagine."

"Yes," he agreed, after meditating on it a while, "if they love enough, I'm sure it is."

13

THE QUEEN IS DEAD;
LONG LIVE THE KING!

Oak: Symbol of strength, maleness and virility. The acorns
refer to male sexuality; the alternation of light and dark to
the spiritual and physical aspects of masculinity

*Seth says that even in this life, each of us has
various egos; we only accept the idea of one ego as
a sort of shorthand symbolism. The ego at any
given time in this life is simply the part of us that
"surfaces"; a group of characteristics that the inner
self uses to solve various problems . . .*

—Jane Roberts

*. . . There are some interesting episodes when a
severe psychological shock or deep sense of futility
causes a short circuit so that one portion of the self
begins to experience one of its other probable reali-
ties. . . . Personality and identity are not dependent
upon physical form. It is only because you think
they are that you think this sort of performance so
strange . . .*

—"Seth," speaking through Jane
Roberts in trance

*Subtract us into nakedness and night again, and
you shall see begin in Crete four thousand years
ago the love that ended yesterday in Texas.*

—Thomas Wolfe

Fortunately at twenty-one, I already knew that I had many identities.
Actually, everyone has. Some are past; some are present; and some are
future. Some are realized, and more are only potential. It may be man's
ultimate goal to bring all possible identities together, so that in himself
he finds the identity of everyman, and in everyman recognizes his own
identity. Thus he can see all men with compassion and understanding,
suffer as they suffer, and experience their joys. Then he can say of any
other person, not "This is my brother," but "This is *I*, and because I see
myself in him, I love him." Such a man would indeed cease to be an
island unto himself; he would be universal.

208

An identity, I now believe, is merely a group of characteristics. It is not the self, for the self is the complex of identities existent at any given time. Neither is it the spirit, for the spirit is *all* selfhoods—past, present and future, realized and unrealized.

The self, or ego, groups itself around a dominant identity. In most cases, for obvious reasons, that identity is the one of sex. If the body is male, one is likely to take it for granted that the selfhood is male. Generally it is. However, at twenty-one, my dominant identity was that of a person who loved a man and yearned to bear his offspring! To consider *that* identity male is out of the question. Yet my physical body was unalterably male, and the fact that society expected and demanded a man's behavior of me was also unalterable. My ego demanded fulfillment in parenthood, and to create life, the male body requires a female partner—that too was unalterable.

What would you have done in my place? Suppose that the love and need between you and your lover were so great that a mere passionate kiss brought you both to orgasm. Suppose that what you loved most in him demanded that his ego be kept intact, and his decency be maintained. Would you have taken his sacrifice, or would you have sacrificed your own incomplete satisfaction?

Grandmother, when faced with some situation requiring tools, materials, strength, or skill that she did not have, usually improvised a solution possible with what was available. After rolling a huge box with half a ton of potatoes across the floor on a pocket-full of my marbles, or some similar feat, she would turn to me and say with satisfaction: "Always remember, there are always more ways than one to skin a cat." I still remembered Grandmother's saying, and never yielded to the destructive, despairing futility which tends to bring about a disintegration of personality. To preserve Stud intact and find a tolerable happiness without him was my problem—and to skin *that* cat, I realized that I must find another self which could overcome the circumstances, or even use them to advantage.

I searched inward until I found identities which implied an unexpressed self that was male. I now know that he was at one time an Italian duke, then a Salzburger, and after that, thrice, an American, but in each case a man; so when I went to William and Mary, it was not—yet it was—the same student who had graduated from Marshall.

Two things occurred during the first semester which greatly helped
seat the new ruler on his throne. On December seventh, the war I had
expected began, opening the way for me to enlist in the service. And, a
few days before the Christmas holidays, I was accused of witchcraft.

Our hypnotic demonstrations had begun to draw crowds too great
for our rooms, so Coz and I moved them down to the lounge, where
girls began attending. Among them was a baggage who felt that anything a man can do, she could do better. She immediately got a book,
and began to study hypnotism. When she felt herself proficient, she
attempted to hypnotize her roommate, and succeeded in inducing light
trance. Then her boyfriend called, and she went to the phone, where
she talked forty-five minutes without a thought to the half-hypnotized
girl.

The subject somewhat came out of her trance, went to look for the
other girl, came to the stair without seeing it, and tumbled down all the
way to the first floor. Her housemother happened to be at the foot of
the staircase. The girl was limp, and broke no bones, but in the excitement, the cause of her state came to light, and the discussion led to Coz
and me—the truth, more than the whole truth, and nothing like the
truth. The matter of the sabbat was brought up; I was pointed out as
the presiding warlock of a coven, and as a familiar consort of Satan.
The report of our communication with spirits somehow was retold in
terms of "intercourse with the dead," and in the next repetition the
rumor started that we were practicing necrophilia! Coz and I received
notices from the Dean of Men to report to him the day after the vacation, preliminary to a hearing of our activities by a board.

Before leaving, I lined up Coz a band of witnesses, including the two
who had been present in my room during Coz's supposed visit to the
sabbat. Several promised to testify that I had Coz under such control
that I could place him in trance by a mere look, and compel him to do
things merely by willing the command. As the college might look in any
refrigerator or closet in the dormitory without discovering any corpses,
I felt that he stood in no danger. Then I packed, left town, and never
went back—I wanted no part of an inquisition involving witchcraft in a
place of yesterday such as Williamsburg.

When I told Grandmother I intended to enlist, she surprised me by
saying that no youth unwilling to risk his life to defend his country

deserves to live in it, and that the decision made her extremely proud of me. It made me feel very manly.

Stud called Christmas morning to exchange gifts, and Grandmother made him stay for lunch with us. He betrayed his feelings only by the unusual warmth of his handshake, and his conversation was carefully impersonal. Then when he prepared to leave, and I walked to the front gate with him, he looked me in the eyes and asked, "Are you doin' as well as you seem to be?"

"It's over, Stud. I swore I wouldn't look back."

"I'm sorry I went and wrote you, when I said I'd let you alone," he murmured.

"It didn't hurt me; that part of me is dead," I said tonelessly. "I *want* you to write me from time to time—we're still friends, I hope."

"It won't make it any harder on you?"

"The news won't. Have you found a nice girl yet?"

"Not yet—I haven't felt like looking for one."

"As soon as I do, I'm going to get married," I declared.

"Don't do it on account of me—I'm not worth it."

"I told you one time, Stud, I want children. I'm not doing anything for *you*. I'm thinking of my *own* happiness now. I made up my mind not to ruin your life, and I'm sure not going to *let* it ruin mine because I used to love you."

"Don't you still love me a little?"

"I admire you; you're a great guy. But *love*, Stud? What *were* we thinking about! There's nothing in loving each other for either one of us."

"You're goin' to make a real good soldier," he murmured. "You've got courage. You'd kill anybody for what you think is right, and you'd die for it yourself. You've killed all the sweetness and tenderness in you, and all the kindness and warmth. You're nothing but a man now, and you're real hard."

Once in the Army, new identities quickly strengthened the feeble hand of the new self. The uniform, the military haircut, the marching, held a masculine identity constantly in view. Soon the identity of soldier was reinforced by that of comrade, and out of that, the identity of buddy. Military life was my first taste of hardship, and it toughened and strengthened me. Six months after I was in the Army, I safely could have told Stud that I loved him, but when I thought of him, I saw him in his Marine uniform, and as I did think of him, I felt no sick inward hunger. "Military service made a man out of me" far more than I think the expression means to most of those who use it.

Around 1785 Peter Brickey married his first cousin, Elizabeth Brickey. Later, their great-grandson, Peter Gabriel Brickey, married their great-granddaughter, Emma Carper, and they became my grandparents. Grandmother had forever reminded me that when I started looking for a wife, I should be certain to investigate and avoid marrying anyone in any way related to me; so, in the Air Corps—at last away from areas where almost anyone might be a cousin—I began looking for a suitable girl. Often when my barrack-mates, comrades, or buddies headed for town to enjoy the whores who abounded around the air bases, I was greatly tempted to go with them, though I felt strongly that the best things in life are free and—illogically, perhaps—that paying for sexual satisfaction made it so cheap that it was valueless. Still I was thrilled to be so tempted. It was agreeable to stand before a mirror and think of utility rather than futility. A kid who had lied about his age to enlist confided that I seemed like an older brother to him, and I undertook that role. I rather liked myself as a man, once I got the hang of it, and kept wishing I could meet the right girl.

I met three women I would have felt safe in marrying, but three lucky husbands already had found them safe and entrusted them to bear their children.

Almost as soon as I was stationed at Savannah, Georgia, I met a girl who was interested in the best things in life. And I might have become interested in them with her, had I not met her mother and found her much more interesting. I introduced the daughter to my two closest buddies, Glenn and Olaf, and they said she freely gave them the very best of things. With her occupied, I spent my off-duty time with the mother, who had something much more nearly unique to her account. For though she was quite prominent socially, and sang in the Episcopal choir on Sunday morning, on Sunday night she was a Mam'bo at the Voodoo "temple" in the black heart of Yamacraw.

So while my buddies spent this interlude parked under a live oak off Thunderbolt Road, they let me out and picked me up in front of the temple, which was camouflaged as a tin garage-warehouse, the least likely place anywhere to expect to find jungle gods. However, Damballah the Serpent, was there, and so was Erzulee Freda, the voodoo Venus, and I saw them fill black and white alike with ecstacy, as a few on Gabe sometimes were "filled with the Holy Ghost." I once, myself, saw Damballah descend the iron pipe which held up the main H-beam, just as in Haiti he descends the painted center-post of an Oum'phor peristyle. He is not "real" perhaps, but he seems tangible. The priestess told me that with my qualities, a young man could find great satisfaction and great rewards in her religion. Indeed, I found its drums, its dancing, and its primal passion an intoxicating experience. It was religion, but nothing like Christian Science!—though the gods sometimes did dispense healings.

About nine months after I enlisted I took my first furlough, and decided to visit Grandmother the whole time. I had no intention of getting drunk before I started, but my buddies, who took me to the station, insisted that I have a beer with them while I waited for the bus. So, I put my travel case in a locker and went out to have *one* beer—I, who once when under the influence of the Stanley spirit, on a bet downed eighteen bottles in one evening!

Next morning I woke in a hotel room with a fat Puerto Rican corporal named Jesus—a barrack-mate, but neither comrade nor buddy—snoring laboriously on the other four-fifths of the bed. I felt wonderfully relieved, then delighted, my male selfhood gloating that this was the kind of situation one might even expect of Stud—getting too drunk to make it back to camp, and waking up with his tie and shoes on. Then I was filled with a sinking, lost-and-undone feeling as I suddenly realized I had not taken my bus.

"Jesus!" I exclaimed, jumping up, "What time is it!"

"*Son las diez menos viente y cinco. Por qué?*" the corporal mumbled, looking sleepily at his watch.

"By now I ought to have been in North Carolina!" I lamented.

It was a wretched morning. My head ached, and the air which blew into the uncooled old bus was hotter than that already inside it. I tried to sleep, but prickly heat kept breaking out where my back touched the seat, and I was far too uncomfortable. Even the scenery was depressing, for lower South Carolina is flat, covered with scrawny, monotonous pines. Most of the houses were small and poorly built, and the natives seemed to prove that a poor land makes poor people. Beaufort, and

Jasper, and Hampton Counties, like the hills where I was born, were places from which the strong and wise birds flew and left the sparrows. Town after little town appeared and vanished. I was thankful, at least, that my ticket did not name them. I felt so miserable that I would have groaned aloud had I been in privacy. Then the bus pulled up to its stop at Denmark, South Carolina, and I looked out, since there was nothing else to do.

What I saw electrified me. Standing outside, waiting to board the bus, was my wife! Tall, slender, without cosmetics, her hair cut as the boys at the swimming hole used to wear theirs, dressed in a chambray dress that I felt sure some woman like Grandmother had made her, her face too strong and full of character to be called pretty, she was unmistakeably—though I had never met her—the mother of my children. I hardly breathed until she boarded the bus, and I had seen her hand, and satisfied myself that it wore no wedding ring. I took the seat with her at Columbia, and we talked until—almost instantly—the bus was in Rock Hill and she got off.

At Thanksgiving I went on a three-day pass to Rock Hill to see her. When my next furlough came, I returned and married her. We were joined in holy matrimony on March 7, 1943, in the Baptist Church, before God and the company assembled.

My wife told me that she had been visiting relatives, and a cousin had driven her to Fairfax to catch the bus, only to find that it had gone five minutes before. So he drove her to Denmark to take the one she boarded. It convinced me that Fate arranged the meeting. And it had the ironic symbolism of Fate—two people meeting because they missed the buses they wanted.

The metaphorical Bus she wanted was an education.

The woman for whom she worked in Rock Hill was just like Grandmother, and that lady's son-in-law—as old as his wife's mother—a retired professor of Latin and Greek, had taught my wife English; and in the atmosphere of learning and quality of that unusual household, she had become like a member of that family, with which she had lived ten years, since she was fourteen. Later, in Mexico City, at the University of the Americas, she embarrassed me by making higher grades in some courses than I did. Having missed our Buses, what choice had we but take other Buses? Where else could we have met, other than on the road?

Often I have wondered where mateless wild geese meet, if not on the trackless road across the sky; and where the eagles meet for their life-long pairing.

Grandmother adored my wife. My father looked upon her as a very daughter; my brothers became attached to her, and their wives liked her. Ray loved her so much that a few hours after he died—before we learned of his death, and while we supposed that he had been released from the Army medical center the previous afternoon—he woke her by heavy footfalls on the porch.

She did not wake me, but eagerly went to open the door to let him in, and when she looked out and found the huge, shadowy porch empty, she came back, woke me, and sobbed, "Ray is dead! He came up the steps and to the door in his heavy Army boots, knocked, and called 'Sis!' three times!"

"You must have dreamed it," I muttered. "He was to get out and go home yesterday."

"I know," she said sorrowfully, "but he's dead now." About a half-hour later, my father phoned from Florida to inform us.

Nine months and thirteen days after our marriage, our first daughter was born. For over twenty-seven years, through thick and thin, she has stuck with me. We had another daughter, and at last a son. That should say enough about the marriage, about the woman I married, and about me. I should hesitate to say more about her, even if I wished to, for she has already been the subject of the last chapter of Proverbs.

The only unsettling discovery, some ten years after the marriage, was that my Altman ancestor in West Virginia was a brother of her Altman ancestor who emigrated from Pennsylvania to South Carolina before the Revolution. Despite Grandmother's admonitions never to marry a cousin, I had, after all, married a first cousin—seventh removed!

Stud sent me a card congratulating me on my marriage; betrayed surprise when he learned of my wife's immediate pregnancy; wished me a son next time when my daughter was born, and said, "I reckon now you did the right thing after all, maybe. I guess now I'll look around for somebody to marry, too, after the war." His two uses of "now" hinted to me that right up to the time of the birth, he kept alive the hope that I would repent my marriage. Though he did not seem to begrudge me my own happiness, he seemed despondent, puzzled, and confused.

"Somehow I just can't picture you with a wife and kid," he wrote. "I thought you were only putting on. You sure have changed from how you used to be. Even your handwriting."

It was true. My delicate, rounded, backhanded, curlicued scrawl gave way to a plain angular script—the cross strokes like flying lances, the dots like the tops of exclamation points.

Of my family, only Mother did not like my wife. She would not have liked *any* daughter-in-law. Mother loved her sons so with such possessive psychological need that anyone they loved filled her with intense, jealous insecurity.

Mother gave Ray the house and lot adjoining hers and held on to him. There he tried to live, daily torn on an emotional rack between wife and mother. I do not say that this resulted in his two heart attacks, but I do say *I* would have chosen death under his circumstances. He was the strongest of us, and with his passing, Mother began to disintegrate both physically and mentally.

She and Father had been divorced shortly before my marriage. Father soon married a wonderful woman almost young enough to seem my sister, and at last found the love and happiness that were due him. Mother married a rich old misanthrope—a niggardly, mean-dispositioned man—thinking to outlive him and enjoy his wealth. She ended by paying for her own divorce and counting herself lucky to be granted one. Then she married a very kind, understanding, lovable old soul who always called her "little Mary" instead of Delcie. In jealousy of his children Mother soon divorced him, but she found that if she could not live with him, neither could she live without him, and they went back together, intermittently, for months at a time, and he remained devoted to her until her death.

At her funeral, he silently stooped, kissed her cold forehead—which I myself could bear to touch only with my fingertips—broke a red rose from his wreath and placed it in her hand before the casket was closed.

"Poor little Mary," he choked. "In life you wasn't ever satisfied or happy, and when you died, you had to die alone!"

I felt deep compassion for this mother who was mine in fact, but never quite in reality. The undertaker had composed a smile upon her lips, but beneath it were frozen defeat, utter weariness, and cold resentment. The sad, bitter, angry lines of her face made the painted smile sardonic, unreal, distressing, as her laughter always had seemed to me.

We had been associated a long, long time—though *how* long was not revealed to me until shortly before her death. Centuries ago, in Renaissance Italy, she was my mistress and bore me a son. For an urgently needed military alliance, I contracted a marriage of state with the daughter of a more powerful duke. When I was forced to prepare to send away my inamorata and her child, she poisoned me and killed herself.

In the irony of karma, she who had killed me was fated to give life to me, and having killed the thing she loved, was fated to love it and find it dead to her. I, who sired a bastard, was fated to be called one as long as the word still held a sting. I know that in her own way she loved me, and in middle life she did all she could to make me love her, but though I understood her in manhood, and my resentment softened, I never tried to conceal the fact that Mom Eva was the only mother I knew.

Poor soul! She was burdened with dark karma, for besides the guilt of murder and suicide, she had left our Italian son an orphan, to be reared by poor peasants (even as I was left with strangers to rear me). Thank God, they cared for him well! Only he knew that his father had been a duke, and his nobility made peasant life harder for him. (I paid for that with my flour-sack shorts and made-over clothing. Mother had more to pay, and was herself left motherless at four.)

I believe that prayer for the dead is greatly availing, so I prayed for her, releasing her from any remaining karmic debt she owes me. For any and all other things that I fail to mention, O Adonai, I forgive her freely and fully and release her! May she come to rebirth to a life of love and understanding, though never again to a life in any way linked with mine. I know that in this life she was unseeing, and I blame no blind man for his sightlessness.

Over two years after my marriage, while I was in Newfoundland and my wife was waiting behind in Maine, I received a letter from Grandmother which filled me with dread before I opened it.

"I don't know how to break the news to make it easier for you," she said, "so I'll have to say that all of us must die sometime. Stud's folks got word Tuesday that he's been killed in action. I can't tell you how sorry I am, for it won't be the same any more without his grin, and his guitar and his singing. I cried when I looked in the cupboard this morning and saw a jar of the Dutch Honey he used to love so. I know how much he always meant to you, and they say it almost killed his parents. He was so fine. I know he wasn't baptized, but from about the time he had that trouble, I think he tried to live right. So if you live right you'll see him again in Heaven. Try to take comfort in that, for it's the only comfort I know to give you . . ."

I was flabbergasted. She had known of his gonorrhea, and still had loved him! I realized that Grandfather had had the same disease—perhaps she had spent her lifetime forgiving. I had more respect for her God after that. Did she know—no, no one but God knew the rest!

All afternoon I methodically processed personnel data cards on the men in the detachment in Iceland. I was saddened, of course, but did not feel sharp grief. As the afternoon wore on, the sadness more or less dissipated. I was more concerned about what I supposed was a gas pain in my chest. It did not go away when I alkalized my stomach, but grew more acute, and finally it dawned on me what it was. "Oh God!" I thought, "It's not my stomach—it's my *heart!* I buried Zaïda so deep inside me that if I can't let her out to grieve for him, my heart's going to burst to set her free!"

Since Jesus said, "Let the dead bury their dead," I felt that to release her to grieve for him would not be disloyalty to my wife and child. Zaïda's love was not now for the living. So after duty I borrowed a Common Service Book from a Lutheran Chaplain, and set out to climb the cliff across the pond from the runways.

As I walked, I was mocked by the words of Ecclesiastes: "Vanity of vanities, saith the Preacher, . . . For that which befalleth the sons of men befalleth beasts; . . . as the one dieth, so dieth the other; yea they all have one breath; so that a man hath no preeminence over a beast; for all is vanity."

I had sacrificed my very ego for Stud's. "If I had known that it was in vain, Stud," I apostrophized, "I would have made you let me give you every pleasure and sensation that a man can give any other man!" Then I spoke to God: "What joy, what fatherhood, what happiness did it give!" (I did not then realize that it had brought *mine.*) "He kept on loving and wanting me. Is this how You reward those who make sacrifices because they believe in You?" But God never answers until the opportune time.

Still I was more angry with man than with God, for I had received Stud's letter saying that he did intend to marry, and I knew that the war was of man's doing. It is man, not God, who makes sacrifice vain.

When I reached the hidden glade above the rocks, I carefully took off my clothing and my wedding ring, putting aside my identity as soldier and husband so that I could reassume them afterward, and naked, as Stud and I had loved, said, "Come forth, Zaïda! I give you back the body so that you may weep. Stud is dead. Take it and grieve for him."

Gradually the dull sadness I had felt all afternoon became a burning agony in my throat, for the woman filled my whole body and every fiber of it was tortured with her grief. The other self withdrew to make room for her, and began to read from the "Service for Burial:"

"*Kyrie Eleison*," it intoned soundlessly. I wished to speak aloud, so I willed myself back into the suffering body with Zaïda and again shared her anguish.

"*Kyrie Eleison*." Below, over the bay, the gulls cried "*Kyrie*," and the waves against the cliff whispered "*Eleison*."

"Out of the depths have I cried unto Thee, O Lord.

"Lord, hear my voice.

"Let Thine ears be attentive to the voice of my supplications.

"If Thou, Lord, shouldst mark iniquities,

"O Lord, who shall stand?

"But there is forgiveness with Thee . . .

"Shall we receive good at the hand of the Lord,

"And shall we not receive evil?

"The Lord gave and the Lord hath taken away,

"Blessed be the name of the Lord.

"O God, the Father in heaven:

"Have mercy upon us:

"O God, the Son, Redeemer of the world;

"Have mercy upon us:

"O God, the Holy Ghost, the Comforter:

"Grant us Thy peace. . .

"Amen."

I hoped that Zaïda would find resignation, which I felt was the only peace that God could give her. My face was contorted in agony. At last my body sank forward, and the suffering woman pressed her face to the ground and clutched at it with her fingers, and lying thus uttered an agonizing moan. "Oh God," I thought, "that is *my* body, and that is my *real* self grieving!"

"Zaïda," I said, "I love him with you! Try to find peace. I can't help suffering with you. You are my own spirit." I began to feel the completeness of her anguish. "O God," I sobbed, "was it sin for her and Stud to love each other as they did? Is that why You punished him with death and compel me to punish her with death-in-life? Forgive them, forgive *us*, for she and I are the same being. At least forgive Stud and let me bear his punishment."

There was only silence, and I heard myself give a wordless moan of grief. The hemlocks sighed. They had not comprehended the Service, sensing only that it was a solemnity demanding silence, but they understood the moan. I was their sister the wind, lamenting the end of summer, the setting of the sun, and the onset of the long, dark, silent, arctic winter night. God's silence was like that of the space between the stars. The trees, however, breathed sympathy.

"O Stud!" I cried. (It was my voice—the same deep voice with which a thousand times I had told him "I love you".) "Why wasn't it I? You were real and whole—you could have forgotten me and found happiness! I am only fragments: a real woman, a soul without a body; and an unreal man, a body without a soul! Why did it have to be you?"

Something touched my shoulder and I sat upright, my eyes opened, startled. Stud was crouching there, dressed in a Marine uniform, but shimmering and radiant like summer heat.

"Cut out goin' on like that over me!" he said. "You always were kind of crazy—that's what I loved about you. Of course you're woman and man! You're an entire person. Remember how I gave you my ragged old wool shirt to cry on, and how much better it made you feel? Cry now!"

"Stud?" I strangled, reaching to touch him, but finding him intangible.

"Yeah," he said, "It's me. I can't take seein' you tear your heart out and go on so! Our loving was no sin, and you don't need to worry your mind one bit about me. It's better for us both this way. I never could have found anybody I wanted except you, and I know now we'll be together again. It'll be just the way we wanted it to be. They say your wife's goin' to be our oldest son the next time, and that she was your father once. She's a damn fine woman! Love her as you loved me— that's what you've got the body for now; and when you come I'll be ready, waitin'."

I was weeping with joy, not sorrow, my eyes so flooded with tears that I could not see. When I could see again, he was gone. Zaïda was no longer imprisoned within but reunited with me—again I had a soul, and was one person. I dreaded to put my clothing back on, but I put on my ring and waited breathlessly to see whether it was on a man's hand or on Zaïda's.

"Stud's dead," Zaïda whispered. "You have the finger to wear it." Then I put my clothes back on, and again was a soldier.

(How good it felt to Zaïda again to love, with hope—with *certain ty*—and how good it was to be alive again in the light of the world! Even if the man did wear his ring and put on his uniform—well, let him enjoy them! After all, he is part of me; I resurrected him!

How good to the man it felt to thrill again to beauty, to take delight in rhythm and color, and form! Even if he realized that the woman shared the body—the woman who had abdicated for him—how good it was to feel that along with mind and sensation, the body was again instinct with a living soul!

When Stud said, "Of course you're woman and man! You're an entire person," I supposed he referred only to my individual case. But now I believe that he meant something far more general. "Seth" says, "The ego at any given time in this life is simply the part of us that "surfaces.'" I think what Stud meant is that the soul is *both* male and female, and that it "surfaces" at birth in a male body or a female body according to the role the ego is meant to assume in incarnation. Otherwise how could my wife be our son the next time, or how in a former life could she have been my father? I can visualize her as the son, her clean-lined limbs, her wind-blown, carefree haircut, her strong firm face a little altered—she looked much like a handsome, fine-featured boy the day she boarded the bus. Give her Stud's stubbornness and headstrong disposition, my unpredictable moods, and her own willpower—that boy's father is going to have his hands full with him, and I'll have my hands full with both of them! But Stud said, "They say. . . ." You would think anybody would realize that from then on, as long as I might live, all I could do is wonder *who* says! I should have supposed that God says, but *they* is plural, and I can't believe that he meant the Fates.

One has to be ready for anything before it is given. Unless a person

has his present life situation well in hand, and has attained a construc-
tive sense of balance and serenity it is only kindness that keeps him
from glimpsing his past lives. Only after I could tell dispassionately of
our passion, secure in the pattern of my second ego, was it granted me
to see how it was with Stud and me in the beginning.

All my rarest knowledge comes during moments of detachment,
when consciousness is let drift without chart or helmsman until it
moors itself at some wharf of time. At some ports I step ashore into
yesterday; at some, today; and at some, into tomorrow. Some are on
nightmare coasts such as Earth has not been since man entered animal
form. Others may be on the shore of Paradise, or perchance on the New
Earth told of in the Revelation, kept like a garden or returned to forest,
its sky limpid, its waters crystalline, its people at peace and as fair as
the children of God.

Much is certainly fantasy. A great deal of what passes for reality is,
and what makes it difficult to distinguish is that so much of reality is
fantastic—at least *my* reality seems so. But I know when I am merely
daydreaming. If I see things first take form of lights and shadows, then
take on color, movement, sound, and all the other characteristics of the
real, then I am sure that what appears was, or is, or is to become. I
know that I am reliving, living or pre-living something with profound
psychological significance.

After I had written the experience on the mountain for this book, I
was emotionally exhausted. When I looked at the clock it was four
hours past midnight, and I sighed deeply as my head sank onto the pillows. I felt terribly lonely for Stud, and wondered if his spirit knew
what I had written. Of course it knew! Had I not sensed him with me
again as I wrote, even as I had sensed him with me countless times since
his death?

His nearness enveloped me, and I could feel love and sympathy
soothe my loneliness like balm. "Zaïda must have taken full control of
me tonight," I said to myself. "I wonder what she did that brought
about all that unhappiness." And I fell asleep wondering; visualizing the
black-haired, voluptuous woman that Coz had seen and described, trying to relate her to the strange island with the temple—the island where
great white rocks rose in a froth of foam in a deep-blue sea—of which I
had dreamed until it seemed a homeland.

Again I dreamed, and it was a dream such as those on which my

unshakeable faith in reincarnation is founded, in which the consciousness escapes the illusion of time and enters the timeless universe of the
spirit, in which the entire experience of a whole lifetime, is relived in
just a few moments. These dreams have as much reality as has any waking moment of the present life. They are intensely natural—so natural
that in them one may be conscious of a fly crawling on a wall beside
one's bed. It is this kind of dream which has made me doubt the reality
of time, for in our wakeful state we measure in years the time in which
we are young, grow old, and die. But in the dreams these things occur
and we awake not appreciably any older than when the dream began.

I think that this must be true of consciousness without the body.
"One day with the Lord is as a thousand years, and a thousand years as
one day," said good Saint Peter. It comforts me to think so, for my
beloved waits; he has waited now for a generation, and has longer still
to wait. I should hate to think that time seems as long to him as it does
to me. Still, even in the body, it seems only yesterday that I was born,
and even though I must live a century, what is a hundred years when
one has eternity!

These dreams have even made me speculate that our lives may also be
dreams; perhaps that which I have dreamed, and that which I have lived
and do live, are exactly alike. I may be no more "real" and the things
about me no more substantial than are the people in those dreams and
their clothing, their food, their houses and their homelands; for while
the dreams last, *those* things are reality. I remember them when I wake,
and I have drawn many a strange design that I recall seeing painted on
some wall, or vase, or embroidered on some chlamys in such a dream.

Now I shall tell you of Zaïda's lifetime, for if Stud appeared and told
me the future of Zaïda, the story seems incomplete without her past.

Long ago in the age of Cretan thalassocracy, the Minoan civilization
influenced the way of life from Sicily to Canaan, and Cretan ships
sailed to trade at Egyptian and Phoenician ports, and with the beautiful
Greek barbarians of the northern mainland. During this era I was born a
girl on Cyprus of a mother I cannot remember, and a father who may
have been a sailor, or a visitor to the temple of Aphrodite. I never
knew, nor do I suppose did she.

She died, and a weaving-woman took me, taught me to weave—and
how to please men before I was fully a woman. She was very clean, and
taught me cleanliness, and showed me how—by means of a tube and a

goat's bladder filled with a preparation of vinegar and strong herbs—I might enjoy men at any time without having children. She taught me to make perfumes and sweet-smelling ointments, and to apply cosmetics brought from Egypt. By the time I was thirteen, the price she received for me was as great as that received by the women who served the temple.

Men said I was beautiful, and I could have married had I wished to. I had tiny feet, and beautiful full breasts which I wore uncovered, as was the custom of Minoan women. My hair, the blond Greek men said, was as black and beautiful as that of the women of Egypt, and I thought it made me look Phoenician. I knew how to dye with *phoinix*, and whether in purple or crimson or dressed demurely in white, men said they mistook me for a temple girl.

When I was about eighteen, the weaving-woman died. In return for fifty garment-lengths of linen, my friend the Phoenician *phoinix*-seller made oath that she often had heard the weaver say that she was of unknown parentage, a whore's daughter like me, and that as I seemed like a daughter to her, she intended to leave me all her property. For ten additional lengths she procured two dyeing-wenches who swore they had been in the shop on one occasion when the old woman said that. And in gratitude (for I had taken him into the chamber behind the weaving room and been very kind to him on more than one occasion), her herdsman, the young shepherd who brought wool, testified that the old woman had told him the same thing. Thus I fell heir to a comfortable house with a shop and weaving room, a fine loom, and the weaver's sheep-pasture inland, as well as a hundred gold coins that she had buried in the floor under her bed.

I began specializing in weaving chlamydes—jaunty Greek mantles, very popular with the barbarian Athenians, which had caught the fancy of young men on Crete and Cyprus and throughout the thalassocracy. I dyed the best of the chlamydes scarlet or purple, and embroidered them and a few of the finest white ones with symbolic borders—waves, scallop shells, coral, or myrtle leaves—as symbols of love, for all these things were sacred to Aphrodite. And in one corner I embroidered "Made by Zaïda for one whom the goddess favors," with the name of the town. (It is now called Kouklia.) Sailors told me that they had seen my chlamydes on rich young voyagers from Athens to Ilion, in Crete,

and even one or two in Egypt; for the temple drew those in love with
love from near and far, and they bought the garments as souvenirs of
their pilgrimage.

The price of a fine chlamys was a gold piece, and if a young man
admired a chlamys on one of his companions who had bought it at my
shop, often his friend would whisper to him to bring the price of two
chlamydes—for the weaver could be had for the same price as the weaving, and of the two, gave greater satisfaction. If the man had only the
price of a chlamys and chose me instead, when he left I would give him
a plain chlamys without a border, one of those that girls in the village
wove and brought me to sell on commission. Why not? They paid me for
my pleasure no less than theirs, and whatever my faults, I was not un-
grateful. Besides, as long as they wore the garment it reminded them of
me, flattered them as lovers, and sent them away telling not only of
Zaïda the beautiful weaver, and Zaïda the skillful at love, but also of
Zaïda, the generous,—a whore, but no prostitute, since she sold the
garment and gave the love for pleasure. So I grew rich, and had buried a
large jar of gold pieces.

Then one day came a sailor from Crete, a half-barbarian who looked
half-god. He said his mother was Greek when I praised his eyes, which
were less brown than hazel and less hazel than grey—though they
seemed very dark when afire with passion. He had only the price of a
plain white chlamys. When I asked him if he would rather have the
weaving or the weaver, he grinned and said that for the weaver he
would gladly go naked; then he took off the garment and handed it
back to me, squeezed one of my breasts in each of his hands and kissed
me.

His impudence in no way displeased me, but when we were in the
inner room and I saw the size of him, I trembled, not sure whether such
a man would rack me with pleasure or with pain. But he had housed
himself in many rooms not a whit more spacious, and entered so gently
and deliberately that nature had time to prepare the way. Besides, when
he was half lodged, his path was flooded with his preliminary ejaculation, and pausing only to give me a long, gratified kiss, he inched himself all the way in. He gave me both pleasure and pain; but had the pain
been double, and the pleasure only half, I would have bitten my lips
and clung to him. When he prepared to leave, I embraced him, kissed

him, and gave him a fine chlamys—white, but rich with scarlet embroidery. That afternoon I ruined the web I was weaving—I who seldom made a flaw in a single thread because of lack of concentration!

I feared he might never come back, for men so handsome can afford to be casual. And I had supposed he said, "I love you," to every woman who lay with him. As I stabbed the scissors through the ruined cloth, I realized that though I had said the same to each man, to him I spoke sincerely.

But the next afternoon he returned, wearing his old garment. When I asked him where the chlamys was, he grinned. He declared that he would rather have me than any chlamys and that he had sold it for a gold piece. He pressed the coin into my hand, and opened the inner door without asking me. The fool!—to suppose he needed gold when I would have paid *him* for such delight! I closed the shop, told him that I would not lie with him unless he took back the coin, and we enjoyed each other until we fell asleep. It was dark when we woke, and he said he was hungry and must go seek food. I kissed him and bade him lie still and rest; then I rose and baked bread, prepared him a meal, and gave him goat's milk and costly Samian wine. Then all night we lay in each other's arms, whether in pleasure or resting to renew it.

His vessel sailed next day. When he left I gave him a scarlet chlamys with a triple border, the finest in the shop, telling him not to sell it, that though I could not deny that hundreds of men had shared my body, my love was his alone.

"Take the coin," he said. "It is all I have to offer you. Take it not as pay, but as a keepsake—have it beaten into a ring and wear it for me."

So I wore a ring, removing it when I was with any other man. When we were together, I wore it almost as might a wife; he was almost like a husband to me, for each time his ship made port he stayed with me till it sailed. I wore the glass gauds he brought me from Egypt as if they were rubies, and made room by my household gods for a god he brought me from Athens.

Whenever he was home I put a weaving-girl to tend the shop, and took him to a cottage I bought near Petra (which still is called Petra Tou Romiou). There, from the window, we could look out at the white rocks, and could swim to the very spot where the goddess had appeared. As I played in the water and sometimes surfaced in the froth of foam, he impiously declared I *was* the goddess of love, and she in the temple but a cold, stone image. And at night—or by day—in bed, or on the shore, or whenever and wherever he desired me, I strove to play the goddess for his delight, knowing that any pleasure I might give him was but pale satisfaction compared to the ecstacy of giving.

It was at Petra that he first asked me to marry him. Boys of fifteen had asked me when I was twelve years old. After I was twenty, usually it was youths of eighteen—whetted keen by their delight in an experience. But the Cretan was no youth of eighteen; he was almost thirty, and he asked in perfect seriousness.

"You know what I have been," I whispered.

"How could you have been anything else?" he asked (for I had told him how the weaving-woman had trained me and taken hire of me). "Even if a thousand men have paid you for love, I have paid a thousand women. Is it any greater shame to take pay for love than to offer pay for it?"

His idea that the shame was no greater for the woman than for the man was entirely new. Who but a barbarian would speak of it as shame! (But I realized that because of his love I *felt* ashamed.) Somehow it endeared him to me.

As a whore can, driven by nymphomania, I loved him sincerely and desired no one else—as long as he was at my side. Each time as we lay resting, he fondled and kissed me and begged me to marry him. At last I consented.

So, we were married, and the festivities were hardly over when he began urging me to put away my preventatives and bear him a son. (I suppose his ego was so great he felt he could father only *sons*!) I could imagine myself, my belly bulging, my breasts dragged down by the weight of milk, my weaving interrupted, my freedom hampered—my privacy broken by some brat's opening the door to the inner room.

"Most women have children because they don't know how to keep from it," I replied.

He told me that his mother had borne nine children, and once he remarked that she had never known any man except his father. My husband proved to be very unreasonable. He even demanded that I give up casual lovers.

I pointed out that lovers had made me rich. I dug up the jar of gold and offered it to him to buy a ship of his own, but he smashed it on the floor, stalked out cursing, and came back late, almost too drunk to stand. Later, the sailors told me that barbarians all demanded chastity of their wives, however little they observed it themselves. It seemed unfair, for many Greeks had fondled me with hands that wore wedding rings.

However, I know my husband kept his vows, for his shipmates laughed about it; they asked if I had him bewitched, or if he had lost his manhood—and offered theirs if the latter were the case. I felt sorry for him lying alone in some Egyptian inn or on the galley as the others wenched. I did not ask or want such faithfulness: It was very difficult to live with a man whose ideas were so different, who spoke of fatherhood as if it were a golden armband, and of marital chastity as a virtue, and of a virtue as if it were a precious stone.

Besides, I had been married to him hardly more than a year when I met a sailor from Khios five years younger than I who if anything was more perfectly made for enjoyment than my husband, and much more skillful in pleasing. At first, I had been so aflame for my husband that his businesslike dispatch and single-minded pursuit had not mattered, and I caught up with him and timed myself for his second or third climax. But the Khian did not cheat me of the first and second, and if we chose to vary our pleasure, he knew and enjoyed the Phoenician variations that my husband actually called perverse!

For almost five years I lay with him as often as with my husband, who pretended not to know about him. He was too vain to admit that he could have a rival—or he loved me too much to admit my infidelity. He took up heavy drinking and grew morose. He never beat me, but he made me suffer perpetual guilt, saying and doing all he could to prove he loved me. When he was home I wove continually, and if he was drunk when he wanted me, I refused him. Then the Khian was drowned in a storm off Crete, and at thirty I found myself with only a husband who often vexed me.

One evening a Greek of the mainland stock, blond and blue-eyed, absolutely barbarian, novel and exciting, stuck a Phoenician gold piece in my hand, and came to bed almost as if afraid of me. As I toyed with him, expecting more virility, he blurted, "I guess you can tell—I've never had a woman."

I could hardly imagine any boy's reaching eighteen without having enjoyed dozens of girls. As far as I knew he was the first in my life for whom I was the first. "Then I must make your first woman one you can never forget," I murmured, as I put my arms around him and kissed him. "Your hair is spun of golden sunlight, and your eyes are the sea when the sky is clear. Tell me about yourself—where were you born; what is your homeland like; what made you decide to be a sailor?"

He began boasting that he had been on the sea since he was sixteen, saying that he had gone to Egypt on his first voyage, and later to Crete and to the Phoenician cities. I laced my fingers with his, and stroked and patted his forearm. When he seemed sufficiently at ease, I placed the hand I had been holding on one of my breasts. Soon he took the other one in his other hand.

Nevertheless, I did pretend not to notice, and kept on talking, and after stroking his hair, I began letting my fingers stray down his cheek to the throat, and began to stroke the sensitive hollow where his pulse could be felt quickening. I let my fingers move to his chest, then with tantalizing slowness, fingering the silky hair of his abdominal midline, I moved down, feeling his stomach muscles shiver in spasms. And when I reached the inevitable destination, I found him entirely ready, burning with eagerness, and conscious only of the pleasure of my hand. I moved in such a way that he could not possibly take a wrong position. From his face, I judged he found the experience as delightful as he had dreamed it might be, and I found it much more so than I had at first anticipated. However, just like my husband, he finished before he should have been well begun. He started to get up, but I held him, and asked if once had been enough.

"But I have only enough money to pay for the one time," he sighed.

It made me feel more like a whore than I ever had felt before in my life.

"You must not have understood," I murmured. "It was not just for the one time you paid me, but for as many times as you like."

The youth set out to benefit all he could from his piece of gold. Half amused, and entirely pleased, I made it a rare investment for him. I undertook that night to teach him, so that at least one Greek might pass muster as a lover among civilized women.

After sixty days of instruction, training, demonstration, and practice, my golden barbarian could have enraptured even a Phoenician woman. I absolutely dreaded the day when my husband would return, for I felt sure the youth would risk any peril to make and keep rendezvous with me in spite of my husband's presence.

After a keen youth of eighteen, most men of thirty-five would have seemed dull, and this was the case when my husband came home. He stayed drunk most of the time, and I merely submitted to him without enjoyment. Finally he left again, and I sent the weaving-girl to take my lover word that my husband was at sea.

She came back, saying that he had been gone for two weeks from his boardinghouse, and that he had left no message should anyone inquire. So I wandered to the marketplace and confided in the old *phoinix*-seller.

"Huh," she said. "The yellow-haired Greek boy? I see him every day, headed for the Greek market. They say he works for the old fish-merchant, and is living with one of the temple girls. I saw him with her, a barbarian with blue eyes and yellow hair like his, and if any two ever were in love, I'd say they are."

I pronounced an oath that I had picked up from some outlandish heathen from the coast of the great sea second beyond the Dardanelles. I had no idea what it meant, but it expressed my feelings perfectly, for the sound of it suggested human sacrifice, fire, blood, and disembowelment.

The ingratitude! The callousness! It was exactly what one might expect of a yellow-haired, blue-eyed barbarian—of any younger lover! I felt compassion for my husband, keeping his marriage vows while his wife made a fool of herself, and left the dye-shop determined to be a true wife to him.

But a young kinsman of the Khian saw me as I went past the inn, and followed me home. He reminded me greatly of my former lover, and I found myself wondering if he were such a man as the other had been. I let him in, realizing by his almost insulting self-assurance that he was a youth I had no need to guide.

He kept coming back, and one day, arriving, unexpectedly, my husband found us together. He would have killed the young man with a wicked-looking knife, but I clung to his arm and pleaded with him.

"I'm to blame," I cried, knowing that he would not kill me. "I brought him here! I told him I'm a widow."

My husband suddenly looked old, broken, and pitiful. He gave a great despairing sigh, tossed the knife to the youth, who looked as if he accounted himself the same as dead, and said, "Pick up the knife, boy.

Please take it and kill me!" and tears began rolling down his wind-bronzed cheeks.

The astonished youth made no move, but my husband turned to me. "I was just like him at that age," he said, almost patiently. "How can I blame him? And you are what you always were, and you can't help that. I'll always love you, but I've put up with all that I can take." He picked up the sea-bag that he had dropped, wiped the tears from his eyes, and walked out, leaving me with the naked stranger from Khios.

"With a husband who loves you like that," the youth exclaimed as he threw on his garments, "you were my cousin's whore until he drowned, and were just as willing to be a whore with me! He should have cut your throat!"

"He's gone," I said numbly. "My husband is gone."

It was a statement of realization and despair, but the contemptuous youth heard it as an assurance. He gathered his mouth full of saliva, spat full in my face, and strode out too.

Five long years later, in the year of the centennial of the temple, two of my husband's former shipmates appeared at the door, carrying him on a litter. They explained that they had found my husband sick, without friends or money, lying many days without food on an Egyptian wharf. They had put him aboard their vessel and brought him home to die; for the leech they had brought to him in Egypt told them that it was a mysterious fever that did not spread, whose cause and cure alike were unknown.

When I had assured them that I would care for him and offered pay for their kindness (which they refused), they took his hand and bade him farewell. I threw myself down by the bed and kissed his wasted cheek, weeping uncontrollably.

The Cyprian leeches were as helpless as had been the Egyptian. I bathed my husband, cooled him with damp cloths, bought rare medications—even pearls dissolved in wine—and waked day and night tending him, but slowly his life burned away. I buried him in the cemetery beyond the Temple of Love, sincerely wept for him, and had his name cut on the stone which sealed the tomb. I hired double the usual number of paid mourners, and the path to the tomb rang with their lamentations. The watchers who saw me said, "Zaïda looks as if she mourns sincerely," and the *phoinix*-seller nodded.

Not long after that, coming back from the tomb, I found a newborn boy under a bush by the path. I brought him home, gave him my husband's name, and loved him as my own, cursing myself for having denied my husband the sons he desired. He grew strong, straight-limbed, sturdy, and beautiful—somewhat, I fancied, as a son of my husband might have been. The child awakened my heart, and I rejoiced that the town called the boy not the whore's son, but the son of the widow. I planned great things for him—a ship of his own, or if he preferred commerce, the weaving shop, which I enlarged and used to train weaving-girls until chlamys-making became the distinction (next to the temple) of the town.

My boy loved the sea, swimming like a dolphin. But when he was fourteen, he dived, became tangled in a net and drowned. I had the tomb opened and buried him by my husband. At least now he had with him a beautiful boy who bore his name. "What will become of Zaïda now?" the people asked each other.

All that was left was my weaving-shop, and I became rich, dealing in chlamydes with merchants in Crete and on the mainland. I wove barbaric striped ones for the outlandish people inland in Asia, and when the *phoinix*-seller died, I bought her dye-shop. Along with the scarlet and purple dyes prepared with *phoinix*, I added blue, and orange and green—some from Egyptian dyestuffs, but the orange from a secret dye I discovered, using *phoinix* and saffron.

All that I touched prospered, and they called me "Zaïda the rich." A few called me "Zaïda the peculiar," for I laid aside my gauds and finery, went barefoot like a peasant woman, and dressed in undyed linen like a poor sailor's wife. I wove no longer, for my eyes had grown dim from weeping. When I was old and my wealth seemed but a burden, I bought a great old house, and employed a one-legged sailor and his wife to keep it. And on the street I found a dozen homeless boys and took them to him, bidding him to treat them as sons and teach them skills until they were old enough to earn their own livelihoods. One of them brought me a cat from Egypt, and I sent for a mate for her. Soon I had cats everywhere.

It occurred to me that if my husband had had eight brothers and sisters on Crete, I might find some of his kinsman. So I took a weaving girl to care for me, and journeyed to the town where my husband was born, and found one of his brothers living and a sister, too, an aged widow.

And with her was an orphan grandson who so greatly resembled my husband that I wept on seeing the lad. They were very poor, and I besought them to come to Cyprus, and before witnesses named the boy to inherit everything I had.

One morning soon after that I fell asleep, and the dust covered me, and I became dust myself beside my husband, forgetting and soon forgotten.

From a time afterward, I began to dream strange dreams that seemed reality, but knew that I was asleep. Then one morning in spring, I awoke in a strange new land beyond the lost Atlantis of which the sailors told tales they heard in Egypt. More accurately, I awoke one day in summer when my body was thirteen and my heart skipped several beats when I saw again he who had been my husband—a youth called Stud. I tell you this, as I told you of my expiation, because among you may be a wife who has a faithful husband. Such men are so few that the gods know them by name, and single out—for their most ironic punishment —wives who do not keep faith with them.

14

NI; UARI! GO; DIE!

The Sign of the Horns: Protection against the "Evil Eye" and Black Magic. Looking here, the evil eye stares into the eye of God, and the devil is balked in all directions by the "horns" of the Earth Star

. . . Arrebatado de un entusiasmo diabólico
ponía con fiereza increíble los ojos en un pobre
indio, y le decía en su lengua: ní uarí (anda muér-
ete); con esto se dehabajan aquellos miserables
poseer de un terror pánico y profunda melancolía
que les quitaba la vida. . .

*. . . Filled with a diabolical intensity, he used to
fix his eyes with incredible fierceness on a poor
Indian, and say to him in their language, "Ni;
uari! (Go; die!)"; with that, those miserable
wretches were left possessed by a panic terror and
profound melancholy which took their lives. . .*

Juan Josef Moreno

After the war, it was delightful to visit with my father and his new wife
in Florida. But Mother came back to Winter Park after her second divorce and like the Goddess of Discord, at once set things at sixes and
sevens. I decided that the more distant from Florida we might go, the
greater our happiness would be.

I thought of going to West Virginia to be near Jess and Grandmother,
but Gabe held too many memories for me. Further education seemed
the logical thing, so making no mention of having gone to William and
Mary, I applied at Mexico City College (now The University of the
Americas). And having (during the war) come to regard romantic
poetry as irrelevant, if not silly, and the antics of the Victorian poets as
absurd, I changed fields. As Mexico City seemed a fine place to study
Latin American history, I chose that as my special area. So I quit my
job with the Air Force, sold my equity in the house I had bought in
Winter Park, stored my antiques in Father's garage, paid a visit to
Grandmother, and started for Mexico.

In New Orleans we paused to see the fabulous French Quarter, which
at that time sagged forlorn, midway between its former charm and its
present restored beauty. A young man can find a great deal of interest
in New Orleans—even a young husband with a child. I paid a visit of
respect to the tomb of Marie Laveau, the great Voodoo queen, and was

almost tempted to hunt work and stay in town. However, finally, after waiting on unbribed Mexican officials, I prayed to St. Jude and burned a Voodoo candle to St. Expedite. The Voodoo saint whispered, "Offer a very small bribe"; my student visa was issued, and we proceeded.

From New Orleans to Mexico City is a long trip for a pregnant woman with a small child, but we were sentimental about buses. My wife declared that if many a pregnant woman crossed the Plains and the Rockies in a covered wagon, crossing the *Cordillera* in a bus held no terrors for her. (It was her last sentimental—and economical—journey. When we returned, she was no longer pregnant, but she flew.)

At first, until we reached Monterrey, I could not imagine any human mind with resourcefulness enough to find a living in such country, but once out of the chaparral, I thought Mexico beautiful. When we became established, I found a deep bond of sympathy and understanding with the poor of Mexico, who are on intimate terms with life and death, and accept both philosophically. They were the first genuine realists I ever encountered.

It is a very poor country, and Nature does all it can to keep the population in bounds, even if the population itself does nothing to as-sist Nature in doing so. Instead, it lets Nature sort the children. The stupid starve, and the weak die of disease—Nature's way of maintaining quality. An Indian woman who had borne nine children, six of whom were *"angelitos,"* opened my eyes by saying, "Well, yes; when they died I grieved—but we can keep the three we have left from going hun-gry." In my mind, three fed children are much better than nine starving ones, and, of course, just two or three to begin would seem much better still. But the Mexicans cannot practice birth control because they are Catholic.

In that respect, the modern Mexicans have retrogressed. The Puré-pecha women used a mountain lion's bladder with a terra cotta nozzle and a spermicidal herbal douche—as I discovered when in Tzintzuntzan I started to buy one of the nozzles as an archeological relic, supposing it to be a whistle. The Indian who had plowed it up cried, "Senor, you don't want to put that thing in your mouth!" He and his wife had not retrogressed—he introduced his son to me—his *only* son. But they were mere Indians, and in their hut, besides the handsome, well-fed boy, I saw the Fish (one of the Tarascan gods) on a little shelf with Our Lady of Guadalupe. I blame the Catholic Church for Mexico's dead children.

I naturally felt like a fool to have thought the object a whistle, but I found one in a Mexican Museum catalogued as that. The curator said that it made only a very low sound, so he supposed that either some perishable part was missing, or that the Indians had known some special method of making it work. I suppose, too, that if a bronze or ivory nozzle of the Minoan period were discovered on Cyprus, it would also be listed as a whistle.

In Mexico City I found a type of shallow pseudo-intellectual whom I despised as intensely as I do their counterparts in the United States. But I also met men of great learning and profound culture. Most notable of these was Dr. Juan O'Gorman who taught The Philosophy of History, using Augustine's *City of God* and Machiavelli's *The Prince* as foundations for penetrating insights into the Medieval mind and the Renaissance. Study under him opened whole wide new dimensions of understanding, not only of man during these periods, but of man himself. We today are perilously near the situation which drove Western man into Medievalism after the collapse of Roman civilization. There is a strong similarity between the "alienated youth" of this day and the people who filled monasteries in the Middle Ages: the wish to escape a reality too ugly for the human spirit to endure.

I soon went to work on my thesis, "The Beginnings and Nineteenth-Century Developments of Protestantism in the Republic of Mexico." (Years later, it served an unexpected purpose: a Regional Loyalty Board in Atlanta cleared me for Government employment, convinced that however Red I had been at Marshall, no Communist could have written that particular thesis.)

The research was fascinating, for Mexican Protestantism has a history red with the blood of martyrs, frought with racial overtones, cultural conflict, political intrigue, and miracles. I met Protestant missionaries (some of whom I would have stoned had I been Mexican) who scorned the heritage of Spain; called Aztec and Maya civilization "heathen"; and all Mexicans "natives." But on the other hand, I found some who had enriched their own culture among the Mexicans, and had come to revere the proud, clean, patient, devout Indians. A few had even for the first time seen God—not the God of theology, but the Lord of Nature, the *Tloque Nahuaque* of the Aztecs, the "Lord of the Near Vicinity" who inheres in all things—my own God, *Ehyeh Asher Ehyeh,* —and comprehended that the "Lord of the Four Directions" is the Lord of the Universe.

The Mexican metropolis offered wider vistas than ever had stretched before me. I revelled in the glorious colonial architecture; I touched the Toltec carvings with reverence. I climbed the Pyramid of the Sun, from which—not literally of course, but inevitably—one looks across sub-merged Atlantis and sees Egypt. I climbed the Hill of the Star, where Aztec astronomers and priests had kindled fire with starlight. I went to the Shrine of the Guadalupana, and—sentimentally—to the Whores' Chapel by the flower market. I stood where the Lutheran martyrs were burned at the stake. I saw the Church that had been headquarters for the Inquisition, but it now housed the garage for the City garbage trucks. I was pleased that the building was being used, for many of the old churches have fallen into ruin. In the Presbyterian Church I saw the majestic, gold-leaf baroque reredos which fanatic Protestants had paint-ed battleship grey at the same time they covered the inset colonial reli-gious paintings with plywood—the spaces like closed eyes in a dead face. The sight almost made a Catholic of me!

When Thanksgiving came we bought a turkey from a flock that an Indian drove into the patio, and the patio maid shared the meal with us. She insisted on preparing the turkey, and served it with a green *mole*, prepared with many ingredients including chocolate and chile peppers. I bought a picture of the Lady of Guadalupe from a street vendor, who said that since I had paid him his price for the saint, he could make me a very good offer on his photographs of nude couples in various sexual positions and perversions.

I made friends with an old crone who sold orchids and other flowers at our corner. The first time I saw the orchids I told her I wanted ten pesos' worth; she gave the lot and the old slop jar she had them in—twelve dozen less six she said she had sold a maid to put on her baby's grave. The hundred thirty-eight orchids seemed worth far less than one ever had before. Sometime after that, the old woman told me she sold thousands of orchids to the poor for use in cemeteries—very cheap flowers that do last well—and said that if I wanted flowers for my *wife* I should buy her red carnations. In Mexico, I discovered, men give or-chids only to whores! The old woman introduced me to a crony of hers from Oaxaca who sold love charms, herbs, and ingredients for magic. The latter recommended a reliable *brujo* or witch who she said could teach me to use them and told me fascinating tales of Mexican witch-craft, and legends of the *Llorona*, the Mexican national Banshee who is heard weeping when some catastrophe is about to befall the nation.

Our only experience with the uncanny in Mexico City came one night when I was working on my thesis. My wife had the children asleep, and tiptoed in occasionally to see about them. I heard her utter a low, shocked, frightened cry, and I rushed to the bedroom. Faintly illuminated from the window onto the patio, I saw a shape—clearly a casket—floating over the bed where the older girl slept. Slowly it opened, and a man's figure showed indistinctly inside. I assured her that it was not meant for the child, and that since she first saw it, it was a death token for some man in her own family.

"I know; it's Uncle Luther," she murmured. "He has just died. I feel it inside me."

The shape dimmed away. I brought a crucifix and hung it over the bed, but we were not afraid for our daughter. We felt that the apparition had come from afar, from where Luther Phillips lived near Varnville, South Carolina.

When a letter had time to reach us, we received word that he had died just a little while before we saw the casket. Certainly we did not expect his death. I, and my wife, too, I think, had believed that his complaints of ill health were merely an excuse for avoiding exertion— any kind of labor, particularly.

When I asked Dr. O'Gorman how such things can happen, he replied that it is enough that they do. The patio maid said, *"Entre nosotros, cosas parecidas no son raras,"*—either "Between the two of us, things like that are not uncommon" or "Among us [Mexicans], such things are not rare." I think she meant the latter, since she did not seem to keep her beliefs confidential.

I received my degree of *Maestro en Artes, cum laude* at Mexico City College, though the work was much more advanced than that at Marshall, where I had not distinguished myself. A couple of very small children were distracting, but not nearly as much as the Barr's Run Spirit; *having* a wife was much less wearing on the nerves than wanting to *be* one. The new ego was more studious and perhaps more logical.

But after I secured my degree, I enjoyed Mexico so much, and my wife was so happy there, that I did not wish to leave. To find employment in Mexico one had to secure a special permit and work of a type that would not compete with Mexican labor. Many of my college friends had found work with the *Comicion Aftosa,* a joint Mexican-

American organization for eliminating hoof-and-mouth disease. I was taken on as an office manager, and eventually stationed at Pátzcuaro, on Lake Pátzcuaro in Michoacán, only six miles from the site of the old Purépecha royal city Tzintzuntzan (now an archeological zone) and two miles from Janitzio, the volcanic island in the lake, which is the center of the Cult of the Dead.

The whole city of Pátzcuaro is a Mexican cultural monument, for it is to sixteenth- and seventeenth-century provincial Mexico what Williamsburg is to Virginia. It is a religious center, too, the site of the basilica built by the most illustrious Don Vasco de Quiroga, whose bones are preserved in it, and whose memory is venerated in Michoacán as if he were a saint—which he probably was. The Indians loved him so much that soon after his death, they built a shrine to preserve tracks he had made in the mud on his last journey among them.

The basilica also houses a little image known as Our Lady of Health, whose four-hundredth anniversary was celebrated the year I was there. A minor fiesta in her honor is held monthly by one of the twelve villages around the lake, and an annual grand fiesta is held in Pátzcuaro. All twelve villages join in a spectacular celebration in which her image is dressed in jewel-embroidered garments, diamond rings, ropes of pearls, and a golden crown, and carried in a procession. The leading citizens jealously vie for the honor of walking barefoot on the cobblestones and carrying the enthroned miraculous image through the thronged streets. There is much sincere devotion to Our Lady of Health among the Indians, but none are louder in their praise of her than the merchants and innkeepers of Pátzcuaro.

I had read much of the Tarascos in Mexican history. This nation is not as well known as are the Nahuas of Anahuac (the Aztecs), the Mayas or the Toltecs. But they were too powerful for the Aztecs to conquer, and Tzintzuntzan, which had about 75,000 inhabitants, stone temples, a stone palace, and a line of remarkable kings, was in many ways comparable to the Aztec capitol Tenochtitlán. If anything, the Tarascos—with a peace-loving, flower-growing, artistic disposition and a religion which required none of the bloody sacrifice of the Aztec cult— were more civilized than the Aztecs, the two peoples being rather in the same relationship as the Greeks and Romans.

However, when attacked by the Aztecs, about two hundred years before the conquest of Mexico, the Tarascos inflicted a humiliating defeat upon them, in which the Purépecha women were the deciding factor. Soon after conquering the Aztecs, the Spaniards destroyed Tzintzuntzan by allowing a smallpox-infected soldier to be captured and carried into the city, and the plague destroyed nine out of ten of the inhabitants, spreading to the other towns and utterly demoralizing the Indians. Many of the Spanish soldiers married Purépecha wives. And this, in fact accounts for the change in the name of the tribe, for *Tarasco* is the Purépecha word for son-in-law. The Spanish heard it so frequently they mistook it for the tribal name!

It was, then, to the center of this ancient kingdom that my work took me, and I came already prepared to admire and understand the intelligent, proud, independent, clean people who would be working under my supervision. The Tarascans are superficially Europeanized, though when I lived there, some 75,000 still spoke only the Indian language. They are still dreaming of a time when the Indians will overthrow the rule of the hated white minority and return Mexico to its own people, to Indian rule and *Indianismo*—whatever that may mean in the next century.

Superficially they are Catholics, but the Cult of the Dead is much closer to the old religion than it is to Rome. In general, their religion was not unlike that of the Toltecs—belief in an invisible, all-pervasive creative Spirit (the life and consciousness of all living things, and the essence of all that exists); worship of the sun and moon as symbols of the male and female principles; veneration of a black obsidian altar at Tzintzuntzan; acceptance of a host of nature-spirits; and use of fetishes and personal idols. They also worshipped the constellation called the Southern Cross—which their Andean ancestors believed to be the center of the universe and the home of the gods. How well their chief priests must have kept their traditions, for the Tarascans had not seen the Southern Cross for five centuries or more, yet the priesthood knew its position in the sky. And even today the tribal dance of the Cross honors the constellation. Probably only the elite understood the concept of the invisible God, and the worship of the sun and moon as symbolic. The common people worshipped the sun and moon rather than the creative principles—as they did the black stone, the Fish, the Monkey, and the Frog, their usual household gods.

At the head of the priesthood stood the *Petámuti,* the high priest; after him in descending rank were the *axháni-echa* (the Wise Ones); the *curip-echa* (sacrificial priests); the *hirip-echa* (those who lit the sacrificial fires); the *guandatzecuarecha* (who maintained the perpetual flame on the obsidian altar); the *patzari-echa* (prayermakers); the *xuríquiecha* (keepers of treasure); the *étzcuti-echa* (temple physicians); a group of soothsayers charged with interpreting the smoke from the altar fires and the incense burners carried by the army when the Purépecha and their gods took to the field to defend their homeland. And last was a group simply called the Venerable Ones, aged persons of both sexes who cared for the cleanliness and adornment of the temple, and who were treated as sacred.

The function of the *Pétamuti* was to serve as the voice of the whole Tarascan people, speaking to the gods for them on most solemn occasions, or directing the psychic power of the whole nation in collective curses—rather in the curse *"Ní; uarí!"* when some individual transgressed sufficiently to deserve death. It was typical of the Purépecha that they believed that he who spoke to the gods and for them should have the power of life and death, and also that when he said *"Ní; uarí!"* the cursed one was "left possessed by a panic terror and profound melancholy" which made him unable to sleep, to eat, to take interest in his surroundings, or to escape until death mercifully released him. The concentrated power of a whole nation is a psychic force which can be imagined only by those who have felt the psychic influences generated by a sorcerer in a simple ritual of black or white magic. Death from the curse was unspeakable. With the mind disoriented, the metabolism paralyzed, the endocrine activities disorganized, and the secretions and excretions of the body stopped, the doomed sank into helpless lethargy unable even to pray or cry out in pain.

I have some reason to suppose that the old religion is still practiced in the forbidden caves behind Erongaricuaro, even as I am convinced that the *xuríquiecha* concealed the enormous treasure of Tzintzuntzan in caves much nearer the temple. The Spaniards believed that the royal barge was laden with gold and sunk in the depths of the lake, but that is what the Indians *wished* them to believe. Young Tarascans have told me the wise ones say that enough remains hidden to provide every Tarascan boy and girl a college education when the people again rule themselves.

How much of the old religion is incorporated into the Cult of the Dead I cannot say. Though not a day passed during my year in Pátzcuaro that the Cult did not make its presence felt in some way, it remained the secret of those who belong to it, and to whom it belongs. Yet I did come in contact with phenomena attributed to it, and had an opportunity to observe what it can do. What I went through makes the word *opportunity* a questionable choice, unless you consider it desirable to experience any unusual thing, however unpleasant.

Without knowing that any curse existed, I rented a house which, with the owner and his family, had been placed under a curse by the chief wizard, the chosen one called *el Supremo*. If the Cult's only interest in me was to drive me out of the house so as to deprive the owner of his rent money, God help anyone whom the Cult really has it in for!

This house stood on land which was anciently ejidal farmland of the village of Janitzio in the lake. This unfortunate village has barely enough soil in which to bury its dead, and clings to the volcanic hillside, depending upon fish from the surrounding water, and on reed-mat weaving for the food it must buy from the surrounding towns. The Tarascan kings realized the need of the islanders and allotted them communal land adjoining that of Pátzcuaro, but the Spaniards siezed the rich shores for themselves and held them until the Zapata Revolution, when in a burst of *Indianismo*, the government restored the ejido system wherever practicable. It is a kind of communism in which an area belongs to a village and is parcelled out to the individual on the basis of how many mouths he has to feed or on his ability to care for it—usually both. It is by no means Communistic in the Marxist sense, but a system based on the concept that the gods gave man the earth to tend, and that each man must be given the opportunity to enjoy use of enough of it to feed himself and those who depend upon him. It is ideally suited to the way of life of an agricultural Indian village. I greatly admire the ejido system for those for whom it was worked out, and would return all such villages their ancient communal lands. Every man should have the opportunity to feed himself and his dependents, and he has the obligation to do so if he is physically able.

So thought the village elders of the Tarascans. They provided for those who *could* not support themselves because of age, sickness, or infirmity, but if individuals could and *would* not, the land was taken from them, and they were allowed to starve until they decided to work. That, too, to me seems wisdom on the part of the Tarascan elders.

When the Zapatistas restored Janitzio its ejidal land, the island enjoyed almost-forgotten plenty. The islanders rowed their dugouts across the lake to the tiny garden plots and tended them with such love and care that the island produced more than it could consume. Children grew strong and lived to adulthood; and the Cult of the Dead held fiestas. (Its traditional Day of the Dead is not a fiesta at all but its most solemn observation. After dark, the sound of weeping and wailing drifts across the water to the mainland and tourists watch the procession of lights climbing the hillside to the cemetery and glowing there as the women take food to the graves hold their strange supper with the dead. And with smoking incense, weird chants and hypnotic motions they pass into mass trance, conversing with the dead, and producing every phenomenon known to Spiritualism—and some that are as unknown to Spiritualists as to you and me.)

This bountiful life lasted for Janitzio until the Cárdenas regime. President Cárdenas was a great liberal—to himself. Next was he liberal to the cutthroats and criminals around him. This benefactor of the people (his brother was put in office as Communist Governor of Michoacán the year I left Pátzcuaro) appropriated a choice portion of the ejido and built an enormous stone mansion near the railway station, calling it "Erindira," after a Tarascan princess. He surrounded it with spacious pleasure grounds, and parcelled out the rest of the Janitzio land to his cohorts, several of whom built houses on the *Carretera del Embarcadero*, a road near the station. The one I rented had been built by a Cárdenas "general"—officially a general of the Mexican army, but a thug nevertheless.

This house on the *Carretera* was a large stucco dwelling in what cultured Mexicans call the *estilo California,* delicately refusing to recognize either that the style is supposedly Spanish or of their own Mexican heritage. This bastard-Spanish monstrosity would have been ugly anywhere, but it was a blasphemy in the vicinity of the fine colonial houses of the upper town—a monument to four centuries of degeneration in Spanish architecture.

To the injury of robbing the island of its ejidal land, the Cárdenas crowd added the insult of taking Janitzio as the base for a grotesque,

poured-concrete monument which defames the memory of the Revolutionary hero Morelos, for whom Valladolïd, the Capitol city of Michoacán, was renamed Morelia. Already hideous, this statue was made into a
deformity. The builders saw that the money was about to run out, so
they stuck on the statue's arms and head right where they were at the
time—about the middle of the chest. I do not think that the Cult would
have cursed anyone for the loss of the land, or the desecration of the
beauty of the lake by this grotesque concretework. But as I was to discover, its Supreme One was given a more personal reason.

I had been rooming at the boarding house kept by the lady Maria
Solorzano, a middle-aged, unmarried, energetic, astute, talkative woman
of high reputation who boasted that she was all Spanish and all Galician. She served such fine food in the Galician tradition that her estab-
lishment became the Mecca of all traveling salesmen in the area—who,
to an amazing degree, are successful in proportion to their Galician
blood, for these people are very like Scots, even to bagpipe music and
similar folk-dancing.

Doña Maria and I got along delightfully. When I told her I had rented
the house on the *Carretera* (its ugliness notwithstanding, it had a bathroom, hot and cold running water, gas, electricity, beautiful grounds,
and was only a three-minutes walk from my office), she pressed both
fists against her bosom. "You can't go there!" she exclaimed. "You
have your wife and the babies to think of. I would bet pearls to chick-
peas that those shameless creatures did not tell you a word! Did they
tell you that the house had been exorcized?"

"Exorcised?"

"Well, it hasn't been, and it never can be. They tried—the priest went
there with holy water and everything. Such a nice young man—so earnest and so innocent. The bishop ought to know what a poor priest
would be up against if he tried to undo something that the Cult had
done."

"What happened?"

"When the priest went there? Two men of the congregation went with
him, and he learned the rite for exorcism if he didn't already know it,
and took the Crucifix and holy water, and the Mass-bell, and the Book,
and I suppose candles, and maybe the Blessed Host, and walked in on it
as if it were a mere noisy spirit. The men stayed out on the piazza.
Then the priest screamed and ran out. He was in such terror they could

make no sense of what he said. They all ran, and the men brought him
up from the station to the doctor, and that afternoon, when he was out
of shock, took the bus to Morelia—to tell the bishop, I suppose. When
he came back, he hired two young men to sit in the room with him at
night. They pulled his bed out in the middle of the floor under the light
and poured a ring of salt around it, and wet down the door. Then, with
the men sitting there, and the light burning over the bed, he sometimes
could fall into a sort of sleep, though they say he cried out and woke
up continually; and that kept up till the Church transferred him to
Oaxaca."

"What on earth *is* it?" I shivered.

"I suppose the Indians have a name for it. It's something they
formed in darkness out of darkness, gave a dead man's mind, and put
there to destroy. It's a thing, a power, a presence, a horror—but who
knows what to call it in the Christian language?"

"Those people must truly hate the ones who stole their land from
them," I considered.

"I suppose they do," she replied, "but if you want to find out the
reason they put a curse on that house, you'll have to ask somebody
else." She gave me the name of an employee I had recently hired.

So I sent for him; and he came to the office and waited apprehensive-
ly until I took him aside. "I am told that you are familiar with the
house I rented. I am told that it has a very bad reputation."

"Es verdad."

"Is it dangerous for me to try to live there?"

"Mi patron, it will be impossible for you to live there."

"Are you free to tell me about it?" I murmured.

"If the *patron* will never say it was I who told you."

"I promise."

"They say that when the house was begun, the general made one of
his soldiers guard the materials. One night the general came to check on
him, found him asleep, and found some of the cement stolen. He shot
the soldier in the lower spine so he could not move and would die slowly, and then he kicked him into the trench at the footing of the wall.

"You have no doubt noted the outside staircase resting on the slab of
concrete? The plan was for the staircase to rise from the vestibule, not
senselessly under the drip from the eaves as it does. The soldier is under
the slab. The boy said he was buried before he was dead."

"The general was never punished?"

"One of Cárdenas' generals? For killing a poor Indian boy? We expect no justice of the courts. Even for white persons there is none, unless they are rich. The murder was taken before the Council, and the Cult called the twelve principal men, and they authorized the Supreme One to avenge the murder."

"Did he say *'Ní; uarí?'*" I breathed.

The man turned a ghastly color. *"Señor!* That is forbidden knowledge! You do not even speak Purépecha. You are not of the Race!"

"They are told in the book the *Licenciado* Eduardo Ruiz wrote about Michoacán," I said. "I am much interested in all such things."

"Please, as a favor, never speak the two words aloud."

"But what about the Supreme One?"

"Well," he considered, "He did not speak the two words of course—if he had, the general would have died—and *El Supremo* wished him to live a long, long time. He commanded; he was obeyed."

"Was the boy's father important in the Cult?"

"He was the Wise One of Erongaricuaro. That year he was serving as *El Supremo* himself!"

"What proof did he have of how his son died?"

"The boy himself testified before the entire Council, and again before the Twelve."

"Do they go into trances when they receive such messages?" I asked. "Or does the spirit itself speak so anyone can hear?"

"Señor patron, are you yourself an *hechicero?"*

"No," I grinned, "not even a *brujo.* But is the thing at the house dangerous? Someone said something about a child that died there."

"The son of the general. The soldier was the only living child of the Old One of Erongaricuaro, so in retribution, the general's son had to die. It was regrettable, for the child was not to blame—and the *hechiceros* have made the Señora, the wife of the general, unable to conceive. That also is part of the retribution, for the soldier's mother was past the age of bearing another son. So as *El Supremo's* lineage must perish because of that murder, so must the general's. It is just."

"You have not answered me," I persisted. "Is it dangerous to me and my family?"

"Señor, the Cult desires you no harm, only to prevent your money from benefitting that *coyote.* A man of the Señor's perception and discretion will know when it is no longer safe to remain there. You will feel before you see, and see before it would do you harm. Only if you did something foolishly presumptious would you see its elemental form, as did the priest and the child—or would it do to you or your family what it did to the child."

Later when I reported to Doña Maria what I had been told, she nodded. "Yes, how sad that a son should die for the wickedness of the father!"

"How did he die? I forgot to ask that."

"He was such a beautiful little boy," she mused. "It occurred when the house was finished that the general had his family and friends for a very great fiesta. They were drinking and dancing in the *sala*, and people from Morelia and even from Mexico came to attend it. The boy wandered out onto the piazza and was heard to give a loud cry. They rushed out and found him in convulsions. The doctor here could do nothing to help him. His father drove him to The American Hospital in Morelia—flew like a madman, they say—but even those splendid doctors were without power. He died that selfsame night, still in convulsions."

"Was there any autopsy?" I asked. "Were there any marks on him?"

"What could an autopsy have shown? If the sorcerers used poison it would have been one unknown to the physicians. The marks of sorcery are invisible. It was supposed that he died of shock or due to an internal injury to the brain. The family never lived in the house from that day on, though they say the place is still furnished. Have you still not seen anything there?"

"No," I reflected. "The only thing is, the general had a wooden partition built to close the arch to the *sala* so that he could store his own furniture there. There must be a rat or something in there. It sometimes scrabbles on the other side of the partition."

She made the sign of the cross. "That is no rat, you may be sure! The *sala* was where the priest saw it!"

Soon after I rented the house, my wife sent our furniture out from Mexico City and came with the children and the maid we had hired as soon as I began working for the Commission. Something seemed wrong with the lights, so we sent her to the store at the station for candles, for I did not wish to be there at night with only a flashlight. She came back greatly disturbed, claiming that a telegram had come informing her that her child had taken suddenly and desperately ill. So without having unpacked, she forthwith took the train back to Mexico city.

I was anxious about the child, for she was a dear little girl, so later I

sauntered to the telegraph office to ask if any further message had
come for her. The operator informed me that only two telegrams had
come from Mexico City that day—one to inform the Señora Gutierrez
that her brother had died, and the other ordering a shipment of corn
from the grain merchant uptown. So, I went to the store, beginning to
realize what must have happened. I asked the proprietor, and he replied
that she came in and bought candles, and some candy, and began talking with two local maids, boasting of the unconscionable salary her em-
ployer had to pay her to get her to come to such a hole.

"They must have told her about the house," I considered.

"Seguro que sí," he chuckled. Mentally I heard it as "You bet your
life they did."

"Well," I sighed. "If you know of a girl who is looking for work, the
wages are good."

"Señor, I do not believe that in the twelve towns around the lake
there is one who would work in that place."

"The general keeps a family of caretakers living over the stable," I
reminded him.

"Otomís!" he said with the scorn that only a Tarascan or an Aztec
can express for the slow-minded Otomís. "The Cult would be ashamed
to do anything to them. It would be like bewitching dogs."

"Will you please let it be known that we want a maid?" I told him I
was prepared to offer a wage which took into account the reputation of
the house.

Then one day the man who had told me about the murder asked to
see me and dispensed with the formalities of indirection: "It is reported
by everyone that the Señor desires to employ a maid."

"Es verdad," I confirmed, "but no one has come to see about the
job."

"Naturally," he smiled. "It would honor my family if the Señor
would employ my daughter. She is a girl of very good reputation, and
though she never has been employed, she is clever and quick to learn."

"Isn't she afraid?"

"Naturally, but under certain conditions she would go."

"More money?"

"No, Señor, the wage is of no importance. It would only be necessary that she remain upstairs after dark, and under no circumstance be
asked to go outside between nightfall and daybreak."

"Then the upstairs is safe," I said with relief, thinking of my wife and children.

"In its present form, what is there cannot climb," he agreed. "I told her that a child of Tangaxhuan should be ashamed to fear anything that belongs to the Race."

Tangaxhuan was the last Tarascan king. I stared at him in surprise. "Is your family of the royal blood?" I asked.

"*Sí*, we are of the lineage," he said with dignity.

"Tangaxhuan was a man of supreme heroism," I smiled. "If she has any of his courage, let her come."

She came the next morning and proved to be a most excellent girl—industrious, keenly intelligent, beautiful, and wonderful with the children. She, my wife, and the children all wept when we left Pátzcuaro—I will not admit I did.

The lights kept giving trouble. The current weakened each evening, and the five bulbs in the iron chandelier often gave less light than would have a candle—sometimes none at all. This was particularly exasperating since the lights along the *Carretera* always seemed to burn well, and we could see lights in the houses near the station. It would have been annoying anywhere, but in *that* house it was unbearable. Candles seemed to grow worse with each purchase, for they were hard to light, and harder to keep burning. Repeatedly I sent word to the electrician to come and check the wiring and the switchbox and transformer, and went personally one afternoon to demand that someone attend to it that very day.

"I would be a waste of time," the employee declared. "We have been there too many times before. There is nothing wrong with the wiring, or the switchbox, or the transformer. The maestro himself installed the whole system when the house was built, and he, personally, has gone back repeatedly to check it."

"What does he think could be the matter?"

The man shrugged. "He thinks that the current may encounter a stronger force-field which interferes with it, but I cannot follow his thinking, for he is speaking of advanced electrical theory. I just know the damned lights never would burn right, and nothing we knew to try ever did any good."

"Let me talk to him," I implored.

"Señor, he left particular instructions to tell you that if a thing is there that is strong enough to interfere with the flow of electrical current, as you yourself must realize, it is a force which could certainly kill. If you must have the truth, he is afraid to go, and I am just as afraid. He says you would be very wise to find a house where the lights burn by night as they burn by day, and let the general worry about what his lights do."

That very evening, after the chandelier went dark, the candles sputtered and flickered and one went out. When the rat began scrabbling at the partition, I gave up on trying to read, took the flashlight, and visualizing the skeleton under the footing, started upstairs to join my family. I thought I heard something and paused before I started up, directing the beam to the potted plants at the end of the piazza. Under a large palm I glimpsed a huge dog or something. I ran up the stairs, still hoping that it was only a dog, but a dog hardly could be that large, and a dog has a much more familiar shape.

From that night on, it appeared just as I was about to start upstairs, and each time it grew perceptibly more distinct. It was not a dog, but a Van Meckenem print or a Grimoire drawing come to life. It was much more human-looking than my first glimpse of it had seemed, though what had seemed animal now seemed much more beastly. In fact, if it looked half human, and half beast, it looked altogether like a demon. I saw why I had been told that it could not climb, for it dragged itself as a man might if he had enormously strengthened his arms and shoulders and learned to crawl without use of his legs, which dragged useless and atrophied. I thought of the boy, shot in the spine and paralyzed from the waist down—and perhaps those who gave the thing its shape had thought of him. But the soldier had not been covered with long, lank, moldy-looking hair, nor had his face, nor any human face, looked similar. Conceivably, in the lost dawn of evolution, some carnivorous thing between ape and man might have looked similar if wounded and infuriated, and bent on killing.

This horror dragged itself slowly at first, but in a fortnight its speed increased enough to bring it to the foot of the stairs as I reached the top, yelling for my wife to get the door open. I suppose she hurried, but it seemed to me that she fumbled with the key an eternity before she turned it. She saw no real cause for haste in any case, for she could stand and shine the light straight into the thing's eyes as it soundlessly snarled and bared its teeth, grasped the iron railing, and strove vainly to drag itself up the steps, and say, "You have got to quit working so hard seven days a week. There isn't a thing in this world down there!"

She was right about that, anyhow. It was *not* in this world as something normally part of it. It belonged to another world, to another dimension, perhaps—that of nightmare!

Very soon after it began trying to climb the stairs, it appeared in daylight as I dashed across the piazza on the way back to the office from lunch. It slithered off the piazza and took after me, following out the walk to the front gateway. I ran all the way to the office, and the workers gathered around me in grave concern as I burst in. The veterinarian took me in hand, and dragged me out to the jeep. "You are going to the doctor uptown right now!" he declared. "If you were a horse in this shape, I'd shoot you!"

"I'm not crazy!" I said pitifully. "I swear I saw it! It took after me! It's going to kill me!"

"You sit on that side of him," the veterinarian said to the interpreter who spoke Tarascan, "and I'll sit on this side. Get one of the boys in the garage to drive. It may take two to hold him if he tries to get away."

The Señorita Romero, the secretary, a native Pátzcuareña, said, *"I believe you, Señor. If you go back there, it will kill you!"*

"Maybe he'd be quieter if we *all* humored him," the veterinarian whispered.

The Mexican doctor had the two others wait when they delivered me into his hands, but when he learned my name, and where I worked, he seemed greatly relieved. "I have been expecting that you come," he said engagingly. "Now just how does this thing affect you?

"It fills me with a—*un terror pánico"* I said, recalling the exact words of the *Licenciado* Juan Josef Moreno.

"I should think so," he said. "Now, tell me what it looks like. No two people agree on exactly what it is, you know."

"Do you believe me, or are you trying to see just how crazy I really am?"

"It was I to whom the general first brought his son, and it was I to whom they brought the young priest. I do not think there is anything at all the matter with your mind. Now tell me the appearance of the thing."

When I described it, he looked to be in deep study. "It had a different form when the priest saw it," he said. "You are fortunate not to have had a much worse shock."

"I wish my wife could believe that I see the thing," I sighed.

"Your *wife?* I should think that with a more delicate, nervous constitution, a woman would be the first to be affected!"

"Mine doesn't have a delicate, nervous constitution," I sighed. "All she can ever see is a token if somebody dies."

"Remarkable!" he commented. "It is probably quite dangerous for her to be there if she is not aware of it. Do you have a history of psychic sensitivity?"

"Yes, all my life," I admitted.

"I'm going to give you some pills to tranquilize your nerves," he considered. "Take two now, and one each night before you go to bed. But if you stay there, I cannot be responsible for your health, your sanity, or your life. Doña Maria said the Villa de San Miguel is for rent now. That is where you should go. Apply to Cuca Cerda next to the Post Office, and you will be your normal self in a few days."

I had seen the villa on top of the hill and admired it because it looked like a great, half-derelict, galleried Louisiana plantation house. So I sent the Jeep back for my cot and bedding, and ordered my family to leave the general's house and spend the night at Doña Maria's. At first my wife came up, and declared that she would not budge an inch, but she liked the Villa better than the other house once we were established—and the maid certainly did. At the villa, when I opened the closet door the first night and a mouse jumped off the shelf, I screamed, but as the doctor predicted, my nerves grew calm, even tranquil. And I was delightfully happy as I relaxed on the upper gallery, gazing out across the centuries-old town, the enchanted lake, and the blue and purple hills of Erongaricuaro. I believe the view from the upper gallery of the Villa de San Miguel is one of the loveliest in the whole New World.

When the general found that I had left in the middle of the month, he made a special trip from Morelia to see me, threatening to bring a lawsuit for ruining the value of his property by the things I said I had seen. "I still have legal possession of the place till the rent is out." I reminded him. "If you plan to sue, I shall have the dirt under the stair footing dug out, and tabloid photographers from Mexico City brought to take pictures of the skeleton. Is that what you want?"

"Dog!" he snarled. "Damned gringo!"

"Coyote!" I replied. "Murderer!"

He left, and I heard no more of the lawsuit. It seemed proof that he did not want publicity. The house stood empty while I was in Pátz-cuaro, and the Indians still ran past it when they traveled the *Embarc-adero* road. Then, some time after we returned to South Carolina, we received a letter from Pastor Ramirez, the Baptist minister in Pátzcuaro, saying that the General's ne'er-do-well nephew, whom he supported, had been made to live in the house when he married. He said that the town believed the girl would have left her husband, but her own family would not take her back, and one day he found her upstairs in the bed, a pistol still in her hand, with a farewell note to her husband saying that though she loved him, she preferred suicide and the prospect of hell to life in that house.

"Ní; uarí!" Please, as a favor, never speak the two words aloud!

15

"BAPTISTS ARE SO UNREASONABLE"

Pomegranates: Ancient symbol of fertility, prosperity, and happiness

> *How shall we escape, if we neglect so great salvation; which at first began to be spoken by the Lord, and was confirmed unto us by them that heard him; God also bearing them witness, both with signs and wonders, and with divers miracles, and gifts of the Holy Ghost, according to his own will?*
>
> St. Paul (Hebrews, 2:3-4)

However strange I found the phenomena caused by the Cult of the Dead, of even greater fascination to me were the miracles which preceded, accompanied, and followed the founding of the Baptist Church in Pátzcuaro. Somehow Baptists are far too stable, too respectable, and too fundamentalist for one to expect anything extraordinary to happen to them. One does not associate miracles with chicken stew, cole slaw, and iced tea. So in Pátzcuaro it was extraordinary to hear a Baptist preacher referred to as "the Baptist *priest,*" voiced in the same tone of respect as the word for a man of power in the Cult's own wonder-working religion. The Cult lost no members to the Baptist church but it regarded Baptist miracles with respect and wonder and conceded that the Baptist God must be as powerful at least as *Tata Huriata* and *Nana Cuerápperi,* the Father and Mother of Being.

The first two known Protestant proselytes in Mexico were Baptist converts who in 1867 were dunked in an irrigation ditch, much as I had been in the swimming hole at the mouth of Gabe. Before the end of the nineteenth century, Mexico was swarming with Baptist missionaries—Northern Baptists in the south, and Southern Baptists in the north. Considering their Gringo origin and attitude they had surprising success, and Baptist churches and schools appeared in practically every large city in Mexico. The Baptist missionary school was the first in the state of Michoacán to teach bookkeeping and shorthand to women. Forty years ago, such training was so rare in Mexico that girls attended the school even though they had no expectation at all of becoming Baptists. Occasionally, a Catholic girl was proselyted, or as the missionaries say, "converted."

The Baptist church in Pátzcuaro is there, I feel sure, because of the will of God. But His instrument was a business-course student who was converted in Morelia. This girl was the only surviving child of a store-keeper, who allowed her to attend because he felt that her training would be of great benefit when she inherited the business after his death. After her conversion, her father also became a Baptist, and the Catholics in Morelia boycotted his store.

Even worse, from the girl's point of view, her fiancé, Ascención Ramirez, renounced her as a heretic and sorrowfully joined a combine crew going to the United States to follow the wheat harvest. In Kansas he took sick, was robbed, and left behind. A ranch family found him too ill to travel, brought him into their home, provided a doctor, and the rancher's daughter and his wife cared for him day and night, prayed for his recovery, and nursed him back to health. He tried to express his undying gratitude, and the family assured him that what they were doing was what they regarded as their Christian duty and what they wished to do in love of their fellow man. He saw no images, and the women prayed without rosaries (those who had robbed him and aban-doned him were sons of women who prayed with both), so he demand-ed to know what wonderful religion theirs was. When they replied, "Baptist," Ascención took it as an act of Providence—he had fallen sick in order to see what manner of religion his fiancée's heresy really was. (She, of course, had been praying constantly for him to return and be converted, so maybe it *was* Providence.) As soon as the boy was able to earn enough to take him back to Morelia, he returned, told the girl that he wished to marry her if she would take him back, and that in any case, he wished to become a Baptist.

Soon after the marriage, the girl's father's ill health obliged her to take over the business, and the Baptists in Morelia kept it from going bankrupt. The missionaries convinced Ascención that he was called to preach, and his wife and his father-in-law mortgaged the store to pay for his training. He was ordained, but no church was available for him to serve, so he and his wife found themselves with two sons, a dying business, clamoring creditors, and no money.

The mortgage-holders and creditors joined forces and seized the property. The Baptists took them in temporarily, but Morelia was too hostile to permit them to hope for any future in that city. The loss of his life savings and his property was too much for the sick father, so his death added to their woes. Their plight was becoming desperate, so after the burial, they decided to return to the wife's ancestral village in western Michoacán beyond Parangaracutiramicuaro, where she had ejidal right to land and had inherited a hut in the village.

There are two ways to view such a situation: one may feel that he is down so low that he cannot rise, or that he is down so low that all he can *do* is rise. The Ramirez couple were of the more optimistic viewpoint. They took their few remaining pesos and bought tortillas, bundled a few clothes, and set out on foot from Morelia to walk with the two little boys almost to the border of Jalisco.

The rainy season had not yet begun, so the road was hot and dusty. The boys were too young to walk much, and there was no food for them except dry tortillas, cactus fruit, and such seeds and roots as they could find along the road. They left the main highway at Quiroga, and about noon the third day found themselves below the Cerro Colorado east of Pátzcuaro, in sight of the lake, but a mile or more from it. Their water gourds needed refilling, and they were famished and weak with fatigue, with the journey only a third completed. They decided to seek shade on the rugged hillside, found a tree, and prepared to eat the last of the tortillas and seek grasshoppers, lizards, and any other survival food that nature provided.

They blessed the basket with its few tortillas and when they removed the cloth they found it overflowing. In it were *tacos, enchilladas, carnitas, salchichas,* sweetcakes, French bread, soft fresh tortillas, and delicious fresh fruits—a bountiful feast. They looked at each other in desperation, believing that in their hunger and weakness they had begun to hallucinate, but one of the little boys grabbed a piece of the illusion and began wolfing it down, and when they dared touch the food, they found it real. They gave thanks again for the miracle, and ate till they were filled. The basket still looked as if it contained enough to take them to their destination.

After they had eaten, Ascención arose and seeing that a little shower from the lake had fallen recently, decided that water might still be found in the bed of the arroyo. So he took the water gourds and began climbing up the rocky bed of the one nearby. It was dry, but he found holes that were still moist, and hoped to find a deeper one with water remaining in it. As he clambered over the rocks he saw a small bright light ahead, which disappeared behind a large boulder. When he reached the rock, the light was visible beyond, floating over a tiny pool where the stream fell over a low ledge and had washed a hollow. As he watched, the light sank into the water and disappeared.

As he knelt to fill the gourds, he saw the light again, dancing on the bottom of the pool, where it turned the gravel into nuggets of bright gold. They were so beautiful that involuntarily he dipped in and scooped up a handfull. To his amazement, when he looked at them in his palm, they were not gravel transmuted by a trick of light, but something that continued to shine. He dropped them back into the pool and scooped them out again—they did not change. He decided it must be God's day for working miracles, filled the crown of his sombrero with them, and took them to his wife.

Ever since she began helping in the store, she had seen the raw gold that the Indians of Paracho use whenever they wish to buy anything, so by scrutinizing them, biting them, and testing their weight in her palm, the Señora declared the nuggets pure gold. Her husband went back and secured all that were in the pool.

Here I should say that I lived for a year in sight of the Cerro Colorado, and talked with persons who had lived in Pátzcuaro upward of seventy years, and I never saw even a grain of gold on the hill, and never found anyone who had heard of a single nugget's ever having been found there aside from the treasure which came into the hands of Pastor Ascención Ramirez. I find it impossible to imagine what effects of such happenings would be, but I do know that along with wonder and awe, it would leave me with a kind of certainty that nothing else could give, and perhaps with a belief that there must be something I should do for God in return. Ascención Ramirez, not given to overstatements, said that he and his wife were "greatly encouraged."

They decided that two such remarkable miracles surely meant that they should stay in Pátzcuaro and establish a Baptist church where for over four centuries Catholics had come on pilgrimages to the shrine of Our Lady of Health. What irony that God should grant two miracles to Protestants under the very nose of the miraculous image! The Lady had grown very niggardly with great miracles herself, to the degree that some Catholics impiously said that as old as she was getting, her hearing must be all but gone. But the faithful still could not imagine Pátzcuaro without her as its patron saint—its protectress—its tourist attraction. What courage it would take to call *her* an idol—no better than a clay

image of Cuerápperi! What audacity it would require to preach that
Catholicism is mere superstition and establish a Protestant church in the
shadow of the basilica! As for winning converts in such a town, they
felt it would be easier in one of the most remote of the mountain villages where Rome was an unknown power.

There, the Purépecha still told their children that in the beginning,
Tucup-Achá formed the first man and the first woman of clay, but
when they went to bathe in a river, they dissolved; then he made them
of ashes, but was disgusted because of their lack of cohesiveness and
threw them out; then he made them of metal, and when the man of
metal and the woman of metal went to the river to bathe and saw each
other, instead of dissolving as did the clay man and the clay woman,
they mated, and produced a great family of children. (It is much easier
to point out the absurdity of this legend in the Tarascan language than
in English, because in English *metal* is so likely to be heard as *mettle.)*
Some of the Tarascan beliefs lend themselves nicely to Baptist teaching,
for the Indians tell their children of the good man Tezpi, who foresaw
that the earth would be destroyed by a great inundation. Tezpi hol-
lowed out a tremenduous canoe, put his family in it, loaded it with
provisions and pairs of each kind of animals (except the great lizards),
and when the waters came, remained afloat on them until his wife became impatient and told him to send out birds to fly and bring word
whether land had reappeared anywhere. So Tezpi sent a *curitze,* but the
buzzard found a great number of dead bodies afloat, and fed on them,
and did not return; so Tezpi sent a *Tzintzuni,* which brought back a
petal in its beak and darted off to sip nectar from the flowers it had
found—which is why to this day it is a sign of good fortune to have a
hummingbird fly near, and an indication that good news is coming, and
why flowers mean joy and happiness. The *Tzintzuni* remained sacred to
the Tarascans, and their city, Tzintzuntzan's name meant "City of
Hummingbirds."

Pastor Ramirez and his wife decided that since God had given them
proof that nothing is impossible with Him, they would remain in Pátzcuaro whatever the obstacles. They exchanged some of the gold for
pesos and bought a good tract of land near the station, with a house
ample for their needs. There, they could grow all the food they needed,
make friends with the Indians, and by the example of a good life, kind-
liness, and help in time of need, prepare the way for the presentation of
their religious teaching. It is in itself a kind of preaching—the most

effective kind. When they had shown themselves compassionate. helpful, friendly, and hardworking, they began to preach, and presently won a few converts. When they felt they needed larger quarters, they placed a family of converts in the house at the station, turned over the land to them to use in providing food, bought an ancient Episcopal residence just off the main plaza uptown, and set up a mission in it, using the large chapel as the church.

The Catholics were apparently unaware that the old residence had been sold to heretics—until the Baptists sent stonemasons up to cut away the Romish symbols on the façade and throw down the images of saints from the niches in which they had stood for four centuries.

Mexican Protestants are usually iconoclasts, and though the destruction of saints' images meant nothing to me, I felt that it was both foolish and unnecessary—they would have brought a very high price as garden ornaments. A great number have been converted into lamp bases that tourists are happy to buy, and if this practice leaves Catholics speechless and seems in questionable taste, many colonial images are fine enough to be displayed as art, undrilled, without compromising one's Protestantism. I brought back a primitive vestment chest, inset with scraps of worn-out religious paintings when it was made a century and a half ago, and find St. Joseph with the Infant Jesus and Saint Lucy with her eyeballs in a golden tray quite interesting. Still, all said, the Catholics have little justification to complain, for they themselves desecrated and destroyed Indian idols wherever they found them, and I myself would consider it as poor taste to electrify an image of Quetzalcoatl as one of Saint Francis, and to destroy one, a greater cultural offense.

After the chapel in the bishop's residence was de-Catholicized as fully as possible, the building was opened as the First Baptist Church of Pátzcuaro, and the back patio was turned into a refuge for such dregs of humankind as were willing to take refuge in the mission, whatever their religion. And usually if the Baptists succeeded in making self-respecting, useful men and women of a few of these outcasts, they won them as converts as well.

One such was a personable, handsome young rascal who had disgraced himself, his girl, and both their families, and after being disinherited had become an alcoholic. As he lay drunk in an alley somewhere, someone stripped him of all clothing except his shorts. The Ramirez family heard that he was lying there, brought him to the mission,

sobered him, and nursed him back to health. They discovered that
he was a fine craftsman in tooled leather, and got him interested in
earning a living. With infinite patience and subtle persuasion, the Señora
Ramirez got him baptized, but enough of his original, carefree deviltry
persisted for the good lady to feel sorely uneasy about the depth and
sincerity of his professed conversion.

She was in that frame of mind when the youth's body was brought
to the mission; one of the ruined girl's brothers had stabbed him to
death.

They buried him—I think at the *terreno* they owned at the station—
but the Senora's grief was mingled with intolerable uncertainty. "I
loved that unfortunate young mischief-maker almost as a brother," she
told me. "There was so much good in him, and so much folly—that it
seemed to me that only in Heaven could anyone say with certitude
whether he had been saved or lost, so that my heart could rejoice, or so
it could be sad with resignation."

The impulse to pray came to her in the patio, where stood a long row
of fig trees. "Blessed Jesus," she prayed, "I pray Thee that if Thou
didst receive him unto Thyself, that Thou wilt grant me a sign. If he
was saved, wither Thou one of these fig trees—this one that beareth
such evil figs—and let it be a sign unto me when it dieth."

The family thought it rather presumptious to ask a sign from Heaven
for such a scapegrace, and particularly to point out which tree Jesus
should use. But the Señora Ramirez was on such close terms with Jesus
that she would have thought it no more than to ask the postmaster to
give her two five-centavo stamps instead of a ten-centavo one.

Now I would be the last to say that she did not kill the tree herself,
for she wished for its death as fervently as she wished for the salvation
of the youth's soul, and I have seen plants die from far less fervent
wishing. But the tree did wilt that selfsame day, and from wilt passed to
yellow blight and to utter death, root and branch, all in a very short
time. It was generally admitted in Pátzcuaro, even by devout Catholics.

I do not mention it here as a miracle, but as a very peculiar instance
which should intrigue persons interested in parapsychology—or botany
I do not think that any spiritual power is involved, for once in furious
anger I cursed a whole orchard of peach trees, making the square Hex
cross against them, reversed, with my clenched fist as I told a young
man that they would never bear again. That orchard died before the
following spring. I was extremely sorry later on, for the owner had

done me no wrong, and his insolent, insulting son was too young to be held responsible for bad manners. I would have recalled the curse had it not already taken effect when I went past to see the trees. And I was more than repentant when the boy himself died later, and a man asked me if I put a death curse on him also.

"Oh, my God, no!" I gasped.

"He thought you did," the man murmured. "And when the orchard died he started telling his friends that he knew he was done for. He worried himself to death. He said that if a witch could make a motion and mutter something that would kill acres of peach trees, he knew what it was going to do to him—it was a heart attack that took him."

"But you know I'm not a witch! Anyhow that was the year that so many other orchards died," I reminded him. "You don't think I cursed all of them, do you?"

"Just please don't motion over any trees of mine," he replied.

When Pátzcuaro, which had regarded the transformation of the young reprobate as something of a miracle in itself, heard of the sign of the dead fig tree, two or three respectable Catholics were converted. And others began saying that Our Lady of Health must be going blind as well as deaf, not to observe heretics desecrating buildings that once had belonged to the Church. Some of the most impious, thinking of the half-million-dollar treasure of jewels and gold belonging to the image, muttered the Mexican equivalent of "She's got it made—why should she worry!"

Since practically everyone who came to Pátzcuaro came to see the basilica, and since Our Lady of Health was the main attraction inside the building, the wavering faith in her greatly distressed the merchants, filling-station owners, innkeepers, and anyone else who profited from the tourists and pilgrims. "It is not that Our Lady is in any way less efficacious than formerly," the fireworks merchant began saying, "but in times past, there were no heretics to keep people dissatisfied with their own so-called miracles."

"It is the heathenish use of blood in their cult that disturbs me," the innkeeper frowned. "I have stood outside the building and heard them. The priest works himself up into a frenzy calling upon those inside to wash themselves in the blood of a lamb, and they have a song about it. It is truly barbaric!"

"Who knows what goes on in that place when they bar the doors and

shutters and begin those rites!" the woman who sold handicrafts shuddered.

"They should be driven out of the municipio."

"They should be stoned!"

It was the Indian masses from the villages around the lake who held
genuine devotion for Our Lady of Health. It was decided that when
they came to celebrate the great fiesta, they should be stirred up—in
part so that the townspeople could testify before the authorities that it
was the nameless, uncontrollable, irresponsible Indians who formed a
mob, and spontaneously attacked the mission.

The Baptists were gathered in the chapel for their Sunday-evening
service when the rioters were assembled. The Indians were harangued to
rock-throwing, machete-wielding, yelling fury. Those in the chapel
fastened every shutter and door, and prayed for God's protection, for
the handful of Protestants had heard stories of what had happened in
other places—at Acapulco, where the first Presbyterians had been
slashed to death by such a mob; in the State of Tamaulipas, where not
far from Ciudad Victoria, the Indians had hacked a fourteen-year-old
Quaker convert to pieces, severed his head, and carried it on a tray to
lay at the feet of their local saint. Hearing the frenzy of the mob when
it saw the defaced building, the congregation feared that Pátzcuaro
would become the Baptist Acapulco.

The rioters brought a long pole which was too light to make a good
battering ram, and too unwieldly for effective use in the narrow street.
The great iron-bound doors easily withstood its ineffectual blows, and
the cobblestones did no damage to the massive shutters. So, after a
short time the mob went in search of a shorter, heavier log, and the
noise somewhat subsided. Then it began anew, and a much heavier blow
shook the great doors. Time after time they were struck. Then inexplicably the noise ceased, and those inside feared that the Indians had gone
for oil or gasoline to burn their way inside, as had the Revolutionary
horde which massacred the Spanish in the Alhóndiga at Guanajuato. As
they waited, a girl not yet converted approached the Señora Ramirez
and whispered, "If you please, Señora, may I leave the Mission?"

"If you can escape," she sighed. "You are not yet one of us; there is
no reason why you should die on our account."

Señora Ramirez opened the small wicket door, and the girl slipped
through and disappeared into the shadows. Then she barred the little

door again, not able to imagine what the mob might be planning. For a very long time the street was perfectly silent, so finally she began to hope that the rioters had dispersed. At last she ventured to open a shutter and peer out. The two poles lay in the gutter, and the street was littered with stones and rubbish, but not a person was in sight. All night the group stayed in the chapel, mystified but not daring to hope that they were out of danger.

Early next morning, the girl knocked at the door, asking to be readmitted, and apologized for leaving.

"We understand," the Señora said gently. "They would have killed you, too, if they had broken in."

"Oh, I was not afraid of *them*," the girl said scornfully. "They had lost all their courage and run away. I was scared of the soldiers. Mother said you can't ever trust a soldier."

"What are you talking about, child? There were no soldiers here!"

"Those in the back patio. They kept coming and going, and some looked in where I was. I was afraid; with everybody else up in the chapel, I didn't know what they might take it into their heads to do to me."

"There were no soldiers," the Señora declared.

"What of those with the machine gun on the parapet?" the girl persisted. "Those who frightened away the mob?"

Before the morning was advanced, the *Alcalde* of Pátzcuaro appeared at the Mission, and apologized for the nocturnal tumult.

"I hope you realize I was powerless," he told them. "I must make it clear that I do not like you or the Mission. I am Catholic, and I wish you had never come to this city. But the law gives you the right to practice your cult unmolested, as long as you remain in the building and do not create disturbances. You have kept within the law, and it is my official duty to uphold the law and protect you. When I was informed that a mob was forming, I tried to telephone the *Cuartel* in Morelia to secure soldiers, but the wires had been cut. Tell me how you were able to get the soldiers here in time—or perhaps you knew the attack was being planned, and had them already secreted in the building?"

"*Señor Alcalde*, there were no soldiers here!" Pastor Ramirez exclaimed.

"*Señores*, did I not see them myself, with my very eyes! When I realized that I could not secure help, I went to try to persuade the mob at least not to kill any of you. They had a log and were about to break down the doors. Then the soldiers stood up behind the parapet, and set up the machine gun they had, commanding the street, and the colonel in command ordered the crowd to disperse and return to their homes or suffer the consequences."

"We know nothing of this," the Ramirez couple declared.

"Furthermore, the Senor López informed me that someone brought a ladder to scale the back wall and when he looked down into the patio, he observed other soldiers there with carbines—at least a full company of them."

Pastor Ramirez was dazed. "We in the chapel did not see anything," he murmured. "If soldiers protected us, they were of the Army of Heaven!"

"Saint Michael in a Mexican colonel's uniform I suppose, and the angels carrying carbines! I want to see the roof behind that parapet wall. Heavenly soldiers would not break the tile, and I dare say not a piece of it is whole this morning!"

The Ramirez family invited him to look as he saw fit. And when he walked into the patio, from whence the back of the parapet and the roof could be examined, the *Alcalde* blanched with awe, for not a tile was out of place, and not a one was broken.

"If they were not soldiers, what were they!" he gasped.

"God knows," the minister breathed.

"When word of this is spread, the whole city will come to look at this roof, and you will not be molested again. If those were not flesh and blood, then they *were* of the Army of Heaven!" the poor *Alcalde* trembled.

All day, singly and in little groups, awe-stricken people came and stared at the unbroken roof. One man even demanded to be allowed to scale the roof, but his weight crushed the first tile he stepped on, for ancient Mexican tile is extremely fragile, and a man's weight crushes it like an eggshell.

Soon from one border of Municipio Pátzcuaro to the other, the people related that a great miracle had occurred to the Baptists at the Mission. And it gained in the telling, until St. Michael was said to have worn the insignia of a full general, and the lesser angels, that of corporal, at the very least. The Mission added members every day from those who witnessed—or claimed to have witnessed—the miracle with their own eyes.

Doña Maria Solorzano was as devout a Catholic as any I hoped to find in town. I decided to ask her how much of the story I had heard was true.

"I suppose it *all* is true," she frowned. "I was in bed asleep as any decent woman my age should be at that time of night, so I can't say what they saw or didn't see. But whatever it was, it saved those heretics from being dragged out and beaten to death. Those Baptists are so unreasonable—if St. Michael appears for them, that's a great miracle! But if the Blessed Virgin appears at Fatima, then that is superstition!"

"Do you suppose they really were dressed in army uniforms?" I mused.

"If God sent them at all, He could send them with uniforms and a machine gun just as easily as with robes and spears. They did not come from the *Cuartel* at Morelia. I have to suppose God sent them. And since that day, I will say nothing against the Baptists, for if God is for them, who is Maria Solorzano to be against them? But I could not face death without St. Joseph, nor live day by day without the Virgin to comfort me. To hear some of those *convertidos* boasting, you'd think that their miracle was the only one that ever took place in Mexico. The Guadalupana appeared when the whole country was pagan, and St. Michael appeared down below your place at the *pila* back when Pátzcuaro was first Christianized. We also have had miracles."

"Yes," I agreed, thinking of Lourdes, and of St. Anne de Beaupré. "Are you not glad that God has room for all?" I asked.

"It confuses me, for I was taught to believe that the Catholic Church is the only true church, and I supposed that all heretics were terrible, wicked people. But I feel toward you as if you were of my own blood, and do not say to myself that you are an enemy of God. Yes, in a way I am glad that His inn has many rooms."

16

A MIRACLE FOR MADAME ADELINE

Rain: The basic sign. Do not leave exposed after rain be-gins—has been held responsible for disastrous floods when left outdoors during rainstorms. Also a black-hex sign for storm and flood

*Where America has built the great Harmon Air
Base in the West, the tourist may still listen to the
Acadian language that Evangeline and Gabriel
spoke by the Minas Basin . . .*

L. E. F. English, M. B. E.

*On December 12, 1931, the annual fiesta was
the four-hundredth anniversary celebration of the
apparition of the Virgin . . . But even bigger than
this was the fiesta on October 12, 1945, in honor
of the coronation of the Virgin as La Reina de la
Sabiduría y de las Americas, The Queen of Wisdom
and of the Americas . . .*

Frances Toor

Before I left Mexico, I had occasion to know personally how great the
miracles sometimes given Catholics can be. Here I must digress at
length, to make clear how I, of all people, became involved in a situation in which a Catholic miracle seemed the only possible solution, and
acting on a leading of the inner light, aided in bringing it to pass.

For my last several months in the Air Force, I was stationed at Harmon Air Base, at Stephenville, Newfoundland. Newfoundland was then
separate from Canada, as was Labrador. Stephenville is on the western
shore of the island, called the "French Shore" by those who live there.

When I was there, the town had been a settlement just a hundred
years and unclaimed Crown Land was still only a mile or two back from
the shore. Most of the *Habitants* descended from a few pioneer families,
the Le Blancs, the Bourgeoises, the Gallants, the Le Jeuns, the Ro-
maines, and a few others, most of whose homes had formerly been on
Cape Breton Island, at and near a place called Cheticamp (which I always heard pronounced as "Shady Camp," and searched for in vain
until someone showed it to me on a map). Most of the Le Blancs had
begun calling themselves "White," and the Le Jeuns "Young," explaining that they formerly had the French names.

The Le Blancs, the first couple to locate at Stephenville, were newly
wedded when they left Cheticamp. Madame was pregnant before winter, of course, and the hardships she and her husband endured that season were inexpressible. They were reduced to digging fern roots from

beneath the snow, and scraping frozen lichen[...]
doubtful that either Madame or, much less, [...]
have survived had she not despaired in her h[...]
Virgin, who appeared to her in a dream and led her to [...]
nized by a large stone. The vision showed her a rose—like tho[...]
meadows at Cheticamp—blooming in the snow and bade her send her
husband next day to dig it up and plant it at the cabin door. And
though both she and her husband felt sure that no rose grew there, she
insisted until he went.

At the rock he found not only a rose brier, but also a moose floun-
dering in the snow. He killed the moose and cut it into small pieces that
he still had strength to carry, and brought it and the rose home. Madame regained strength and courage to live, and in the spring gave birth
to her firstborn son. They took him in the *bateau* and his father rowed
them back to Cape Breton Island to have him baptized. He was named
Etienne, or Stephen, and it is for him that Stephenville is named. It is
perhaps a hundred miles each way that Monsieur rowed the little boat
across open sea with his wife and son. It suggests both the religious
intensity of the first pioneers, their strength and courage.

Among the first Newfoundlanders I met at Stephenville were Madame Adeline White and her sister Marie, who much preferred to be
called Le Blanc. Madame Adeline was in fact Madame Adeline Alexander. But Monsieur Alexander had remained with her only long enough
to father a son, Pius Alexander, and the town called her "Madame
White" more often than "Madame Alexander." They held her in great
esteem, and pitied her a little.

She reared her son well, helped by her sister Marie, who was a bit
eccentric and remained unmarried, fearing that she might, like her sister, have the mischance to fall in love with some man without resolution and solidity enough to bear the responsibility of a wife and family.
With Madame's earnings as postmistress and telegraph operator, and
Marie's tireless husbandry—working in the fields, mowing and raking
hay in the meadow, growing such vegetables as the short seasons allow,
tending her cow, her sheep, her pigs, and her poultry—the three of them
lived in modest comfort, making their own clothing, spinning, knitting,
and hooking rugs which they sometimes sold for a few extra dollars.
They had innumerable cousins, nephews, nieces, and other connections,
so in spite of Monsieur's absence, theirs was a happy family life. The
original Le Blanc house still stood on their land, now in use as a barn

for Marie's cow and her hay, but as quaint as any cottage in Acadia.

Most people in Stephenville could speak English understandibly. A few old people still spoke only Acadian; a few others only Acadian and Breton. The nuns at the school taught the children Parisian, of which their parents understood less than they did English. But whatever any of them spoke, it was spoken with fluency and inventiveness, and to Acadian were added words and expressions picked up in the street from English, Parisian French, Breton, Micmac, and Gaelic, using a grammar not intended for any of them. By trying to recall my struggles with the poetry of François Villon, I could recognize their speech as closer to the fifteenth century than to the twentieth—and indeed some of their ideas seemed much closer kin.

I went to Newfoundland after an endless winter in New Hampshire and Maine, and when lilacs, delphiniums, and musk flowered in the Stephenville dooryards, they set me a little mad. I am enchanted by the sea—even the icy sea of the North—and I soon found that the flowers in the village did not compare with the springtime blossoming along the shore. When I was off duty, I would hike along the coast from the Indian Head to Stephenville Crossing, where for some six miles there was not a human habitation, only some of the most beautiful seascape anywhere—fields of huge blueberries, and acres where millions of wild iris bloomed. I was perishing for sunshine, and so often I would swim in the sea until I was blue, thaw dry on the warm sand, scale the cliffs and hike naked save for my shoes until I came to the ridge above the air base. Nowhere else have I been able to enjoy the matchless ease and freedom of nakedness with such certain privacy, to feel so completely natural, or find nature so completely unsullied by man. I took no food with me, for I fed on fern crosiers and roots, on rushes, on berries and lichens. I also ate raw mussels and clams. On such hikes I could imagine myself an Indian—even a more primitive man.

However, I digress too far, for I did not meet the two sisters on any of these hikes. The one which led to our meeting was a much more conventional stroll below the village meadows by the sea. The iris sheeted the ground with their rainbow of loveliness, and so hungry for beauty was I after New England winter, that from the plethora of flowers I gathered an armload to keep with me as long as possible, not thinking of myself as a soldier, not looking ahead to the time when I must throw them down.

Each flower seemed a living jewel, and I felt rich as only one who has had nothing for a long time feels when he has abundance. Only when I glanced up and saw St. Stephen's Church above me did I realize that a staff sergeant wandering aimlessly with an armload of iris is hardly a military sight. The cemetery seemed to offer a suitable repository, so I climbed to the church close and arranged the flowers at two of the graves.

Marie was making hay in her nearby meadow. So when I came out of the cemetery, she crossed Gallants' little field and called out to me.

"Ey, soldier!" she demanded. "You arrange the flowers and pray at our parents' graves. Are you one cousin of mine that I have never seen, of those who went to the land of Massachusetts?"

"No," I replied. "I gathered them up the shore, and when I saw the cemetery, I put them on the graves out of respect. They were too beautiful to throw down on the beach."

"Our dear mother loved those flowers," she said. "You are not an American, are you?"

"Yes," I replied. "I'm stationed at the base."

"You will come with me to the house," she said, more as a command than as an invitation. "I desire that my sister meet you. She will know what to say about the flowers. But me, I do not speak well the English."

"I hope I did not do anything wrong," I murmured, hoping that I had broken no local taboo.

"No. That was admirable," she replied.

When Madame Alexander opened the door, Marie loosed a torrent of Acadian, and the older woman listened to the end without comment. Then she turned to me, smiled, and invited me to enter.

The room was old-fashioned, far more so than anything I remembered from early childhood, with a spinning wheel and spindles of yarn, oil lamps and hooked rugs and a set of ancient-looking foreign Windsor chairs. It was immaculate, and the house was full of the delectably fragrant odor of fresh-baked bread.

"Marie tells me that you entered the cemetery and placed a great armfull of iris on the graves of our mother and father, and that you bowed your head and made a prayer. She desires that I thank you. Are you Catholic?"

"No," I murmured.

"Yet you make prayer for the dead?" she asked.

"Oh my church does not teach it—I just always do it when I go to a cemetery," I explained. "It can do no harm."

"That brings me to the second point my sister wishes me to make. Only yesterday she was declaring that Americans are without feeling, without religion, and without any good qualities whatsoever. She wishes me to say that she is ashamed to have judged a whole people by the few that she had seen.

"I had fear of Americans!" Marie exclaimed. "They blew the horn of the Jeep behind me and struck the metal, and made me jump. Then they laughed at me!"

"They are a bunch of boys away from home, full of mischief, who like to show off," I minimized. "But they would not hurt anyone."

"But I was saying my rosary and lost count, and I must have looked like one great—how you call him?—like one great frog, as I jumped off the roadside into the ditch. I shook my fist after them, and they laughed more and louder at me."

"When I was young, I would have laughed, too," Madame Alexander chuckled. "When you are angry, Marie, my sister, you are very amusing."

"But no matter," Marie shrugged. It was not this one who did that thing. We offer him of the coffee, no?"

"*Certainment*," Madame replied. "Would you like to have a cup with us before you go? There is nothing made, only some fresh bread."

"We have of the conserve of *fraises*," Marie reminded.

"I haven't tasted real home-baked bread and strawberry preserves since I was five years old," I said eagerly. "I hope it is not an imposition."

This was the beginning of a friendship that grew so warm and deep that I came to feel sincere devotion for the two women. Madame Alexander was of almost the same age and appearance as Grandmother, and Marie came to seem like an eccentric, lovable little old-maid aunt. Not long after my first visit, I brought Marie a bunch of iris, and she handled them as if they were made of glass. I do not believe anyone ever had given her a flower before, and when I told her I gathered them because I hoped she would enjoy them, tears came to her eyes.

When they learned that I had gone on furlough to Québec and had visited the shrine of St. Anne de Beaupré, they interrogated me until I described in minute detail the beautiful, unfinished church, the golden vessels, the jewels, the crutches and other mute testimonials of healing, the "Holy Staircase," the Calvary, and its other features. I had bought some medals and rosaries and had them blessed as gifts for Catholic friends, and when I gave Marie a rosary from Beaupré, she was speechless with delight. They confided that since childhood they had yearned to make a pilgrimage to Cheticamp, and to go on to St. Anne de Beaupré, the spiritual well from which all French Canada drinks. Protestant as I am, if I had some incurable disease and could not go to Lourdes, I would go there—not because I believe in St. Anne, but because I know that thousands of devout persons do and expect miracles to occur there. Such expectation is a factor which makes miracles possible, even probable, at such shrines. A shrine becomes a focus of psychic or spiritual power, be it Lourdes, or a Voodoo wishing-tree by a Louisiana bayou.

Marie then showed me a tally-book closely pencilled with marks recording the times she had repeated a prayer to St. Anne written on a card from the shrine. They prayer gave dispensation from time to be spent in purgatory and by her bookkeeping, her dispensation came to over eighty thousand years. Since like most other Stephenville women, she went to church every day and paused to pray at Matins, Prime, and Angelus, I began to wonder whether, if she found that she was dispensed from purgatory altogether, with time left over, she could request transfer of the excess.

My theology holds that man is saved by faith, but faith that keeps a tally-sheet record has visible proof that it exists. And to pray as one washes dishes, rakes hay, or walks along the road as Marie did evidences a faith that one seldom encounters. Marie did her praying to the Mother of God, and to the Grandmother of Jesus, because they were women, and she felt less embarrassed to address them than she would have felt to address the Lord Jesus, who reproved Martha for being just such a woman as Marie knew herself to be. Marie could not have imagined *le Dieu Tout-puissant*, who concerns Himself with empires, nations, principalities, and powers, as having a second to spare a poor, middle-aged, unknown woman, unable to pray in proper French or correct English.

One day she showed me a sick hen that she called Geneviève, and sighed, *"La pauvre petite poule!*—I have prayed twice to St. Gall that he make her well, but if he does not, after the third time it would be better that she die."

"Why to St. Gall?" I asked her.

"He takes care of chickens," she replied. "He is one very small saint."

"Wouldn't it be better to pray to a more powerful one?"

"*Parblieu!*" she exclaimed. "They would make jokes of it in Heaven if I should ask St. Joseph, or the Blessed Virgin. And St. Anne might say, '*Ma foi*! What does she think I have to do with my time—am I to drop everything and intercede for one sick chicken?' "

"This hen is eaten up with lice," I said, examining her. "Grease her with lard and sulphur, and you won't need to bother even St. Gall."

"Lard? The grease of hogs?"

"Yes, with sulphur in it—scald the roosts—you'd better clean out the whole hen house and scald it all; then sprinkle sulphur around. But scald the roosts especially, or all the rest will get like her."

She did as I suggested, and though poor Geneviève looked miserable and stood around picking forlornly at her greasy feathers, she recovered and began to lay. Marie was delighted. "St. Gall hardly ever fails when it is a concern of chickens," she beamed.

"St. Gall! *I* was the one who told you to grease her and scald out the hen house."

"*C'est vrai*," she shrugged. "But why do you suppose I mentioned poor little Geneviève to you? Because St. Gall was aware you could tell me what to do."

I cannot deny that chance remarks made to just the right person at the right time seem to serve the purpose of an external consciousness, so I did not object to her opinion that St. Gall had used me as his instrument. Who am I to say that he didn't?

It is very easy to smile at or to pity such childlike faith, but if one does, he is certain quite soon to have some reminder that Jesus said, "Whosoever shall not receive the kingdom of God as a little child, he shall not enter therein." Sophistication has its place and its use, but one must deal simply and directly with God and Nature, maintaining the kind of communication with the Being he venerates that Marie maintained with St. Anne and her other saints.

Considering that Stephenville had around two thousand inhabitants, and had existed a hundred years with only one crime serious enough for the offender to be imprisoned (a murder, committed in uncontrollable rage by a man whose sanity seems questionable), I could only stand in awe of its people's religion. But from what I have seen, I believe that Stephenville was a case apart, and its faith a faith apart, a survival of the

ancient peasant faith of France, which in its own day brought forth
Joan of Arc, built Rheims, raised Chartres, and made even a gargoyle
part of a mystical beauty.

I also found Stephenville a goldmine of folklore. Never did I leave
Madame Alexander's at night when the Northern Lights were in the sky
but that she or Marie would caution me not to whistle. "Whistling
draws something down," they would whisper, "and persons who have
whistled have disappeared and never been seen again." For the same
reason, they abhorred the sound of a violin at night when the lights
were in the sky. I think what they feared is called "the Wendigo." But
the *loup-garou*, the werewolf, was also deeply part of their fear.

"Fortunately, the sea is wide," Marie whispered one night as she sat
knitting a sweater, "for they infest that accursed island which lies to
the west of us."

"Anticosti?" I asked.

"Do not speak the word! When ships were in distress, men who could
have swum ashore there have drowned rather than be found alive on
that place. Did you never demand of yourself why so large an island is
uninhabited?"

"They say it was inhabited once," Madame Alexander mused. "It is
said that after it became impossible to live there, a few of those who
escaped came here and settled on the *Bras d'Or.*"

"A pirate lived there," Marie narrated. "He had two beautiful daughters, and they were all werewolves. He would lure ships onto the rocks,
and when they went aground, he would plunder them. Then he would
hold dances, and the devil played the fiddle for them. And if those he
captured would join his crew, he kept them alive. But the others were
put outside when the dance ended, and the werewolves came from the
forest for them. Then, they themselves became werewolves. At last they
began to destroy the inhabitants, and all who were not already changed
went away. I have heard that those who were made to attend the dances would count the persons when they went in, and always later, after
the doors were locked, there would be more, not noticed until the dancing ended."

"How did they get in?" I shivered.

"Through keyholes and cracks, I suppose. Wherever air could enter
they could come in. Only they cannot cross running water or the sea."

"That pirate den was destroyed," Madame Alexander continued.

"The devil went away with the pirate, and his daughters joined the others in the woods. And to this day, the wonderful timber on that island remains uncut because no one can be found who will go work there."

"That is not all," Marie took up. "Not a great many years ago there was a sensation in the papers. A rich Frenchman who fabricated chocolate built a grand chateau on the island, and came each year with servants from old France. Then in the autumn, when he returned, he always told those of Québec that the servants had run off and mingled among the people. But once a *bateau* was washed ashore with a half-dead woman in it, and she related what had passed. He had killed all those poor unfortunates to drink their blood. She had the wounds on her throat, and was almost without enough blood to live, so the police went to that island, searched the chateau and found all the skeletons. Only that one poor woman ever escaped.

"So even yet they become more and more," Madame added. "Do *loups-garou* infest the United States?"

"No," I considered, "there are a few persons with lycanthropy, but that is a kind of insanity. People there do not believe in them."

"Then assuredly there are none there," Marie said with conviction, "I assure you with all my heart, where they exist, people believe in them."

The French shore wove its spell upon me. I liked the people from all parts of Newfoundland, but the unspoiled, childlike, warm-hearted Acadians had more warmth than the others. And the British elements were not unlike those in West Virginia, for essentially they were the same people—rural English or Scotch, or Scotch-Irish, lifted from their eighteenth-century homelands and cut off from later influences. They had first-rate ghost stories, and their apparitions and haunts were always a bit more macabre than the French ones, which often enough had a Gallic sort of humor. They involved no saints in their tales of the grotesque and improbable, and the gray mist and the cold had rimed their imaginations with a sort of hoarfrost. I heard many words in Newfoundland that I never have heard anywhere else except on Gabe. Besides, those of the North Shore speak a kind of English that was spoken in Devonshire three centuries ago. The Devonshire dialect's transposed cases of pronoun, its regular plurals and past participles only hindered understanding, for the grammar took away from the thought. A sentence such as "'Er wuz good an' 'omely e'er 'er comed 'ere, but now

look at she!" requires thought, even if one is aware that the speaker
meant "homeloving" by *homely*.

When the time came to depart, I told the two women that I would
always remember them, and that some day I would return. As the plane
soared up and the church and the village became as toys, I glimpsed a
black speck in the Le Blanc meadow, and knew it was Marie—crying,
and praying to St. Anne or to St. Christopher for my safe journey. Poor
Marie. She never needed St. Christopher for herself, for she had never
been farther from Stephenville that to St. George, in sight across the
bay, but she liked to pray to him for other people, so that he would be
aware of her if she ever should travel.

Until I was thirty-five, I kept thinking that next year I would go back
to find a lost gold lode. It is an outcropping so rich that it gleams in
morning sunlight, and the piece that was taken from it assayed at
$70,000 a ton. However, I saw the original finder, who had spent forty
years in searching since he lost it, and I knew friends of his wife and
children, and I did not want to become what the gold had made of him,
or see my wife in rags and my children unfed. The dream of gold is a
cruel, hard, cold dream, and each year I preferred the wakeful, warm
reality. When I am so aged that warm flesh means no more than gold to
me, it will be soon enough to take to the hills prospecting. By then my
children can choose, themselves, to seek an El Dorado and go hungry,
or go to work on Main Street and be fed. Until then, I felt duty-bound
to provide for them, seeking certain sufficiency rather that uncertain
riches. The gold is still there—and I have a long lifetime ahead, a son, a
grandson, and three other boys I love the same as sons.

I wished, also, to go to a place in the north where a Viking village
stood a thousand years ago, where the inhabitants find Norse axes and
battle-blades and iron flinders. Perhaps I shall still go there. Helge
Ingstad has found the site of a Viking village, but the one he found was
a mere outpost at L'Ance-au-Meadow. The other, I feel sure from an
Icelandic saga, is the main settlement where a woman killed one of the
men in an argument over a calf. Vinland does not mean "land of wild
grapes," as so many believe, for *Vin* means grassland or pasture. The
iron wound-givers and stone arrowheads mutely reiterate the saga, for
this village would have been wiped out utterly by the Indians had not
that redoubtable woman who killed for a calf gone berserk, taken out
her breast, whetted a war-knife on it, and screaming war cries, charged

the savages. Thinking, no doubt, that if a woman were made of stuff to
whet an edge on iron, what must the men be! They took to the woods
in confusion.

The lad who told me of the village site was so untaught that he could
not have told other than truth, and the truth was evidential. Somewhere near his village are stones cut with runes, and a field where broken swords, axes, and bosses from Viking shields lie awaiting me among
the mounds of vanished buildings.

But dreams are dreams; time passes; and becoming rich and famous
somehow eludes or gives way to things more important. I never went
back; I never took any of the gold to buy Madame and Marie fine trav-
eling-clothes in which to go in style to visit Cheticamp and Beaupré.
Still, I wrote them regularly for many years. Madame's letters filled me
with nostalgia, and kept green the lonely, beautiful island. Sometimes
even in Mexico, at 154 Bajo, Calle De Medellin in the Colonia Roma,
the noise in the patio stilled and I could see and smell it—half forest and
half sea—its haze of fragrant smoke, its aromatic balsam, its damp fields
fertilized with wagon loads of capelin. Sometimes I could feel its tex-
tures—the rough softness of undyed hand-spun wool such as Marie knit-
ted into stockings and sweaters; its sharp sand. Sometimes I glimpsed
the sheen of its enormous blueberries, and saw the whiteness of its
birchbark. Sometimes I could hear its plovers and the mad laughter of
its loons. As are all things I have loved, it lives unchanging in my heart.
As Marie would have said, "I have still of the nostalgia, me."

After I was living in the Villa de San Miguel in Pátzcuaro, I received
an unhappy letter from Madame Alexander, who said that dark misfortune had befallen them. The Le Blanc well—one of the few in Stephenville that was not brackish—had suddenly and inexplicably gone dry,
and she and Marie were compelled to bring fresh water from her sister's,
a long distance up the road toward Romaine's Brook. It was a difficult
task in summer; in winter it would be a great hardship to depend on
melted snow or carry water in the icy gales. She had prayed for the
water to return, she said wistfully, and asked me to pray for it.

Not long before, I had read a study of psychic phenomena which
stressed the frequency of miracles involving *water*. It told of the appearance of the spring at Lourdes, of Moses who smote the rock in the wil-
derness, of the parting of the Red Sea; and of the water which was
made wine. As I pondered the inconvenience and misery of the two

good women, in that place which has so much water and yet so little—fresh lakes and ponds and streams, but salty wells—that which leads
me from within whispered that their faith was great enough to em-
power a miracle.

I knew that they had exhausted themselves praying to St. Anne without avail, for the Grandmother of Jesus, like Our Lady of Health, is
growing very old. I knew that they had sought the aid of the five or six
other most powerful saints favored in the Church of St. Stephen. The
saint to produce this miracle would have to be a very powerful one, and
one they had not yet tried.

Then it occurred to me how my letter telling of visiting Tepeyac had
fascinated them, and how they had thrilled to the story of the apparition of the Virgin on Mexican soil. She was not in any of her familiar
guises—not Our Lady of Sorrows, Our Lady of the Olive Trees, Our
Lady of Good Help, the Immaculate Conception, or any other familiar
to them, but Our Lady of Guadalupe—"Mother of the Poor," "Refuge
of the Sorrowing," "Queen of Wisdom," and "Queen of the Americas"!
Her titles are formidable. I bought a picture of her and had a priest
bless it for them. Then I gave him a few pesos and besought him to pray
for a good intention.

When I sent the picture, I directed Madame to hold a secret novena
beginning the first morning after the new moon, (pointing out that the
Guadalupana in her mantle of stars stands on the crescent moon). I
wrote her to place the picture over the well, and to go barefoot before
dawn, without eating or drinking, to pray nine times for the restoration
of the water, in no wise doubting that the Guadalupana has power to
perform that or any other miracle. I told her of the *Capilla del Pocito*,
the Chapel of the Little Well, inside which is the well which opened at
the feet of the Virgin on one of her apparitions.

I refused to think what the novena would do to her faith if it should
fail. The impulse and the instructions did not come from my conscious
mind, and when I obey such instructions there is no expectation of
failure. Though I could never be a Catholic, I do believe in the communion of saints—and *communication* is a legitimate meaning of the
word *communion*. If the Angel Gabriel could say unto the Virgin,
"Hail, thou that art highly favored, the Lord is with thee: blessed art
thou among women," I hold myself no whit embarrassed to say,
"Hail, Mary, full of grace; blessed art thou, and blessed is the fruit of

thy womb, Jesus." And if I do not count myself too pure a Protestant
to speak to her, neither do I hold it unavailing to beseech her to do
what a woman can to comfort other women. Who else should have
more influence!

So I prayed to the Guadalupana myself, but more to the *Dieu
Tout-puissant* (whom I call *Ehyeh Asher Ehyeh* and the Aztecs called
Tloque Nahuaque), nine mornings after the new moon, imagining Ma-
dame as she walked barefoot through the stinging dew praying to her
new manifestation, to the Mother, to Tonantzin, the Dark Virgin, the
Great Mystery of Tepeyac, the Queen of the Americas, therefore of
Newfoundland. "Surely the Queen of Wisdom would know how to
bring back water to a well," I could hear Marie saying.

In a few weeks a letter from Madame Alexander came. She had done
as I suggested, affixing the picture to the shed over the well. Then she
walked barefoot and fasting to it each morning just before dawn to
accomplish the nine prayers. But on the seventh morning she was
shocked by stepping into a pool of water near the well, and ran back to
bring Marie with the lantern. They found that not only had the water
returned, but the well had become a spring, overflowing the surface.
They dug a little channel for it so that it could run across the meadow
and down toward the sea. When they tasted it, it was pure and free
from a brackish taste.

Moreover, as time passed, Our Lady of Guadalupe wrought other
miracles on the French Shore. One of Madame Adeline's nephews was
gravely ill of tuberculosis. I remembered him as a handsome, fair-haired,
blue-eyed, thick chested, burly young man, industrious and not as wild
as some of Madame's nephews. His illness was all the more tragic because when the disease struck him, he was about to marry a fine girl. He
was given no hope of recovery, and I sympathized deeply with his family and his fiancée.

But after the miracle of the well, Madame and Marie took the picture
to him at the hospital, took him some of the water to drink, and began
a novena for his recovery. He immediately ceased coughing up blood,
and within three months went home, resumed his work, and was married. The doctors had pronounced him perfectly cured.

Whatever I did not learn to do in Mexico, I learned to believe in the
power of faith. Almost daily I read the Bible. The consistent message
was, is, and ever shall be, that faith has power. It is "the substance of

things hoped for, the evidence of things not seen: for by it the elders obtained a good report. Through faith we understand that the worlds were framed by the word of God, so that things which are seen were not made of things which do appear . . ." And as for what else I might say of it, I quote the Scripture: ". . .What shall I more say? for the time would fail me . . ."

17

THE NEW-FOUND EDEN, CAROLINA

The Whirling Star: Advancement through movement or change. A sign to use when seeking a promotion or moving to new work or a new locality

1745, Aug. 16.
Oswald Widmer, born in Lützelflüh in the dis-
trict of Brandis, a bachelor, in poor health, who
can only walk with crutches, wishes, in spite of all
this, to emigrate to Carolina . . .

Bernese *Ratsmanuale* 187, 34/35
(translated by Albert Bernhardt Faust)

It is strange that when I first passed through South Carolina on my way to visit my parents in Florida, I felt great psychic excitement as the bus neared Columbia, and I felt that I recognized the landmarks west of the Congaree River in Lexington County. I knew then that I had been there before, and that I must return. Ever since, when anywhere else, I have had the same desire which obsessed the above-mentioned Oswald Widmer. Lexington County is now my home, and I live surrounded by descendants of such men as Widmer. In South Carolina, that name is now Whitmire, and in adjoining Newberry County there is a little town of that name. Several Widmers emigrated from Canton Bern.

From 1732 until 1740 (and to a lesser degree until 1750) such emigration fever raged in Switzerland that a Bernese official coined the expression *rabies Carolinae*—"Carolina Madness"—to describe it. In 1737 an emigration brochure, the *New-Gefundenes Eden* (the *New-Found Eden),* presented South Carolina almost in terms of man's lost Paradise. Hundreds, mostly from Zurich, Bern, Appenzell, and the Graubünden came to Saxe-Gotha Township, where some of their descendants still live on land granted their ancestors through the royal Bounty of King George II. They are hardworking, self-respecting, honest, thrifty, loyal folk; religious, given to devoted friendship, bound by family feeling so strong it often leads to self-sacrifice. Here in Saxe Gotha Township, which became Lexington County after the Revolution, they were joined by Germans both from the Fatherland and from Pennsylvania. Until after 1800 they retained their language, their customs, and most of their superstitions. Even yet they form the basic population of Lexington, Orangeburg, and Newberry Counties.

Nearly all their immigrant ancestors came from Calvinist villages. Those from Zurich had lived under a Puritanism stricter and more intolerant than that of seventeenth-century Massachusetts, for though they

288

were allowed to drink beer in taverns, they durst not sing in them unless they sang hymns. Nor durst they give a wedding gift above a certain
value, or wear braid over a certain width. Those of the other Cantons
had lived under less repression, but the Bernese Oberland was haunted
by near-famine; taxes were high everywhere, and Appenzell was still not
recovered from its Cantonal civil war. Land was scarce.

When the Tobler *Schreib-Kalendar* or almanac with note space appeared in Appenzell and Grisons in 1753, those who remembered Tobler as an honest man before he went into exile at New Windsor on the
Savannah River believed his account of the conditions in South Carolina. He said that Christian Minnig, Myny, or Minnick, of Bern had
become a Captain of Militia, and in Oranienburg (or Orangeburg) had
accumulated 900 acres of land, over 2,000 head of cattle, and in ad-
dition, many horses, Negroes, and other property and had become a
British subject with all the rights of a native.

To be sure, the clergy warned of the serpent in this New-Found
Eden, but the hungry heed their bellies. So by 1755, Saxe Gotha was
full of families cut off from their accustomed mode of life, an alien
people, faced with the task of carving homes out of a frontier wilder-
ness. Their loneliness was perhaps their greatest hardship, and the incredible heat of the Carolina summer the next greatest. Those from the
high Alps sometimes died of it.

Swiss records show that Heinrich Weber (born October 6, 1715), his
fiancée Anna Urner (born November 6, 1718), and Heinrich's brother,
Jakob Weber (born December 30, 1725), emigrated in August 1739,
from the village of Under-Rifferschweil in Parish Rifferschweil, Canton
Zurich. Heinrich and Anna were married before reaching Carolina, and
were granted land for three persons—a town lot in Saxe-Gotha village
and 150 acres nearby. In his "Confession," written not long before his
execution, Jakob Weber stated that Heinrich died very soon after reaching the new land, and implied that Anna either died or remarried, leaving him alone at fourteen, among strangers, to survive or perish.

Nevertheless, the boy was keenly intelligent and had a remarkable
personality, so in spite of his plight, when he next appears in the records in 1756, it is as a man well-educated for the time and place, and
possessed of considerable property. His "Confession" is a strange doc-
ument—though it might have been written by a Puritan in Massachusetts a century earlier. In part, it says: "I was forsaken of man, and

without father or mother. But God had compassion on me amid much trouble and sorrow. He planted the fear of the Lord in my heart, so that I had more pleasure in the Lord, in godliness, and the Word of God, than in the world. . . .

"... but the judgment of God became manifest in me, so that I judged myself, and confessed that I deserved a thousand-fold to be cast from the presence of God, and wondered that the forebearance of the Lord had not long since hurled me, poor and condemned wretch, into the lowest pit of destruction; . . .

"Then Jesus revealed Himself to my soul. Then there was great joy in heaven over me, a returning sinner. Then all my sins were forgiven me, and I was full of the Holy Ghost, and rejoiced with a joy unspeakably great. This occurred, or I experienced this joy *A. D.* 1756 in the month of May. . . . This peace and communion with God I possessed about two years. . . . Upon this followed the great misery and awful fall into sin, already, alas! too well known; the devil bringing me into greater temptation and fall than was ever known, of which Peter Schmidt was the origin and instrument . . . [This is only a small portion of the "Confession"] "

Even so, shortly before he was hanged in 1761, Jakob Weber experienced another period of joy in which he fancied himself forgiven of all his sins. His exhortation to his children might have been written by Increase Mather, so sacrosanct is its tone, and so pious its admonitions. It was religion of this stripe that Dr. Quimby blamed for the psychoses and psychosomatic ills of the New England of his day. At Salem, it resulted in the witchcraft delusion. In Saxe-Gotha it bore even stranger and worse-twisted fruit. And just as Tituba precipitated the crisis at Salem with Obeah, the delusion called the Weberite Heresy in Carolina came to a head because of Voodoo. Calvinism and black magic are a lethal mixture.

"The origin and instrument" of Jakob Weber's downfall (his full name was Hans Georg Peter Schmidt) is a figure of sinister shadows and grotesque, lurid highlights. He is said to have been driven out of Pennsylvania, where he had already attracted a following and formed a disreputable sect called the "Gifted Brethren." The reputation he had in Pennsylvania was that of being a *Zauberer* or sorcerer—far more sinister a word than *Hexenmeister*. But I infer that he was forced to flee from Pennsylvania on account of some carnal offence against Nature.

Whatever else he was, he was a master hypnotist, and schemer, utterly without scruples. Evidently he was also a masochist, for he delighted in the use of the whip in religious ceremonies. (Incidentally, in Germany before the Reformation, another man named Schmidt had organized a cult called *Flegler*, which was mercilessly stamped out by the Holy Inquisition. It also practiced nakedness and flogging; but in telling of the perversions of Schmidt, Lutheran historians usually say, delicately, that his were similar to or remindful of the "Knipperdolling abominations," without saying just what those particular abominations were. It is enough to say that they were quite abominable.)

When Schmidt arrived in Carolina he found the settlers already formed into congregations, but with only one regular minister to serve the Calvinists within a forty-mile radius of Saxe-Gotha Village. This man, a God-fearing, stern shepherd after Calvin's own heart, served well and faithfully. He taught school too, but his zeal took him afar, to shepherdless flocks in Georgia and quite often to North Carolina, where he founded congregations. His contract with the colony called for visits to several stated places four times yearly, but with such responsibilities, he could not maintain adequate religious life for any of his congregations,—and in any case, the Lutherans did not like him. Even Calvinists who had left Zurich to find a freer atmosphere did not like the rigidity of his doctrines.

Schmidt's land grant lay quite near Zion Church, which appears first as a "union" organization, meeting its first years in the mill which Gottfried Dreher, a staunch Lutheran, had built twelve miles from Saxe-Gotha, near the mouth of Twelve-mile Creek. Here one supposes the Lutherans occasionally heard Pastor John Georg Loeff, who was in the area by 1754. And when he did not preach, they met to hear sermons read by Gottfried Dreher from the Sermon-book he brought from Germany. (Considering that Calvin had said he would have burned Luther at the stake along with Severtus, one imagines that the Calvinists liked these sermons only indifferently.)

Gottfried Dreher did not deny the Calvinists use of his building when Christian Theus, the Seminary-trained Swiss contract pastor from Chur met them for his quarterly appointments. And it seems likely that Jakob Weber exhorted at the mill at other times.

But records show that many of the nearby settlers traveled to Orangeburg, some fifty miles distant, to take communion, for the purpose of getting married, or of having an infant christened, so it seems evident that the hunger for church life was great, and the food scant in old Saxe-Gotha.

When word spread that the new settler, Hans Georg Peter Schmidt, was a preacher, no doubt he was asked to preach at the mill, and from what is known of him, it seems likely that he was very circumspect at first. Wherever he went, he quickly acquired a following, among them Jakob Weber and his wife Hannah.

The settlement still had a number of Indians and half-breeds, some Negroes, both slaves and escaped, and some mulattoes and mustees. In general, the Swiss and Germans had no use for these people, though a few married Indian or part-Indian wives, and the Trader's half-Wateree "natural" son was a favorite with everyone. Among the blacks was an individual called Frederick Dubber or Du Bard (or familiarly, "Cudjo"), who probably had escaped from some Huguenot owner near Charleston. He organized the blacks and began holding Voodoo rites shortly before Schmidt's arrival—though the law forbade Voodoo ceremonies on pain of death on account of their potential danger in organizing the blacks for a slave uprising.

Many Germans and Swiss came from villages which had a *Sonnenwendfeuer* to mark summer and winter solstices. This pre-Christian fire ceremony calls—in the summer ritual—for the throwing of embers down a hillside, or the rolling down of a burning wheel to symbolize the descent of the sun. No records prove that *Sonnenwendfeuers* were held in Saxe-Gotha, but if they were, the eminently suitable place is a strange monadnock called Little Mountain, as inviting for witch ceremonies as the Brocken Mountain or Blocksberg in Germany—which it somewhat resembles—or the Puy-de-Dôme in Auvergne. Whether Cudjo saw the settlers holding sabbats or *Sonnenwendfeuer* ceremonies there, or merely decided that it was ideal for his own purposes, he began holding Voodoo rituals on the barren mountaintop. The blacks, Indians, mustees, and mulattoes built a fire, sacrificed goats and chickens, and maddened by blood, rum and dancing to voodoo drums, culminated in an orgy, as similar rites still do in Haiti.

Schmidt presently grew lax in his decorum. He stripped to the waist while preaching, and as if to give vivid realism to the text "with His stripes we are healed," gave some handsome stripling or buxom virgin a small scourge and bade him lash him. Now Gottfried Dreher had

brought a sixteenth-century *Book of Concord* from the Fatherland, and
in it is no countenance for such excesses, or justification for them in
either Lutheran ritual or doctrine. He called the behavior to the attention of Pastor Christian Theus. And though the two seldom agreed on
any other matter, they both declared such goings-on a scandal and a
disgrace, and forbade their followers to have anything more to do with
Schmidt or the so-called "Gifted Brethren."

Denied the use of the mill, Schmidt merely began holding his meetings in the forest at night. The settlers were given the thrill of meeting
at a bonfire, with no restraint such as the presence of the strait-laced
Lutheran purist.

Pastor Theus grew even more outraged, for no one ever heard of a
half-naked, outdoor midnight Calvinism, and the Chur-Zweibrückischer
Classis of the Reformed Church was not a step behind Lutheranism in
the matter of decorum.

However, the common settlers thought Theus too strict and Dreher
too formal and for them the innovation of nocturnal meetings occasioned great excitement. By all that is known of him, Schmidt preached
intoxicating sermons, induced trances, and whipped up emotional
frenzy amounting to hysteria. His meetings were opportunities to throw
off repressions, forget the monotony and loneliness of day-to-day life,
and purge tensions away. Such "religion" is a psychological drug, and
those who experiment with it are very apt to become addicted. If a tent
revival provides a kind of spiritual marijuana, Schmidt's meetings provided "the hard stuff."

As Hitler knew, if one can excite a crowd, fix its attention upon a
speaker, and dazzle its eyes with flickering firelight, it is possible to
hypnotize it into believing anything. Schmidt began to introduce rhyth-
mic handclapping and stamping, and presently his fires became little
other than Voodoo rituals—even to the orgies. Perhaps his cult was
more pernicious than Voodoo, for the whip is a very dangerous instrument to introduce into either religious worship or sex. And when religion and sex combine, the whip brings together sadist and masochist in
unions as religious as they are unholy. Add drunkenness, the holding of
husbands and wives in common, hypnosis, and black magic, and one has
the "Gifted Brethren."

Cudjo was fascinated to discover White people who also danced
naked at ceremonial fires and held fertility rites afterward. Apparently

he made inquiry of Schmidt and was well received. In any case, he began to take interest in the strange white religion, so different from the frigid Huguenot and sedate Anglican. He learned the names of its three deities, and in Old Testament Hebrew sacrifice of doves and sheep, he found something that struck a familiar chord. If doves and sheep, why not chickens and goats? Indeed, here was a Christianity that a Voodoo might accept. Perhaps Cudjo felt that there would be no death penalty risked in holding rites in the name of the white men's gods.

After mass hypnosis, Schmidt began to hypnotize individuals. He singled out twelve important men—among them Beat Räbensemen, who was as strong as Samson; Jakob Burckhardt, who would obey in anything; and Abraham Geiger, who was very dignified and had a cousin in Saxe-Gotha in political exile who had been a Cantonal Governor in Switzerland. Schmidt convinced them that he, Schmidt, was Jesus Christ; that Carolina was the New Earth foretold in the Revelation; and that they were the twelve apostles ordained to rule with him in the heavenly New Jerusalem. He made them behold the city in the clouds above Saluda river—waiting, he told them, only until he had legal title to the land on which it was to descend.

At once they gave him title to their own land, and went forth with great joy to proclaim the good news to the people. With twelve leading citizens, including Geiger, telling that men of deserving character could see the city above very clearly, individuals began to make out at least the dim outlines. And whether or not they fancied they saw anything, they told their neighbors that they did. When they were under the spell of Schmidt's sermons, it appeared very distinctly to some of them, and their ecstatic descriptions suggested to those who saw nothing what they *should* see. So the description became reasonably standardized—heavenly, but still a little on the order of Geneva.

So great was the apostles' faith that they went forth to other German settlements and won converts as far distant as Maryland. Schmidt did do extraordinary things, bringing many to healing. One does not need be Jesus Christ to do that, but if he were *thought* to be Christ, he could hardly fail.

Please note that I say Schmidt "brought people to healing" rather than that he brought healing to them. Since Jesus Christ was on earth, that is all anyone ever has done. The technique has to be suited to the person seeking the healing. Great faith in God is highly desirable, but

not necessary if one has it in himself. It does not require particular holiness, or *any* holiness. I have done it depending solely upon faith in God;
I have also done it depending upon sheer dramatics; when I attempt it, I
use what I am told will best reach the person in need.

Among the German settlers, few were as rich as Schencking Mohr
(whom the English called Moore). Seeing his great herds, his land, and
his money as the largest single haul possible, Schmidt undertook to
make a proselyte of this rich man. But Mohr had not grown rich
through luck alone—he was shrewd. Let their Master bring a dead man
back to life, he told them. Germans that they were, the apostles agreed
that a man should be prudent, and concurred in Mohr's opinion that to
Jesus Christ, raising a dead man would require no more than mere utter-
ance of a command.

So Schmidt got Jakob Weber, his overseer, to help him and hypnotized a poor wretch until he could be made to enter a state superficially
like death. When he was satisfied that Mohr would be deceived,
Schmidt had a coffin prepared, and suggested to the man that he would
fall gravely ill. When the settlement had seen him, Schmidt induced the
death trance and sent word to Mohr to come and receive his sign.

Mohr made haste and arrived, and Schmidt convinced him that the
man was a corpse. Then Schmidt called upon the man to arise—but he
remained lifeless looking. Greatly upset, Schmidt all but dragged him
out of the coffin trying to revive him, but without avail.

Mohr's face clearly showed his feelings, and he muttered that for
imposters, all he had was the toe of his boot. It looked as if Schmidt
might soon suffer something more physical than loss of face.

Then Jakob Weber—who must have realized fully what Schmidt had
been doing and commanded the "corpse" to respond to no voice but
his own—said loudly to Schmidt, "You are not Jesus Christ, you are
Satan!" and shoved him aside. Then he commanded, "Rise! Come forth
from the coffin and live."

And as the crowd gasped, the "dead" man rose up in his winding
sheet, and when he was oriented, struggled out of it and clambered
down from the coffin.

"Only God can bring the dead back to life!" one of the apostles said,
awe-stricken.

"My land, my cattle, my body, and soul are yours," Mohr babbled,
kneeling before Weber.

"Thy wealth perish with thee!" said Weber austerely. "Thou shalt not tempt the Lord thy God! Is not the world and all it contains God's to do with as He wishes? But thou wert deceived by this wretch. Give alms to the poor and thou shalt be forgiven."

"I did not demand a sign of *Thee*," Mohr said, "only of *him*, remember?"

"That was not thine offense," Weber said. "It was in offering me what is mine already."

From that hour, many in the cult worshipped Weber as God. As Frau Hannah had borne his children, they renamed her Mary. When Jakob bade the cultists bind Schmidt and cast him into a place of darkness, they had no suitable chains, but trussed him up with rawhide instead and dumped him into apostle Jakob Burckhardt's turnip-cellar, where he was given the bread of adversity and the water of affliction—barely enough of either to keep him alive.

Not even Mohr was more impressed by the "resurrection" than was Cudjo. He fell to his knees and worshipped Weber with the others. "You is God," he declared. "The Holy Ghost say you *is* God!"

Perhaps Jakob misunderstood him. He turned to the black man and raised him to his feet and made room for him by his side.

"Hear me," he said, perhaps in intended irony. "Even as much as I am God, this is the Holy Ghost. He will lead his people, and they shall obey him as henceforth you will obey me. There is room for all in the New Jerusalem!"

So Cudjo and all his people were added to Weber's following, and on some occasions they met together. Cudjo found someone to read him the Bible, and his mind was filled with new ideas about oblations and burnt offerings, for he had progressed hardly farther than Leviticus when time came for his next great fire on the mountain.

Among the settlers, as it happened, was a young man named Jakob Hentz or Heinz, known for his staunch Lutheranism and his godly life. His wife was pregnant with her first child, and they lived at a considerable distance from Saxe-Gotha, west of Little Mountain. He had gone to the Trading Post on the day of the fire, and was riding home past the mountain when he saw the fire and heard the drums and commotion.

He decided to go spy on the ceremony to learn if it were as abominable as he had been told, but when he came near, he was discovered and hauled into the firelight. Had he been one of the "Brethren," certainly Cudjo would not have allowed him to be harmed. But Hentz was known as an avowed enemy of the white God and his people, and Cudjo was afraid that the Voodoo ritual would be reported. So instead of sacrificing a white goat, he called for the blood-basin and cut Hentz's throat. Then he sprinkled the worshippers, poured out the remaining blood as an oblation, and had the body cut in pieces and carried in a procession to be thrown into the flames as a burnt offering to the new God. The Voodoos were delighted with the sacrifice, for not even to Damballah or Aida Wédo had they ever been given a human being to sacrifice, and human blood is much more powerful than that of a goat in working magic.*

Next day, Cudjo, expecting praise, came to Jakob Weber to tell him of the killing of his enemy. But Weber called the apostles together, and they decided unanimously that if the witch-doctor were not punished, the Cult itself would share the blame when the white settlers found out the truth. So they decreed that Cudjo be hanged, and hanged him.

There is a proverb to the effect that even the devil can quote Scripture, and friends of the imprisoned Schmidt began asking others if they had doubted that Schmidt could raise the dead man in the first place. The honest ones said they had been skeptical. So Schmidt's friends came to Jakob Weber and protested in Schmidt's behalf, saying that in the light of such unbelief as they had encountered, it proved nothing that Schmidt had failed—since the Bible says in plain words that Jesus had been unable to do anything remarkable (or anything more than heal, which Schmidt had done) on a previous occasion when those a-round him had known him familiarly, as they had known Peter Schmidt. Frau Hannah, who rather enjoyed being called the wife of God, made light of them, pointing out that Peter Schmidt was no son of hers, and if she were Mary, he could not possibly be Jesus Christ! People in the Cult gathered from near and far in great confusion to argue out the matter, and Schmidt was brought out to speak in his own behalf.

Pastor Christian Theus had heard of the assembly, and rode to the Dutch Fork to try to bring them all back to their senses, but as soon as he appeared he was seized and tied to a tree, and the two factions united in saying that however their internal dispute might result, he

*The *History of Newberry County, S. C.*, by Chapman relates that when Jakob Hentz's wife learned of her husband's fate, she took refuge with her own family on Little River, and in due time bore a son, from whom the excellent Hentz family of Newberry County all descend.

must be killed. They then began to argue the merits of hanging, which was very exciting; or drowning, which could be explained as accident. But as they disputed, Pastor Theus worked loose from his bonds and dashed to the river, where by good fortune or Divine Providence he found an untended boat and escaped.

The Schmidt matter was then resumed, and the majority decided against him. He was thrown down; a mattress was placed on him to smother him, and the apostles stood on it and stamped; so finally his spirit left him. His body was thrown into the great fire and consumed, and Weber gave back the deeds to all the land that Schmidt had been given.

Meantime the terrified Pastor Theus made his way to Dreher's Mill. When the two men ascertained that Schmidt had been murdered, they rode to Charleston to inform the Royal Council and secure help from the authorities, for the cult was beginning to use force to convert those who could not be won by persuasion, and the two now knew that their own lives were not safe.

The militia was called out to arrest Jakob Weber, his wife, and the twelve apostles. Ten of them escaped or hid, but Weber and his wife were captured along with Abraham Geiger and Jakob Burckhardt. The four were taken to jail in Charleston, where Weber was placed in chains to await trial, as perhaps were the other two men. Weber was eventually hanged, his wife and the two men banished from the colony; and they and Frau Weber went to the Lutheran Salzburger settlement at Ebenezer in Georgia.

I think it safe to say that had these events taken place in seventeenth century Massachusetts, they would be as well known as the Salem witchcraft delusion, for seldom in America have three men set themselves up as God the Father, God the Son, and God the Holy Ghost, and been so acclaimed by perhaps thousands of believers in an area involving four states. Penetrating psychological studies of the principals would have been made; books would have been written, plays produced, and films made. But these things occurred on the South Carolina frontier, among persons of alien speech in an area where few records were maintained, and where Revolution and Civil War have wiped out most that were kept. Those who were involved tried to forget the whole matter, and in any case were plunged very soon first into a war with the Cherokees, then into the Regulator trouble (when the frontier was overrun with outlaws after the breakdown of frontier organization in the

Cherokee War. One of the former apostles, Bartholomew Räbensemen, called Beat Rapesome in the Regulator records and Beat Turnipseed after he translated his name, distinguished himself as a Regulator); and then into local Civil War during the Revolution. Still, Pastor Christian Theus is thought to have sent the great Lutheran organizer, the Rev. Henry Melchior Muhlenberg, a full account of the matter. Scholarly research is at last being done to recreate a clearer understanding of the Delusion; perhaps someday Theus' account may come to light. How I wish I had it before me! for Muhlenberg thought very highly of Christian Theus.

I do not know yet how the story of the Weberite Heresy connects with mine, but when I was a very young child, Little Mountain was one of the landscapes that appeared in the pictures of light. Each time I see it, it fills me with disquieting, puzzling emotions, for I am both drawn and repelled by it—much more strongly drawn than repelled. If I stand alone on it, I am strangely excited. My inner hearing or my heartbeat recaptures the rhythms of a voodoo drum and I see a fire. Besides, in childhood any nocturnal fire filled me with intense excitement, which had I been less stable might well have made me a pyromaniac. From the time I was eleven, when I watched Grandfather burn brush heaps on dewy nights, or arose before dawn to build fires to heat rocks for boiling water to scald hogs at butchering time, the mere sight of the leaping flame against the dark so aroused me sexually that sooner or later I would ejaculate even without other stimulus.

I know that I died in 1781 at the age of about eighteen, so in that life I was born about two or three years after the Delusion *ended.* Could I have had another earthly life only a few years before? For a long time I felt that such quick reincarnation was impossible, but in the twenty cases suggestive of reincarnation reported in Dr. Ian Stevenson's scholarly study, several of those supposedly reincarnated were born less than two years after the deaths of the persons they claimed to have been. A few of the "suggested" (Dr. Stevenson is far more objective than I would be, and more scientific in his choice of words) cases were of persons who were reborn in less than a year. So by that authority, there *was* time for me to have reincarnated by 1763—and I think I did. But who was I? The Cult was accused or suspected of several murders, so I could have been anyone who took pleasure in the fires and the orgies. Any choice among a sexually-twisted, masochistic *Zauberer,* a hanged Calvinist "God," and a Negro witch-doctor is not very appealing, and I do not think Jakob Hentz would return capable of being anything but appalled by the strange, bald mountain.

Interestingly, sexual excitement always has been characteristic of my first intimations of reincarnative recognition, for it seems that my psychic system and my sexual sensitivity are very closely associated (perhaps because sex is my preferred emotional outlet and release from tension. If I ever dream *that* life, I expect I shall not soon wish to forget it.) I am not a Freudian. When I dream a sex dream, it is in full technicolor, as naked and natural and enjoyable as life. I despise sneaky squeamish dreams that hide behind masks of symbolism, and I leave it up to you—would you prefer a lifelike dream experience of climbing a stair, or one of making love? If I dream that I am having intercourse with a woman, so what? If I dream that my partner is a male, when I wake up I can always shake my head and mutter, "That Zaïda!" In either case, I merely turn over and fall back asleep hoping I can resume dreaming where I left off—a very healthy attitude, I think, though certainly a hedonistic one.

But up until I knew about Zaïda, homosexual content in a dream disturbed me somewhat. Little did I think that homosexuality would prove to be the most convincing detail in my recall of the life that ended on November 7, 1781.

Homosexuality appalled me in that life—I was a naïve farm boy, one of several children of a German farmer who lived just east of the head of Cloud's Creek on the western border of what is now Lexington County. I recall nothing of my life before the Revolution brought excitement into it. My father said the Whigs were fighting for independence and freedom, and told me to join the militia if I wished. My mother said that our land was a gift from the king, however, and that the quarrel did not concern us Germans in any case. So I compromised, joining a band of local irregulars, and we did a great deal to keep outlying Tories from stealing cattle to sell the British who were fighting in Georgia and soon at Charleston.

I had never slept away from home before, but on our patrols we lay out in the pine woods, sharing our scant cover with a companion. Mine was another German youth—I think a cousin—and late one bright moonlight night he woke me and whispered, "I want you should see a sight! Take a look over there at the two others."

I turned my head, and was astounded to see the two young men in a grotesque position, their heads and hips moving rhythmically in unison. They continued for some time, then straightened out and lay in close embrace. The next morning we started in on one of them, a German boy. But he gave us each a shilling—all he had—if we would say nothing about it to anyone. We agreed, if the other youth would pay us—and if both would give us each another shilling each time the lieutenant paid us.

So for several months we enriched and amused ourselves at their expense, for the German boy was high-strung, sensitive, and profoundly embarrassed. We could tease him until he actually burst into tears. And quite cruelly, we made him teach us the English words for parts of the male body and with gestures and these words, made life just as miserable for the English-speaking boy, who never cried, but writhed in helpless humiliation.

Whenever we encountered Tories and exchanged shots with them, they both kept well concealed and were not of much use on patrol. However, when we pursued some cattle and caught up with the raiders, the Scottish boy did shoot from behind a large tree and killed one of the Tory ringleaders. We killed several on that trip and brought back the cattle. Our lieutenant said we had put an end to raids for a while, so we penned the cattle until their owners should reclaim them and got quite drunk, as did most of the other men, at the tavern nearby.

We had used most of our powder and ammunition, and some of the men said we should hide in the swamp until we had more, and let the owners worry about the cattle. But the lieutenant declared that it would take days to assemble enough revengeful Tories to be dangerous, saying that they were just as short on powder and lead as we were.

We bedded down in the tavern that night, but just at daylight we were awakened by gunfire outside, and the lieutenant's bawling orders to take positions at windows, and to punch out chinking between logs—that the Tories were upon us!

Our munitions were exhausted very quickly, whereas the Tories kept up steady fire. Two men in the room with us were wounded, and I noticed that the two youths were so unnerved that both were crying. "Damned girls!" I thought in disgust. "A brave show they'll make when it comes down to the end with gun butts and knives!"

But the lieutenant knew that those outside outnumbered us three to one. He was afraid they would burn the tavern with us alive in it, and so, when the enemy offered terms, he ordered us to surrender without resistance on their promise that all except those known to have killed Tories would be spared. Surrender was our best chance—our only hope of life.

We were ordered to come out with our hands up. The last to leave the building were the two lovers. When they appeared, they were clinging to each other almost too terrified to stand. Someone asked them something, but neither could answer. Then a brawny young Tory scowled at the Scottish youth, cried, "You shot my father!", and split his head almost in half with a claymore. The German boy swooned like a woman and collapsed; his friend's body fell on top of him and covered him with blood. Then a little red-haired Tory who could scarcely have been fifteen leveled a flintlock at me, and as others began firing, he shot. As smoke puffed from the barrel and the bullet tore into my chest, I awoke.

What I do when I dream reincarnative experience is very difficult to describe. Though part of my consciousness is dreaming with the very similitude of life itself, I am preternaturally awake with another part of consciousness which knows that the dream *is* a dream, analyzes it, relates it to facts known to my conscious mind and recalls previous related dreams to determine whether the dream being experienced adds any details.

This part of my mind stood at a slight distance from the dream and in a sense made the following estimate of it: "This seems to be one of the "reliving"-experience dreams, but you know you were reading of that very skirmish just two days ago. You know the traditions of what took place. The cattle were recaptured at the battle of Tarrer's Spring and driven back to Carter's, and you know very well that the people in the tavern were all said to have been killed except a man named Hughes who ran off with the cattle when they stampeded. You know that the bodies were hacked to pieces to such a degree that they could not be certainly identified, and all but two Butler men were buried in a mass grave. You know all that; so as many movies as you have seen of battles and costume, and as much research as you have done, you don't need to take this as real experience."

I had that dream maybe five years ago; it remained very clear and occasionally I redreamed 't, once with the two youths enjoying each other in broad daylight. I was just as disgusted with myself for dreaming that as I was for having dreamed the original version.

Something like two years went by, and I undertook to read the Draper Manuscript documents of Series VV—twenty volumes of three or four hundred pages each, pertaining to South Carolina in the Revolution, collected by Dr. Lyman C. Draper over ninety years ago and now owned by the Wisconsin Historical Society. I sought in them a map which my intuition told me must be there, showing the Revolutionary battle sites in Lexington County. I secured microfilm, and spent my evenings running reels of it, (also abstracting genealogical and historical data for use in a History of Lexington County for which I have been gathering material the past fifteen years or more). I found a map—in fact more than one—with detailed accounts of skirmishes and events which have passed completely from local tradition.

Then as my weary eyes were giving out, I came to a letter written May 5, 1874, by John Langford, whose family lived near Carter's Tavern in 1781 (It is in Volume 6VV, beginning at page 221). A kind of chill ran over me as I read it.

Langford wrote: "... Two men only escaped—Benjamin Hughes and Bartley Blucher. Hughes ran off with the frightened cattle and hid himself under some driftwood that had caught against a pine log ... Blucher and Benjamin Rabun came out of Carter's house, when ordered by the enemy, *hugged together, each with his arms around the other's neck; they were asked their names but would not tell. Rabun's skull was cleft with a saber, & he died with his arms around Blucher's neck.* I have heard my father say that Blucher never had his right mind afterwards ... [Italics mine, of course]."

I stared at the letter until I could not see it. Yes, that *was* their names! I could now remember the lisping softness of "Rabun" or Raeburn's voice when he said "Bartley," as if no "r" were in it; and how Bartley—we had called him Beat—trying to call the other youth "Benjamin," never had been able to make the English sound, and had to be satisfied with "Benchamin," however much the other youth tried to teach him. Hair stood up along my forearms as I realized that I must have seen the whole group of men exactly as they looked in 1781 on

their death date. I did not doubt at all that my cousin and I had
watched the two together or that I had once experienced the other
dream of spying on them.

I could all but feel their guilty shillings in my pocket, and realized
that I had paid a dear price for tormenting Beat until he cried; for
though no one had teased me or blackmailed me over my love for Stud,
I had cried enough.

Those who kill shall be killed. Those who mock shall be mocked.
Those who torment shall be tormented.

18

THE STRANGEST PRAYERS ARE PAINTED

Earth, Rain and Sun: A prayer for plenty, fertility, or for a balance of life's sorrows and joys. It is sun-rain and fertility sign

*It is He who sitteth upon the circle of the
earth. . . Lift up your eyes on high, and behold
who hath created these things, that bringeth out
their host by number: He calleth them all by
names, by the greatness of His might, for He is
strong in power; not one faileth.*

` Isaiah 40:22, 26.

The expenses of establishing ourselves in South Carolina, of
Grandmother's long terminal illness and burial, and of entering the
University of South Carolina where I planned to secure my doctorate,
consumed all of what I had earned in Mexico. I soon came to feel that
our financial straits imposed too great a hardship on my wife and children, and after a short time at the university, I reluctantly dropped out
and took the only work I could find in Columbia—which, like the university, had not yet manifested its incredible potential for expansion
and improvement. It was a grotesquely inappropriate job; that of ware-
house clerk in a concern dealing in filling-station supplies, and it paid
only $35.00 a week.

Our apartment was probably the only one in the Assembly Street
slum area furnished with antiques. It was large enough—six big rooms
and a huge hall—but it was noisy, with a family of inebriates in the six
rooms upstairs and day-long heavy traffic at a busy corner. The porch
roof leaked, and water from the upstairs bathroom fixtures frequently
dripped through the kitchen ceiling. A broken sewer pipe under the
house drained raw sewage onto the surface, and the house seemed all
the meaner because we had so recently lived in the Villa de San Miguel,
where even the maid's quarters and bath were luxurious by comparison.

Here we ate turnip greens, corn pone, and fat-back with sterling silver-
ware from antique Staffordshire plates because we could not afford an
everyday set of stainless steel and ten-cent-store dishes. The intolerable
conditions demanded a demonstration, even if it be of Christian Science. And as I strolled on Arsenal Hill to enjoy the beauty of the fine
old mansions fronting the governor's lawn, I gazed longingly to the west
at the green woods and fields of Lexington County across the river. I

felt compelled to see what dwellings they offered. I felt in my pocket. My total cash amounted to $2.50, and a round-trip bus ticket to Lexington cost 70¢. We had to buy groceries from Friday to Monday out of the $2.50, but a family of four can live three days on $1.80 almost as sumptuously as on $2.50, and a dealer had offered a price for our Georgian-style antique Sheffield-plate candlesticks, which we could always replace with sterling (when we could afford it). So I bought the ticket and took the next bus to Lexington.

Just on the outskirts of the village I saw a little house with a "For Sale" sign in the yard. It stood under a large oak tree in a jungle of flowers and weeds with a woodland just behind it. It looked homelike and inviting, so I yanked the pull cord, got off the bus and walked back to look at it. It proved to be a five-room dwelling with an acre of land, and the price the neighbors said the owner asked seemed reasonable—$3,000. I decided I must have it, and I told my wife so when I returned home.

"I'd be glad to move there or anywhere else," she sighed. "But it can't be much of a place if you can get it for a dollar-eighty."

"Well, I'm going to buy it," I declared.

"How?" she asked voluminously.

I could not answer that just then, so I went back to Arsenal Hill and closed my eyes to *see* how. After I had shut out Columbia and was in a world unlimited, something or someone whispered "Hex," and I saw what I must do.

I made an incantation, and when I went home I drew a picture of my right hand. In the palm I drew the house and oak tree, over it drew the "Eye of God" symbol, and enclosed both inside a circle. Then I took Monday afternoon off and went to see the owner, whispering an incantation inaudibly all the way to Lexington.

I still cannot explain how the transaction was brought off, for it still seems totally unreal and illogical. But before I went back to Columbia, a lawyer had been instructed to draw up a contract and deed. I sold a spinning wheel and a few other unnecessary antiques, palmed off on a Negro conjure woman a "unique" earthen Haitian voodoo bottle sold to me as containing a spirit. (The Mam'bo from whom I bought it as a curio imported them by the gross directly from the manufacturer in Tokyo and sold them at too low a price for the spirits to be very choice.) This provided money for moving to Lexington. We lived in the house for several years, renovated and improved it, cleaned up and beautified the grounds, and when I found exactly the house I really wanted I bought it the same way I did the first. By that time, though, I had sixty dollars in the bank and a decent job, and I sold the first house for twice what I paid for it.

Subsequently I have bought two other houses in Lexington, both when I had less than one hundred dollars in the bank, and have sold them at a profit. In fact my proceeds from these transactions and from sale of unwanted land has more than paid for the big house where I live—an ante-bellum farmhouse whose builder oriented it four-square with the four directions, using the pole star for true North, and fenestrating it so that sunlight shines into every room each day of the year. (Hexed for protection and built according to Hex symbology and geometry, the house was visited by federal looters when Lexington was burned in the Civil War. The women in the house concealed everything of value and made the house look already looted—turned everything upside down, poured molasses on the floor and wearing men's shoes, trampled it and flour over the floors. Instead of stealing anything, the enemy *gave* them a large piece of bacon they had just stolen from a neighboring family.)

My wife is a canny woman with a dollar, even in the archaic meaning of canny, but management alone could not have paid for four houses, four automobiles, the rearing of three children, the purchase of antiques, sufficiency of food and clothing, and my capricious extravagancies—my books, pipes, matches, and tobacco—on a salary which never exceeded $6,000 a year even when I taught college. Those who know my doings are convinced that what I really want, I Hex, and what I Hex, I get. It is true that when I wanted my museum-quality 1824 Dutch Fork Hex-painted punched-tin pie-sideboard, I drew a picture of it against the very wall where it now stands. This piece has twenty Hex rosettes, four of them centering sun-discs, besides eight half-suns, so to draw it required me to make enough Hex prosperity signs to provide plenty in the house from that day henceforth. And when I timidly asked the price of the sideboard the owner asked only sixty dollars.

After my second daughter was born, we tried for seven years to have another child, for I was told in a dream that I would have a son—though the doctors averred that my wife could not conceive any more children for obscure reasons that varied from doctor to doctor. After I knew of my Italian reincarnation, I knew that the reason was karmic, since then I had a son and did not want him—or at least, did not want him enough to sacrifice for him. I did all I could to release myself from that karma, and painted an Empire sideboard with a unicorn (symbol of the miraculous), a tree of life with lilies and pomegranites, four Hex signs, and on the doors a woman surrounded by the fruitful vine, and a man with a son, surrounded by oak-leaf and acorn motifs.

I also made the prayer of the seven secret stones. As I have not read of their use anywhere, maybe I'd better explain what they are. The Bible tells of stones of witness (Gen. 21:30, 48:52; Josh. 24:27; etc.), and the earth is called to witness (Deut. 4:26). So since a Hex believes that Stones are conscious and are in league with him (Job 5:23), and since Christ said that what one prays, believing, he will receive, somehow the idea arose that if one wishes to make a prayer that will continue as long as a stone remains a stone, he should find seven unbroken stones and lay them in a heap somewhere where they will not be seen, call them to witness that he prays believing, and charge them to bear witness continually that the prayer has been made. In praying for a son, I used seven pebbles and kept them in a metal saucer hidden on top of my tall clock. I have also laid prayer-heaps in seldom-visited thickets in the woods, and each time had answers. It is "magic" of this kind that I feel one can find all through the Bible. The Bible calls for unbroken stones for the building of altars, saying that using a tool on a stone profanes it; so if for altars, all the more for stones of witness—they are to be left as nature shaped them.

See how superstitious I am? Anthropologists say that Australian Bushmen and certain other primitive folk believe that stones have spirits and consciousness, and here I am saying it. No wonder they let me go at Lenoir Rhyne College! It's going to shock some people when it filters down to them that the philosophers of avant-garde physics postulate a kind of consciousness in *all* forms of matter. It's a perfect illustration of the concept that if you go far enough you'll end up right where you started; that if you travel east far enough, you'll find yourself in the west or *vice versa;* a suggestion that the more primitive the mind, the closer it is to the truth about nature.

A week after I set the praying stone to testify, I was again visited, and told that my son would be born on a day of wonder and of hail, and as it eventuated, he was conceived a few days afterward. I was in the swamp visiting an Indian mound and was bitten by hundreds of mosquitos. The acid injection into my body by the insects completely overcame my alkalinity, and while I was acidified, I sired the boy. Not for several years after that did I read a scientific account of experiments in which it was shown that an acid condition tends to further the conception of male children. Remember that if you want a boy—sire him when you are happy, preferably after a day spent outdoors doing something you thoroughly enjoy; eat things that will leave your body acid—drink vinegar and honey if nothing else; lie with your head toward the north, and I'll give odds you'll get your son.

Midway of my wife's pregnancy, as I stepped out of a bright room into a shadowy hall, Grandmother appeared, smiled with satisfaction, said "I just wanted to tell you how glad I am for you about your boy," and disappeared; and as I fidgited at the Camden hospital waiting for my wife's long labor to end, those in the room discussed a phenomenon which had occasioned great excitement soon after the previous midnight, when a great light passed over Camden. Some declared that it had been seen in other counties besides Kershaw, and opined because of its flight pattern that it was a flying saucer of enormous size. Others declared that it had to have been a meteor, but whatever it was, it sufficed to make me remember that July 19, 1956 was to be a "day of wonder." As the people speculated someone came in and said, "If you have your car windows open, you better go see to them. The sky's as yellow as saffron, and there's a mighty strange feel in the air."

I went out, and the sky was frightening. A man by me said, "That's a hail cloud. It's too high for here, but someplace they are getting an awful hailstorm." Almost as he spoke, the hot wind began to chill, and it grew cold. No hail fell at Camden that day, but it did in nearby counties, and unusual hail was reported from at least fourteen widely separated states. Nowhere was it more abundant than over Gandeeville, West Virginia, where mother happened to be at that time. She said that the oldest people could remember no hail to compare with it, and it lay two feet deep along the highway through Gandeeville and did not wholly disappear for three or four days. Thus, as the spirit had whispered in the night, my son was born on a day of wonder and of hail "that it may be a sign . . ."

I did not make a Hex drawing again, except to heal a few people and buy the big house, and I do not count those anything extraordinary—I draw those kinds all the time—until people I love began to become endangered by involvement in the Vietnam conflict. The first was a youth I'll call Mark, who took part in the grave-lamp scrying I will tell of in the next chapter. His father was murdered when Mark was an infant, and as Mark was his mother's only child, and the light of the world to his widowed grandmother, the two women were distraught when he was drafted. He had just married, and his wife was also beside herself. I painted a sign to insure him safe and pleasant surroundings— for I saw no danger for him—and provided it with a German inscription. As soon as he completed basic training he was assigned duty in Germany. There until his service was completed, he was stationed in a tourist region of south Germany not far from the Swiss border, and within fifty or so miles of the villages from which his ancestors and mine emigrated in the eighteenth century. He told me that his quarters were in a former tourist hotel that the Nazis had taken over as a rest center for army officers, and he averred that he enjoyed more conveniences and comforts than he was accustomed to at home, his only hardship being separation from his wife and family. When he returned, he looked stronger and healthier than I ever had seen him before. He found a good job and has worked diligently at it ever since.

The next case was for my nephew Jesse, my brother Jesse's only child. His mother was almost prostrated when he went into the Army, and Jesse was worried as only an adoring father of an only child can be. As I prepared myself to make his Hex, I went into trance and saw the young man surrounded by fire and smoke, with blood on his clothing and skin and a look of numb fatigue. I knew that he would be sent to Vietnam, so since his comfort was beyond hope, I concentrated on protecting his life. I drew a ghastly dragon trampling a skull in a fire-blasted wasteland, with thorns and thistles to signify the horror and devastation of war, and closed it off with a triple border from the panel above. There I placed Jesse and his protective inscription under a top panel representing the arch of heaven and in the latter drew the Eye of God.

When he was trained, he was sent to Vietnam immediately, and assigned duty in a field hospital. There, daily, he tended men wounded in battle. I suppose often his clothes and hands were smeared with their blood, and sometimes in emergencies he worked continuously until he was too weary to do more. Yet he did not receive a scratch, and in the care of the wounded, the practical, methodical, common-sense nature of his father at last found unity with his mother's tender compassion. He discovered therapy as the life-work he had sought in vain at college. Now out of the Army, he has just turned down a $12,000-a-year offer to work as a practical therapist in order to finish college and continue educating and training himself for a career in therapy, perhaps as a teacher.

The third draftee for whom I made a Hex prayer was my younger son-in-law. I saw no danger ahead for him, so I merely made him a Hex for happiness. He was sent to Germany, almost on the border of France, where my daughter soon joined him. Neither was particularly happy with their marriage, and it was neither better nor worse in Germany than it had been in North Carolina. He deliberately asked for transfer to Vietnam, and his wife returned home. He never saw action, and as they had decided upon divorce my daughter proceeded with one as soon as he returned. Their experience should forever stand as a warning to Piscean men not to marry women born in Leo, and to Leo women not to marry Piscean men, but if a fish and a lioness should not marry, neither do they have anything in common over which to quarrel, so the divorce came off as casually as the marriage had occurred. Then after visiting with the rest of us a few days afterward, this youth drifted out of sight, and in a month my daughter married a Scorpio, a delightful boy of a birthsign compatible with Leo and very congenial with Taurus.

The uniformly gratifying outcome of these Hex prayers has left me with the feeling that while verbal prayer is adequate for many things, painted prayers are far more certain to accomplish their purpose. I began studying Pennsylvania Dutch folk art seriously, and came to have as much faith in symbolic drawings as the old Daughertys had in them.

All my experience suggests that "magic" power is derived from the action of the mind at the subconscious level. A symbol is more potent than a naturalistic representation simply because a realistic drawing is interpreted mainly at the conscious level. I am left quite unmoved by all pictures of the Crucifixion that show the scene as it was, or might have been. The only one which ever reached down to the level of my subconsciousness showed it as it could *never* have been—on a German hilltop, with somber fir trees and brooding hillsides, but not a living

soul—only the dead Christ and the dead malefactors, all forsaken equally. Even though the details were all but photographic in their realism,
that painting was a symbol. In fact the realism was the strongest symbol, for that is how it *is* with the crucified!

In solitude and secrecy, the mind thinks in symbols—as is proved best
by the graffiti found in public latrines. There the subconscious turns to
sex, protesting that sex is as natural and necessary as defecation or uri-
nation. So if the repressed individual is responsive to the subconscious,
and has a pencil or pen, he draws sexual symbols on the wall. Here he
reverts to the most primitive pattern of thought, seeing the part as the
whole, and drawing stylized sketches. If any body is represented, usually the genitals are greatly exaggerated, as in African fetishes and idols.
It is quite revealing that such symbols drawn in college and art-school
washrooms are not noticeably different from or superior in technique
to those scribbled by truck drivers, coal miners, or stevedores. Below
the belt all men are brothers, and so are they below the level of the
conscious mind. For thousands of generations, man's subconsciousness
has used symbol as the language of instinct and emotion and the phallic
symbols made by prehistoric man are so like those made yesterday by
your neighbor's son that they could be interchanged without exciting
professional comment.

As biological man evolved into philosophical and spiritual man, he
began to speculate if the creation hadn't been the result of some trans-
cendant or deific copulation. Anthropologists find legends everywhere
in which a god and goddess bring forth the created universe through
sexual union. It does very well to represent human sex with phallic
symbols, but one cannot as easily represent abstract concepts such as
the magnetic attraction of positive and negative polarity. Hex found its
symbol for generation in a square cross, which signifies the union of
opposites. Its four arms point to the four cardinal directions, so it also
means "to the four corners of the earth," or everywhere, and as the
figure is the same on either side of an imaginary line drawn midway
through the horizontal bar, it is an affirmation of the magic principle
"That which is above is like that which is below . . ." which Jesus called
the keys to the kingdom of heaven when he worded the formula less
cryptically (see Matthew 18:18).

Down through the millenia and centuries of his history, man has
evolved a vocabulary of other symbols to express almost any idea or

emotion. Many are so familiar that anyone recognizes them. A heart stands for love; an olive branch or a dove for peace; a blindfolded woman with a balance, or the balance alone, justice; a five-pointed star, luck; an oak, strength; or a four-leafed clover, a horseshoe, or a rabbit's foot, good fortune; a crown, sovereignty; a lamb, innocence; a lion, strength or courage; a palm branch, triumph; a lily, purity, and so on. The symbols are so numerous that anyone wishing to learn them must do so by perusing books on symbology, including a work on the "language of flowers" such as Victorian romantics used in conveying sweet nothings or innocent-looking communications of serious meaning by sending bouquets. From such books one learns that roses stand for love, that a red rose indicates passionate love; a pink rose, respectful love; a white rose, spiritual love; and a yellow rose, jealous love—in fact, a bouquet of yellow roses expresses jealousy as the primary message. Various religions have also contributed their symbolism to the "collective unconscious," and the Hex artist is free to appropriate any symbol from any source in making his Hex designs.

A certain little old Sicilian lady once wrote from Utica asking me to break the spell of the "Evil Eye" some Mafia miscreant had placed on her for influencing her son to cease and desist in some scheme the Mafia wanted him to help carry out. (People have written me for such services from places as distant as Hong Kong and Lusaka, Northern Rhodesia.) As I was working on the Hex signs for this book, I thought of what her reaction would be: "Signor Gandi, you no make-a for book sign you send me for Evil Eye? Lotsa people need-a help for da *Mal'occhio.*"

I recalled how relieved she had seemed after getting her sign ("It work right away for me and break the spell."), saying that in Italy people hung pairs of horns on building to nullify *mal'occhio* spells. So I tried to remember the design I worked out for her, and sent to help her visualize the protective horns.

I suppose I was guilty of duplicity in letting the Signora suppose that I knew the Sign-of-the-Horns Hex, for I reasoned that a Sicilian would take it for granted that if a Hex knows *anything*, he should know the thing for the Evil Eye, and not have to create something special.

Here I've put it atop Chapter XIV just for good measure. It's a beautiful design with four devils in gesticulating rage and frustration trapped between the horns of the earth star issuing from the Eye of God, the horns on their own heads forced to make the sign of the horns in the four directions. I defy any art form other than Hex to make a beautiful design of *that* motif! If it worked for a Sicilian to break a *mal'occhio*, it should break any kind of hoodoo.

All of the Hex signs included in this book, unless they are purely geometric ones determined by the inherencies of geometry and number, are personal. Again I must emphasize that Hex is a creative art. A Hex needs not copy slavishly the work of any other Hex. He draws ideas from it, and makes it his own by selection of motifs, by subordination through placement or size of components. If no standardized design exists to express an idea, affirmation or prayer, he racks his subconscious for suggestion—as I did when faced with the challenge of finding a design to express the Hex belief of reincarnation and settled upon the Triskelion of Fishes, which you'll find printed over Chapter I. Fish are symbols of spirit; their habitat is water, also a symbol of spirit; they live in the ocean, which is a symbol of eternity, and three is the number of spirit. So my subconscious related these observances to the fact that the head is the symbol of consciousness and gave one head three bodies to symbolize the certainty I have that the spirit that moves in the ocean of eternity has a succession of bodies, but the consciousness remains intact, and its eye (awareness) is that of *all* its bodies, the sum of all its experience. I think I remembered this design from my Cretan lifetime, for as Zaïda, I used to embroider the stylized ocean waves as borders on my chlamydes, and the whirling triskelion is an eastern Mediterranean motif, still in use as the heraldic symbol of the island of Sicily. It refers to progressive motion and the geometry of rhythm, to balance not static but dynamic—a very good symbol for life, in my opinion. I use it as my own symbol of total identity.

A Hex *drawing* may be of any shape, but a Hex *sign* is circular. This is itself symbolic, for as a Hex conceives God as present throughout the universe, and manifested in every atom of which it is composed, it rejects out of hand any anthropomorphic concept that presumes to represent Him. In seeking a sign to represent completeness and all-inclusiveness, the Hex recognized the only perfect wholeness without beginning or end as the geometric circle. So when he sets the point of his compass to a surface, he says silently, "This is I; my consciousness is the radius." And as he draws the circle, he says, "This is God; He surrounds me. The design that I make in the bounds of my consciousness must be laid out with reference to Him."

Then as he meditates upon the relationships of basic inherencies (laws of geometry), he discovers that by using the radius with which he drew the circle he can set the point anywhere on the circumference and by progressing from point to point, segment the circumference into six equal segments. By moving the compass to alternate points on the circumference and sweeping the pencil from the inner circumference through the middle and to the opposite curve, he forms a six-pointed rosette:

The Basic Hex Rosette: A Good Luck and protection sign:
The sign of creation through spiritual law

This six-pointed figure is the primitive, first sign of Hex, which states the basic truths of being, namely: that the relationship between God and man, and between God and every created thing is one of law and order. It is an ancient sign of protection against evil, found carved on pre-Christian Jewish coffins; inlaid in the floors of Byzantine churches in the second and third centuries; used in rose windows in the Middle Ages. In placing oneself symbolically in the center of the symbolic universe, and using the six lines to guide the arrangement of the motifs used as symbols, one places his ideas in the right relationship with those forces which act to create form and substance out of energy.

A Hex knows a thought to be a *thing*—a form with an electronic force field, so when he arranges his motifs what he really is doing is sending out into the universe a telepathic blueprint image of what he wishes materialized. Nature is so constituted that the image tends to be materialized and sent back. To be a witch, one must be able to send *sustained* images *far enough* out to attract enough energy to effect the materialization, and to draw this basic rosette sign with concentration pushes the signals across the entire universe, which, like Diriac's ocean, is without resistance. Space is no obstacle to telepathy.

Internally, any structure (the universe or an atom) has certain lines and points of balance. In a Hex sign these are diagrammed by connecting alternate points around the circumference to the points opposite. In a six-segmented circle, these lines form two equilateral triangles so ar ranged as to have six equidistant points arranged around an internal hexagon. To surround oneself mentally with these six lines is to establish oneself within the strongest balance in the universe. For thousands of years, this symbol has been that of the Jewish religion, and the figure has been called the "Star of David" or "King Solomon's Seal." The drawing that opens Chapter VII, "Testimony of Healing," is one copied from a *Wunder-Sigel* or Wonder-seal. Hexes stamped it on sick folk in soot made from ritually-prepared candles to establish the balance of good health in their bodies—for Hexes know that sickness is an imbalance. The geometry involved in the star of David is that of the universe—the type employed by space physicists.

If based on squares, an eight-pointed figure of the same type would diagram the points of balance which result in the greatest stability and permanence in terrestial structures. The Egyptian pyramids were built according to the rules of this terrestial geometry, and a Hex sign drawn as a four-sided or eight-sided figure is constructed according to it.

Naturally, all such signs refer to earthly things—prosperity, temporal happiness, the physical body, one's possessions, sex, crop yield, rain, and the like. The six-oriented signs, and certainly the ones of three motifs, refer to spirit. Thus to draw my own sign of masculinity, the oak, which appears at the beginning of Chapter XIII, I arranged both the leaves (the masculine qualities) and the acorns (male sexuality) in an unusual six-oriented sign. I already had the male body and the male organs: my need was a man's spirit. Moreover, a wreath is a symbol of victory awarded the winner in a contest or struggle, so when I drew the sign, it referred to the dominant role the male portion of my spirit assumed after Zaïda surrendered my body in order to be given new life in the body she desired.

In a general way, four- or eight-sided figures better express the male, and three- or six-sided ones the female. But spirit is of greater significance than body, and I should not hesitate to draw a woman a four-sided Hex sign of oak leaves (certainly not with the acorns, however!) if she needed strength to assume alone the task of rearing a family of sons, or to perform other duties requiring the qualities of a man.

Compare this sign with the Fruitful Vine I drew for the Zaïda who was and is to be:

The Fruitful Vine: Symbol of womanly qualities. Since woman is not woman unless she loves and is loved, the heart design is included, as is clover, symbol of sweetness and modesty

The grapes represent ova and the leaves life (balanced in the creative arrangement). The tendrils represent the certainty that she will cling to the man she loves as long as her spirit exists in eternity, and I could not refrain from adding clover leaves (clover is a symbol of modesty) to the love that encircles her inner universe. Stud will probably come back with a certain hang-up about modesty due to his misfortune with the two girls. I don't think he ever got over that experience emotionally, and Zaïda doesn't want to scare him off next time by being too bold. Anyhow, it will take more than six clover leaves to make a prude out of Zaïda.

Anyone who wishes may find Hex signs in any work on Pennsylvania Dutch folk art or observe them painted on barns in the Pennsylvania Dutch country. Not much literature on Hex art is available. Jacob and Jane Zook, who operate a gift shop in Paradise (Paradise, Pennsylvania 17562, that is) prepared a booklet, "Hexology," in association with the late Hex artist, "Professor" Johnny Ott, of Lenhartsville, which they sell along with Hex sign patterns, folk art stencils, and similar regional items. Henry Kauffman's *Pennsylvania Dutch American Folk Art,* Dover Publications Inc., N. Y., 1964 includes two pages of Hex signs without explaining the motifs (which include three rain signs, two rain-and-fertility or rain-and-sun signs; an earth-rosette or flower for happiness due to abundance; a six-pointed rosette forming a flower for happiness due to creativity; an eight-pointed star for prosperity; a five-pointed star for "luck," and a triple six-pointed star for well-being of mind, spirit and body.) Hex signs and symbols on everything from piecrust perforators to tombstones are illustrated in John Joseph Stoudt's *Early Pennsylvania Arts and Crafts*, A. S. Barnes & Co. Inc., N. Y. 1964, and some mention of them may be found in almost any work on American folk arts and crafts. Usually the author will say that the Hex signs are "just for nice." They do make colorful decorations. But if the authorities were told that by those who were asked, either the informers were not Hexes and did not *know* what the signs meant, or they *were* Hexes who would not *say*. True Hexes, witches, and Christians often are very reticent, and often they are very justified in being so.

If anyone wishes to prove the effect of a Hex sign, let him make one prayerfully and use it without explaining to anyone what it intends. Any in this book may be copied—I do not care—and all but the ominous-looking rain sign that opens Chapter XVI are white-hex signs. (I could not resist putting in one black-hex sign just to show the contrast.) In it there is no earth-star to call for rain as a blessing to the earth, but only furious raindrops whirling in from all sides. It calls for storm and tempest, flood and destruction. Johnny Ott always liked to tell of a flood in the Delaware River that did $5,000,000 damage merely because one of his ordinary rain signs was left out after the rain started. I certainly would not want to leave the one I drew outside after the rain began—and because of the lightning drawn on it, I wouldn't want to go out and bring it in, either.

The signs may look hard to draw, but all the ones in this book were laid out with only a ten-cent-store compass and ruler, and a pair of scissors for cutting out freehand-drawn shapes of the fish, oak leaves, grape clusters, and pomegranates. Fish and grape clusters do not lend themselves to the trick, but perfectly symmetrical leaves and pomegranates can be formed by folding paper and drawing only half the motif, then cutting it folded.

A last word or two about color: the Hex sign on the front of the dust jacket is one I designed some years back for a man in California who wanted to make amulets. It is the strongest "good-luck-and protection" sign I could devise. To facilitate printing, my editor asked if they could substitute navy blue for black, adding—not wholly in jest—"Will this subject our offices to tempest and devastation? Please advise."

No. Hex signs can be made in one color as well as another *unless* you *mean* for the color to have a specific significance. Black is not a good color if you give it a black meaning (for instance, if you drew the Chinese yang and yin and put black over red, it could call for darkness to overshadow someone's life—or if over yellow, to darken his reason). But blue stands for serenity, and deep blue, I suppose, would stand for deep serenity. Psychologically it is not a good color to use if one wants to attract a person to spend money—you want red for that. Did you ever see a prostitute wearing navy blue?

19

"GO FETCH ME MY THIGHBONE"

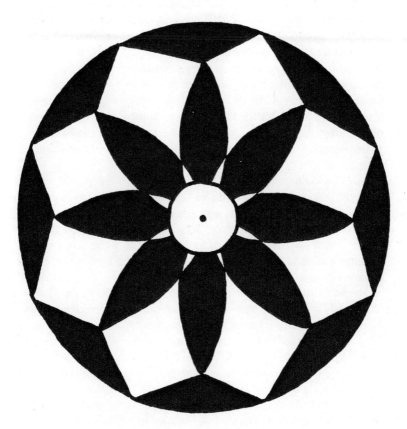

The Flower of Happiness: For Good Luck in any situation. The flower is for happiness, the sun centering it for brightness and joy

> *There is not much doubt that the procedures of*
> *ritual magic are likely to cause hallucinations.*

Richard Cavendish

I should like to tell of every event which has caused me to change some belief or supposition. Many have been without dramatic interest, however; others I am restrained from telling of because of the same ethical obligations which bind priests and physicians. Nevertheless, nothing has caused me to accept, change, or discard more beliefs than what Cavendish refers to as "ritual magic." I make no claim to knowledge of it but on one occasion I tried to create a reasonable facsimile to head off the effects of breaking a taboo and to create the psychological atmo sphere necessary to break spells a witch had placed upon a man and his wife.

Any condition resulting from belief in witchcraft is apparently beyond the reach of ordinary medicine—and beyond the reach of ordinary religious faith, because anyone with enough faith to break a spell is not subject to a spell in the first place. Breaking a spell is as formidable a task as a *Hexenmeister* ever needs to undertake, so if one is to undertake it, he must do everything possible to create the illusion that he *is* a *Hexenmeister*.

The wife, whom I'll call Ruth, came to me first, relating facts that I had already accepted as true—namely, that she had believed herself to be in poor health for a long while and that her nerves and disposition were deteriorating. She had gone the round of the best doctors and taken the medicines they prescribed without obtaining any relief. Ruth understood that I was on familiar terms with certain Dutch Fork individuals who are supposed to have "the power." Those "certain individuals" are old-believers, so I knew she was about to tell me she believed herself bewitched. But even so, I was startled when she flatly stated that someone had placed a witch-crab in her stomach to devour her vitals and kill her!

That is not in the tradition of Germanic Hex, but is a thing of Voodoo. During two years when I taught school in New Orleans and studied things not taught in school, I heard several references to witch-crabs. Usually an old Mam'bo on St. Claude Street broke the spell, and the victim vomited up the witch-crab, or crabs (or crayfish, snails, frogs, or spiders), and glimpsed them just long enough to be certain that they were gone. If she did not get the case soon enough, or if she failed with it, reports told of autopsies which revealed the stomach mysteriously eaten away as if consumed by gastric ulceration.

Ruth went on to tell me she had not dared tell the doctors what was really wrong with her, since they would have only referred her to a psychiatrist. I was inclined to agree with her; besides, I do not think psychiatrists are trained to deal with witch-crabs.

However, what magic has done, magic should be able to undo. I prescribed a midnight visit to a murdered man's grave, told her to secure nine handfulls of dirt from it, and gave her a ritual to perform with the dirt at sunrise, nine mornings following the next new moon. (This dirt, "goofer dust" in the Voodoo jargon, is sold commercially, but I have seen some offered as genuine that I would use for nothing more exacting than potting a geranium. If anyone wants any, he would do well to get it himself—at midnight on a night of the new moon, of course.)

Then, on the ninth morning, Ruth drove up, bounced out, and before she reached the porch, began exclaiming that the crab was gone. Radiant with delight, she explained that as she threw the last of the dust and repeated the incantation, she felt the crab let go of her stomach wall and start scrambling about in a frantic effort to escape. Soon, it somehow made its way down through her body and leg, and as she stared at her bare foot, it forced its way to the tip of her toe. She glimpsed it as it passed out onto the ground and scurried off in the direction of the grave, where I had told her it would wait until the witch returned on the night of the full moon.

She very quickly regained her health and a cheerful, pleasant disposition, too. She began saying that her husband, whom I'll call Luke, had not believed she had the crab in her stomach, as long as it was in there. But now that it had left her, he was convinced. So, since Luke was in poor health himself, and had been going to the same doctors without benefit, he decided that he too was under a spell. She asked me if I would try to help him.

I had no idea that goofer dust and sunrise incantations would do him any good. Generally speaking, Luke is a very long-headed man of the type who might begin such a treatment, and midway of it demand of himself, "What can grave dust do?" and start using reason.

Reason is a wonderful thing, but it is as destructive to a process dependent upon emotion as is emotion to a reasoning process. Witchcraft, like religion, is an emotional matter. In order to make money out of religion, a priest, tent-revivalist, or pastor must learn to play upon instinct or emotion, and these things are not without a logic beyond logic. In order to succeed with magic, so must a Voodoo or Hex. Love, hate, fear, and faith are quite outside the bounds of ordinary reason, but they are much nearer the wellsprings of life. Whoever seeks the water at the Fountainhead has to follow paths that lead far past the formal walkways. Pure reason and its logic never sent adrenalin to a man's heart or gave him an erection. They do very well for day-by-day routine, but they fail utterly when asked to prepare a man for loving, or for breaking a spell.

So in seeking an approach to Luke's problem, I felt I had to seek out an area in which unreason held undisputed rule. The only "weak" spot I found in him was a lingering belief in the reality of spirit communication. His grandparents had been Spiritualists, and in his youth he had learned a method of automatic writing. He went through a ritual with five other persons, after which he could take a pencil and paper and write names. The signatures he produced were identical with those written by persons now deceased, persons he supposed guided his hand.

He could not get messages, though, and the ability to secure mere signatures seemed to me only a pitiful vestige of the power the old people had—for he told of seances at which the dead materialized and spoke, and of sessions at which they levitated tables, made hats revolve, and caused brooms to stand up and sway to music as they swept about the room. I have found traditions of hat-turning and broom-dancing nowhere in America save in the Dutch Fork and in Lexington.

But then, nowhere else have I found such books as I have found in the Fork. In one old library I found the 1809 edition of Davies' *Mythology and Rites of the British Druids* and the two-volume work of the remarkable Count Agénor de Gasparin, *Science vs. Modern Spiritualism; A Treatise on Turning Tables, the Supernatural in General, and Spirits.* It may seem extraordinary to find such books among German farm people in South Carolina, but the Dutch Fork was a remarkable place. Not all its witches were old, uneducated farm women. Little Daniel Koon, the most powerful of them, somehow learned to read in five languages including Hebrew and Latin, and had seven grimoires which his eighteen children feared even to touch! The only German-language Hex incantation surviving from the Fork was recorded by a doctor who descended from immigrants in the Fork at the time of the Weberite Delusion—but he himself studied at the Sorbonne and at Heidelberg.

It is his name incidentally, which is inscribed with the date "1856" on the flyleaf of de Gasparin's strange book, now the pride of my own collection. The introduction to this work states that it deals with ". . . the Supernatural in general, the Agency of Spirits, False Miracles, Animal Magnetism, Spirit Rappings etc. . . . treated at length, with the vivacity which characterizes the French mind." The Count was a Calvinist, married to a rich Swiss lady from Vaud, and "vivacious" is hardly the term I should use to describe his writing. "Logical" or "realistic" would be much better choices—but the Count used the logic and realism of *un*reason! For instance, the book makes the point that supernatural phenomena are not the result of the causes generally supposed. But to do so, it argues that the phenomena themselves are real! Knowledge of the real causes is vital to the production of the phenomena, and that is equally true for magic. So what the good Calvinist Count did as a disservice to the Spiritualist religion, turned out (I *think* unintentionally) to be a great service to anyone who wishes to produce Spiritualist-type phenomena outside a religious context, and to anyone who wishes to work Hex in any context whatsoever. De Gasparin's theories are actually sufficient to serve as a foundation for a science of unreason. They allow one to work out formulas, using specific ideas as one does chemical elements. It is the fun of Hex to experiment in the laboratory heating the mixture to a certain emotional degree, adding a given quantity of instinct, and precipitating a phenomenon. However, it is a hazardous pastime if one uses the elements of fear and hate or adds the instinct of sex at the wrong time.

In his effort to be "modern" in 1856, the Count found himself handling the human mind as a physical force, which occult circles of course considered it to be when "Animal Magnetism" was in vogue. How he and Dr. Quimby would have stimulated each other! They would have agreed that thoughts are things, exerting physical force; that an individual creates what he thinks and determines his results by his expectation—but then they would have entered into disagreement. And had "Seth" come along to inspire them, or had Edgar Cayce, Parapsychology might have become a respectable study a century earlier than it did.

At least Quimby and the Count would have had great fun and I should have been happy to join them had I then been in Vaud instead of plowing cotton fields in South Carolina. The Count tells of one poor soul who was convinced that his seances had become infested with demons. Knocks such as the Barr's Run Spirit made on the headboard of my bed began to bother this man's wife—but let the Count tell it—

". . . Madame L — had placed some holy water within reach, hoping thus to preserve herself from all nocturnal terrors. After remaining there about two hours, the same knocks were again heard, and as they seemed especially to come from under the chair of Madame L — , she dipped her fingers in the holy water, and sprinkled it on the spot whence the sound proceeded. Her hand was instantly seized and bitten above the second joint of the thumb, and she could with difficulty withdraw it. Her husband did not at first comprehend the cause of the cries she uttered, and great was his astonishment to see on her red and swollen flesh, the print of two rows of teeth . . ." (This is only one paragraph after which three or four pages relate even stranger things.)

It would be enough to suppose that such a phenomenon could be produced by a demon (as I thought myself that night in Huntington). It is the genius of the Count de Gasparin to make it comprehensible as a *natural* phenomenon—the result of activities in which you and I, or any other normal person might take part if we wished. I believe the Dutch Fork "witches" did take part; so by the logic of unreason, anything and everything they did was quite natural and what one might expect. But let me continue and tell what happened when I deliberately set out to follow the procedures of unreason.

I decided, then, that only a reasonable facsimile of spirit communication would keep my bewitched patient from interjecting ordinary reason in the course of the procedure. And of all the kinds of Spiritualistic phenomena I know anything about, none is more impressive than what may occur when one uses a grave lamp and a dead man's mirror. I have personal interest in the method because neither Grandmother nor James Andrew would ever teach me to descry—the proper Hex word is *scry*—in such a mirror.

Actually, though, they had good reason for this refusal. About ninety years ago, the girls in the community had grown very casual with Hex, and prepared a real grave lamp and took a dead man's mirror to serve as the main entertainment at a jolly Halloween party to be held in an abandoned house. A *Hexenmeister* would regard such festivities much as a Catholic would a party where consecrated wafers were served with onion dip.

The girls meant to scry their future husbands. Five or six had done so, either declaring that the boy who appeared in the mirror was the only one that the scrier would think of marrying, or that under no circumstance would she marry the boy who appeared. (All did marry as the glass predicted, however.) But when the next girl peered into the glass, she gasped in horror and sat frozen, then gave a stricken cry and fainted.

That ended the hilarity. The girls revived her and when she was somewhat coherent she told them that as the mirror cleared, she saw a door open into darkness. An open casket stood upright with the corpse of her fiancé in it, and before she could look away, her own open casket stood up beside it, and she saw herself laid out for burial.

They hurried to take her home, but when they got there, they met her father already on his way to the abandoned house to get her. Shortly before, he told them, the fiancé's brother had ridden up with tragic word: the youth had been killed in a buggy accident near Walter late that afternoon.

The girl fainted again, and her family spent half the night with her, making her eat raw onions and keeping a cold compress at the base of her skull until she grew calmer and passed into a fitful sleep. Finally she seemed to be settled, so they went to bed. As soon as her mother arose next morning, she went to see about her. She found the girl dead, the bed soaked with blood from her slashed wrists and her father's razor by the bedside.

I never heard of anyone in Roane or Kanawha County's using a dead man's mirror after that. Though the girl might have killed herself in any case, it was thought that the vision had fixed the idea in her mind; some even said it was punishment for having used the mirror as a parlor game, when any Hex knows that only the most serious purposes justify its use. (In murder cases which defy solution, for example, a Hex might resort to use of the mirror to see the crime reenacted and thus identify the murderer. Or a girl considering a man of doubtful character might scry to decide whether the picture of their future life justified accepting or rejecting him.)

If Luke *had* been bewitched, I seriously hoped to use the mirror to

scry the witch and observe what he had done. Failing that, I expected
to be shown the outcome of his condition, for even a Hex likes to know
what to expect. Seeking that sort of information is considered legitimate.

The lamp I wished to use had been standing prepared on a grave in an
adjoining county ever since its owner died unexpectedly in 1916. For
forty-five years it had stood unmoved. The elements turned the glass a
beautiful amythest, the metal parts corroded away, and the chimney
was broken by accident or by hail. When I inquired about it, I was told
that if it were moved—except to be put to the intended use—the person
who moved it would die within three days. But when I said that was
what I meant to use it for, the family joyfully said to take it at the
earliest need. It was a lovely old lamp, but they found it embarrassing,
because the whole congregation who saw it each Sunday knew that
their grandmother had placed it on her husband's grave, and it was a
reminder that the family had had witches in it.

Anyway, I visited my friends in Dutch Fork and inquired until I was
told how to set up the grave lamp and use the mirror—that the lamp is
filled with oil and set on the grave before midnight on a night of the
new moon, with repetition of certain prayers and incantations. Then
the grave is circled with salt, and the lamp is left burning until after
sunrise. Then it is extinguished and left on the grave until after dark on
the evening when it is used—normally before the next new moon,
though once prepared, it may be used at any time.

Before sunrise on the day of use, the "user" secures water from a
spring on the eastern slope of a hill. Sunlight is not allowed to fall upon
it, and it is kept in a dark place all day. Then, after dark it is taken to the
place where it is to be used, and placed in a clear glass container. (I used
an old half-gallon vinegar jug.) The lamp is stood on a closed Bible and
lighted. The scrier seats himself with the lamp behind him, so that when
he holds the mirror before him, he sees the lamp reflected over his left
shoulder. If it is properly arranged, the flame of the lamp is reflected
through the container of water, and appears to be burning in the center
of the glass container.

The scrier states what he wishes to have shown, and concentrates on
the reflection of the flame. If "it is intended" that he be shown, his
eyes soon become dazzled; the mirror becomes unbearably bright, then
opaque as if filled with thick fog. And when the mists clear away, he

sees in the mirror a television-like scene that clarifies the matter in question. For example, after the question "Did John kill himself or was he murdered?" the enactment of suicide or murder should appear as it actually took place. As I found out, however, the glass shows what it wishes, and the information may seem impertinent, though I suspect that it is often far more pertinent to the situation than the answer to the given question itself could be.

Much to everyone's consternation, particularly mine, on the way from the grave to my house the antique lamp mysteriously broke of itself. Luke took it as a sign that he would be punished with death for disturbing it, for I had sent him to bring it. The broken lamp unnerved me temporarily, almost as much as it did Luke for I had to prepare a new one—and here I was left on my own. I had been told merely that there *are* a ritual and incantations—without having them given me since the lamp I was planning to use from then on was already prepared.

Luke kept saying that he knew he was done for, and I had to do something to keep him from a nervous collapse. I tried to express annoyed disappointment rather than apprehension. I told him how fragile rotton old glass becomes, and pointed out that the break probably occurred because the lamp was blazing hot from the sun, and the shade, and the air blowing inside the car cooled it too rapidly and caused it to crack. It had not yet broken all the way around, so I said, "Maybe we still can use it," and took it to the sink to wash off the sand. When the cold water touched it, the crack continued around the bowl and the top fell off. This only supported my theory that no more than temperature change broke it. It eased Luke a little, but he still lamented that we could not hold the scrying. When I told him we would simply have to prepare a lamp of our own, he asked me if I knew how—in tones which contained something close to awe.

When truthful answers must not be given, sometimes a question does as well. "You don't think I'd risk messing with one if I didn't, do you?" I demanded.

A young friend of mine I'll call Mark, who is often mistaken for my son, was with me, and when they left, he said, "Are you going to let me in on this? Can I go with you?"

"You bet," I smiled, for I counted on Mark's terror for most of the psychological "power" or mana that I hoped to attach to the lamp.

"Here's fifty cents. Get a box of salt before you come tomorrow, and I'll cut some holly and make a cross, and hunt a clear jug for the water. Go fetch me my thighbone and my crooked knife."

This thighbone when I first got it was merely an historical relic. Washed out by a gravel-washing machine within two hundred feet of the first fort site in Lexington County, it may date back to the first white outpost in 1718. More likely it belonged to one of the settlers of the first Swiss group—maybe even to Heinrich Weber. At first I intended to rebury it, but when I found that it kept my children out of my room and away from my books and papers, I soaked it with varnish to preserve it. Later, when it convinced my first Cuban son-in-law that my room was a *"nudo de brujos"* (witches' nest) and kept him from pilfering my Confederate money and old coins, I became downright attached to it. I now have honest sons-in-law, but the bone remains very useful. It makes a very impressive wand, and when I use it, I can do anything I please with my left hand, which is not noticed because everyone is watching the bone. Not that I do any sleight of hand, you understand, but a free left hand is always useful for motioning and giving cues for special effects of lighting, interruptions, or sound effects for the desired psychological reactions. Since then I have added a second-hand skull and a few odds and ends of Indian skeletal remains, and in the atmosphere that they create I can forget a word of an incantation, or a whole line, and go right ahead without the visitor's taking note. Besides, they liven up the room, and the skull cheers me up when my spirits are low. However poorly I may feel, I realize I am much better off than he, missing his whole body.

He was a local do-it-yourself medical student's anatomical specimen, prepared about 1850 from a cadaver supplied by body-snatchers, the poorfarm, or the executioner. I understand that such students then boiled the flesh off the bone, and this example has the cranium sawed off maladroitly just above the eyebrows. He still has a wicked grin, and it is impossible to feel alone in the house when the grandchildren are at school, my son is gone and my wife is out, as long as he grins from the top of the shrine on the mantle, sharing the room with me. If I ever get a whole skull, I probably will plant an African violet or a cactus in his brain-cavity, and use him as a window decoration. As a symbol of life rising out of death, he should be a very inspiring planter.

I counted on enough's having come down, in however garbled a form, for use of ritual magic to affect Mark and Ruth and Luke, so I decided to make it as dramatic as possible. My request to Mark to bring the thighbone and knife was a step to prepare him, for he was reluctant to touch either one—the bone because it was human and the knife, a homemade tool used by a blacksmith in paring horses' hooves for horse-shoeing, because it was said to have been used by the blacksmith's wife when she cut his throat.

"Huh-uh," he grinned resolutely. "That's *your* old thighbone—you handle it if you want to!"

"Well, just bring me the knife so I can cut some holly," I told him.

Mark brought it, held gingerly in his handkerchief between finger and thumb. "Some *Hexenmeister* you're going to make," I chided. "What are you going to do if sometime you have to undertake something that calls for a dead man's blood or the powdered bones of a suicide victim?"

"I'll make a deal with an embalmer for the blood, and send off to the mail-order house in Chicago for the bone powder," he said practically.

"Fat chance," I snorted. "I'd be willing to bet they get the bones from a slaughter-house, and when you called upon the spirit to answer some question of life or death, you'd feel pretty funny if a steer showed up and bawled at you."

"People wouldn't pay five dollars a packet for it if it doesn't work all right," he said confidently.

"What is Hex coming to!" I grumbled. "You kids lack the feel for it. In the old days you got your own powdered bone, no matter how, and those old *Hexenmeisters* had *power*. Some first-rate magic you'll ever get with a powdered soup-bone!"

"You take it too seriously, Dad," he grinned.

Of course Mark was perfectly right. Chaucer had the final word when he wrote that the Pardoner of Roncesvalles had a glass vessel full of pigs' bones which he displayed—or more likely sold—as holy relics. I dare say such "holy relics" have wrought miracles comparable to those attributed to the wristbone of St. Anne at Beaupré—if it *is* a wristbone, and if it *is* St. Anne's. At five dollars a packet a powdered soup-bone *would* work just as potent magic as that of a genuine suicide victim. Neither has an effect except for faith and suggestion, and five dollars' worth of faith is forever equal to the faith one has in five dollars' worth. After I had had my fun with Mark, I told him so.

Even religion works better if it is not too deadly serious. Jesus performed one of His major miracles at a wedding party where the guests were already too drunk to know the difference between good wine and poor, and nobody knows how much drunker they got on the wine He provided for them. I am impatient with disciples who would have it supposed that they are holier than Christ in such matters, and I like jolly witches much better than grim ones.

When the night to prepare the lamp came, I took Mark, the salt, the holly cross (a square Hex cross of holly boughs lashed together with linen, since Hex avoids iron—the cold, killing, mutable metal used by cynics to dampen lightning), the wand, the knife, and the lamp to the old couple's house. Ruth and Luke brought a lantern and we went to the cemetery and to the grave of the murdered grandfather. On setting out I admonished them not to speak, not to take flight whatever they might see, and under no circumstance to step outside the nine-foot ring of salt I would draw around them, telling them to stand exactly where I placed them after I drew the pentagram with salt upon the grave.

A sliver of moon haunted the sky, and the stars seemed very bright. A night wind stirred the graveyard shrubbery; crickets chirped, and bats flew down after the moths drawn to the lantern. It was a perfect time and place for magic. When I reached the grave I stood the three beside it, drew the pentagram and the circle invisibly with the point of the knife, raised the holly cross in my left hand, held up the salt in my right, and offered it to the moon. As I did so, I intoned solemnly, "Radmiel, Ithiel, Zophiel: *Acer saccharum; Quercus nigra; Quercus phellos; Quercus falcata. Celtus occidentalis; Morus rubra. Crataegus intricata; Aralia spinosa; Maclura pomifera; Oxydendrum arboreum: Taxodium distichum.*" Then I retraced the pentagram and circle with the salt, which I am sure they believed had been offered to a number of spirits whose names it is not lawful to utter. The wife clutched her husband's arm, and the boy edged over until he pressed against him.

I then leaned the cross against the tombstone, and drew a triangle with salt at the foot of the grave. *"Ilex opaca, Asimina triloba, salix nigra, salix babylonica, Populus deltoides:* against all demons, evil and malevolent spirits, we beseech thee preserve us. *Betula papyrifera; Betula lenta; Betula populifolia;* Amen, amen, amen. We beseech thee, protect us from the dragoman; preserve us from the melanochroi; keep us safe from the notornis; defend us from the papilionaceous ranuculus. O *Caria ovata*, we implore thee, against the primigenial varicocele, forfend!"

Then I raised the dreadful wand and with it drew the Hex cross in the air, and with lugubrious, prayerful voice chanted: *"Castanea dentata* thou of the thousand spines, we summons in thy name those who will grant us success in this our undertaking! *Aesculus glabra,* thou of the unpleasant smell, drive all the guardians from the graves; keep not back the spirits within. *Tilia vulgaris,* cast thy shadow between us and those who would stay us in our endeavor. *Quercus stellata,* thou of the great strength, grant us fortitude to withstand all terrors of this night."

I then solemnly elevated the salt to each of the four directions and slowly taking handfuls, cast it north, east, south, and west, saying "Tetra, tetrad, Tetragram, Tetragrammaton!" Then I bade the others hold one another's hand, gave Mark mine, and holding the cross aloft led them out of the circle, leaving the lamp flickering on the grave.

When we were back in the house, Ruth said, "I had the most awful feelings! Will any of those things come tonight and bother us here at the house?"

On impulse, I said, "Some of the salt is left. It has been lifted up to the four directions. I will draw a barrier in front of the steps. If any evil spirit or fiend should come, or any creature or person who intends harm, he cannot step across the salt."

Then chuckling inwardly at how amused Stud would have been by the sonorous Latin names of various trees intoned as a priest might, and at the awed uncomprehension on the boy's face as he listened to the solemn nonsense, I came home. Mark sat so close against me that it was almost uncomfortable, and he was actually holding to my arm. At last he breathed, "What was it out there just beyond the light?"

"Did you see something?" I whispered.

"I didn't dare to look, but I know something was there; I could feel it," he shuddered.

"The dead were out there. They were all around us." As we had been in the middle of the cemetery, this was very true in one sense, but I am sure he did not take it that way nor did I expect him to.

"I'm afraid I'll never be a *Hexenmeister,"* he sighed. "I'm too cowardly."

"Oh, you'll get over that," I said lightly. "Just be thankful that something you *could* see didn't come up." (It could have well been a

post oak, and then where would I have been?) "You aught to read some
of the accounts I have seen of what can happen at a grave ritual."

"I wish I could stay all night," he said. "I'll keep hearing those awful
incantations all the way home."

"Ilex opaca, Asimoina triloba, Salix nigra. . . ?"

"Uh-huh, but please don't repeat them now."

"If you won't tell anybody, I saw a big male *Ilex opaca* in the yard
one night on the full moon. It had a dark, somber stateliness, I
thought."

"What was it doing?"

"Just standing. It didn't move a foot the whole time I watched it."

"Was it very big?"

"Goodness, yes!" I replied, "It looked to me as if it were fifty feet
tall at the very least."

"Aaah, you got to be pulling my leg!" Mark protested. "If a thing
that big prowled around, people would see it!"

"If you want to stay a while I'll do something so *you* can see it, if
you *want* to," I said earnestly.

"I can't," he said quickly. "Mother would be worried sick if I stayed
out all night, and it's too late to phone her!"

Mark came very early next morning for we were doing some repairs
we wished to get completed as soon as possible. We were having breakfast together when the couple drove up in great excitement. As Ruth
ran up to the porch, she called out, "You caught a man. You caught
him with the salt!"

"What happened?" I asked, astonished.

"We were awake until two or after, trying to calm down after what
we went through at the grave, and were just dozing off when all the
dogs ran out. They sounded as if they were about to tear up somebody,
so we jumped up. Luke grabbed the pistol and jerked his pants on and
ran to the porch. The dogs were snarling at a man frozen at the steps."

"Frozen?"

"Like a stone image, with one foot raised to step up. His other foot
was outside the salt and he couldn't move. I've been told that to break
a spell like that you have to touch the person, or speak his name and
release him in the name of St. John the Baptist. So I hollered to touch
him, and when Luke did, the man could set his foot down and speak,
but he was so muddle-headed he didn't make any sense!"

"Did you know him?"

"Why yes, he lives just across the creek—in sight if the trees weren't in the way. He's lived there sixteen years, but he didn't know where he was, and he didn't recognize us. He didn't even know his own name! He said he didn't know where he was, or why he came in. He said something went over him as he started up the steps, and he offered us a dollar to take him home if we knew where he belonged."

"Was he drunk?" I asked weakly.

"We couldn't smell anything on him. He didn't seem drunk—just completely addled. We took him home and his sister let him in, and we heard him hollering and going on like a crazy person right on till sunup. Now you know as well as I do he had no business at our place at two in the morning! I bet he's been the one who was stealing stuff all the time."

As soon as they left, the awe-stricken Mark stared at me and murmured, "Dad, just what *did* you do to that salt?"

I tried to *look* as wise and mysterious as I *felt* confused. "You saw what I did, and I hope you remember the incantations," I replied. "But It may be a long time before I'm ready to explain it to you. Maybe after you've seen the *Ilex opaca,* and can bear to look at the notornis, and are not afraid to stand face to face with a dragoman, you'll understand without having it explained—especially if on some night of the full moon you take one of the melanochroi into your bed."

"I'll never do that!" he cried, aghast.

"It wouldn't be as bad as you think," I shurgged. "You could keep your eyes shut if you couldn't bear to look at one's face."

"Did you ever go to bed with one of them?" he shuddered.

"Yes," I breathed, "when I was even younger than you are, and on up almost until I went into the Army, I sometimes lay with one in my arms."

"God! I'll bet you never told your wife. Was it warm or cold?"

However I made it *sound,* I always told Mark the truth, as I tell you. And never was I more truthful than when I said it might be a long time before I felt ready to explain what happened to the salt. Since there was not a word of real magic in the incantations, except the word *Tetragram maton,* and since the whole ceremony was merely staged for effect, mostly to minimize the importance of the broken lamp and to give mana for the mirror-scrying, I realized that the salt-spell took its effect from something else. The salt was merely the iodized common variety from the supermarket, and that was all I supposed it to be when I made the ring in front of the steps. *I had no real faith in it, so I did not give it power* to immobilize the prowler and thrall his mind into confusion. Yet something gave it psychic power which impelled me to dig a deep hole and bury what was left in the box, and I threw the broken lamp into an unused well.

Later, as I pored through de Gasparin's eldritch pages, I came to realize that I had worked very potent magic at the grave, and that my incantations were filled with words of power equal to those of any grimoire. If you do not know what a notornis is, how would you like to see one at a murdered man's grave at midnight? If you do not know that an *Ilex opaca* is an American holly tree, how would the thought strike you of seeing one fifty feet tall, standing without moving a foot, in the light of the full moon?

The ritual manipulated the unknown in an atmosphere of very strong suggestion, and that is the way of magic. The salt took on mana from the fear of the three unknowing, terrified people. It gave it power to produce the effect I told them it could, and since then I have learned that all ritual magic is contrived to fill substances with mana. There are many kinds of mana and mana alone suffices to do many very remarkable things. Religious relics take on power to heal. The Sacrament takes on perhaps the greatest power of any substance. Vervain juice and leaves do become irresistible love-charms, and Voodoo dolls become death-dealing images. This is de Gasparin's contention, and I have found it absolute truth.

To fake magic and secure magical results is a profoundly instructive experience. I shudder to think what the incantations of Satanists, uttered with rituals utterly more terrifying than the mere lighting of a lamp upon a grave, can do. Emotion fixes mana; it may also be the force that fixes spirits to the same spot, inducing them to repeat the odd, often shameful, activity that engendered the original emotion. Where men believe that they have power to kill, they have it. If they, themselves believe in their magic, I do not discount the power they believe it has. Similarly, if one believes in the power of religion, then it has the power.

De Gasparin was not the first to set forth this axiom. It has been stated by the highest authority recognized by the western world. But maybe because it was Jesus Christ who stated the ultimate truth as to magic, men have read it piously for nearly two thousand years and paid no heed to it—no more than they have to the rest of what He said. *"According to your faith be it unto you,"* he said, addressing blind men whose sight had been given them. *"All things are possible to him that believeth."*

Those sayings were among the first things that I read in childhood. Yet like everyone else, I did not pay any attention to them because Jesus said them. Yet when Count Agenor de Gasparin said them in a book that I read because I sought to learn how to practice witchcraft successfully, I paid attention, and common table salt struck a man motionless and unable to recall his name or recognize a house in hearing distance of his own, simply because I told three people who believed me, ". . . if any evil spirit should come, or any creature or person who intends harm, he cannot step across the salt." Verily, verily, I say unto you, according to your faith be it unto you! It is magic. Like many other outrageous things I have said to you which tax your credulity, it is truth. If you do not believe Jesus Christ, take *my* word for it; if you do not believe my word, take *His.*

We got on with our scrying. I was on summer vacation at home; my family was at Hickory, North Carolina; so Luke, Ruth and Mark and I made up the group. We met in the old couple's kitchen, using the kitchen table as the lamp-stand, and their old family Bible to make the illumination rest on truth.

The mirror was a small, pine-framed one about 150 years old that I bought in Dutch Fork which had reflected four or five generations now dead. We sought control by the spirit of the murdered man from whose grave the dust was taken—the old man's grandfather—and since it was the first experience with the lamp for us all, we waited in breathless expectancy, not very sure what might happen.

I discovered I could attempt to scry until I am ninety without seeing anything more than a surprising display of underwater pyrotechnics. The flame seems to move about, divide, reunite, disappear, and reappear—I cannot concentrate enough on the unreasonable. Neither could the old man, and his wife was able to get as far as the fog, but could not see it clarify. I felt sure I had fouled up by making a farce of preparing the lamp, and had little hope that the boy would see anything.

However, when his turn came, he went into trance from looking at the flame, and presently from the movement of his eyes and the rapt interest in his expression we could tell that he was seeing something in the glass.

"Tell us what you see, son," I murmured.

"I see an old man on a porch," he breathed. "It's sure a funny-looking old house, away up off the gound on brick pillars—must be ten feet up to the porch. Long steps coming down. The porch has a sharp roof. It's a big old house with big trees all around it, and it's here, I think, only the road is a lot further from the house than it is now."

"That was the old house that burned when I was a child," Luke said. "What's the old man you see like?"

"He's got on a fork-tailed coat that hangs to his knees behind, and he has a beard that comes to his waist, and long white hair, and he's got only one hand—no, he's got a hand on that arm, but it's all crooked around and he can't use it."

"That's your grandpa!" the woman exclaimed to her husband.

"Yes," he agreed, "he looked just like that when he was murdered, and he was wearing that old forked coat when they brought him in."

"What is he doing?" I asked.

"He looks all excited. He keeps pointing back toward the distance behind the house, and now he's making as if he has a shovel and is digging something."

"He's trying to show us where he hid the gold!" Luke exclaimed, utterly forgetting that he had been in hope of finding out the details as to how he was bewitched.

Without anything much more revealing than this, the old man in the glass kept on pointing and imitating digging for perhaps ten minutes. Mark's cheeks were flowing with tears from eyestrain, so when he said that the old man went inside and shut the door I told him to close his eyes and rest a while. He remained in trance, though, and was apparently unaware of anything except my voice when I questioned him.

As Mark rested, Luke related that when he was about ten years old—shortly before the house burned—his grandfather became distrustful of his youngest son, and unknown to anyone except his wife removed about five thousand dollars in gold that he had kept concealed under the bricks in the hearth in his room. He hid the gold outside, then he openly took the empty pot in which it had been kept and went with it and a shovel into the swamp, making sure that his son observed him. He buried the empty pot by a peculiar tree, and kept alert until he heard his son sneak out one night. The old man followed him and watched unseen as the youth dug up the pot. When he came back, his father confronted him and would have driven him from home had not the young man begged forgiveness, and had not his mother interceded so pitifully for him. The old man agreed to let him stay until he could earn enough to take him to Texas, which was what the son had in mind.

The young man worked diligently and raised a fine crop of cotton on land his father provided for him. Pleased with his son's industry, the old man began to feel that the youth had changed and they became on better terms than they had been since the young man's childhood. When the crops were gathered, father and son took their cotton to Columbia together and as usual, the old man was paid in gold—about two thousand dollars.

The youth pointedly told his father to go on home ahead of him, as he wished to celebrate a bit before returning—but he was seen driving through New Brookland only a short time after his father had passed through. Then about three o'clock he burst in at home in great excitement, saying that he had found his father's wagon near the mill dam, where a bush had been cut to block the road. He had stopped to clear the bush out of the way, but could find no trace of his father. The other members of the family hurried to alarm nearby neighbors, and the young man took the swiftest horse and rode off, saying he wished to bring the sheriff.

A search party soon gathered, and soon after daylight found the old man's murdered body in the mill pond. As the sheriff had still not come, someone hurried to town and found that the young man had not reported his father's disappearance after all. His description was wired to points west, and he was apprehended crossing the bridge at Augusta. He had the old man's gold as well as his own cotton money, and confessed to the murder.

"That just about killed the poor old lady," Ruth sighed.

"That *was* what killed her." Luke said. "The grief and the shame—it right near killed Ma and the rest of them, too."

Mark looked rested, so I told him to open his eyes and see what was then in the glass. When he started following movement he said, "I see

men with a team and wagon. It's a blue wagon with red wheels, and two
big black horses with a white spot on one's head, and the men are load-
ing old lumber on the wagon."

"That was Pa's old wagon," Luke declared. "I traded it in when I got
my first car, back in 1921, and the horses were old Ben and old Blaze.
Ask him what the men look like."

"One is a great big man; one's heavy-set and has a fierce long mous-
tache, and the other one is a big, gawky guy about eighteen, barefooted, with a red shirt hanging out of his pants."

"I see them just as if they were here," he chuckled. "Tell him to take
a good look. That was Big Jim, and his son Ed and my pa. They were
tearing down Grandpa's old sheep barn. Big Jim was this kid's great-
grandpa, and the gawk was his grandpa. Big Jim was dead twenty years
before this here boy was born—it ain't many boys that see their folks as
they were in another lifetime."

"What are they doing now?" I asked.

"The big man is unloading the lumber, and the heavy one is stacking
it, and the young guy is leaned back against a tree with his hands in his
pockets, chewing on a straw, and just looking on."

Luke laughed again. "That's Ed, plainer than life," "Before he got
married, and this boy's little old grandma put some get-up-and-go into
him, that was the do-lessest white boy in the whole county. Ask him
what they seem to be doing with the lumber."

When I did, he replied, "They have another barn or something started, and I guess they are using the old lumber in the new one."

"They built it out of the old barn," Luke confirmed. "I wonder why
he's seeing that? His sheep were Grandpa's pride and joy and he was
always hanging around the sheep barn."

"Do you reckon he could have buried his gold there?" Ruth wondered
aloud.

"I'm trying to think," Luke murmured. "It seems like Grandpa went
there a lot of times when the sheep weren't penned up."

"You could hide digging under the litter and manure," she
considered.

Mark reported that the men went back for another load, and at last
saw his grandfather helping work, for he did help load the heavy timbers. But as the scrying seemed to no purpose and as his eyes were again
watering, I stopped him and let him rest. On the third scrying he saw

only a rock sticking up out of some low weeds and near it a cedar tree. It meant nothing to me, but Luke seemed excited, and said that the rock was just behind where the sheep barn had stood, and that the cedar had come up just where the corner of the old building had been.

"Grandpa is trying to show us something," Ruth declared. "I reckon the gold is all that he has on his mind."

We closed the seance soon, and later as I assessed it, I found it baffling, though I did feel certain that all that had appeared in the mirror had come directly from Luke's memory and had only seemed to Mark to appear visually in the glass. It took me no nearer Luke's physical trouble. However, lack of interest in life had been one of his problems, and revival of interest in the gold broke his lethargy. I know that he dug around the old barn site, and that very soon he bought a new car and had a deep well drilled. But I always suspected that he had a great deal more money than he appeared to, and he could have bought the car merely because he again felt that one might be of use to him. He sold some land about that time, too, so I have no real reason to suppose that he did find any money. The dead man's mirror rather disappointed me. I had expected more of it than proof that my young friend was clairvoyant. I tried him later, and found that he could go into trance and see just as clearly in a glass of water. Still, I would not have missed preparing the lamp for anything.

Since the mirror did not proffer the desired information, we held a simple session with a table, and Luke's mother's spirit—or what purported to be her spirit—gave a message saying that he was under a death spell, placed upon him by a man whom she named. She said that the curse was to cause cancer, and that Luke already had a cancer in his chest. He was instructed to burn on a bed of salt certain things found marked with black Hex symbols, along with something belonging to the man who placed the spell. Luke burned an ear of the man's corn, and as instructed, threw the salty ashes over the fence into the other man's field.

I do not say that there is any connection between this act and the events which followed, for too often one assumes cause and effect when there is only coincidence or sequence to suggest it. But very soon after the spell was supposedly turned back upon the sender, that man developed a cancer which killed him inside ninety days. A doctor, in giving a very thorough examination, detected a tumor between Luke's lung and heart. That has been his condition ever since, for the tumor has not grown or given him any apparent trouble, and for the first time in several years he found a job and went to work at it. I do not know that the tumor ever was cancerous. I only know what Luke believed: that if the spell were broken, he would get well and be able to work again.

20

"I WOULD THAT
THOU WERT COLD OR HOT"

Tulips: Symbol of faith—refers to "The Time of the Lily" when righteousness and peace shall reign on earth, and man shall love as brethren. The leaves form hearts, for without love there can be no faith

*He that hath an ear, let him hear what the Spirit
saith unto the churches.*

*And unto the angel of the church of the Laodi-
cians, write; These things saith the Amen, the faithful and true Witness, the beginning of the creation
of God; I know thy works, that thou art neither
cold nor hot; I would that thou wert cold or hot.
So then because thou art lukewarm, and neither
cold nor hot, I will spue thee out of my mouth;
because thou sayest, I am rich, and increased with
goods, and have need of nothing; and knowest not
that thou art wretched, and miserable, and poor,
and blind, and naked. . .*

Revelation 3:13-17

Grandmother believed that the reference to the seven churches of Asia
in the Revelation is to successive periods in the history or life of the
Church, and that the Church of the Laodicians is that of the last days. I
do not believe in the end of the world as did she, but I do believe in the
end of the age. In fact, I believe we have reached and passed it, for I
feel that I was born in another age, and I know that in my time man
loosed atomic power and set foot on the moon, and not since the end
of the Age of Atlantis (be it fact or fable) had man previously done
either. I am told that the age past was that of the Fishes, which corre-
sponds more or less to the Christian Era, and that the present age is that
of the Man with the Watering Pot, the characteristics of which are on
the one hand, energy and violence, and on the other those of the gardener, for the man with the watering pot is a gardener. Those characteristics appear already in the Aquarian young, for they wreck in order to
make ready to build anew, and they are greatly concerned about their
garden, the environment. But the Age of Aries did not end with the
beginning of the Age of Pisces, nor will the Ram be forgotten until the
last shophar is blown. Neither will the Age of Pisces be over until the
last bishop takes off his fish-head mitre. The old age is still very much
with us, and we shall be reminded of it yet a long, long time. It has
historic value and antiquarian interest, and may be studied to advantage. No man can know where he is unless he knows from whence he

started his journey, or know what he is unless he realizes what he has been. Still, though it is good to know the past, it is not wise to live in it.

I can have little doubt that the Church of the Laodicians does refer to the church of our own day, if only because it characterizes it perfectly Nothing better describes the present state of the church than "neither cold nor hot." It does not reject religion outright, for even the God-is-dead concept offers the deity decent Christian burial, and though the Church seems to have lost sight of man, the individual immortal soul, it is greatly preoccupied with Man, the abstract mass social phenomenon.

The Church of this day suffers a number of conditions any of which singly could be fatal. It is wealthy, it is secular, it is privileged: on all these accounts it is woefully vulnerable. However eternal its underlying truths may be, it has buried them in a dungheap of theology. No sect rests on doctrine capable of scientific proof.

Even the Romish church, for centuries the epitome of ecclesiastical authority, is full of people who reject its dominion. The Dutch church is in almost complete schism with Rome over the matter of celibacy of the priesthood, and in almost every other advanced nation the priesthood is divided by this controversy, as are the laity over the matter of birth control. Nothing but calamity faces the Roman church. This tottering ruin, half of which fell in during the Reformation, creaks and sags on the verge of total collapse. When the government of Italy turns Communist, which may be very soon, the Vatican (already stripped of its princely lands) will lose its remaining autonomy. Confiscation of the Papal treasures will impoverish the church, and serve as a precedent for other governments.

The proper function of religion is to awaken, nurture, and satisfy the soul, and give man the dominion willed for him by his creator. It should give each man conviction that he is more than mere flesh and blood, that his life is more than the little moment between birth and death. It should fill him with a sense of individual meaning, identity, and uniqueness, yet relate him to other men and show him something higher than himself that he can always strive to attain. It should not allow him to feel that he has attained enough to warrant him to stop and bask in self-satisfaction and spiritual pride, yet it should allow him a sense of inner peace in assurance that his striving is itself of as great worth as the goal. It should give him an understanding of mankind, and a sense of harmony with nature, provide him with a philosophy of peace, and bring him serenity, health, and happiness.

The Church should be a group of individuals with similar interests, beliefs and goals who work together for spiritual, social, and emotional enrichment, finding with each other that friendship and love which develop among people of similar interests when they meet and work together. Needless to say, such intimacy is impossible in a congregation of hundreds or thousands, and one seldom knows more than a few persons in such congregations even by name. All the more now, since family ties are so difficult to maintain, the church and religion should provide something akin to family feeling among its people.

A witches' coven of twelve, and a leader (or the twelve disciples and Jesus, if one prefers), is an ideal group for what I consider a good church to be. As many as thirteen persons can be close friends and feel devotion, even love for one another. Such a group cannot finance great buildings, but a church is not a building, even though that is what the primary meaning of the word has become. It cannot do most of the things that a large congregation can do, but it can do more important things that the large group cannot. I should not care to found a new church or another denomination, but if I should, I would enjoin my followers to form a church in spirit—a body which if it acquired property at all would own only centers for renewal in remote and scenic areas in the mountains, on the seashore, and in the desert, where members might go to enjoy natural beauty and drop for a healing moment the unreality which so universally is mistaken for the real. If more than twelve should wish to unite with this invisible body, I should insist that they form new units—little separate intimate confraternities to work with God.

Jesus said, ". . . if two of you shall agree on earth, as touching anything that they shall ask, it shall be done for them of my Father which is in heaven. For where two or three are gathered together in my name, there am I in the midst of them." He said no such thing of groups of two or three hundred, or two or three thousand; for where there are so many, there can be no such singleness of purpose, or unity of thought as can exist between two or among as many as thirteen. Without this unity, there can be little spiritual power; for conflicting interests and

ideas dissipate it, fragment it, and bring it to confusion. In this knowledge the witches of the earth have been wiser than the clergy. It is
noteworthy that when the Lord had seventy disciples, He "... sent
them two and two before his face into every city, and place, whither He
himself would come." The combined spiritual strength of two men is
much greater than the mere sum of their individual strengths. Two together can work miracles: two hundred cannot. Moreover, I should
advise these little confraternities to end each year owing nothing and
owning nothing, for when property is involved, a church ceases to be
human and becomes a thing. My church would first of all be in any
place one of one man and one God, as it is now with me; then one of
men and women going two and two with God; and never anywhere
more than a group of twelve and its leader going with Him. Thus there
could be nearness, intimacy, and the opportunity to walk close enough
together that each could hear the others' voices, and all could hear God
even should the speech be in undertones. God often whispers to those
near to Him, and when one walks with Him alone, at most He murmurs.
It is far better that God need not raise his voice, for when He must
shout, the whole earth trembles. It vexes Him to have to shout in order
to be heard by those at a distance. But soon He must.

It is the materialism and impersonality of the church which make it
seem irrelevant to millions who hunger for spiritual food. What it *does*
may be praiseworthy, for it engages in an effort to obtain social justice
and it speaks out for all sorts of humanitarian ideals. However, one may
question whether the church or a political organization is the proper or
more effective agency for social action, and it is not the one that young
revolutionists choose. When anyone tells me that the Church is the
spearhead of social action, I shall remain dubious until I see Black
Panthers flocking to Sunday School and hippies going to Mass.

I do not know any young people who regard the church with the
same feeling as those whom I consider old. Even the aged speak as if
their parents and grandparents were much more devout than they themselves. Dark days truly lie ahead, if it commands only the loyalty of
those who are about to die.

Well-meant persons have asked me why I ceased attending Divine
Service. I feel minded to retort that to me Divine Service is not something one *attends*—it is either a way of life or it is nothing. I could say

that I left the church in order to enjoy more meaningful religious experience. Those who best know me know I left because I am not Laodician—either I am cold or I am hot. Furthermore, I had about had it up to here with a church to which I could not bring any non-white friend I have without embarrassing myself, my friend, the congregation and the pastor, a church which nevertheless preached brotherhood and racial equality.

My decision to leave my church came shortly after it made an investigation of spiritual healing and rejected it. Jesus Himself commanded, "Heal the sick," and said, ". . . These signs shall follow them that believe . . . they shall lay hands on the sick and they shall recover." I had myself healed a student the week before—I, a sinful, ordinary man, not ordained, and not entitled to offer him consubstantiated bread and wine for the strengthening of his spirit, as could a pastor. Deliberate rejection by the church of a thing specifically commanded by Christ Himself was the last straw. Had the clergy admitted simply, "We have no power to heal," I should have accepted their statement, for I know it takes faith. But Christ never commanded anything that a man cannot do if he has faith.

The rags of dogma and theology that I took off were of the cut that Torquemada, Calvin, and the Holy Roman Emperor wore, and those which more recently clothed the Puritans when they hanged Mary Dyer on Boston Common because of her Quaker teaching, and in which the vigilantes were clad when they murdered Joseph Smith. When I took them off, I washed myself as clean as possible of contact with them. I stood before God as naked as when I was born, my head held high, proud that I am—good, evil, or both—made in His image and likeness and as He created me.

It was the second time in my life that I deliberately rejected a basic identity. I was no longer theological man: I was natural man. I am free now to say that I am an eternal spirit housed in, clothed with, and given the mechanism of a temporal, material body. I accept the teachings of science that the body evolved on earth over millions of years. As regards the spirit, I accept its own testimony, and to borrow a Quaker expression, follow it as my inner light. What other theology is necessary or possible? Is it not enough that God reveals Himself in all His creation and speaks with the voice from within me? Is not the inner light the only one by which a man can see?

How beautiful was the good earth when I walked out into the fresh clean air and climbed a mountain! How sweet seemed newness of identity. I lifted up my eyes and questioned, "Father, here I stand: what do you wish of me?"

The Lord spoke to my Lord: "The Lord hath sworn and will not repent, thou art a priest forever after the order of Melchizidek."

The only priests after the order of Melchizidek of which I knew are high dignitaries in the Church of Jesus Christ of Latter Day Saints. I knew that one of them I could never be. So I sought to learn who or what Melchizidek was, and found that he was king of Salem (which is by interpretation, Peace). So what my spirit heard was, "Thou are after the order of the sovereign of Peace."

Luther himself said each man is his own priest. That day when I was made ruler of my own inward Salem, I became also its priest. So does each man who has the courage to live by his own beliefs. Any man whose spirit calls God Father in joyous recognition becomes a king of Salem and a priest.

I could feel God, Spirit of my spirit, Mind of my mind, Life of my life; my strength; my intelligence; my consciousness—and felt Him in all living things. Trees were my brethern, and all living creatures my kindred. Even the earth and stones were filled with Him, and had being of Him. I was His thought, but He formed them before He embodied me. A lizard ran across a stone and stopped to watch me. I said to him, "Little elder brother, you whose people have been on earth so long, did your kind seek out inventions, or did you keep your knowledge in its purity?" He replied silently, "God is our life." I think that all of Nature, excepting Man alone, has kept its knowledge.

How different it is to say "Our Father which art in heaven" inside four walls as mechanical repetition without feeling, and to say it on a high hill in recognition of identity. The God of Salem is the God of Nature, Creator of the Universe, and a child of his is most at home in natural surroundings.

A priest must have an altar, and the earth is mine. In Exodus, the Lord spake unto Moses, saying: "An altar of earth shalt thou make unto me and shalt sacrifice thereon thy burnt offering and thy peace offerings . . . in all places where I record my name I will come unto thee and I shall bless thee."

In former times, in a religion which worshipped the God of Nature under the symbol of the sun, it was held fitting that on the darkest hour of the year, a service of rejoicing be held to proclaim faith that Light shall overcome the darkness. In German it is called the *Sonnenwendfeuer* (Sun-turning-fire). From its ceremonies come the traditional evergreens and lights of Christmas, and the date of Christmas itself, for the *Sonnenwendfeuer* is held at midnight on December twenty-fourth.

So wishing to offer a peace offering of prayer and praise to the Lord of Light, last year I dried pine and cedar branches indoors and built a pyre to provide a towering flame, using the whole earth as the altar for it. I kindled it at midnight, feeling in no wise pagan. My excitement mounted, for as far as I know, I am the last, or the first priest of the Father of Lights to worship Him with fire from the altar of earth in many generations, and this was my first ceremony.

It was a cold, clear, radiant night, with a full moon. No one seemed awake in miles, and the moonlight flooding the dark pool and the silent woodland beyond gave the illusion that I was alone in a place both distant in time and location from the busy, crowded world of illusion around us.

I kindled the sweet-smelling pyre, and flame leaped up with showers of sparks toward the starlit heavens. My eyes followed, and as I stood with my arms raised, my eyes rested upon the moon.

Then a wondrous thing happened. A ring of darkness began to extend outward from the moon, covering the stars or blotting them out, and the light which was uniform before formed a shining circle at about twelve diameters distant from the lunar orb leaving the space between the moon and the circle empty. I felt the impulse to fall down and worship in awe, for then I know I saw what Elijah saw—the Wheel of Heaven, the Shekinah, which he said is the likeness of the glory of the Lord, for it was like no other circle I ever saw. It was more beautiful than the rainbow, the most splendid display I ever have seen in the sky.

Did not my Lord say in Exodus, ". . . In all places where I record my name, I will come unto thee"? God to me is perfection, wholeness, completeness, as near my consciousness at any point as at any other. The only symbol I can find for this concept is a perfect circle. Even in childhood I saw visions of circles and wondered at their meaning. Now I knew what they meant. Even then, God was the circle at the center of which I exist. He is the outer margin of my consciousness, that which contains me, surrounds me, and protects me. The Bible says Man cannot behold the Lord God and live. Even the likeness of His glory suggested by the Shekinah, the Wheel of Heaven in the midnight sky, almost caught my soul out of my body and left me weak and faint with ecstasy. As long as it shone above me I was one with Light, not merely on earth but throughout the universe, and one with everything. I was at the same time on earth and on Arcturus—here and among the Pleides. All through the Milky Way I was a spark in communion with Light. It was a drunken, out-of-the-body, expanded experience, a kind of trip I never even have heard mentioned. It was contact—not atonement, but at-one-ment with God. I knew it to be the Lord keeping his word—no more, but no less!

As long as the pillar of flame lifted, and my heart reached up to touch this glory, it remained. Then as the fire burned low, it faded away, the stars came out again, and the sky was as it always is.

In the old religion, ashes from the sacred fire were considered protection from all evil, and the guarantee of good things through the new year. I sent to a friend perhaps the strangest and rarest gift he ever had received, an envelope of ashes.

I am well aware that some are sure to call the *Sonnonwendfeuer* a witch ceremony (all the more since the ideal group to hold one is thirteen). It is true that the first *Sonnenwendfeuer* known to have been held in America was the summer fire on St. Johannes' Eve held by the first Hex group to arrive in Pennsylvania, only a few hours after their vessel, the *Sarah Maria*, docked in Philadelphia in 1694. Indeed, there may be some who call me a witch. Like Grandmother, I say "What I want, I get." I always do, if I want it badly enough to pray, concentrating until I see it coming into existence in spite of all appearances to the contrary. That sounds like witchcraft, but it was Jesus who said, "All things whatsoever ye shall ask in prayer, believing, ye shall receive." It applies the same principal as does the Emerald Table of Hermes Trismegistus, to be certain—and that has been called magic for many centuries—but in my study of magic, I find that magic best which is like the teaching of the Master.

If it is witchcraft, I use it only for benevolent purposes. It can be used for evil, however, if one is willing to pay the penalty. Jesus said, "Do unto others as you would have others do unto you." It sounds so pious and so impractical that the church saw no harm in leaving it in the Bible. There is nothing pious about it—it is intensely practical, and it applies to witchcraft as to anything else. The good one does with Hex always returns to benefit him, and likewise, evil returns. Woe to the Black *Zauberer* when his chickens come home to roost. If he has sent a death spell to kill with cancer, a cancer will return to punish him. There is allegorical truth in the Faust story.

I try to use Hex for good, I want to give freely in order to be given freely—love in order to be loved.

Reports of strange experience continue to reach me. Four generations of a family have lived on a farm about seven miles from here, and during the whole time, they have been plagued by something that they and their neighbors call "Old Buncombe." Dogs very often bark at it, and cats bush out their tails and spit. It makes noises, used to pull an old man's hair whenever he sat down to eat, pinches people at embarrassing times and in embarrassing places, and when the old man died, it came down the chimney as a ball of fire, skipped across the floor, jumped up on the coffin, and the watchers saw something pull the dead man's hair—not hard, but just about as much hair as you could take between thumb and finger, and about as hard as you could if you didn't mean it to hurt, as when the old man was alive. They always have found mysterious holes dug on the farm at night, and people hear walking, or running, and never see anything plainly.

The farm is quite near a Revolutionary War skirmish site, and they seem to think maybe it's a soldier who was killed and buried there, or maybe buried before he died, or face down, or something. He sounds like a poltergeist to me, but a poltergeist comes when an adolescent has a sex problem. They can't have had a sex problem that lasted four generations, and considering the size of that family, they *never* had any.

I have been thrilled to learn that my house stands on land where people lived as long as ten thousand years ago, and I felt it explained something I heard once, back near the spring at the pond. It was dusk, and I heard mournful chanting, very low and indistinct, but clear enough to be heard as in a totally alien language. In ten thousand years, it would be surprising if some Indian spirit did *not* become fixed here.

But my house is so full of symbols and substances that an evil spirit would not be at ease in it, and the land is planted with trees that they avoid—cedar, holly, and oak—and now my holly I planted to cast sunrise shade on the wall is tall enough that the shadow touches the foundation. Though these are still small, other holly trees grow so that no one can approach from any direction without being in sight of one, while the builder's Hex tree (the majestic *Ilex opaca*) stands, taller than the chimneys, out in the side yard, so that it casts shadow on the house on the 24th of December and on the important nights of the full moon. So, nothing malevolent can get at me of those things that wander to and fro finding no rest. *Sonnenwendfeuer* ashes in a glass box are on the mantle, and rue and the fiend's aversion (love-bringing vervain), nettles and amaranth are dried in a cedar box. I am a bizarre man, bizarrely helped and protected.

The bizarre has its own special logic and consistency. That is why people seldom show surprise when they come into my room and find its jumble of antique furniture, books, occult and magical symbols, its prehistoric artifacts, skeletal remains, weird masks, and symbolic draw-ings. It is littered with old bottles, some of them corroded, irridescent, encrusted with centuries of patina. I have one that has turned to the sheen and colors of opal, and one the colors of a peacock's plumes. I grow plants, and each window is a jungle. Even in January vivid flowers bloom.

It is logical that I should have such things around me, and though the skull on the mantle is made diabolical-looking by a pair of goat horns and a crown contrived of cast-off trinkets, and though a pair of human thighbones now stand beside it, and a painting of a ghost hangs above, visitors chuckle, for they know that I do not take death seriously, and nobody ever thinks the display morbid. It never occurs to them that by the logic of ordinary reason, it is insane to stick horns into the top of a skull, and contrive only a trumpery crown for death to wear. It is part of the same special logic that hardly anyone who is ruled by the logic of reason ever sees inside my room. I take them into the living room where the furniture is upholstered in good, durable, solid-color homespun-weave in keeping with early American farmhouse décor. There the cabi-nets have gaudy Dutch earthenware in them; my mother's portrait in oils stares down—like an early American primitive, and another painting shows water birches by a shore. A television set consecrates this room to the banal and ordinary, and there are copies of *Reader's Digest* on the table. Of course, *my* friends hardly ever enter the living room. They head for my bedroom. (Be quiet, Zaïda!)

There they know they can find an ear to listen, a hand to clasp for comfort or sustainment, and a heart that glows like a hearth in a snow-bound room. It is good for me and for them to have such a refuge, for the room in which all of us live *is* truly snowbound.

The age is in December; or if January, the spring, if there *is* a spring, seems far away. Of course there *must* be a spring—there always has been—but the blizzard howls, the roads are closed, and men perish in the storm. The ache in my bones presages more cruel weather; night is about to fall, and the wind is bitter cold. Tomorrow, (if morning comes) a thick white blanket will cover everything. When talking grows still on such a night, there is time for reading, and for reading on such a night, there is the Bible.

Mine opens of itself, I have read so often, and this is the passage that I shall read my friends:

"The Spirit of the Lord God is upon me; because the Lord hath ap-pointed me to preach good tidings unto the meek; he hath sent me to bind up the broken-hearted; to proclaim liberty to the captives, and the opening of the prison to them that are bound; to proclaim the accept-able year of the Lord, and the day of vengeance of our God; to comfort all that mourn; to appoint unto them that mourn in Zion, to give unto them beauty for ashes, the oil of joy for mourning, the garment of praise for the spirit of heaviness; that they might be called Trees of righteousness, the planting of the Lord, that he might be glorified. And they shall build the old wastes, they shall raise up the former desola-tions, and they shall repair the waste cities, the desolations of many generations. . ."

Blessed Israel! The above was spoken on a dark and bitter night of that eternal people. It was their promise through cruel centuries. It was their hope that sustained them in their exile, and for those who are still in exile, it is their dream.

Am I not Israel, too, who worship the one God? Is not this promise like so much else given Israel truly mine? Yours? Everyone's?

In another place I read: "In that day when my people of Israel dwell-eth safely, shalt thou not know it? [I *do* know it, for Israel has returned to the land of promise in my own time] And thou shalt come from thy place out of the north parts, thou, and many people with thee, all of them riding upon horses, a great company, and a mighty army: And thou shalt come up against my people of Israel, as a cloud to cover the land; it shall be in the latter days, and I will bring thee against my land, that the heathen may know me. . .

"For in my jealousy and in the fire of my wrath have I spoken; Surely in that day there shall be a great shaking in the land of Israel; so that the fishes of the sea, and the fowls of the heaven, and the beasts of the field, and all creeping things that are upon the face of the earth shall shake at my presence, and the mountains shall be thrown down, and the steep places shall fall, and every wall shall fall flat to the ground. And I will call for a sword against him throughout all my mountains, saith the Lord God; every man's sword shall be against his brother. And I will plead against him with pestilence and with blood: and I will rain upon him, and upon his bands, and upon the many people that are with him, an overflowing rain, and great hailstones, fire and brimstone. Thus will I magnify myself, and sanctify myself; and I will be known in the eyes of many nations, and they shall know that I *am* the Lord."

I have brought all of you into my room to hear me read this. It is of the cruel weather that twinges in my bones. I do not prophecy; I read the prophets, and I have seen part of the prophecy fulfilled. I said before that I should bless Israel—how can I bless her? If God has blessed a people, can a man? Or, if God has blessed a people, can a man do otherwise? *Peace,* I say unto the people of David—but unto all men everywhere, may the Lord be gracious unto you and grant you peace!

I have shown you many cherished things in the chamber of my consciousness; I have told you strange true stories, and offered you my hand. The fire of my inward hearth—I have hoped to warm you with it, for to give warmth in such a time as this is to give life through the winter storm.

How I should like to tell you more, but there is tomorrow. Yes, no matter what the night may be, there *is* tomorrow!